DEBATES IN
INTERNATIONAL POLITICAL
ECONOMY

DEBATES IN
INTERNATIONAL POLITICAL ECONOMY

2nd EDITION

Thomas Oatley
University of North Carolina at Chapel Hill

Longman

Boston   Columbus   Indianapolis   New York   San Francisco   Upper Saddle River
Amsterdam   Cape Town   Dubai   London   Madrid   Milan   Munich   Paris   Montreal   Toronto
Delhi   Mexico City   Sao Paulo   Sydney   Hong Kong   Seoul   Singapore   Taipei   Tokyo

Senior Acquisitions Editor: Vikram Mukhija
Editorial Assistant: Beverly Fong
Senior Marketing Manager: Lindsey Prudhomme
Associate Production Manager: Scarlett Lindsay
Project Coordination, Text Design, and Electronic Page Makeup: PreMediaGlobal
Senior Cover Design Manager: Nancy Danahy
Senior Manufacturing Buyer: Dennis J. Para
Printer and Binder: RR Donnelley – Crawfordsville
Cover Printer: RR Donnelley – Crawfordsville

For permission to use copyrighted material, grateful acknowledgment is made to the copyright holders on pp. 381–82, which are hereby made part of this copyright page.

Library of Congress Cataloging-in-Publication Data

Oatley, Thomas H.,
    Debates in international political economy / Thomas Oatley.—2nd ed.
        p. cm.
    ISBN-13: 978-0-205-06061-0
    ISBN-10: 0-205-06061-7
    1. International economic relations.   2. International finance.   3. Globalization.
4. Multinational corporations. I. Title.
    HF1359.O245 2012
    337—dc22   2011000896

1 2 3 4 5 6 7 8 9 10 — DOC — 14 13 12 11

Longman
is an imprint of

www.pearsonhighered.com   ISBN-13: 978-0-205-06061-0
                           ISBN-10:   0-205-06061-7

BRIEF CONTENTS

DETAILED CONTENTS

PREFACE

In the summer of 2010, the world's government confronted a compelling public policy problem. Although the global economy had emerged from the recession that followed the great crisis of 2008–09, many North American and European economies appeared to be slipping back into recession. Governments disagreed sharply about how to respond to the possibility of a "double dip" recession. In Europe, the German government, with support from other European Union friends, advocated fiscal consolidation to restore market confidence in the face of large government deficits and debt burdens. In contrast, the U.S. government argued that consolidation would further depress economic activity and suggested instead that fiscal consolidation be deferred in favor of short-run stimulus until economic growth resumed. German policy makers rebuffed U.S. calls for stimulus on the grounds that additional stimulus would do little to boost growth. Who is correct? How can governments facing similar economic choices embrace such different policy responses? This disagreement is more common than one might think. Rarely do important problems lend themselves to simple policy solutions that evoke unanimous agreement. Almost always policy questions are complex and associated with competing views about appropriate responses.

An undergraduate striving to understand the global economy must clear three hurdles. First, she must become familiar with a broad range of theories from both political science and economics that have been developed lo study the global economy. Second, she must become familiar with the historical development of the global economic system. Third, she must become familiar with the issues and debates that are at the center of contemporary discussion among governments, international economic organizations, think tanks, and academics.

Existing textbooks and edited international political economy readers provide faculty with a wealth of options for material that promotes the development of core theoretical knowledge and historical background. Professors have fewer options when selecting a textbook that introduces students to contemporary issues and debates in the global economy. For this purpose, I suspect that most teachers rely on infrequently revised textbooks and a set of photocopied (or more commonly now online) readings taken from some of the more policy-oriented journals. This book is intended to fill that niche by providing paired articles that feature contemporary debates over enduring policy issues in the global economy.

NEW TO THIS EDITION

This second edition includes six brand new debates. In selecting these new additions, I have sought to dedicate greater attention in particular to the causes and consequences of the financial crisis.

- Chapter 1 explores whether transition from American hegemony to a multipolar world poses a fundamental challenge to the liberal international order.
- Chapter 6 examines whether governments should employ trade restrictions to support climate change objectives as well as whether such trade restriction are with the requirements of the world Trade Organization compliant.
- Chapter 10 explores whether the financial crisis was a consequence of too much or too little government intervention.
- Chapter 14 explores the contribution to poverty reduction we should expect from microcredit.
- Chapter 15 explores whether the rise of China has created a model to challenge the Washington Consensus model of development.
- Chapter 16 explores whether the global financial crisis will produce a fundamental realignment of the global economy.

FEATURES

This book's central pedagogical tool is reasoned debate between informed observers with distinct viewpoints. Every chapter contains two articles that offer alternative and in most instances contending visions of policy solutions to pressing global economic problems. Each chapter contains a concise introduction that places the debate in a broader context and briefly summarizes each article. Each introduction concludes with a few "Points to Ponder," questions that students can usefully keep in mind as they read through the chapter. The debate format encourages students to evaluate the quality of arguments and to see that most complex problems have more than one solution and that no single solution is obviously better than all others.

The chapters cover all of the major substantive areas of international political economy: the trade system, multinational corporations, developing countries, monetary and financial issues, and global governance. In addition, the book provides discussion of policy debates at the domestic and international levels. My selection of articles was governed by two concerns. I sought articles that focus on issues that are the subject of current debate and discussion, rather than focusing on issues that are of largely historical interest. These current debates should be contemporary manifestations of enduring problems in the global economy.

SUPPLEMENTS

Longman is pleased to offer several resources to qualified adopters of *Debates in international Political Economy* and their students that will make teaching and learning from this book even more effective and enjoyable.

Passport for International Relations With Passport, choose the resources you want from MyPoliSciKit, and put links to them into your course management system. If there is assessment associated with those resources, it also can be uploaded, allowing the results to feed directly into your course management system's gradebook. With over 150 MyPoliSciKit assets like video case studies, mapping exercises, comparative exercises, simulations, podcasts, *Financial Times* newsfeeds, current events quizzes, politics blogs, and much more, Passport is available for any Pearson introductory or upper-level political science book. Use ISBN 0-205-09287-X to order Passport with this book. To learn more, please contact your Pearson representative.

MySearchlab Need help with a paper? MySearchLab saves time and improves results by offering start-to-finish guidance on the research/writing process and full-text access to academic journals and periodicals. Use ISBN 0-205-10909-8 to order MySearchLab with this book. To learn more, please visit www.mysearchlab.com or contact your Pearson representative.

The Economist Every week *The Economist* analyzes the important happenings around the globe. From business to politics, to the arts and science, its coverage connects seemingly unrelated events in unexpected ways. Use ISBN 0-205-00263-3 to order a 15-week subscription with this book for a small additional charge. To learn more, please contact your Pearson representative.

The Financial Times Featuring international news and analysis from journalists in more than 50 countries, *The Financial Times* provides insights and perspectives on political and economic developments around the world. Use ISBN 0-205-00249-8 to order a 15-week subscription with this book for a small additional charge. To learn more, please contact your Pearson representative.

Longman Atlas of World Issues (0-205-78020-2) From population and political systems to energy use and women's rights, the *Longman Atlas of World Issues* features full-color thematic maps that examine the forces shaping the world. Featuring maps from the latest edition of *The Penguin State of the World Atlas*, this excerpt includes critical thinking exercises to promote a deeper understanding of how geography affects many global issues. Available at no additional charge when packaged with this book.

Goode's World Atlas (0-321-65200-2) First published by Rand McNally in 1923, *Goode's World Atlas* has set the standard for college reference atlases. It features hundreds of physical, political, and thematic maps as well as graphs, tables, and a pronouncing Index. Available at a discount when packaged with this book.

The Penguin Dictionary of International Relations (0-140-51397-3)
This indispensable reference by Graham Evans and Jeffrey Newnham includes
hundreds of cross-referenced entries on the enduring and emerging theories,
concepts, and events that are shaping the academic discipline of international
relations and today's world politics. Available at a discount when packaged
with this book.

Research and Writing in International Relations (0-205-06065-X) With
Current and detailed coverage on how to start research in the discipline's major subfields, this brief and affordable guide offers the step-by-step guidance
and the essential resources needed to compose political science papers that go
beyond description and into systematic and sophisticated inquiry. This text
focuses on areas where students often need help—finding topic, developing a
question, reviewing the literature, designing research, and last, writing the
paper. Available at a discount when packaged with this book.

ACKNOWLEDGMENTS

This reader was strengthened by the very helpful comments I received from
external reviewers, including

Gordon Bennett, *University of Texas*
Charles R. Boehmer, *University of Texas at El Paso*
John A. C. Conybeare, *University of Iowa*
Jonathon Crystal, *Fordham University*
Michelle Dion, *Georgia Institute of Technology*
William M. Downs, *Georgia State University*
Daniel Gibran, *Tennessee State University*
Dorothee Heisenberg, *Johns Hopkins University*
Peter B. Heller, *Manhattan College*
Ian Hurd, *Northwestern University*
Moonhawk Kim, *University of Colorado–Boulder*
Steven Livingston, *Middle Tennessee State University*
Waltraud Queiser *Morales, University of Central Florida*
A.L. Morgan, *University of Tennessee*
Linda Petrou, *High Point University*
Rebecca Steffenson, *DePaul University*
Strom Thacker, *Boston University*
Jaroslav Tir, *University of Georgia*

Finally, I owe my students a large debt for helping to convince me that
sometimes one can grasp abstract theoretical concepts more easily by ap-
proaching them through the more familiar territory of contemporary issues
and debates.

THOMAS OATLEY

PART I
THE LIBERAL INTERNATIONAL ORDER

International political economy explores how the interaction between politics and markets shapes the creation and distribution of wealth. The focus is international due to its primary interest in how the construction of global markets for goods, services, financial capital, and, increasingly, labor shapes the global division of labor. For example, China's emergence as a major economy has been greatly facilitated by international trade. China's development strategy rested upon producing products it could export to the United States and the European Union. China's determination to pursue an export-led development strategy in turn attracted American and European and Asian companies to move part of their production to China.

Global economic institutions structure global markets. Global trade is possible in large part because of the rules and decision-making procedures embodied in the World Trade Organization (WTO). Governments have used the WTO to progressively eliminate barriers to cross-border trade in goods and services. Cross-border investment is possible in large part because of common agreement on rules about how governments can and cannot treat foreign investors. Here governments rely upon bilateral investment treaties rather than a multilateral organization. The principle is the same: Common rules establish a structure that enables cross-border economic exchange. Finally, the global financial system is supported in part by cooperation within the International Monetary Fund and the Group of 20. These structures provide financial assistance to governments facing unanticipated difficulties attracting financial capital into their economies.

Global economic institutions rest on political foundations. The contemporary global economic system reflects the power of the United States and Great Britain. Current organizations emerged from World War II and embodied the interests of American and British policy makers. The system's emphasis on global markets and multilateral organizations was an American response to the protectionist system organized around colonial empires that had emerged during the 1930s. Since 1945, this

1

Anglo-American project attracted more and more adherents as societies abandoned alternative economic models.

Two current events have generated discussion about the long-term future of the current order. Rapid economic development has thrust China into a global leadership position that was impossible to imagine twenty years ago. China's rapid ascent has caused many to question whether an Anglo-American global economy can survive in a world in which power is more evenly distributed. Such concerns have grown as a consequence of the recent financial crisis. To what extent will the Anglo-American model of capitalism retain its appeal if its consequences are periodic large crises? And if China (and other East Asian economies) can develop rapidly based on a different model, will we see a shift in the global economy from the Anglo-American to an East Asian model?

In short, recent developments suggest that fundamental change might well be in progress. We thus begin and end our exploration of politics in the global economy with debates that focus on these two dimensions of change. Chapter 1 explores whether the changing distribution of economic power—China's relative rise—will produce major changes in the institutional structure of the global economy. In the final chapter, we consider whether China's developmental success provides a coherent Beijing Consensus that offers an alternative to the Washington Consensus.

CHAPTER 1 GEOPOLITICAL CHANGE THREATENS THE LIBERAL ORDER *v.* THE LIBERAL ORDER REMAINS ROBUST

Geopolitical Change Threatens the Liberal Order

Advocate: Mathew J. Burrows and Jennifer Harris

Source: "Revisiting the Future: Geopolitical Effects of the Financial Crisis," *The Washington Quarterly* 32:2 (2009): 27–38

The Liberal Order Remains Robust

Advocate: G. John Ikenberry

Source: "The Liberal International Order and Its Discontents," *Millennium* 38:3 (2010): 509–21

How robust is the global economy? In the wake of the financial crisis, analysts have begun to debate the future of the global economy and the broader liberal international order of which it forms one part. The contemporary global economy was constructed after World War II on what are essentially classically liberal principles. As such, it emphasizes markets rather than states to allocate resources. It strives to bring the rule of law into international politics to regulate the interaction between governments. It strives for inclusive multilateral cooperation as the basic mechanism for adding and amending international rules. It has constructed international organizations as the core institutional foundations of this liberal international order.

At the time of its creation, this liberal international order was very much an American and British project. Its founding economic principles reflected Anglo-American beliefs about how best to structure the global economy. Its emphasis on multilateralism and rule of law reflected a peculiarly American reformist orientation toward international politics. Over the postwar era, this Anglo-American project attracted more and more adherents as societies abandoned the alternative economic models. Although this liberal order has flourished for the past seventy years, the financial crisis and China's rapid ascendance have sparked discussion about whether the liberal international order can remain robust moving forward.

GEOPOLITICAL CHANGE THREATENS THE LIBERAL ORDER

Some analysts argue that the liberal order faces fundamental challenges as a consequence of far-reaching changes in the broader global distribution of power. Rapid growth in China, India, Brazil, and Russia is pushing the world away from hegemony toward multipolarity. These rising powers are only loosely connected to America's "liberal vision" of international order. Some are autocratic rather than democratic. Many embrace economic models that assign to the state an important role in allocating resources. Consequently, geopolitical change that alters the global distribution of power will pose more fundamental challenges to the liberal order.

Mathew J. Burrows and Jennifer Harris, both of whom are analysts at the National Intelligence Council, develop this argument. Revisiting the conclusions they drew in the report entitled *Global Trends 2025*, they suggest that the international system is in the midst of fundamental change; by 2025, the United States will no longer be the dominant power it is currently. Rising powers are less democratic, more statist, and less attached to the principles of the liberal order. A global power shift will thus reduce support for the liberal order and create greater potential for global conflict.

THE LIBERAL ORDER REMAINS ROBUST

Other analysts assert that the liberal order remains robust. Some of these observers caution against simple projections of past growth rates into the distant future and thus question whether a fundamental redistribution of power will occur. Some point to parallels with Japan's rapid ascent during the 1980s and equally sudden relative decline ever since. Others argue that, even if the world is transitioning toward multipolarity, the liberal order remains robust. Not only do these rising states benefit from the liberal order, but also the rising powers offer no coherent alternative to the liberal order.

G. John Ikenberry, the Albert G. Milbank Professor of Politics and International Affairs at Princeton University, develops this argument. He suggests that, although the liberal order is in crisis, the crisis is a result of rising powers questioning the quality of recent American leadership rather than of fundamental questions about the liberal order itself. Consequently, the liberal order will persist, and perhaps even strengthen, in the face of the United States' incipient hegemonic decline.

POINTS **TO PONDER**

1. To what extent do the two articles agree that the global distribution of power is shifting from hegemony to multipolarity?

2. What does Ikenberry mean by the distinction between a crisis of authority within the liberal order and a crisis of the liberal order? Which type of crisis do you think the liberal order is experiencing? Why?

3. What do you think will be the most important in determining whether a shift away from American hegemony generates a fundamental challenge to the liberal order?

Mathew J. Burrows and Jennifer Harris

Revisiting the Future: Geopolitical Effects of the Financial Crisis

Every four years, the National Intelligence Council (NIC) publishes an unclassified report projecting global trends over the next fifteen years. The intent is to help incoming decisionmakers lift their sights above the here-and-now, focusing on longer-term trends likely to shape the strategic future of the United States. Inevitably, the NIC's estimations find a far wider audience. The most recent edition, *Global Trends 2025: A Transformed World* (hereinafter the report), was published November, 2008 and already has received substantial media attention both within the United States and overseas.[1] Completing the report in the midst of the financial crisis required the NIC to make risky predictions on the world's most volatile issues, from youth bulges and climate change to odds on a nuclear Iran, from whether the International Monetary Fund (IMF) might soon be spelled SWF for sovereign wealth funds in the developing world, to a Russia (and a Gazprom) rising, even as the ground was shifting day to day beneath its feet.

The report highlighted the emergence of a multipolar global order with rising states like China and India economically overtaking most of the older Group of Seven (G-7) powers by 2025. The United States' traditional partners, Europe and Japan, would increasingly be challenged to maintain economic growth in view of their aging populations. While the rising states would want sears at the international high table, the report anticipated that they would be cautious about assuming global burdens, despite a packed agenda composed of new challenges like climate change and energy security in addition to growing threats such as nuclear proliferation and weapons of mass destruction (WMD) terrorism. By 2025 the international order, although unrecognizable from its post–World War II contours, would remain in transition and be one in which the United States, though still preeminent, would be less dominant even as others would still look to it to shoulder many of the global burdens.

Such was the world the NIC foresaw as the crisis unfolded. Now, emerging markets the world over have lost more than half of their value since September 2008 alone. Banks that have never reported a net loss earnings quarter were dissolved in a matter of days. The proportions of the current crisis hardly need familiarizing. As the panic has not yet given way to a lucid picture of the impacts, most economists and political forecasters are smart enough to shy away from sweeping predictions amid the fog of crisis. Yet, in the post-crisis world, it seems conceivable that global growth will most likely be muted, deflation will remain a risk while any decoupling of the industrialized from developing countries is unlikely, the state will be the relative winner while authoritarianism may not, and U.S. consumption as the engine for global growth will slowly fade. Whether U.S. political and market clout will follow, and whether U.S. political leadership will come equipped with knowledge of the strategic forces affecting the United States remains to be seen.

How Much of a Geopolitical "Game Changer" Is the Financial Crisis?

Mapping the NIC's predictions against early facts, one of the most interesting observations is less about any particular shock generated by the financial crisis and more about its global reach. If anything, the crisis has underscored the importance of globalization as the overriding force or "mega-driver" as it was characterized in both the NIC's 2020 and 2025 Global Trends works. Developing countries have been hurt as decoupling theories, assertions that the emerging markets have appreciably weaned themselves from the U.S. economy, have been dispelled. This second epicenter of the crisis in emerging markets could also continue to exacerbate and prolong the crisis. Alongside foreseeable exposures, such as Pakistan with its large current account deficit, are less predictable panics like Dubai, whose debt was financed on suddenly expensive dollars. Even those with cash reserves, such as Russia and South Korea, have been severely buffeted.

At the same time, globalization itself may be transformed because of the financial crisis. The spectacular growth in global liquidity that took effect in the past decade, allowing for an era of free money, may be ending. Recent data suggests that the NIC may have underestimated the extent and pace of the contraction in global trade, at least in the short term, and the corresponding diminished appetite for Chinese manufactures. Even if global growth rebounds, it is unclear whether the U.S. consumer, with its large debt overhang, can continue to hold up its side of the bargain and be the engine for continued Chinese growth. China may instead be forced to penetrate the last remaining frontier in global consumer markets: its own.

The 2025 report anticipated such a development happening at some point. It underlined the importance, even before the financial crisis, of China's domestic market in spurring growth and highlighted the likely increased role of China's middle classes. . . . A more domestically driven economy in China would inevitably lead to a more powerful political, voice for the middle class over time, one which might not sit comfortably with China's single-party status.

It is not clear whether China's leaders have woken up to these possible changes on the horizon. In the month since the report was issued, China's trade surplus reached a new high and its authorities appeared to be trying to lower the value of the RMB [Renminbi] against the dollar, in effect trying to restore the status quo ante. Export-led growth models, however, have been unsustainable and prone to volatile unwinding. German attempts to forge export-led growth atop U.S consumption proved unsuccessful in the 1960s. Japan tried and failed in the same manner in the 1970s, and similar attempts by the East Asian tigers met the same fate in the 1990s.

Such lessons also apply to any U.S. attempts to reinstitute past patterns of mutual dependence. After noting the familiar definition of insanity, repeating the same action and expecting a different result, a Wall Street leader recently summarized the future of U.S.–China relations, stating that the incoming U.S. leaders must ask themselves if they are willing to double down again on the country's national debt to facilitate the economic rise of those insistent upon an export-led growth model.

Inauspicious as traditional prospects surrounding the U.S. financing of export-led growth might be, the crisis suggests this may now be an even riskier bet than in previous eras. In 1971, then-Treasury Secretary John Connally simply pulled the plug on Japanese undervaluation by refusing to exchange dollars for gold. Likewise, former president Ronald Reagan issued credible threats that forced cooperation from Germany and Japan in the Plaza and Louvre Accords in 1985. The United States enjoys no such unilateral options today, as the current crisis involves more actors and few willing allies in adjustment. In light of collective action problems, it may be the market, more so than either Beijing or Washington, which dictates the terms of adjustment.

How Much of a Boost for Multipolarity?

. . . [T]he financial crisis appears to have accelerated the trend toward a multipolar world. The G-7/8 looks set to morph into the Group of 20 (G-20), consisting of finance ministers and central bank governors on a permanent basis. The state wealth Beijing has already amassed, over $1 trillion of which resides in U.S. government-backed securities, gives China ample leverage in shaping the future economic landscape. In fact, as the crisis deepens into further paralysis of the real economy, the manner in which China deploys its reserves is among the decisive factors determining global outcomes to the current crisis.

U.S. policymakers guess that, unlike the United States with Bretton Woods after the Second World War, China will not deploy its considerable reserves in order to redraw the financial Landscape. Having assumed global stakeholder status more quickly, perhaps too quickly in Beijing's view, China's decisionmaking remains almost exclusively domestic. This is consistent with the report's view of China as a status quo power which has benefited from the current geopolitical arrangement and now sees itself in a waiting game. Beijing is loathe to play its hand too early for fear of taking on too much risk or disrupting prospects for its continued rise. Hence China's reluctance to use its reserves to come to the rescue of other countries in need, or subsequently to have far more say in how the new economic order is constructed.

An Enlarging State Role . . .

The 2025 report pointed to the resurgence of the state in economic affairs, particularly for the rising powers. As with previous countries whose economies had taken off, such as South Korea and Taiwan in the 1960s and 1970s, the state is playing an important economic role not just in authoritarian states like China, but arguably even in rising democracies like Brazil and India. The financial crisis would seem to have further heightened the role of the state, potentially even more so where governments in the West are funding bailouts and coordinating stimulus packages.

Perhaps the best known, but hardly the only, mark of these collapsing firewalls between state and markets is the upsurge in sovereign wealth funds in recent years. It is worth recalling that sovereign wealth funds came into fashion roughly fifty years ago, initially to aid in fiscal stabilization or balance of payments sterilization. But with the long-term upward trajectory in commodity prices, these funds have evolved from state liquidity buffers to become market behemoths. In all cases, sovereign funds have arisen as byproducts of states with large balance of payments surpluses. . . .

The question is whether this enhanced economic role for the state will be a permanent, enduring feature of the future economic landscape or one that is transitory until some economic stability is achieved and growth resumes. The answer may be slow to emerge, as none of these models of state and market appear close to a steady equilibrium. As those "newly rich" states that willingly collapsed distinctions of public and private now bleed reserves, and as Western governments come to wrestle the costs of fiscal stimulus amid continued economic uncertainty, societies everywhere will repeatedly confront the need to define and redefine the desired role of the state in markets.

Ultimately, we anticipate that the shift toward a greater state role in the economy may be more permanent than not. State-owned enterprises (SOEs), long seen by the report and others as a more insidious threat, may gain greater market prominence and heightened political stakes amid increased state presence in markets and revamped industrial policies. The report recounts how SOEs, once mere exercises in job creation, are not only resurfacing, but are newly aggressive, and in many cases (e.g. Gazprom, Lenovo) are expanding beyond national borders to become global household names. Even before the crisis, state wealth was increasingly deployed to subsidize non-tariff barriers that lend SOEs advantages over private firms. This competitive advantage is particularly concerning as SOEs increasingly operate across national lines. Now, as the state finds itself managing more industries, as job creation again becomes a core concern, and as neo-mercantilism looms ever larger, SOEs may become a dangerous source of attraction.

. . . But Authoritarianism May Face a More Uncertain Future

The report predicts that even for successful state capitalists, authoritarian regimes would face a day of reckoning when, at some point, they would have to loosen the political reins and open up, partly in order to encourage continued investment and greater scientific and technological innovation. Turbulent experiences, such as the growing labor unrest across rural China in recent years and increasing panic among oligarchs in Russia, demonstrate that these state authoritarian models . . . only work so long as the global economy is in relatively solid working order. Each state appears susceptible to some "magic number" such as an average of $55 per barrel of oil in the case of Russia or approximately $60–65 per barrel in Iran, and the benchmark 7–8% for GDP growth in China. The crisis has forced all of these below their respective thresholds. . . . Uncertainty surrounds what level of growth China needs to deflect political unrest. A 1.6 percent drop from a 9.5 percent GDP growth may seem slight to Western countries, but it may spark massive domestic uprising in China.

As the crisis progresses, China and other state-led developers may be finding that free markets and democracy offer certain pragmatic benefits, such as necessary buffers to public hostility during times of economic strain. The admirable growth performances of many non-democratic emerging states moved several economists and commentators to publicly question whether democratic developers, such as India, bear a "democracy tax," and whether China and other strong state developers, enjoying greater concentration and reach of decisionmaking power, might perhaps offer a more efficient growth alternative.[2] But as these "state capitalist" countries fall under severe strain, their leaders are finding that with centralized responsibility comes a conspicuous target for accountability. Without any open election to vent popular frustration, the likelihood of increased domestic turmoil and conflict may be even greater than originally forecasted.

The report hypothesizes that a reversion to more political liberalism in Russia would only happen in event of a prolonged economic downturn. The same may be true for China. While economic growth appears to be falling, the Chinese Communist Party, whose legitimacy has rested on continued growth, may have to reinvent itself and that might include greater accountability. . . .

The Future of the United States

The report projects that the United States will remain the preeminent single power by 2025, but the gap between it and others will narrow. This is the result of several factors, not just due to the increasing economic powers of rising states like China and India. Power itself has for some time been diffused with non-state actors rising in importance. As seen most recently in Iraq, military power, on which the United States will remain technologically superior, can be blunted with the use of asymmetrical strategies and others, like China, are expected to narrow the high-end technological edge with the United States. Cyber and space are two areas where the United States currently has a near monopoly, but by 2025 it will disappear. The financial crisis raises the question whether the United States' relative decline, particularly in the economic realm, will arrive sooner than anticipated in the report or whether the crisis will be an opportunity for the United States to emerge stronger in coming years, helping to maintain a bigger edge for a longer time into the future.

Recessions are a relative game, and historically, the United States has proven more adroit at responding to them than most. The United States emerged from oil shocks of the 1970s far faster than more heavily oil-dependent counterparts like Europe and Japan. It went on to survive the collapse of Bretton Woods in 1971 with the dollar's global reserve status intact, and it escaped the "Eurosclerosis" that descended upon Europe in the trans-Atlantic recession of the 1980s. It graduated from the recession of the early 1990s into a decade-long productivity boom, while Japan, its nearest rival, entered a decade of decline. While China will likely be forced to engineer a new strategy favoring greater emphasis on a domestic economy, one that scales to its unprecedented population and finds sufficient purchase politically, the United States' tradition of openness and the developed skills and mobility probably puts it in a better position to reinvent itself. The sort of Schumpeterian "creative destruction" that appears to have distinguished the United States in the past and helped pull the country through severe downturn is likely to be an asset in this current crisis.

At the same time, the image of the United States may have suffered anew, and this time not because of the global war on terror or Washington's policies in the Middle East. Hostility toward the United States as the source of this global crisis, warranted or not, may have received too little credence. With the decoupling myth now gone but U.S. antipathy not forgotten, the commonly described "unhappy marriage" between China and the United States could metastasize into a mistrusting union between Beijing and Washington, spilling over into widespread distrust of the United States among swaths of emerging and mature economies. Global financial protectionism, while not a big feature in the report, represents a new danger. Its forms, such as numerical leverage ceilings and outright bans on entire markets, may be greater and more systemic than traditional trade and investment protectionism. Should imminent domestic regulatory battles aggregate into destructive and futile "what touches here, clears here"–style regulation, credit markets would be left Balkanized even as regulatory blind spots would grow.

The dollar's recent strengthening suggests that the NIC was perhaps unwarranted in flagging concerns over the dollar's ability to maintain its role as the world's leading global reserve currency. Comforting as it would be to believe in such an eternal flight to quality, the dollar's rebound may have more to do with the unwinding of dollar-denominated assets than any safe haven effect. Even so, the scale of recent fiscal stimulus efforts would seem to suggest that the United States is indeed relying on an exorbitant privilege that may not always exist. Even beyond national economic decisions, the United States has built its foreign policy and military positions atop these privileges. Lasting dollar declines would force difficult tradeoffs between achieving ambitious foreign policy goals and the high domestic costs of supporting those aims.

Wider Ramifications of an Enduring Global Financial Crisis

The report's 30,000 ft. lesson that historic changes in the global economic and financial landscape require corresponding shifts in foreign policy thinking, is, if anything, even more apt. Artificial divisions between "economic" and "foreign" policy present a false dichotomy. To whom one extends swap lines and how the IMF is recapitalized are as much foreign policy as economic decisions. Several states openly hinge support for NATO and U.S. coalition efforts upon domestic economic conditions which in turn, they insist, are contingent on U.S. monetary and fiscal aid. Others blend the two with even greater calculation: China using its SWF to compel Costa Rica to disavow Taiwan, Russia resorting to military tactics to scare would-be investors away from competing pipeline projects.

Economics as High Politics

As markets prove truly global in reach and risk, as margins progressively thin, and states assume ever-more market presence, the fictional barriers between "economic" and "foreign" policy will be increasingly difficult, even dangerous, to maintain. Finance and markets are now high politics. Mere days after the G-20 convened in Washington and promised to "refrain from raising new barriers to investment or to trade," Brazil supported hikes in Mercosur common external tariffs on a range of goods, China tightened its dollar-peg and announced a new round of export tax-breaks, India levied a new duty on iron and steel manufactures, and Russian leaders increased auto import tariffs. Inability to hold ground on these old and familiar problems will exacerbate progress on new, arguably more difficult tasks such as managing stimulus efforts, coordinating their eventual drawdown, and not least, undertaking any meaningful financial regulation. Against these odds, and in the face of untold consequences of failure, the price of admission onto the international high table, whether indeed the G-20 or some successor entity, must be more than aggregate GDP, and include increased responsibility for shouldering global burdens if new institutions are to be effective.

Increased Potential for Global Conflict

Of course, the report encompasses more than economics and indeed believes the future is likely to be the result of a number of intersecting and interlocking forces. With so many possible permutations of outcomes, each with ample opportunity for unintended consequences, there is a growing sense of insecurity. Even so, history may be more instructive than ever. While we continue to believe that the Great Depression is not likely to be repeated, the lessons to be drawn from that period include the harmful effects on fledgling democracies and multiethnic societies (think Central Europe in 1920s and 1930s) and on the sustainability of multilateral institutions (think League of Nations in the same period). There is no reason to think that this would not be true in the twenty-first as much as in the twentieth century. For that reason, the ways in which the potential for greater conflict could grow would seem to be even more apt in a constantly volatile economic environment than they would be if change would be steadier.

In surveying those risks, the report stressed the likelihood that terrorism and nonproliferation will remain priorities even as resource issues move up on the international agenda. Terrorism's appeal will decline if economic growth continues in the Middle East and youth unemployment is reduced. For those terrorist groups that remain active in 2025, however, the diffusion of technologies and scientific knowledge will place some of the world's most dangerous capabilities within their reach. Terrorist groups in 2025 will likely be a combination of descendants of long established groups—inheriting organizational structures, command and control processes, and training procedures necessary to conduct sophisticated attacks—and newly emergent collections of the angry and disenfranchised that become self-radicalized, particularly in the absence of economic outlets that would become narrower in an economic downturn.

The most dangerous casualty of any economically-induced drawdown of U.S. military presence would almost certainly be the Middle East. Although Iran's acquisition of nuclear weapons is not inevitable, worries about a nuclear-armed Iran could lead states in the region to develop new security arrangements with external powers, acquire additional weapons, and consider pursuing their own nuclear ambitions. It is not clear that the type of stable deterrent relationship that existed between the great powers for most of the Cold War would emerge naturally in the Middle East with a nuclear Iran. Episodes of low intensity conflict and terrorism taking place under a nuclear umbrella could lead to an unintended escalation and broader conflict if clear red lines between those states involved are not well established. The close proximity of potential nuclear rivals combined with underdeveloped surveillance capabilities and mobile dual-capable Iranian missile systems also will produce inherent difficulties in achieving reliable indications and warning of an impending nuclear attack. The lack of strategic depth in neighboring states like Israel, short warning and missile flight times, and uncertainty of Iranian intentions may place more focus on preemption rather than defense, potentially leading to escalating crises.

Types of conflict that the world continues to experience, such as over resources, could reemerge, particularly if protectionism grows and there is a resort to neo-mercantilist practices. Perceptions of renewed energy scarcity will drive countries to take actions to assure their future access to energy supplies. In the worst case, this could result in interstate conflicts if government leaders deem assured access to energy resources, for example, to be essential for maintaining domestic stability and the survival of their regime. Even actions short of war, however, will have important geopolitical implications. Maritime security concerns are providing a rationale for naval build-ups and modernization efforts, such as China's and India's development of blue water naval capabilities. If the fiscal stimulus focus for these countries indeed turns inward, one of the most obvious funding targets may be military. Buildup of regional naval capabilities could lead to increased tensions, rivalries, and counterbalancing moves, but it also will create opportunities for multinational cooperation in protecting critical sea lanes. With water also becoming scarcer in Asia and the Middle East, cooperation to manage changing water resources is likely to be increasingly difficult both within and between states in a more dog-eat-dog world.

What Kind of World Will 2025 Be?

Perhaps more than lessons, history loves patterns. Despite widespread changes in the world today, there is little to suggest that the future will not resemble the past in several respects. The report asserts that, under most scenarios, the trend toward greater diffusion of authority and power that has been ongoing for a couple of decades is likely to accelerate because of the emergence of new global players, the worsening institutional deficit, potential growth in regional blocs, and enhanced strength of non-state actors and networks. The multiplicity of actors on the international scene could either strengthen the international system, by filling gaps left by aging post–World War II institutions, or could further fragment it and incapacitate international cooperation. The diversity in both type and kind of actor raises the likelihood of fragmentation occurring over the next two decades, particularly given the wide array of transnational challenges facing the international community.

Because of their growing geopolitical and economic clout, the rising powers will enjoy a high degree of freedom to customize their political and economic policies rather than fully adopting Western norms. They are also likely to cherish their policy freedom to maneuver, allowing others to carry the primary burden for dealing with terrorism, climate change, proliferation, energy security, and other system maintenance issues. Existing multilateral institutions, designed for a different geopolitical order, appear too rigid and cumbersome to undertake new missions, accommodate changing memberships and augment their resources. Nongovernmental organizations and philanthropic foundations, concentrating on specific issues, increasingly will populate the landscape but are unlikely to affect change in the absence of concerted efforts by multilateral institutions or governments. Efforts at greater inclusiveness, to reflect the emergence of the newer powers, may make it harder for international organizations to tackle transnational challenges. Respect for the dissenting views of member nations will continue to shape the agenda of organizations and limit the kinds of solutions that can be attempted.

An ongoing financial crisis and prolonged recession would tilt the scales even further in the direction of a fragmented and dysfunctional international system with a heightened risk of conflict. The report concluded that the rising BRIC powers (Brazil, Russia, India, and China) seem averse to challenging the international system, as Germany and Japan did in the nineteenth and twentieth centuries, but this of course could change if their widespread hopes for greater prosperity become frustrated and the current benefits they derive from a globalizing world turn negative.

Mathew J. Burrows is a counselor in the National Intelligence Council (NIC), the principal drafter of Global Trends 2025: A Transformed World, *and can be reached at mathejb@ucia.gov. Jennifer Harris is a member of the NIC's Long Range Analysis Unit who worked closely on the report, and can be reached at jennifmh@dni.gov.*

Copyright © 2009 Mathew J. Burrows and Jennifer Harris
The Washington Quarterly • 32:2 pp. 27–38
DOI: 10.080/01636600902772604

ENDNOTES

1. National Intelligence Council, *Global Trends* 2025: A *Transformed World*, November 2008, http://www.dni.gov/nic/PDF_2025/2025_Global_Trends_Final_Report.pdf.

2. Morgan Stanley Asia chief Stephen Roach articulates this growing view: "What we're seeing is that the Chinese command-and-control system can actually work more effectively than other market-based systems in times of economic stress." Quoted in Rana Foorohor, "Why China Works," *Newsweek*, January 19, 2009. While offering no normative endorsements, Robert Kagan of *The Washington Post* and Gideon Rachman of the *Financial Times* also concede the successes of state-capitalist models.

G. John Ikenberry

The Liberal International Order and Its Discontents

Introduction

The American-led world system is troubled. Some would argue that it is in crisis. But what sort of crisis is it? Is it a crisis of America's position in the global system or is it a deeper world historical transition in which liberalism and the liberal international order are at risk? Is the American-led 'liberal era' ending, or is it transforming into a new sort of liberal order? What would a post-hegemonic liberal order look like? What sort of historical moment is this? Has the 'liberal ascendency' of the last two hundred years peaked, or is it simply taking new twists and turns? If liberal internationalism as it has been organized in the post-war era is giving way to something new, what is that 'something new'? This article takes up these questions.

Many observers see grand changes. Henry Kissinger has argued that he has never seen the world in such 'flux' with so few agreed-upon rules and norms to guide the flow of change. The National Intelligence Council has published its 'Global Trends 2025', arguing that a 'return to multipolarity' is the master trend of the coming decades. This movement towards multipolarity will manifest itself in a gradual diffusion of power away from the West, the rise of new power centres, a decay in multilateral institutional governance and new forms of conflict among great powers and regions.[1]

Some observers see a new divide between autocratic and liberal democratic states. The liberal international optimism in the West has given way to worries about coming breakdowns and divides among the great powers. Robert Kagan sees a rise in influence of authoritarian states that are hostile to Western visions of order. Russia and China are the leading edge of the autocratic revival; unlike the old authoritarian states of the last century, they are adaptive to global capitalism, and capable of sustained growth and development. They are able to trade and invest in world markets. Yet, at the same time, they are anti-liberal and hostile to Western democracy. They have, in effect, found a pathway to modernity and development that bypasses liberal democratic practices and institutions; it is only a step away from this analysis to argue that 'multiple modernities' exist. The great post–Cold War anticipation of a global liberal revolution has been dashed by the 'return of history'.[2] Some see China as an emerging rival wielding a non-liberal strategic orientation. Martin Jacques gives a dramatic version of this view. China is emerging as the next global hegemon; it will build a non-liberal, even anti-liberal, world order. As a result, the world will have two pathways to modernity. One is the old Western liberal pathway. The other is the authoritarian alternative.[3]

These anticipations of coming struggles with Russia and China see the clash between liberalism and autocracy reinforced by other factors. One is historical grievances. Russia feels disrespected and encroached upon in the decades since the end of the Cold War, and China is an emerging world power that nurses resentments from its century of humiliation. The other is the intensification of competition over energy and resources. This great power competition will reinforce liberal and statist models of economics and security and bring mercantilism back into the centre of world politics.

In the great narratives of this moment, the world is transitioning away from the American-led liberal order. It is a story of the return to multipolarity, the rise of new great powers and multiple pathways to modernity. The 2008 financial crisis and subsequent world economic downturn—the most severe since the Great Depression—has also been a blow to the American-led system. Unlike past post-war economic crises, this one had its origins in the United States. The repercussions of this economic crisis are complex and still playing out. But it has served to tarnish the American model of liberal capitalism and raised new doubts about the capacities of the United States to act as the global leader in the provision of economic stability and advancement.[4]

I want to be sceptical of these views. Yes, the American liberal hegemonic order is in crisis. But it is a crisis of authority within the liberal international order and not a crisis of its underlying principles and organizational logic. That is, it is a crisis of the American governance of liberal order and not of liberal order itself. The crisis of liberalism today will ultimately bring forth 'more liberalism'. This is true if by liberal order we mean an open, rule-based relations system organized around expanding forms of institutionalised cooperation. In this sense, liberal international order can be contrasted with alternative logics of order—blocs, exclusive spheres and closed geopolitical systems. The future still belongs to the liberal international order. . . .

American-Led Liberal International Order

Remarkably, we still live in the international order built by the United States and its allies over a half-century ago. It is a distinctive type of order, organised around open markets, multilateral institutions, cooperative security, alliance partnership, democratic solidarity and United States hegemonic leadership. It is an order anchored in large-scale institutions, which include the United Nations, NATO, the Bretton Woods institutions, the World Trade Organization [WTO], alliance partnerships between the United States and Asian partners, and informal governance groupings such as the G-7/8. In the background, the United States played a hegemonic role, providing public goods by supporting open markets and the provisioning of security.[5]

This American-led international order was a very specific type of liberal order. It was a liberal *hegemonic* order. The United States did not just encourage an open and rule-based order. It gradually became its hegemonic organiser and manager. The American political system—and its alliances, technology, currency and markets—became fused to the wider liberal order. In the shadow of the Cold War, the United States became the 'owner and operator' of the liberal capitalist political system. The United States supported the rules and institutions of liberal internationalism but it was also given special rights and privileges. It organised and led an extended political system built around multilateral institutions, alliances, strategic partners and client states. It was an order infused with strategic understandings and hegemonic bargains. The United States provided 'services' to other states through the provision of security and its commitment to stability and open markets. In these ways, the United States was more than just a powerful country that *dominated* the global system. It *created* a political order; a hierarchical order with liberal characteristics.

The liberal imagination is vast—and the liberal vision of international order has many facets. From the early 19th century through the current era, liberals have articulated a cluster of ideas and aspirations: free trade, multilateralism, collective security, democratic community, progressive change, shared sovereignty and the rule of law. The post-war American vision was a specific version of liberal international order. It was hegemonic. As noted, it was an arrangement in which the United States actively managed the wider system. The United States and the wider liberal order were organized into a single extended global order. This type of liberal order can be contrasted with earlier liberal political formations. In the 19th century, liberal order was manifest in open trade and the gold standard, flourishing in the shadow of British economic and naval mastery. After World War I, Woodrow Wilson sought to construct a more far-reaching liberal progressive order, organized around the League of Nations. It was a system that did not rely on American hegemony but rather hinged on the cooperation of liberal democracies adhering to open trade and collective security. After World War II, Franklin Roosevelt again sought to construct a liberal order organized around great power concert and the United Nations. The rise of the Cold War, the weakness of Europe and the complexities associated with opening up and managing post-war order brought the United States more directly into the operation and management of the system. In fits and starts, liberal order turned into American liberal hegemonic order.[6]

This order has also been remarkably successful; it has accomplished a great deal over the last six decades. It provided a framework for the reopening of the world economy after World War II, ushering in a 'golden age' of growth. It integrated post-war Japan and Germany, who went on to become the second and third largest economies in the world, respectively. The Western alliance and the European 'project' provided institutional mechanisms to solve Europe's bloodiest geopolitical problem: Franco-German antagonism and the position of Germany within Europe. This was the quiet revolution in post-war world politics. A chronic source of war and political instability was eliminated. The larger Western-based liberal international order also provided an expansive system in which rising and transitioning countries could integrate and join. Over the last thirty years, over 500 million people in countries connected to this liberal order have been lifted out of poverty.[7] The Cold War was also ended peacefully, with countries in Eastern Europe and the former Soviet Union integrated into the Western order.

Overall, this American-led arrangement is arguably the most successful international order the world has yet seen. At least this is true if success is defined in terms of wealth creation, physical security and hope for justice. This order has not solved all the world's problems and it exists in a world with widespread human suffering and rising economic inequality. But in the context of the savage history of world politics over the last centuries, including the world wars of the recent past, it has been an unusually stable and functional system.

The Durability of Liberal International Order

There are also reasons to think that this liberal order will persist, even if it continues to evolve. Firstly, the violent forces that have overthrown international orders in the past do not seem to operate today. We live in the longest period of 'great power peace' in modern history. The great powers have not found themselves at war with each other since the guns fell silent in 1945. This non-war outcome is certainly influenced by two realities: nuclear deterrence, which raises the costs of war, and the dominance of democracies, who have found their own pathway to peace. In the past, the great moments of order-building came in the aftermath of war when the old order was destroyed. War itself was a ratification of the view that the old order was no longer sustainable. War broke the old order apart, propelled shifts in world power and opened up the international landscape for new negotiations over the rules and principles of world politics. In the absence of great power war it is harder to clear the ground for new 'constitutional' arrangements.

Secondly, this order is also distinctive in its integrative and expansive character. In essence, it is 'easy to join and hard to overturn'. This follows most fundamentally from the fact that it is a liberal international order— in effect, it is an order that is relatively open and loosely rule-based. The order generates participants and stakeholders. Beyond this, there are three reasons why the architectural features of this post-war liberal order reinforce downward and outward integration. One is that the multilateral character of the rules and institutions create opportunities for access and participation. Countries that want to join in can do so; Japan found itself integrating through participation in the trade system and alliance partnership. More recently, China has taken steps to join, at least through the world trading system. . . . Secondly, the liberal order is organised around shared leadership and not just the United States. The G-7/8 is an example of a governance organisation that is based on a collective leadership, and the new G-20 grouping has emerged to provide expanded leadership. Finally, the order also provides opportunities for a wide array of states to gain access to the 'spoils of modernity'. Again, this is not an imperial system in which the riches accrue disproportionately to the centre. States across the system have found ways to integrate into this order and experience economic gains and rapid growth along the way.

Thirdly, rising states do not constitute a bloc that seeks to overturn or reorganise the existing international order. China, India, Russia, Brazil, South Africa and others all are seeking new roles and more influence within the global system. But they do not constitute a new coalition of states seeking global transformation. All of these states are capitalist and as such are deeply embedded in the world economy. Most of them are democratic and embrace the political principles of the older Western liberal democracies. At the same time, they all have different geopolitical interests. They are as diverse in their orientations as the rest of the world in regard to energy, religion and ideologies of development. They are not united by a common principled belief in a post-liberal world order. They are all very much inside the existing order and integrated in various ways into existing governance institutions.

Fourthly, the major states in the system—the old great powers and rising states—all have complex alignments of interests. They all are secure in the sense that they are not threatened by other major states. All worry about radicalism and failed states. Even in the case of the most fraught relationships—such as the emerging one between the United States and China—there are shared or common interests in global issues related to energy and the environment. These interests are complex. There are lots of ways in which these countries will compete with each other and seek to push 'adjustment' to problems onto the other states. But it is precisely the complexity of these shared interests that creates opportunities and incentives to negotiate and cooperate—and, ultimately, to support the open and rule-based frameworks that allow for bargains and agreements to be reached.

Overall, these considerations suggest that the leading states of the world system are travelling along a common pathway to modernity. They are not divided by great ideological clashes or emboldened by the potential gains from great power war. These logics of earlier orders are not salient today.

Fascism, communism and theocratic dictatorships cannot propel you along the modernising pathway. In effect, if you want to be a modern great power you need to join the WTO. The capitalist world economy and the liberal rules and institutions that it supports—and that support it—are foundational to modernisation and progress. The United States and other Western states may rise or fall within the existing global system but the liberal character of that system still provides attractions and benefits to most states within it and on its edges.

Liberal Order and the Great Transformations

Obviously, great shifts are underway, many of them long in the making. The end of the Cold War triggered a slow-motion transformation in the global system. The American-led liberal order has existed within a larger bipolar Cold War distribution of power. With the collapse of the Soviet Union and the end of Cold War hostilities, this 'inside system' became the 'outside system'. The liberal order was thrown open and exposed to the entire world. This has triggered a variety of complex reactions. New questions were asked about the role of alliances and debates about threats. If the Cold War alliances were part of the architecture of the American-led liberal order, that part of the hegemonic framework was rendered less stable. In addition, new questions about political identity were triggered. Are we 'one people'? Is there a 'free world'? Does democratic solidarity still matter in the absence of a common enemy?[8]

The end of the Cold War also ushered in problems with Russia. At first, the Western powers and the Russian Federation had found a peaceful settlement of their bipolar rivalry. But the United States and Europe also found themselves encroaching on Russian geopolitical interests. NATO expansion was in part driven by liberal aspirations to expand the club of democracies eastward, to include newly liberalising post-communist states. But this exercise in liberal expansionism tended to come at the expense of Russia's sensibilities. Other developments also eroded Moscow's relationship with the West. The American withdrawal from the ABM treaty and the failure to go forward with the START II arms control talks signalled a retreat from the vision that American and Soviet leaders articulated at the end of the Cold War. Tensions between the West and Russia have mounted in more recent years over oil and pipeline issues, rights of Russian minorities, borders inherited from the former Soviet Union and the democratisation of former Soviet republics.[9]

The rise of unipolarity has made American power more controversial and raised the level of uncertainty around the world about the bargains and institutions of liberal order. With the end of the Cold War, America's primacy in the global distribution of capabilities became one of the most salient features of the international system. No other major state has enjoyed such advantages in material capabilities—military, economic, technological, geographical. This unipolar distribution of power is historically unique, and it has ushered in a new set of dynamics that are still working their way through the organisation of world politics. But the rise of unipolarity brings with it a shift in the underlying logic of order and rule in world politics. In a bipolar or multipolar system, powerful states 'rule' in the process of leading a coalition of states in balancing against other states. When the system shifts to unipolarity, this logic of rule disappears. Power is no longer based on balancing or equilibrium, but on the predominance of one state. This is new and different—and potentially threatening to weaker and secondary states.[10]

A more gradual shift in the global system is the unfolding human rights and the 'responsibility to protect' revolution, resulting in an erosion of the central Westphalian norm of sovereignty over the post-war decades. The international community is seen as having a legitimate interest in what goes on within countries, its growing interest in the domestic governance practices of states driven by considerations of both human rights and security. In consequence, norms of sovereignty are seen as more contingent. Their gradual erosion has created a new 'licence' for powerful states to intervene in the domestic affairs of weak and troubled states. Over the past few centuries, Westphalian sovereignty has been the single most universal and agreed-upon norm of international politics. It underlies international law, the United Nations and the great historical movements of anti-colonialism and national self-determination. So when the norm weakens, the consequences are not in the least surprising. But the erosion of state sovereignty norms has not been matched by the rise of new norms and agreements about *how* the international community should make good on human rights and the responsibility to protect. Unresolved disagreements mount regarding the standards of legality and legitimacy that regulate the actions of powerful states acting on behalf of the international community.

The sources of insecurity in world politics have also evolved since the early decades that shaped American liberal hegemony. As noted earlier, the threat to peace is no longer primarily from great powers engaged in security competition. The result has been a shift in the ways in which violence is manifest. In the past, only powerful states were able to gain access to the destructive capabilities that could threaten other societies. Today, it is possible to see technology and the globalisation of the world system as creating opportunities for non-state actors—or transnational gangs—to acquire weapons of mass destruction, As a result, it is now the weakness of states and their inability to enforce law and order within their own societies that provide the most worrisome dangers to the international system.

In contrast to earlier eras, there is no single enemy—or source of violence and insecurity—that frames and reinforces the American-led liberal order. The United States and other states face a diffuse array of threats and challenges. Global warming, health pandemics, nuclear proliferation, jihadist terrorism, energy scarcity—these and other dangers loom on the horizon. Any of these threats could endanger Western lives and liberal ways of life either directly or indirectly by destabilising the global system upon which security and prosperity depend. Pandemics and global warming are not threats wielded by human hands, but their consequences could be equally devastating. Highly infectious disease has the potential to kill millions of people. Global warming threatens to trigger waves of environmental migration and food shortages, further destabilising weak and poor states around the world. The world is also on the cusp of a new round of nuclear proliferation, putting mankind's deadliest weapons in the hands of unstable and hostile states. Terrorist networks offer a new spectre of non-state transnational violence. The point is that none of these threats are, in themselves, so singularly preeminent that they deserve to be the centrepiece of American national security as were anti-fascism and anti-communism in an earlier era.

The master trend behind these diffuse threats is the rise and intensification of 'security interdependence'. This notion is really a measure of how much a state's national security depends on the policies of other actors. If a country is security 'independent' it means that it is capable of achieving an acceptable level of security through its own actions. Others can threaten it, but the means for coping with these threats are within its own national hands. This means that the military intentions and capacities of other states are irrelevant to a state's security. This is true either because the potential military threats are too remote and far removed to matter, or because if a foreign power is capable of launching war against the state, it has the capabilities to resist the aggression.[11]

Security interdependence is the opposite circumstance. The state's security depends on the policy and choices of other actors. Security is established by convincing other actors not to attack. During the Cold War, the United States and the Soviet Union were in a situation of supreme security interdependence. Each had nuclear weapons that could destroy the other. It was the logic of deterrence that established the restraints on policy. Each state knew that to launch a nuclear strike on the other would be followed by massive and assured retaliation. States cannot protect themselves or achieve national security without the help of other states. There is no 'solution' to the security problem without active cooperation.

Today, more people in more places matter for the security of the states within the old liberal international order. With the growth of transnational and diffuse threats, we are witnessing an explosion in the complexity of security interdependence. What people do and how they live matter in ways that were irrelevant in earlier eras. How people burn energy, provide public health, treat minorities and enforce rules and treaties count more today than ever before. The result is a rising demand for security cooperation. The demand for universal, cooperative, institutionalised and rule-based order will grow—and not decline—in the decades ahead.

Trends Shaping Future Liberal International Order

In seeking to detect the evolving contours of international order, there are three trends that bear special attention. First, is the so-called 'return of multipolarity'. This is the alleged movement away from American unipolarity towards a more decentralised global power structure inhabited by rival great powers. How quickly is this happening and what are its consequences? In tracking this development, it is important to distinguish between three steps towards multipolarity. The first is the simple diffusion of power: a gradual transition in the systemic distribution of power whereby the United States will experience an erosion of its relative advantages in material capabilities. Its share of world GNP in market size and in military capabilities will shrink. A second step towards multipolarity involves not just a redistribution of power but also the rise of new 'poles'. This entails the emergence of great powers that take on characteristics of a 'hub'. They have their own security alliances, commercial partners, political networks and so forth. A 'pole' is manifest not just as a concentration of power but in the way it builds networks and takes on the role of an organising hub for other states within the larger system. The third step towards multipolarity would involve not just a diffusion of power and the rise of new 'poles', but also the triggering of balancing and security competition. This would be a world in which the restraints and accommodations that the major states have made within the post-war American-led order would give way to more traditional power balancing. My point is that it is possible to witness a diffusion of power and not see the emergence of new 'poles', and it is possible to see the rise of new 'poles' without the commencement of great power balance of power politics.[12]

The most important question in this regard is China. Is it emerging as a geopolitical 'pole'? This, in turn, raises specific questions. Is it becoming a source of attraction? Is it becoming a security provider for states in its region? What sort of alliance partnerships is it developing, if any? What sorts of 'soft power' characteristics does China project as it rises? Answers to these questions are not obvious but the way and extent to which China becomes a 'pole' will help shape the character of the next cycle of international order.

The second major trend to watch is the softening or deterioration of political order in key states. This question concerns the stability of political institutions in late-developing states that have emerged in recent decades and integrated into the liberal international order. Examples are Brazil, Mexico, Turkey and Indonesia. What are the changing political capacities of these modernising states? Do they face common challenges as middle-tier states? What will be the consequences for the global system if these states fall back and experience a decline in their ability to function as stable democracies?

The third trend to watch is the way and extent to which rising states get integrated into the existing liberal international order. As I have argued, the post-war liberal order has been an American-centred and Western-oriented hegemonic order. The great drama of the next few decades will involve the choices and strategies of rising states, such as India, China, Brazil, as they confront this old order.

The analogy might be a big corporation. For over half a century, the liberal international order has been owned and operated by the United States. It can be called American Inc. This American-dominated system emerged out of Cold War circumstances, and the family-owned corporation grew and prospered. But today, the struggle is to 'go public' with the company. Rising countries are seeking a greater role and voice in the global system. The United States is finding itself under pressure to turn American Inc. into a publicly traded company. It has to invite new share-holders and add members to the board of directors. The United States (and Europe) will remain leading members of the board. But their voice and vote will not be what they once were. The challenge of the liberal international order today is to manage this transition in its ownership and governance.

Conclusions

I want to end where I began by discussing the nature of the 'crisis' that besets the American-led liberal international order. My conclusion is that if the 'liberal order' is in crisis, it is a crisis of *success* and not a crisis of *failure*. It is not a crisis in the way that some observers have depicted it in the past—by presenting the 'liberal project' as an idealist enterprise that cannot take hold in a world of anarchy and power politics. The crisis today is precisely the opposite of this classic charge. That is, the liberal project has succeeded only too well. The global system has boomed under conditions of hegemonic rule. It is expanding and integrating on a global scale and creating economic and security interdependencies well beyond the imagination of its original architects. The crisis today is that the old *hegemonic* foundations of the liberal order are no longer adequate, rather than reflect a failure of the order itself.

In effect, my argument is that this is not an E.H. Carr crisis. Rather it is a Karl Poianyi crisis. An E.H. Carr crisis is a moment when realists can step forward and say liberals had it wrong and that the crisis of their project reveals the enduring truths of self-regarding states and the balance of power.

Instead, it is a Karl Polanyi crisis, where liberal governance is troubled because dilemmas and long-term shifts in the order can only be solved by rethinking, rebuilding and extending that liberal order.

Liberal order generates the seeds of its own unmaking, which can only be averted by more liberal order—reformed, updated and outfitted with a new foundation. This is not a story about the rise and spread of Western liberalism. It is a story of modernity and the global search for universal principles of politics and economics. No region or people owns this story. It is a story that is written on a world scale—and it is one of breakthroughs, crises, triumphs and transformations. The liberal international order is in crisis. But after liberalism there will be more, well, liberalism.

G. John Ikenberry is Albert C. Milbank Professor of Politics and International Affairs at Princeton University and a Global Eminence Scholar at Kyung Hee University, Korea. His forthcoming book is Liberal Leviathan: The Origins, Triumph, Crisis, and Transformation of the American World Order *(Princeton University Press, forthcoming).*

ENDNOTES

1. The National intelligence Council, *Global Trends* 2025 (Washington, D.C.: The National Intelligence Council, 2008). On anticipations of a return to multipolarity and the end of American dominance, see Charles Kupchan, *The End of the American Era: US Foreign Policy and the Geopolitics of the Twenty-First Century* (New York: Knopf, 2003); Parag Khanna, *The Second World: Empires and Influence in the New Global Age* (New York: Random House, 2008); and Fareed Zakaria, *The Post-American World* (New York: Norton, 2009).
2. Robert Kagan, *The Return of History and the End of Dreams* (New York: Knopf, 2008). See also Azar Cat, *Victorious and Vulnerable: Why Democracy Won in the 20th Century and How It Is still Imperiled* (New York: Rowman & Littlefield, 2009).
3. Martin Jacques, *When China Rules the World: The End of the Western World and the Birth of a New Global Order* (New York: The Penguin Press, 2009).
4. For arguments about the impact of the world economic crisis on the American neo-liberal model and Washington's leadership capacities, see Joseph Stiglitz, *America, Free Markets, and the Sinking of the World Economy* (New York: Norton, 2010); J. Bradford Lelong and Stephen S. Cohen, *The End of Influence: What Happens When Other Countries have the Money* (New York: Basic Books, 2010).
5. For depictions of the American-led post-war order, see G. John Ikenberry, *After Victory: Institutions, Strategic Restraint, and the Rebuilding of Order after Major War* (Princeton: Princeton University Press, 2001); and Stewart Patrick, *The Best Laid Plans: The Origins of American Multilateralism and the Dawn of the Cold War* (New York: Rowman & Littlefield, 2009).

6. See G. John Ikenberry, 'Liberal Internationalism 3.0: America and the Dilemmas of Liberal World Order', *Perspectives on Politics* 7, no. 1 (2009): 71–87.

7. See Bruce Jones, Carlos Pascual and Stephen John Stedman, *Power and Responsibility: Building International Order in an Era of Transnational Threats* (Washington, D.C.: Brookings Institution Press, 2009), xiii.

8. For a searching reflection on Western identity, see Timothy Garton Ash, *Free World: America, Europe, and the Surprising Future of the West* (New York: Random House, 2004).

9. Daniel Deudney and C. John Ikenberry, 'The Unravelling of the Cold War Settlement', *Survival* 51, no. 6 (December 2009–January 2010): 39–62.

10. An international system is unipolar if it 'contains one state whose overall share of capabilities places it unambiguously in a class by itself compared to all other states'. G. John Ikenberry, Michael Mastanduno and William C. Wohlforth, 'Introduction: Unipolarity, State Behavior, and Systemic Consequences', *World Politics* 61, no. 1(2009): 5.

11. See Daniel Deudney, *Bounding Power: Republican Security Theory from the Polis to the Global Village* (Princeton: Princeton University Press, 2007).

12. For a discussion of the logic and implications of a 'return to multipolarity', see Barry Posen, 'Emerging Multipolarity: Why Should We Care?' *Current History*, 108 (November 2009).

PART II

INTERNATIONAL TRADE

International trade used to be obscure and uncontroversial. Governments would negotiate agreements in Geneva and nobody would pay them much attention. International trade has become substantially more controversial during the last fifteen years. The public and civil society now appear increasingly hostile toward trade and toward global trade institutions. Debates have emerged about whether trade and globalization more generally are good things for American workers. Debates have emerged about whether governments should liberalize trade exclusively through the World Trade Organization (WTO) or also through regional arrangements such as the North American Free Trade Agreement. Debates have emerged about whether global trade rules limit the ability of governments to achieve other desirable social objectives such as protecting the environment and safeguarding human and animal health. Part II examines these contemporary debates.

Chapter 2 explores the impact of international trade, and the U.S. trade deficit, on job destruction and job creation. Trade liberalization promotes specialization in production along the lines of comparative advantage. Societies that trade, therefore, should lose jobs in some sectors and create jobs in others. Robert Scott argues here that these labor market dynamics are compounded by the trade deficit the United States has run for more than twenty-five years. Focusing on the U.S.– China bilateral trade deficit, Scott argues that the excess of imports over exports results in net job reduction for the United States. Douglas Irwin challenges Scott's logic. He argues that the net job loss that may be attributed to the trade deficit is offset by net job creation attributable to foreign investment in the United States. For Irwin, therefore, trade, and even the trade deficit, does not affect how many jobs are available in the United States, but rather the kind of jobs available.

Chapter 3 examines how to maintain public support for trade given its impact on people employed in comparatively disadvantaged industries. Because trade eliminates jobs in some areas and creates jobs in others, some people must transition out of their current jobs to new work. In addition, the Stolper–Samuelson theorem tells us that trade has some permanent redistributive consequences: It reduces the return to society's scarce factor. Hence, some people will earn less than they did previously. How can we best maintain public support for trade in the face of these labor market consequences? Howard Rosen argues that the best approach relies on a variety of instruments that retrain displaced workers and help them find new jobs in expanding sectors. Such Trade Adjustment Assistance offers temporary support for people directly harmed by trade. Kenneth Scheve and Matthew Slaughter argue that Trade Adjustment Assistance is inadequate. Instead of such exclusive reliance on short-term adjustment assistance, they call for permanent redistribution of income from those who clearly gain from trade to those who are made worse off.

Chapter 4 explores the debate over the free flow of people across borders. Whereas governments have greatly liberalized the cross-border flow of goods, services, technology, and capital, they continue to restrict the cross-border flow of people. Philippe LeGrain argues that governments should liberalize flows of people, too. Migrants, he argues, may move to enhance their own position, but they end up providing substantial benefits to their host countries as well. The free flow of people, therefore, is a "win–win" situation. David Goodhart argues that governments should continue to restrict migration. Paying particular attention to the impact of migration to Great Britain from its former colonies, he argues that unfettered migration can weaken a society's cultural, linguistic, and political cohesion. He thereby highlights a tension between liberal commitment to social cohesion on the one hand and multicultural diversity on the other.

Chapter 5 considers the consequences of governments' current enthusiasm for preferential trade arrangements (PTAs). PTAs, which include free trade areas like the North American Free Trade Area and customs unions like the European Union, are trade-liberalizing affairs. Yet debate exists about whether PTAs have a net positive or net negative impact on international trade. Daniel Griswold argues that PTAs are a building block toward a world of global free trade. By this logic, governments will first eliminate all trade barriers within regional PTAs and then eliminate all trade barriers between regional PTAs. Jagdish Bhagwati argues that PTAs are a stumbling block to global free trade. He suggests that the preferential nature of PTAs introduces inefficiencies into the international trade system.

Chapter 6 discusses the impact of international trade and the international trade system on the environment. The central question under consideration is whether governments can restrict trade under current

WTO rules in support of domestic regulations that reduce greenhouse gas emissions. Jeffrey Frankel asserts that such trade restrictions are a useful tool to support climate change regulation and are consistent with obligations under the World Trade Organization. Jason Bordoff argues that even if WTO rules allow such trade restrictions in support of global warming regulation, governments should create new non-trade instruments. He argues that allowing trade restrictions opens the door to disguised protectionism under which governments protect uncompetitive firms and justify the action in environmental terms.

CHAPTER 2 TRADE DEFICITS REDUCE TOTAL JOBS *v.* TRADE DEFICITS PRODUCE DIFFERENT JOBS

Trade Deficits Reduce Total Jobs

Advocate: Robert E. Scott

Source: The China Trade Toll, EPI Briefing Paper #219 (Washington, DC: Economic Policy Institute, 2008)

Trade Deficits Produce Different Jobs

Advocate: Douglas A. Irwin

Source: "The Employment Rationale for Trade Protection," in *Free Trade under Fire* (Princeton, NJ: Princeton University Press, 2002), 70–90

The United States has run persistent trade and current account deficits since the early 1970s. These trade deficits mean that each year residents of the United States purchase more goods and services from residents of other countries than they sell to residents of other countries. Between 1980 and 1999, the trade deficit averaged $94 billion per year. The deficit widened substantially to an average of $629 billion between 2001 and 2008.

Such persistent deficits raise a number of issues that have been at the center of policy debates during the last twenty years. What causes this trade imbalance? Does it reflect flaws or inequities in the international trade system, or does it instead reflect American domestic economic factors? What impact does the trade deficit have on the U.S. economy, especially on the jobs available to American workers? What policies might reduce the trade deficit?

TRADE DEFICITS REDUCE TOTAL JOBS

Some argue that the trade deficit is a consequence of multilateral and bilateral trade agreements that fail to limit unfair trade practices by the United States' trade partners. The World Trade Organization (WTO) does not prevent governments from implementing policies that enable their industries to prosper at the United States' expense. The resulting deficits eliminate jobs in the U.S. economy. A commonly cited estimate suggests that between 2001 and 2006, the trade deficit eliminated close to 2 million jobs in the United States.[1]

Robert Scott, an economist based at the Economic Policy Institute, embraces this framework to analyze the U.S. bilateral trade deficit with China. Scott attributes the bilateral trade deficit in large part to China's determination to keep its currency undervalued relative to the dollar and to the WTO's inability to prevent such policies. He estimates that the resulting bilateral trade deficit eliminated more than 2 million manufacturing jobs in the United States between 2001 and 2007.

TRADE DEFICITS PRODUCE DIFFERENT JOBS

Other analysts attribute the trade deficit to economic imbalances inside the United States. Americans have enjoyed a consumption boom during the last twenty-five years and have saved little. In addition, the U.S. government has run large budget deficits, which it must finance by borrowing. The trade deficit simply reflects these total expenditures relative to U.S. income. Moreover, the deficit does not eliminate jobs, as the foreign capital that finances the trade deficit creates new businesses that provide new jobs.

Douglas Irwin applies this lens to the U.S. multilateral deficit. He suggests that, although a trade deficit does eliminate some jobs, the foreign investment that finances the deficit creates new jobs. Hence, the deficit merely changes the kind of jobs available. According to Irwin, the deficit is caused by an imbalance between U.S. savings and investment rates and has nothing to do with trade policy or tariffs. Irwin's analysis thus implies that the United States can engage in trade liberalization without concern that trade reduces the number of jobs available to American workers.

POINTS **TO PONDER**

1. What does Scott omit from his analysis that Irwin argues is a necessary component of a full accounting of the impact of the trade deficit on American jobs?

2. Irwin argues that the trade deficit has no net effect on the number of jobs in the U.S. economy. Does this mean that trade deficits have no impact on American jobs and American workers? Why or why not?

3. Suppose the Obama administration decided to enact policies to eliminate the trade deficit. What specific policy changes would Scott's analysis suggest? What specific policies would Irwin's analysis suggest? Which approach do you prefer, and why?

---

[1] Robert E. Scott, *Fast Track to Lost Jobs*, EPI Briefing Paper #117 (Washington, DC: Economic Policy Institute, October 2001). Available at http://www.epi.org/content.cfm/bp117.

Robert E. Scott
The China Trade Toll

The growth of U.S. trade with China since China entered the World Trade Organization [WTO] in 2001 has had a devastating effect on U.S. workers and the domestic economy. Between 2001 and 2007 2.3 million jobs were lost or displaced, including 366,000 in 2007 alone. New demographic research shows that, even when re-employed in non-traded industries, the 2.3 million workers displaced by the increase in China trade deficits in this period have lost an average $8,146 per worker/year. In 2007, these losses totaled $19.4 billion.[1]

The impacts of the China trade deficit are not limited to its direct effects on the jobs and wages of those displaced. It is also critical to recognize that the indirect impact of trade on other workers is significant as well. Trade with less-developed countries has reduced the bargaining power of all workers in the U.S. economy who resemble the import-displaced in terms of education, credentials, and skills. Annual earnings for all workers without a four-year college degree are roughly $1,400 lower today because of this competition, and this group constitutes a large majority of the entire U.S. workforce (roughly 100 million workers or about 70% of all workers, Bivens (2008)). China, with nearly 40% of our non-oil imports from less-developed countries, is a chief contributor to this wage pressure. . . .

A major cause of the rapidly growing U.S. trade deficit with China is currency manipulation. China has tightly pegged its currency to the dollar at a rate that encourages a large bilateral surplus with the United States. Maintaining this peg required the purchase of about $460 billion in U.S. treasury bills and other securities in 2007 alone.[2] This intervention makes the yuan artificially cheap and provides an effective subsidy on Chinese exports. The best estimates place this effective subsidy at roughly 30%, even after recent appreciation in the yuan (Cline and Williamson 2008).[3]

China also engages in extensive suppression of labor rights. An AFL-CIO study estimated that repression of labor rights by the Chinese government has lowered manufacturing wages by 47% to 86% (AFL-CIO 2006, 138). China has also been accused of massive direct subsidization of export production in many key industries (see, e.g., Haley 2008). Finally, it maintains strict, non-tariff barriers to imports. As a result, China's exports to the United States of $323 billion in 2007 were more than five times greater than U.S. exports to China, which totaled only $61 billion (Table 2.1). China's trade surplus was responsible for 52.3% of the U.S. total non-oil trade deficit in 2007, making the China trade relationship this country's most imbalanced

Table 2.1 U.S. China trade and job displacement, 2001–07

U.S. trade with China ($billions, nominal)

	2001	2006	2007	Changes in: ($billions)			Percent change
				2001–06	2006–07	2001–07	2001–07
U.S. domestic exports[a]	$18.0	$51.6	$61.0	$33.7	$9.4	$43.1	240%
U.S. imports	102.1	287.1	323.1	185.0	36.0	221.0	217%
U.S. trade balance[b]	–84.1	–235.4	–262.1	–151.3	–26.6	–178.0	212%
Average annual change in the trade deficit				–30.0	–27.0	–30.0	21%

U.S. trade-related jobs supported and displaced (thousands of jobs)

	2001	2006	2007	2001–06	2006–07	2001–07	2001–07
U.S. domestic exports	166.7	425.7	482.3	259.1	56.5	315.6	189%

	2001	2006	2007	Changes in: (thousands of jobs)			Percent change
				2001–06	2006–07	2001–07	2001–07
U.S. imports- jobs displaced	1,188.2	3,376.9	3,799.1	2,188.6	422.2	2,610.9	220%
U.S. trade balance-net jobs lost[b]	1,021.5	2,951.1	3,316.8	1,929.6	365.7	2,295.3	225%
Average annual job displacement				385.9	365.7	382.5	22%

[a]Domestic exports are goods produced in the United States. Total exports as reported by the Census Bureau include re-exports, i.e., goods produced in other countries and shipped through the United States Total exports were $12.8 billion in 1997, $19.2 billion in 2001, and $965.2 billion in 2007. U.S. re-exports to China rose from 2.1% of total exports in 1997 to 6.9% in 2007. The employment estimates shown here are based [only] on domestic exports.

[b]Domestic exports minus imports. This value is sometimes referred to as net exports, since re-exports are not included in this balance. Hence, the trade deficit reported here is slightly larger than the figure report by the Census Bureau.

SOURCE: EPI analysis of Census Bureau and BLS data.

by far. Unless China raises the real value of the yuan by an additional 30% and eliminates these other trade distortions, the U.S. trade deficit and job losses will continue to grow rapidly in the future.

While the overall U.S. trade deficit improved significantly in 2007, largely as a result of the 30% decline of the dollar against major currencies since 2002 (including a 44% fall against the euro), the U.S. deficit with China increased $26.6 billion, in large part because China allowed the dollar to fall only 12% against the yuan between 2002 and 2007. The annual increase in the U.S.–China trade deficit slowed from $31.6 billion in 2006 to $26.7 billion in 2007, reflecting both a decline in U.S. GDP growth (reducing import demand) and the initial effects of the stronger yuan. However, yuan appreciation was largely delayed until late 2007 and 2008— too little and too late to be of any help in slowing the current U.S.–China trade gap to date.[4] Furthermore, the appreciation of the yuan has had little effect on the prices of U.S. imports from China, which rose only 2.5% between July 2005 (when the yuan was first adjusted) and May 2008, much less than the 19% appreciation of the yuan in that period (Congressional Budget Office 2008, 2).

China's entry into the WTO was supposed to bring it into compliance with an enforceable, rules-based regime which would require that it open its markets to imports from the United States and other nations. The United States also negotiated a series of special safeguard measures designed to limit the disruptive effects of surging Chinese imports on domestic producers. However, the core of the agreement failed to include any protections to maintain or improve labor or environmental standards and, prior to 2007, the administration rejected all requests for special safeguards protection. As a result, China's entry into the WTO has further tilted the international economic playing field against domestic workers and firms and in favor of multinational companies from the United States and other countries as well as state- and privately owned exporters in China. This shift has increased the global "race to the bottom" in wages and environmental quality and closed thousands of U.S. factories, decimating employment in a wide range of communities, states, and entire regions of the United States. U.S. national interests have suffered while U.S. multinationals have enjoyed record profits on their foreign direct investments (Scott 2008).

False Promises

Proponents of China's entry into the WTO frequently claimed that it would create jobs in the United States, increase U.S. exports, and improve the trade deficit with China. President Clinton claimed that the agreement allowing China into the WTO, which was negotiated during his administration, "creates a win–win result for both countries" (Clinton 2000, 9). He argued that exports to China "now support hundreds of thousands of American jobs" and that "these figures can grow substantially with the new access to the Chinese market the WTO agreement creates" (Clinton 2000, 10). Others in the White House, such as Kenneth Liberthal, the special advisor to the president and senior director for Asia affairs at the National Security Council, echoed Clinton's assessment:

> Let's be clear as to why a trade deficit might decrease in the short term. China exports far more to the U.S. than it imports [from] the U.S. . . . It will not grow as much as it would have grown without this agreement and over time clearly it will shrink with this agreement.[5]

Promises about jobs and exports misrepresented the real effects of trade on the U.S. economy: trade both creates and destroys jobs. Increases in U.S. exports tend to create jobs in the United States, but increases in imports will lead to job loss—by destroying existing jobs and preventing new job creation—as imports displace goods that otherwise would have been made in the United States by domestic workers.

The impact of changes in trade on employment is estimated here by calculating the labor content of changes in the trade balance—the difference between exports and imports. Each $1 billion in computer exports to China from the United States supports American jobs. However, each $1 billion in computer imports from China displaces the American workers who would have been employed making them in the United States. On balance, the net employment effect of trade flows depends on the growth in the trade deficit, not just exports.

Another critically important promise made by the promoters of liberalized U.S.–China trade was that the United States would benefit because of increased exports to a large and growing consumer market in China. However, despite widespread reports of the rapid growth of the Chinese middle class, this growth has not resulted in a significant increase in U.S. consumer exports to China. The most rapidly growing exports to China are bulk commodities such as grains, scrap, and chemicals; intermediate products such as semiconductors; and producer durables such as aircraft. Furthermore, the increase in U.S. exports to China since 2001 has been overwhelmed by the growth of U.S. imports.

Growing Trade Deficits and Job Losses

The U.S. trade deficit with China has risen from $84 billion in 2001 to $262 billion in 2007, an increase of $178 billion, as shown in Table 2.1. Since China entered the WTO in 2001, this deficit has increased by $30 billion per year on average, or 21% per year.

While it is true that exports support jobs in the United States, it is equally true that imports displace them. The net effect of trade flows on employment is determined by changes in the trade balance.[6] The employment impacts of growing trade deficits are estimated in this paper using an input-output model that estimates the direct and indirect labor requirements of producing output in a given domestic industry. The model includes 201 U.S. industries, 84 of which are in the manufacturing sector.[7]

The model estimates the amount of labor (number of jobs) required to produce a given volume of exports and the labor displaced when a given volume of imports is substituted for domestic output.[8] The net of these two numbers is essentially the jobs lost due to growing trade deficits, holding all else equal.

Jobs displaced by the growing China trade deficit are a net drain on employment in trade-related industries, especially those in the manufacturing sector. Even if increases in demand in other sectors absorb all the workers displaced by trade (an unlikely event), it is likely that job quality will suffer, as many non-traded industries such as retail trade and home health care pay lower wages and have less comprehensive benefits than traded goods industries.

U.S. exports to China in 2001 supported 166,700 jobs, but U.S. imports displaced production that would have supported 1,188,200 jobs, as shown in the bottom half of Table 2.1. Therefore, the $84 billion trade deficit in 2001 displaced 1,021,500 jobs in that year. Job displacement rose to 2,951,100 jobs in 2006 and 3,316,800 in 2007.

Since China's entry into the WTO in 2001 through 2007, the increase in U.S.–China trade deficits eliminated or displaced 2,295,300 U.S. jobs, as shown in the bottom half of Table 2.1. In the past year alone 365,700 jobs were lost, either through the destruction of existing jobs or by the prevention of new job creation. On average, 382,500 jobs per year have been lost/displaced since China's entry into the WTO.

Growth in trade deficits with China has reduced demand for goods produced in every region of the United States and has led to job displacement in all 50 states and the District of Columbia, as shown in Table 2.2. More than 200,000 jobs were lost in each of California and Texas and more than 100,000 each in New York, Illinois, Ohio, and Florida. Jobs displaced due to growing deficits with China exceeded 2.0% of total employment in 12 states including Idaho, New Hampshire, South Carolina, Oregon, California, Minnesota, Vermont, Texas, and Wisconsin as shown in Table 2.3. . . .

Growing trade deficits with China have clearly reduced domestic employment in traded goods industries, especially in the manufacturing sector, which has been hard hit by plant closings and job losses. Workers displaced by trade from the manufacturing sector have had particular difficulty in securing comparable employment elsewhere in the economy. More than one-third of workers displaced from manufacturing dropped out of the labor force (Kletzer 2001, 101, Table D2), and average wages of those who secured re-employment fell 11% to 13%.

Table 2.2 Net job loss due to growing trade deficits with China, ranked by number of job losses, 2001–07

State	Net job loss by state		
	2001–06	2006–07	2001–07
California	270,400	55,400	325,800
Texas	168,800	34,100	202,900
New York	105,700	21,300	127,000
Illinois	85,500	17,300	102,800
Ohio	85,800	17,000	102,700
Florida	83,900	17,000	100,900
Pennsylvania	72,700	12,400	85,100
North Carolina	67,400	12,400	79,800
Michigan	67,300	12,300	79,500
Georgia	62,000	11,500	73,600
New Jersey	56,400	11,400	67,800
Wisconsin	49,800	9,300	59,100
Minnesota	49,300	9,400	58,700
Massachusetts	48,800	9,600	58,400
Tennessee	45,900	8,800	54,700
Indiana	44,900	7,800	52,700
Missouri	38,000	7,500	45,400
Washington	38,000	6,900	44,900
Arizona	36,700	6,600	43,300
South Carolina	35,800	6,800	42,600
Virginia	33,200	6,300	39,500
Alabama	32,600	4,800	37,400
Oregon	31,400	5,400	36,800
Colorado	28,900	4,900	33,800
Kentucky	28,100	5,300	33,400
Maryland	22,200	4,100	26,600
Connecticut	22,100	4,000	26,100
Iowa	19,200	3,100	22,200
Arkansas	19,400	2,400	21,800
Mississippi	19,100	2,700	21,700
Utah	14,500	2,400	16,900
Kansas	14,000	2,600	16,600
Louisiana	13,500	2,400	15,900

(*continues*)

Table 2.2 (*continued*)

State	Net job loss by state		
	2001–06	2006–07	2001–07
New Hampshire	13,400	2,300	15,700
Oklahoma	13,200	2,200	15,400
Idaho	12,200	2,500	14,700
Nebraska	10,200	1,700	12,000
Maine	10,300	1,400	11,700
Nevada	9,100	1,600	10,700
Rhode Island	8,200	1,500	9,700
New Mexico	8,000	1,500	9,400
West Virginia	6,300	900	7,200
Vermont	5,500	1,000	6,500
Delaware	3,900	700	4,600
South Dakota	3,800	600	4,400
Hawaii	3,400	700	4,100
Montana	2,800	400	3,200
North Dakota	2,300	400	2,700
District of Columbia	2,000	400	2,400
Alaska	2,000	300	2,300
Wyoming	1,700	300	2,000
National total[a]	1,929,600	365,700	2,295,300

[a]Totals vary slightly due to rounding errors.
SOURCE: EPI analysis of Census Bureau and BLS data.

Table 2.3 Net job loss due to growing trade deficits with China, ranked by share of state employment, 2001–07

	Net jobs lost	Share of total state employment in 2001 (%)
Idaho	14,700	2.59
New Hampshire	15,700	2.50
South Carolina	42,600	2.34
Oregon	36,800	2.29
California	325,800	2.23
Minnesota	58,700	2.18
Vermont	6,500	2.15
Texas	202,900	2.13
Wisconsin	59,100	2.10

	Net jobs lost	Share of total state employment in 2001 (%)
North Carolina	79,800	2.05
Tennessee	54,700	2.03
Rhode Island	9,700	2.03
Alabama	37,400	1.96
Maine	11,700	1.92
Mississippi	21,700	1.92
Arizona	43,300	1.91
Arkansas	21,800	1.89
Georgia	73,600	1.87
Ohio	102,700	1.85
Kentucky	33,400	1.85
Indiana	52,700	1.80
Massachusetts	58,400	1.75
Michigan	79,500	1.74
Illinois	102,800	1.71
New Jersey	67,800	1.70
Washington	44,900	1.66
Missouri	45,400	1.66
Utah	16,900	1.56
Connecticut	26,100	1.55
Colorado	33,800	1.52
Iowa	22,200	1.51
Pennsylvania	85,100	1.50
New York	127,000	1.48
Florida	100,900	1.41
Nebraska	12,000	1.30
New Mexico	9,400	1.24
Kansas	16,600	1.23
South Dakota	4,400	1.16
Virginia	39,500	1.12
Delaware	4,600	1.10
Maryland	26,600	1.08
Oklahoma	15,400	1.03
Nevada	10,700	1.02
West Virginia	7,200	0.98

(*continues*)

Table 2.3 (*continued*)

	Net jobs lost	Share of total state employment in 2001 (%)
Louisiana	15,900	0.83
North Dakota	2,700	0.82
Montana	3,200	0.82
Wyoming	2,000	0.81
Alaska	2,300	0.80
Hawaii	4,100	0.74
District of Columbia	2,400	0.37
National total[a]	2,295,300	

[a]Totals vary slightly due to rounding errors.
SOURCE: EPI analysis of Census Bureau and BLS data.

Some economists have argued that job loss numbers extrapolated from trade flows are uninformative because aggregate employment levels in the United States are set by a broad range of macroeconomic influences, not just by trade flows. However, while the trade balance is but one of many variables affecting aggregate job creation, the employment impacts of trade identified in this paper can be interpreted as the "all else equal" effect of trade on domestic employment. The Federal Reserve, for example, may decide to cut interest rates to make up for job loss stemming from deteriorating trade balances (or any other economic influence), leaving net employment unchanged. This, however, does not change the fact that trade deficits by themselves are a net drain on employment.

Further, even in the best-case scenario in which other jobs rise up one-for-one to replace those displaced by trade flows, the job numbers in this paper are a (conservative) measure of the involuntary job displacement caused by growing trade deficits and a potent indicator of imbalance in the U.S. labor market and wider economy. Economists may label it a wash when the loss of a hundred manufacturing jobs in Ohio or Pennsylvania is offset by the hiring of a hundred construction workers in Phoenix, but in the real world these displacements often result in large income losses and even permanent damage to workers' earning power (Bivens 2008). . . .

Conclusion

The growing U.S. trade deficit with China has displaced huge numbers of jobs in the United States and has been a prime contributor to the crisis in manufacturing employment over the past six years. Moreover, the United States is piling up foreign debt, losing export capacity, and facing a more fragile macroeconomic environment.

Is America's loss China's gain? The answer is most certainly no. China has become dependent on the U.S. consumer market for employment generation, has suppressed the purchasing power of its own middle class with a weak currency, and, most importantly, has held hundreds of billions of hard currency reserves in low-yielding, risky assets instead of investing them in public goods that could benefit Chinese households. Its vast purchases of foreign exchange reserves have stimulated the overheating of its domestic economy, and inflation in China has accelerated rapidly in the past year. Its repression of labor rights has suppressed wages, thereby artificially subsidizing exports.

The U.S–China trade relationship needs a fundamental change. Addressing the exchange rate policies and labor standards issues in the Chinese economy are important first steps.

The author thanks Lauren Marra and Emily Garr for research assistance and Josh Bivens for comments.

This research was made possible by support from the Alliance for American Manufacturing.

ENDNOTES

1. The $19.4 billion includes losses experienced by workers displaced by growing imports and net losses experienced by the movement of jobs from import-competing sectors to industries producing exports to China.
2. These purchases financed more than one-half of the U.S. $731 billion current account deficit (the broadest measure of all U.S. trade and income flows) in 2007. But for these purchases, the reduced demand would have put significant downward pressure on the U.S. dollar. A substantial depreciation in the dollar would begin to improve the U.S. trade deficit within a few years.
3. The official name of the Chinese currency is the renminbi (RMB). The RMB is convertible for current account transactions but not for capital account flows. "Unlike the United States and many other countries, China uses a different word—yuan—for the unit in which product prices, exchange rates, and other such values are denominated from the word used for its currency" (Congressional Budget Office 2008, note 3). Hereinafter the word yuan will be used when referring to the Chinese exchange rate.
4. The trade balance usually responds to a fall in the dollar with a substantial lag of at least one to two years, due to "J-curve" effects. The major initial impact of a depreciation is usually to raise the price and total value of imports, and hence the trade deficit. In the medium- and long- term, the trade flows usually respond to the increase in the relative competitiveness of domestic products as the rate of growth of imports slows or imports decrease, and the rate of growth of exports accelerates, ultimately leading to an improvement in the trade balance for large currency adjustments. Most of the dollar adjustment against major currencies occurred between February 2002 and December 2004. For example, the dollar

fell 36.4% against the euro in this period, and then fell only 4.0% between December 2004 and December 2007.

5. NewsHour with Jim Lehrer transcript. 1999. "Online NewsHour: Opening Trade—November 15, 1999." <http://www.pbs.org/newshour/bb/asia/july-dec99/wto_11-15.html>

6. Output (gross domestic product or GDP) is the sum of consumption, investment, government spending, and the trade balance. The trade balance is the sum of exports less imports. A declining trade balance lowers GDP. The growth of the U.S. trade deficit with China has therefore reduced U.S. GDP and the demand for labor. Holding all other sources of demand constant, growing trade deficits therefore reduce the demand for labor in the U.S.

7. See Scott (2006) for further details on the model and Ratner (2006) for a technical presentation and details on data sources used. This model has been completely updated for this study using new employment requirements tables for 2001 and related economic data from the Bureau of Labor Statistics (2008). Trade data collected by the U.S. Census Bureau was downloaded from the U.S. International Trade Commission (2008).

8. For the purposes of this report it is necessary to distinguish between exports produced domestically and re-exports—which are goods produced in other countries, imported into the United States, and then re-exported to other countries, in this case to China. Since re-exports are not produced domestically, their production does not support domestic employment and they are excluded from the model used here. See Table 2.1 for information about the levels of U.S. re-exports to China in this period.

REFERENCES

AFL-CIO, U.S. Representative Benjamin L. Cardin, and U.S. Representative Christopher H. Smith (AFL-CIO et al.). 2006. "Section 301 Petition [on China's repression of workers' rights]." June 8.

Bivens, L. Josh. 2008. Trade, Jobs, and Wages: Are the Public's Worries about Globalization Justified? Issue Brief No. 244. Washington, D.C.: Economic Policy Institute. http://www.epi.org.

Bureau of Labor Statistics, Office of Employment Projections. 2008a. Special Purpose Files—Industry Output and Employment. Washington, D.C.: U.S. Department of Labor. http://www.bls.gov/emp/empind2.htm.

Bureau of Labor Statistics, Office of Employment Projections. 2008b. Special Purpose Files—Employment Requirements. Washington, D.C.: U.S. Department of Labor. http://stats.bls.gov/emp/empind4.htm.

Cline, William R., and John Williamson. 2008. New Estimates of Fundamental Equilibrium Exchange Rates. Policy Brief #PB08–7. Washington, D.C.: Peterson Institute for International Economics.

Clinton, Bill. 2000. "Expanding Trade, Protecting Values: Why I'll Fight to Make China's Trade Status Permanent." New Democrat, Vol. 12, No. 1, pp. 9–11.

Congressional Budget Office. 2008. "How Changes in the Value of the Chinese Currency Affect U.S. Imports." Washington, D.C.: Congress of the United States, Congressional Budget Office.

Faux, Jeff, Bruce Campbell, Carlos Salas, and Robert Scott. 2006. Revisiting NAFTA: Still Not Working for North America's Workers. Briefing Paper. Washington, D.C.: Economic Policy Institute.

Haley, Usha C. V. 2008. Shedding Light on Energy Subsidies in China: An Analysis of China's Steel Industry from 2000–2007. Washington, D.C.: Alliance for American Manufacturing.

Kletzer, Lori G. 2001. Job Loss from Imports: Measuring the Costs. Washington, D.C.: Institute for International Economics.

Ratner, David. 2006. "Appendix: Methodology and Data Sources." In Faux et al. 2006.

Scott, Robert E. 2006. "NAFTA's Legacy: Rising Trade Deficits Lead to Significant Job Displacement and Declining Job Quality for the United States." In Faux et al. 2006.

Scott, Robert E. 2008. Increase in Oil Prices, Fall in Investment Income Exacerbates Current Account Deficit Woes. Washington, D.C.: Economic Policy Institute. http://www.epi.org.

U.S. Census Bureau. 2008. "Basic Monthly Survey of the Current Population Survey (Data for 2005–07)." Washington, D.C.: U.S. Department of Commerce.

U.S. International Trade Commission. 2008. USITC Interactive Tariff and Trade Data Web. http://dataweb.usitc.gov/scripts/user_set.asp.

Douglas A. Irwin

The Employment Rationale for Trade Protection

Economic analysis has long established free trade as a desirable economic policy. This conclusion has been reinforced by mounting empirical evidence on the benefits of free trade, and yet protectionism is far from vanquished in the policy arena. Of course, this is nothing new: as Adam Smith observed more than two hundred years ago, "not only the prejudices of the public, but what is much more unconquerable, the private interests of many individuals, irresistibly oppose" free trade (Smith 1976, 471). Industries that compete against imports will always actively promote their own interests by seeking trade restrictions. But, as Smith acknowledges, the general public also has concerns about foreign competition. The argument that resonates most strongly with the public and with politicians is that imports destroy jobs. Is this an accurate view of trade as a whole? And if so, are import restrictions the remedy? . . .

Does Free Trade Affect Employment?

The claim that trade should be limited because imports destroy jobs has been trotted out since the sixteenth century (see, e.g., Viner 1937, 51–52; Irwin 1996, 36ff). And imports do indeed destroy jobs in certain industries: for example, employment in the Maine shoe industry and in the South Carolina apparel industry is lower to the extent that both industries face competition from imports. So, we can understand why the plant owners and workers and the politicians who represent them prefer to avoid this foreign competition.

But just because imports destroy some jobs does not mean that trade reduces overall employment or harms the economy. After all, imports are not free: in order to acquire them a country must sell something in return. Imports are usually paid for in one of two ways: the sale of goods and services or the sale of assets to foreign countries. In other words, all of the dollars that U.S. consumers hand over to other countries in purchasing imports do not accumulate there, but eventually return to purchase either U.S. goods (exports) or U.S. financial assets (foreign investment). Both exports and foreign investment create new jobs: employment in export-oriented sectors such as farming and aircraft production is higher because of those foreign sales, and foreign investment either contributes directly to the national capital stock with new plants and equipment or facilitates domestic capital accumulation by reducing the cost of capital.

Thus, the claim that imports destroy jobs is misleading because it ignores the creation of jobs elsewhere in the economy as a result of trade. Similarly, while trade proponents like to note that exports create jobs, which is true, they generally fail to note that this comes at the expense of employment elsewhere. Export industries will certainly employ more workers because of the foreign demand for their products, but exports are used to purchase the very imports that diminish employment in other domestic industries.

Since trade both creates and destroys jobs, the pertinent question is whether trade has a net effect on employment. The public debate over NAFTA consisted largely of claims and counterclaims about whether it would add or subtract from total employment. NAFTA opponents claimed that free trade with Mexico would destroy jobs: the Economic Policy Institute put the number at 480,000. NAFTA proponents countered with the claim that it would create jobs: the Institute for International Economics suggested that 170,000 jobs would be created (Orme 1996, 107).

In fact, the overall impact of trade on the number of jobs in an economy is best approximated as zero. Total employment is not a function of international trade, but the number of people in the labor force. . . . Employment in the United States since 1950 has closely tracked the number of people in the labor force. And while there is always some unemployment, . . . this is determined by the business cycle, demographics, and labor market policies rather than changes in trade flows or trade policy. For example, unemployment rose in the early 1980s and the early 1990s because the economy fell into recession, not because of the behavior of imports.

• • •

Yet there remains a deep-seated inclination to frame the trade policy debate in terms of its impact on employment. This has motivated many attempts, however futile, to quantify the overall employment effects of trade. Analysts at several Washington think tanks (both favorable and unfavorable to NAFTA) have settled upon the rule of thumb that every $1 billion in exports generates or supports thirteen thousand jobs (implying conversely that every $1 billion in imports eliminates thirteen thousand jobs) as a way of evaluating the employment effects of trade agreements. Some NAFTA proponents argued that, because Mexico was to eliminate relatively high tariffs against U.S. goods while U.S. tariffs against Mexican goods were already very low, the agreement would generate more exports to than imports from Mexico. Using the rule of thumb, it was therefore reasoned that NAFTA would result in net job creation. Anxious to sell NAFTA to a wary Congress, Mickey Kantor, the Clinton administration's trade representative, claimed that two hundred thousand jobs would be created by 1995 as a result of the agreement.[1]

Such formulaic calculations were publicized to fight the dire forecasts that thousands of jobs would be lost as a result of NAFTA. But even if tariff reductions are asymmetric, exports may not grow more rapidly than imports. Trade agreements themselves have little effect on any bilateral trade balance or the overall trade balance, as we will see shortly. And it is a mistake to think that changes in the trade balance translate into predictable changes in employment; a booming economy with low unemployment may be accompanied by a growing trade deficit because people have more money to spend on imports. Thus, any attempt to isolate the portion of the change in overall employment that is due to changes in trade is immediately suspect: it is bound to rest on implausible and arbitrary assumptions, and the predictions are ultimately unverifiable. In addition, stressing the positive employment effects of trade gives the false impression that achieving a higher level of employment is the principal motivation for pursuing more open trade policies. . . . The reason for pursuing more open trade policies is not to increase employment but to facilitate the more productive employment that comes with mutually beneficial exchanges that raise aggregate income.

• • •

Employment and the Trade Deficit

Does the trade deficit injure domestic industries and have adverse effects on employment? In every year since 1976, the value of goods and services imported into the United States has exceeded the value of goods and services exported. Should the trade deficit be a matter of concern and reversing it an objective for trade policy?[2]

The connection between the trade deficit and employment is more complex than the simple view that jobs are lost because imports exceed exports. . . . The correlation between the merchandise trade deficit and the unemployment rate is actually negative: the trade deficit has risen during periods of falling unemployment and has fallen during periods of rising unemployment. As noted earlier, the business cycle may be driving this relationship: a booming economy in which many people are finding employment is also an economy that sucks in many imports, whereas a sluggish economy is one in which expenditures on imports slacken.

A deeper understanding of the trade deficit, however, requires some familiarity with balance of payments accounting. Balance of payments accounting may be a dry subject, but it helps lift the fog that surrounds the trade deficit. That accounting also suggests which remedies are likely to be effective in reducing the deficit, should that be considered desirable.

The balance of payments is simply an accounting of a country's international transactions. All sales of U.S. goods or assets to nonresidents constitute a receipt to the United States and are recorded in the balance of payments as a positive entry (credit); all purchases of foreign goods or assets by U.S. residents constitute a payment by the United States and are recorded as a negative entry (debit). The balance of payments is divided into two broad categories of transactions: the current account, which includes all trade in goods and services, plus a few smaller categories; and the capital account, which includes all trade in assets, mainly portfolio and direct investments.

The first accounting lesson is that the balance of payments always balances. By accounting identity, which is to say by definition, the balance of payments always sums to zero. . . .

Because the overall balance of payments always balances, a country with a current account deficit must have an offsetting capital account surplus. In other words, if a country is buying more goods and services from the rest of the world than it is selling, then the country must also be selling more assets to the rest of the world than it is purchasing.[3]

To make the link clearer, consider the case of an individual. Each of us as individuals exports our labor services to others in the economy. For this work, we receive an income that can be used to import goods and services produced by others. If an individual's expenditures exactly match his or her income in a given year, that person has "balanced trade" with the rest of the economy: the value of exports (income) equals the value of imports (expenditures). Can individuals spend more in a given year than they earn in income, in other words, can a person import more than he or she exports? Of course, by one of two ways: either by receiving a loan (borrowing) or by selling existing financial assets to make up the difference. Either method generates a financial inflow—a capital account surplus—that can be used to finance the trade deficit while also reducing the individual's net assets. Can an individual spend less in a given year than that person earns in income? Of course, and that individual exports more than he or she imports, thereby running a trade surplus with the rest of the economy. The surplus earnings are saved, generating a financial outflow—a capital account deficit—due to the purchase of financial investments.

What does this mean in the context of the United States? In 2000, the United States had a merchandise trade deficit of about $450 billion and a services trade surplus of $80 billion. The balance on goods and services was therefore a net deficit of about $370 billion, but owing to other factors (net income payments and net unilateral transfers) the current account deficit was nearly $435 billion, or 4.4 percent of that year's GDP. This implies that there must have been a capital account surplus of roughly the same magnitude. Sure enough, in that year U.S. residents (corporations and households) increased their ownership of foreign assets by just over $550 billion while foreigners increased their ownership of U.S. assets by over $950 billion. Therefore, the capital account surplus was approximately $400 billion. In other words, foreigners increased their ownership stake in U.S. assets more than U.S. residents increased their holdings of foreign assets, the mirror image of the current account deficit (Joint Economic Committee 2001, 36–37).

The balance of payments "balances" in the sense that every dollar we spend on imported goods must end up somewhere. Here's another way of thinking about it: in 2000, the United States imported almost $1,440 billion in goods and services from the rest of the world, but the rest of the world only purchased $1,070 billion of U.S. goods and services. What did the other countries do with the rest of our money? They invested it in the United States. In essence, for every dollar Americans handed over to foreigners in buying their goods (our imports), foreigners used seventy-five cents to purchase U.S. goods (our exports) and the remaining twenty-five cents to purchase U.S. assets. What assets are foreign residents purchasing? Some are short-term financial assets (such as stocks and bonds) for portfolio reasons; some are direct investments (such as mergers and acquisitions) to acquire ownership rights; and some are real assets (such as buildings and land) for the same reasons. . . .

In running a current account deficit, the United States is selling assets to the rest of the world. These foreign purchases of domestic assets allow the United States to finance more investment than it could through domestic savings alone. In essence, the United States is supplementing its domestic savings with foreign investment and thus is able to undertake more investment than if it had relied solely on domestic savings.

• • •

Because the United States is a net recipient of foreign investment, it is difficult to say much about the impact of the trade deficit on the number of jobs in the economy. The Economic Policy Institute, a Washington think tank aligned with organized labor, regularly issues reports stating that the trade deficit has destroyed American jobs. So why has the unemployment rate fallen during periods of large trade deficits? In recent years, [the Economic Policy Institute has] argued that job losses due to trade have been more than offset by job creation due to consumer spending and business investment (e.g., Scott and Rothstein 1998). And yet that higher business investment is made possible precisely because of foreign capital inflows, the flip side of the current account deficit. If the United States took action to reduce the trade deficit (supposedly reducing the number of jobs lost to trade), those capital inflows would necessarily fall. Then domestic investment would have to be financed by domestic savings, implying higher interest rates, which would reduce the number of jobs created by business investment. In the end, a lower trade deficit's positive impact on employment would be offset by the negative impact of lower domestic investment and higher interest rates.

• • •

So what are the implications for trade policy? The current account is fundamentally determined by international capital mobility and the gap between domestic savings and investment. The main determinants of savings and investment are macroeconomic in nature. Current account imbalances have nothing to do with whether a country is open or closed to foreign goods, engages in unfair trade practices or not, or is more "competitive" than other countries. If net capital flows are zero, the current account will be balanced. Japan's $11 billion current account deficit grew to an $87 billion current account surplus in 1987 not because it closed its market, or because the United States opened its market, or because Japanese manufacturers suddenly became more competitive in international markets. The surplus emerged because of financial and macroeconomic reasons in Japan and the United States.[4]

Trade policy cannot directly affect the current account deficit because trade policy has little influence on the underlying determinants of domestic savings and investment, the ultimate sources of the current account. If a country wishes to reduce its trade deficit, then it must undertake macroeconomic measures to reduce the gap between domestic savings and investment. . . .

ENDNOTES

1. Hufbauer and Schott (1993, 14), for example, conclude that NAFTA and Mexican economic reforms "will create about 170,000 net new U.S. jobs in the foreseeable future. . . . Our job projections reflect a judgment that, with NAFTA, U.S. exports to Mexico will continue to outstrip Mexican imports to the United States."

2. To investigate the causes and consequences of the trade deficit, Congress set up the Trade Deficit Review Commission, which issued its report in November 2000. Unfortunately, the commission split along partisan lines. Democrats viewed the deficit as malign (a serious threat to employment in trade-affected industries), while Republicans viewed the deficit as benign (as reflecting the good state of the economy). The commission's report is available at http://govinfo.library.unt.edu/tdrc/index.html.

3. A country therefore cannot experience a "balance of payments deficit" unless one is using the old nomenclature that considers official reserve transactions (an important component of the balance of payments under fixed-exchange-rate regimes) as a separate part of the international accounts.

4. Japanese exporters became more price competitive in the U.S. market due to the appreciation of the dollar in the early to mid-1980s, but this appreciation was driven by capital flows into the United States. While trade policy cannot directly affect the current account deficit, the deficit does affect trade policy. A large trade deficit puts a competitive squeeze on both exporting and import-competing industries resulting mainly from the exchange rate appreciation that usually accompanies the rising deficit. This pressure fuels protectionist sentiment, as seen by the experience of the early and mid-1980s.

REFERENCES

Hufbauer, Gary C. and Jeffrey J. Schott. 1993. NAFTA: An Assessment. Revised Edition. Washington, D.C.: Institute for International Economics.

Irwin, Douglas A. 1996. Against the Tide: An Intellectual History of Free Trade. Princeton: Princeton University Press.

Joint Economic Committee and Council of Economic Advisers. 2001. Economic Indicators (April).

Orme, William A. Jr. 1996. Understanding NAFTA: Mexico, Free Trade, and the New North America. Austin: University of Texas Press.

Scott, Robert E. and Jesse Rothstein. 1998. "American Jobs and the Asian Crisis: The Employment Impact of the Coming Rise in the U.S. Trade Deficit," Economic Policy Institute Briefing Paper, January.

Smith, Adam. 1976. An Inquiry into the Nature and Causes of the Wealth of Nations. Oxford: Clarendon Press.

Viner, Jacob. 1937. Essays on the Intellectual History of Economics. Princeton: Princeton University Press.

CHAPTER 3 RETRAIN WORKERS v. REDISTRIBUTE INCOME

Retrain Workers with Better Trade Adjustment Assistance Programs

Advocate: Howard F. Rosen

Source: Strengthening Trade Adjustment Assistance, Policy Brief #PB08-2
(Washington, DC: Peterson Institute for International Economics, January 2008)

Redistribute Income with a More Progressive Income Tax System

Advocate: Kenneth F. Scheve and Matthew J. Slaughter

Source: "A New Deal for Globalization," *Foreign Affairs,* July/August 2007: 34–47

The American public is increasingly anxious about participation in the global economy. Recent public opinion polls administered by the Pew Center found that almost half of the American population believes that participation in the World Trade Organization (WTO) and free trade agreements is bad for the country as a whole and for themselves individually.[1] More than 60 percent of the respondents stated that trade reduces American wages and eliminates jobs. Growing skepticism about the benefits of globalization have in turn made Americans reluctant to support additional trade liberalization through the WTO or free trade agreements and more receptive to protectionist measures.

The re-emergence of widespread protectionist sentiment has stimulated concern about whether the U.S. government can maintain its commitment to open trade. The fear that a protectionist public must ultimately generate protectionist governments has caused analysts to propose programs and policy changes that would transform a public skeptical of global markets into free trade supporters. Such proposals share a desire to use government policy to ease the negative impact of the global economy on individual workers. Proposals differ on what policies are best suited to this purpose.

RETRAIN WORKERS WITH BETTER TRADE ADJUSTMENT ASSISTANCE PROGRAMS

One approach to ease the negative impact of the global economy on workers involves the strengthening of programs specifically and narrowly directed at workers displaced by international trade. This approach rests on the assumption that

---

[1]Pew Research Center for the People and the Press, "Obama's Image Slips, His Lead over Clinton Disappears; Section 4: Trade and the Economy," May 1, 2008, http://people-press.org/report/?pageid=1295.

public anxiety reflects falling job security in the face of international competition. Such anxiety may be eased by government programs that facilitate the transition to employment in expanding industries—programs known in the United States as Trade Adjustment Assistance.

Howard Rosen, a resident fellow at the Peterson Institute of International Economics, embraces this strategy. Rosen argues that American workers face more intense competition today than they have in the past. Their anxiety about this competition is lessened, he argues, when government programs help them acquire skills needed to find employment in the expanding higher technology industries. Thus, the appropriate response to public skepticism is an expansion of the Trade Adjustment Assistance programs that help workers transition from declining to expanding industries.

REDISTRIBUTE INCOME WITH A MORE PROGRESSIVE INCOME TAX SYSTEM

Others suggest that American anxiety is driven by widening income inequality rather than uncertainty about job security. Income inequality in the United States has widened substantially during the last twenty-five years. Some portion of this greater inequality is a consequence of international trade. Those groups whose incomes have stagnated are increasingly skeptical about globalization because they perceive that its benefits accrue to a narrow segment of society. Shoring up public support for free trade, therefore, requires a more fundamental redistribution of income so that the gains from globalization are more broadly shared.

Kenneth Scheve and Matthew Slaughter develop an argument along precisely these lines. They suggest that growing public support for protectionism is a consequence of the rising income inequality. Moreover, they argue that Trade Adjustment Assistance programs are too narrowly targeted to remedy the underlying problem. Building strong public support for globalization will require a substantial redistribution of income—the creation of what they call a "New Deal for Globalization."

POINTS **TO PONDER**

1. Rosen argues that Americans would be more supportive of free trade if the government strengthened Trade Adjustment Assistance programs. Do you agree or disagree? Why?

2. Scheve and Slaughter argue that expanded Trade Adjustment Assistance programs will do little to stem contemporary protectionism. Why do they believe this is the case? Do you agree or disagree?

3. Are Trade Adjustment Assistance and income redistribution substitutes for or complements to one another?

Howard F. Rosen

Strengthening Trade Adjustment Assistance

In 1962, when the United States was running a trade surplus, imports were barely noticeable, and manufacturing employment was increasing, Congress made a commitment to assist American workers, firms, and communities hurt by international trade, by establishing the Trade Adjustment Assistance (TAA) program. This commitment was based on an appreciation that despite their large benefits, widely distributed throughout the economy, international trade and investment could also he associated with severe economic dislocations. President John F. Kennedy best enunciated this commitment when he wrote,

> Those injured by trade competition should not be required to bear the full brunt of the impact. Rather, the burden of economic adjustment should he borne in part by the federal government. . . . [T]here is an obligation to render assistance to those who suffer as a result of national trade policy.[1]

More than 40 years later, with a trade deficit above 5 percent of GDP [gross domestic product], with imports as a percent of GDP five times what they were in 1962, and with manufacturing employment falling, this commitment is more important than ever before.

The U.S. economy is currently facing significant pressures from intensified domestic and international competition. There is no "magic bullet" to deal with the pressures from globalization. More worker training alone will not be sufficient to address the large adjustment burden placed on workers and their families. A comprehensive set of integrated efforts is necessary to help the economy adjust to the enormous pressures from globalization. These efforts should not be handouts, but rather targeted, yet flexible assistance aimed at raising productivity and enhancing U.S. competitiveness.

The TAA for Workers, TAA for Firms, and TAA for Farmers and Fishermen programs are part of this strategy. Although the impact of globalization on the U.S. economy calls for strengthening these programs, sound economic policies are the most important prerequisite for responding to the pressures from globalization. In that regard, TAA is a complement to trade policy, not a substitute for it.

Why Targeted Assistance for Those Affected by Globalization?

Assisting workers [to] move from declining, inefficient industries to growing, highly efficient industries, although painful to workers and their families, can contribute to increasing national productivity and raising living standards. Efforts aimed at encouraging this adjustment are central to any effort at enhancing U.S. competitiveness.

The benefits of international trade to the U.S. economy are large and widely distributed. One such study finds that international trade contributes approximately $1 trillion a year to the U.S. economy. These benefits are five times the estimated costs, primarily from job and earnings losses, associated with trade (Bradford, Grieco, and Hufbauer 2005).

Although the costs associated with opening the economy to increased international competition are significant to those incurring them, relative to the benefits and the size of the economy, they tend to be smaller and more highly concentrated. TAA is one means of sharing some of the benefits of trade with those workers and communities paying a heavy price for that policy. . . .

TAA for Workers

The TAA for Workers program is by far the largest of the three existing programs. In order to receive assistance, workers must show that they lost their jobs due to one of three criteria:

- an increase in imports;
- laid off from either an upstream or a downstream producer; or
- a shift in production to another country.[2]

Each of these criteria must have "contributed importantly" to a firm's decline in production and sales. Table 3.1 presents the distribution of certified petitions by reason. In contrast to estimates made during the congressional debate over the 2002 reforms, the number of certified petitions related to shifts in production is much larger than the number of certified petitions for secondary workers.

Workers covered by certified petitions are currently eligible for the following assistance:

- 78 weeks of income maintenance payments, in addition to an initial 26 weeks of Unemployment Insurance (UI), if enrolled in training;
- all training expenses;
- a Health Coverage Tax Credit (HCTC), which provides a 65 percent advanceable, refundable tax credit to offset the cost of maintaining health insurance for up to two years;

Table 3.1 Distribution of certified petitions by reason, 2002–07

Grouping	2002	2003	2004	2005	2006	2007
Number of all petitions submitted	2,796	3,585	3,215	2,594	2,488	1,086
Number of workers covered by all petitions submitted	336,833	304,126	210,153	155,712	168,871	93,903
Percent of petitions certified	59	53	56	60	58	63
Percent of certified petitions due to increased imports	n.a.	47	55	55	53	46
Percent of certified petitions due to secondary workers	n.a.	8	9	6	8	9
Percent of certified petitions due to shifts in production	n.a.	30	36	39	39	44

n.a. = not available
SOURCE: U.S. Department of Labor.

- the Alternative Trade Adjustment Assistance (ATAA) program, commonly known as wage insurance, under which workers over 50 years old and earning less than $50,000 a year may be eligible to receive half the difference between their old and new wages, subject to a cap of $10,000, for up to two years;
- 90 percent of the costs associated with job search, up to a limit of $1,250; and
- 90 percent of the costs associated with job relocation, up to a limit of $1,500.

The TAA for Workers program has had a rocky history, including liberalization of eligibility criteria in 1974, cutbacks in assistance in 1981, and the establishment of a special program just for workers affected by trade with Canada and Mexico—i.e., the NAFTA-TAA for Workers program.[3] In 2002 Congress enacted the most expansive set of reforms in the TAA for Workers program since it was established. The reform . . . included:

- The TAA for Workers program and the NAFTA-TAA for Workers program were merged. The eligibility criteria and the assistance package under both programs were harmonized and unified in one program.
- Eligibility criteria were expanded to include workers who lost their jobs from companies producing inputs for goods that face significant import competition, and workers who lost their jobs due to shifts in production to countries with which the United States has a preferential trade agreement or "where there has been or is likely to be an increase in imports. . . ."[4]
- The HCTC was established.

- ATAA was established.
- The training appropriation cap was increased to $220 million.
- Income support payments were extended by 26 weeks to enable workers to be enrolled in training and receive income maintenance for up to two years.
- Workers undertaking remedial education can postpone their entry into the TAA for Workers program for up to six months.
- The amounts provided for job search assistance and relocation assistance were increased to keep up with inflation. . . .

ATAA and HCTC are two examples of how assistance under the TAA for Workers program has shifted from traditional income transfers to more targeted, cost-effective assistance. Despite the benefits associated with these new forms of assistance, however, enrollment in ATAA and the HCTC is disappointingly low. . . . Less than half of those TAA-eligible workers who visited one-stop career centers were even informed of the HCTC [GAO 2006]. A little over half of eligible workers were aware of the ATAA program.

Wage Insurance (ATAA)

Many workers who lose their jobs due to import competition and shifts in production pay a heavy price in terms or short- and long-term earnings losses. . . . Only two-thirds of dislocated workers from high import-competing industries find a new job within one to three years after layoff (Kletzer 2001). Of those workers reemployed, more than half experience no earnings loss or an improvement in earnings. Wage insurance is designed to assist the remaining 40 percent of dislocated workers. . . .

For example, the average weekly wage before layoff for workers displaced from high import-competing manufacturing industries was $402.97 between 1979 and 2001. Workers who found new jobs faced, on average, a 13 percent loss in earnings. Under the current wage insurance program, these workers would be eligible to receive an additional $5,532 for the first two years after reemployment, an 8 percent increase in their new wage.

Despite its benefits, wage insurance is not a perfect solution to addressing the costs associated with unemployment. The 26-week deadline for eligibility and the inability to enroll in training while receiving wage insurance are two examples of shortcomings in the current program. One option to address these problems would be to remove the 26-week requirement and allow workers to enroll in training while receiving wage insurance. A more ambitious proposal would be to enable workers, with the approval of their one-stop career counselor, to design a mix of income support, training, and wage insurance over a two-year period. The benefits of the program suggest that eligibility should also be expanded to those younger than 50 years old.

Health Coverage Tax Credit

The . . . average cost of health insurance for a family of four in 2006 was $11,500.[5] This equals 85 percent of the average amount of annual income support provided under the TAA for Workers program. For many workers, maintaining health insurance can be one of the largest, if not the largest, expense during unemployment. As a result many workers forgo health insurance. Unemployed workers and their families comprise a large share of the uninsured.[6]

The HCTC provides workers a 65 percent advanceable, refundable tax credit to offset the cost of maintaining health insurance for up to two years. The Internal Revenue Service (IRS) reports that since 2003, approximately 22,000 workers have used the credit, or about 500 to 600 new enrollees per month.[7] This constitutes only a small percentage of eligible workers. . . .

Of those workers who did not use the credit, the GAO [U.S. Government Accountability Office] found that between 50 and 82 percent of workers were covered by other health insurance—i.e., from a spouse. Forty-seven to 79 percent of respondents claimed that they could not afford to maintain their health insurance, despite the credit. Fifteen to 33 percent of workers found the credit too complicated.

. . . The IRS has implemented an outreach effort to inform each worker directly about the HCTC. Despite this effort, additional efforts appear necessary to ensure that all workers are aware of the credit. Congress should also consider raising the amount of the credit in order to make maintaining health insurance more affordable to unemployed workers and their families. Technical problems relating to waiting periods and health insurance options for workers not covered by their previous employer's health insurance need to also be addressed.

The Next Round of Reforms

For the most part, the 2002 reforms "fought the last battle" and did not fully address more recent economic developments, such as international outsourcing of services. In addition, several technical problems were discovered while implementing the 2002 reforms. Following are the major issues that still need to be addressed:[8]

Service Workers

The service sector is increasingly under pressure from outward shifts in investment and international outsourcing.[9] Based on its current interpretation of the statute, DOL [U.S. Department of Labor] denies assistance to workers who lose their jobs from the service sector. DOL argues that workers in the service sector do not produce items that are "similar or like an imported *good* (emphasis added)." Although the law does not specifically restrict TAA eligibility to workers employed in manufacturing industries per se, over the years DOL's interpretation of the law has de facto resulted in such a restriction. A recent GAO study finds that denying assistance to service-sector workers currently accounts for almost half of petition denials.[10]

In response to several recent appeals brought before the Court of International Trade, DOL recently announced that it would consider petitions on behalf of software workers.

The statute governing the TAA for Workers program needs to be updated to explicitly cover workers who lose their jobs from service industries. A simple change in legislative language alone will not be sufficient to achieve this goal, since data do not currently exist to measure the importation of services. The administration and Congress may need to consider alternative methodologies for determining trade impact in order to adequately cover workers who lose their jobs in service industries.

Industry Certification

Petitions for TAA eligibility are currently filed according to firm-related layoffs, meaning that multiple petitions must be submitted by different groups of workers employed in the same firm as well as in the same industry. In an effort to streamline the petition process and remove arbitrary discrimination between workers from the same firm and industry, industrywide certification should be added to the existing firm-related layoff certification.

For example, if the apparel industry was found to experience a decline in employment related to an increase in imports or outward shift in investment, then any worker subsequently laid off from the industry over the next two years or so would be automatically eligible for TAA without needing to go through the bureaucratic petition process. . . .

Training Appropriations

Allocating training funds to states to meet the needs of workers has been a challenge to DOL under successive administrations. . . . On average, states spent or obligated 62 percent of their training allocations in 2006, with a large range among the states (GAO 2007a). The GAO found that 13 states spent less than 1 percent of their training allocation while 9 states spent more than 95 percent of their training funds in 2006 (GAO 2007b).

Currently, DOL allocates 75 percent of TAA training funds according to a formula based on states' spending over the previous two and a half years. Thus states that experience large layoffs in a subsequent year may receive an inadequate amount of training funds to meet the needs of all TAA-eligible workers. Conversely, states that experience large layoffs in previous years may receive more training funds than needed in a subsequent year. GAO also reported that DOL allocates a significant amount of funds at the end of the fiscal year, making it difficult for states to utilize those funds. Since existing legislation does not address this issue, DOL has complete discretion in setting the method by which training funds are allocated to the states.

The allocation of training funds desperately needs improvement. Currently, DOL makes two disbursements—one at the beginning and the other at the end of the year. One recommendation would be to increase the number of disbursements, spread out more evenly throughout the year, based on shorter look-back periods—i.e., six months.

Currently the law sets a global cap of $220 million for training expenditures under the TAA for Workers program. The gap is not adjusted for inflation, changes in the economy, or major plant closings. At a minimum, the training cap needs to be raised on a regular basis. Ways to better link the training appropriation to the needs of TAA-eligible workers should also be explored.

Health Coverage Tax Credit (HCTC)

GAO's survey of workers involved in five plant closings found that almost 70 percent of those workers without alternate health insurance reported that they could not afford to maintain their previous health insurance, despite the HCTC (GAO 2006). In a subsequent report, GAO estimated that even with the 65 percent tax credit, the cost of maintaining health insurance in four sample states was equal to approximately 25 percent of a worker's average monthly UI [unemployment insurance] payment. Although the HCTC appears to have been an important addition to the package of assistance provided to workers, the amount of the credit needs to be increased in order to enable more workers to use it.

Currently, workers must receive income maintenance (or participate in ATAA), which means that they must be enrolled in training, in order to be eligible to receive the HCTC. This restriction severely limits the number of displaced workers who can receive the credit. GAO found that this requirement has forced workers to both enroll in training and receive income maintenance payments or to apply for a training waiver.[11] Some argue that requiring a worker to undertake training promotes "real adjustment," while others contend that it results in workers getting expensive assistance that they may not need or want. One proposal would be to provide the HCTC to all TAA-certified workers for up to two years or until the worker finds a new job, regardless of enrollment in training.

Other technical issues concerning the HCTC, such as the waiting period before enrollment, require immediate attention.

Wage Insurance (ATAA)

The current program is restricted to workers over the age of 50. Although there is some evidence that older workers may have a harder time finding a new job, ATAA can potentially benefit all workers. It is a cost-effective means of cushioning the costs associated with taking a new job. The age requirement for ATAA should be lowered or even eliminated in order to make more workers eligible.

Self-Employed

Under the current program, workers are discouraged from pursuing self-employment. One option would be to continue providing income support, training, and possibly wage insurance to workers starting their own businesses.

Outreach

GAO has consistently found that many workers are unaware of the assistance provided by the TAA for which they are eligible (GAO 2006). This lack of awareness may help explain why program take-up rates are so low. DOL's outreach efforts seem inadequate. More resources need to be devoted to informing workers about TAA and other forms of assistance for dislocated workers. . . .

International Comparisons

. . . Currently, other industrialized countries are devoting many more resources to labor-market adjustment programs than the United States (see Table 3.2). Relative to six other major industrialized countries, the United States spends the least on active labor-market adjustment programs,

Table 3.2 Spending on active labor-market adjustment programs

Country	As a percent of GDP all labor–market	Ratio of spending as a percent of GDP rate	As a percent of total spending on the unemployment programs
France	1.32	0.14	44.4
Germany	1.21	0.16	38.6
Canada	0.41	0.06	36.4
United Kingdom	0.37	0.07	40.0
Korea	0.31	0.08	66.9
Japan	0.28	0.06	34.2
United States	0.15	0.03	32.9

SOURCE: Organization for Economic Cooperation and Development, *Employment Outlook 2003,* data for 2000–2001.

even after taking into account each country's unemployment rate. France and Germany each devote about five times more to their active labor-market programs than does the United States.

On the other hand, the Danish "Flexicurity" system, which is currently getting a lot of attention, is not a magic bullet. In addition to differences in hiring and firing policies, the Organization for Economic Cooperation and Development estimates that Denmark spends eight times more public funds, as a share of GDP, on labor-market programs than the United States.[12] The Danes spend ten times more public funds, as a share of GDP, on training and five times more, as a share of GDP, on income support than the United States.

Conclusion

Public opinion surveys find that Americans are willing to support trade liberalization *if* the government assists those workers, firms, and communities adversely affected by trade and offshore outsourcing. Despite significant changes in the U.S. economy over the last 45 years, including an increase in import penetration and a decline in manufacturing employment, efforts to assist workers adversely affected by increases in imports and shifts in production have remained modest at best. Efforts to reform and expand the program in 2002 were extremely useful in breathing new life into that commitment. But implementation of those reforms has been uneven at best. More effort must be undertaken to ensure that all workers, firms, farmers, and fishermen receive the assistance they need.

Several pieces of legislation have already been introduced, and several others are likely to be introduced, to continue the efforts begun in 2002 to reform and expand TAA. These proposals include extending eligibility criteria to cover workers who lose their jobs from service industries, establishing a process for certifying entire industries, increasing the budget cap on training expenditures, and expanding the HCTC and wage insurance programs. Congress should seriously consider enacting these proposals.

The increased importance of international trade to the U.S. economy and the growing concern over economic dislocations would seem to make assistance to workers, firms, and communities facing these pressures a more pressing issue in 2006 than it was in 1962. Yet despite public support for this kind of assistance and rhetoric on the need to increase worker training, expanding labor-market adjustment programs remains a low priority in the United States. This needs to change if the United States wants to pursue a competitiveness strategy that increases productivity and raises living standards.

ENDNOTES

1. Special Message to Congress on Foreign Trade Policy, January 25, 1962. See Kennedy (1963).
2. Current law limits this eligibility to shift production to countries with which the United States has a preferential trade agreement or from which there is a prospect of an increase in imports.
3. See Rosen (2006) for a more detailed discussion of the history of the TAA for Workers program.
4. Public Law 107-210, Section 113(a).
5. See the Henry J. Kaiser Family Foundation, *Employee Health Benefits: 2006 Annual Survey,* September 26, 2006.
6. US Census Bureau (2007). More than one-quarter of those workers without health insurance, aged 18 to 64, were not working.
7. The number of people covered by the HCTC rises to 37,000 when family members of TAA-eligible workers are included.
8. See Kletzer and Rosen (2005) for additional recommendations.
9. Alan Blinder (2006) recently estimated that as many as 42 million to 56 million jobs, or 30 to 40 percent of total U.S. employment, could be under pressure from possible offshoring. This estimate includes 14 million manufacturing workers and 28 million to 42 million nonmanufacturing workers, primarily workers employed in the service sector.
10. GAO (2007a). Many more workers may be discouraged from submitting petitions.
11. GAO (2006). Some states have issued training waivers in order for more workers to receive the HCTC.
12. Danish labor laws are more protective of workers than U.S. labor laws.

REFERENCES

Blinder, Alan. 2006. Offshoring: The Next Industrial Revolution? *Foreign Affairs* (March/April).

Bradford, Scott C., Paul L. E. Grieco, and Gary Clyde Hufbauer. 2005. The Payoff to America from Global Integration. In *The United States and the World Economy: Foreign Economic Policy for the Next Decade,* ed. C. Fred Bergsten and the Institute for International Economics. Washington: Institute for International Economics.

GAO (U.S. Government Accountability Office). 2006. *Trade Adjustment Assistance: Most Workers in Five Layoffs Received Services, but Better Outreach Needed on New Benefits.* GAO-06-43. Washington.

GAO (U.S. Government Accountability Office). 2007a. *Trade Adjustment Assistance: Changes to Funding Allocation and Eligibility Requirements Could Enhance States' Ability to Provide Benefits and Services.* GAO-07-701. Washington.

GAO (U.S. Government Accountability Office). 2007b. *Trade Adjustment Assistance: States Have Fewer Training Funds Available Than Labor Estimates When Both Expenditures and Obligations Are Considered.* Report to the

Chairman, Subcommittee on Trade, Committee on Ways and Means, House of Representatives. Washington.

Kennedy, John F. 1963. *Public Papers of the Presidents of the United States, 1963.* Washington: Government Printing Office.

Kletzer, Lori G. 2001. *Job Loss from Imports: Measuring the Costs.* Washington: Institute for International Economics.

Kletzer, Lori G., and Howard F. Rosen. 2005. Easing the Adjustment Burden on US Workers. In *The United States and the World Economy: Foreign Economic Policy for the Next Decade,* ed. C. Fred Bergsten and the Institute for International Economics. Washington: Institute for International Economics.

Rosen, Howard E. 2006. Trade Adjustment Assistance: The More We Change the More It Stays the Same. In *C. Fred Bergsten and the World Economy,* ed. Michael Mussa. Washington: Institute for International Economics.

U.S. Census Bureau. 2007. *Income, Poverty and Health Insurance Coverage in the United States—2006.* Washington (August).

Kenneth F. Scheve and Matthew J. Slaughter

A New Deal for Globalization

Globalization has brought huge overall benefits, but earnings for most U.S. workers—even those with college degrees—have been falling recently; inequality is greater now than at any other time in the last 70 years. Whatever the cause, the result has been a surge in protectionism. To save globalization, policymakers must spread its gains more widely. The best way to do that is by redistributing income.

Wages Falling, Protectionism Rising

Over the last several years, a striking new feature of the U.S. economy has emerged: real income growth has been extremely skewed, with relatively few high earners doing well while incomes for most workers have stagnated or, in many cases, fallen. Just what mix of forces is behind this trend is not yet clear, but regardless, the numbers are stark. Less than four percent of workers were in educational groups that enjoyed increases in mean real money earnings from 2000 to 2005; mean real money earnings rose for workers with doctorates and professional graduate degrees and fell for all others. In contrast to in earlier decades, today it is not just those at the bottom of the skill ladder who are hurting. Even college graduates and workers with non-professional master's degrees saw their mean real money earnings decline. By some measures, inequality in the United States is greater today than at any time since the 1920s.

Advocates of engagement with the world economy are now warning of a protectionist drift in public policy. This drift is commonly blamed on narrow industry concerns or a failure to explain globalization's benefits or the war on terrorism. These explanations miss a more basic point: U.S. policy is becoming more protectionist because the American public is becoming more protectionist, and this shift in attitudes is a result of stagnant or falling incomes. Public support for engagement with the world economy is strongly linked to labor-market performance, and for most workers labor-market performance has been poor.

Given that globalization delivers tremendous benefits to the U.S. economy as a whole, the rise in protectionism brings many economic dangers. To avert them, U.S. policymakers must recognize and then address the fundamental cause of opposition to freer trade and investment. They must also recognize that the two most commonly proposed responses—more investment in education and more trade adjustment assistance for dislocated workers—are nowhere near adequate. Significant payoffs from educational investment will take decades to be realized, and trade adjustment assistance is too small and too narrowly targeted on specific industries to have much effect.

The best way to avert the rise in protectionism is by instituting a New Deal for globalization—one that links engagement with the world economy to a substantial redistribution of income. In the United States, that would mean adopting a fundamentally more progressive federal tax system. The notion of more aggressively redistributing income may sound radical, but ensuring that most American workers are benefiting is the best way of saving globalization from a protectionist backlash.

Rising Protectionism

U.S. economic policy is becoming more protectionist. First, consider trade. Trade promotion authority has expired. The 109th Congress introduced 27 pieces of anti-China trade legislation; the 110th introduced over a dozen in just its first three months. In late March, the Bush administration levied new tariffs on Chinese exports of high-gloss paper—reversing a 20-year precedent of not accusing nonmarket economies of illegal export subsidies.

Barriers to inward foreign direct investment (FDI) are also rising. In 2005, the Chinese energy company CNOOC tried to purchase U.S.-headquartered Unocal. The subsequent political storm was so intense that CNOOC withdrew its bid. A similar controversy erupted in 2006 over the purchase of operations at six U.S. ports by Dubai-based Dubai Ports World, eventually causing the company to sell the assets. The Committee on Foreign Investments in the United States [CFIUS], which is legally required to review and approve certain foreign acquisitions of U.S. businesses, has raised the duration and complexity of many reviews. Both chambers of the 109th Congress passed bills to tighten CFIUS scrutiny even further; similar legislation has already passed in the current House.

This protectionist drift extends to much of the world. The Doha Development Round of trade negotiations, the centerpiece of global trade liberalization, is years behind schedule and now on the brink of collapse. Key U.S. trading partners are becoming increasingly averse to foreign investment, as expressed both in their rhetoric (recent public pronouncements by the governments of France and Germany) and in their actions (new restrictions in China on foreign retailers).

At first glance, this rise in protectionism may seem puzzling. The economic gains from globalization are immense. In the United States, according to estimates from the Peter G. Peterson Institute for International Economics and others, trade and investment liberalization over the past decades has added between $500 billion and $1 trillion in annual income—between

$1,650 and $3,300 a year for every American. A Doha agreement on global free trade in goods and services would generate, according to similar studies, $500 billion a year in additional income in the United States.

International trade and investment have spurred productivity growth, the foundation of rising average living standards. The rate of increase in output per worker hour in the U.S. nonfarm business sector has doubled in the past decade, from an annual average of 1.35 percent between 1973 and 1995 to an annual average of 2.7 percent since 1995. Much of the initial acceleration was related to information technology (IT)—one of the United States' most globally engaged industries, at the forefront of establishing and expanding production networks linked by trade and investment around the globe.

Gains from globalization have been similarly large in the rest of the world. China and India have achieved stupendous rates of productivity growth, lifting hundreds of millions of people out of poverty. Central to this success has been the introduction of market forces, in particular international market forces related to trade and FDI. In Chinese manufacturing, foreign multinational companies account for over half of all exports. And in the Indian IT sector, Indian and foreign multinational firms account for two-thirds of sales.

Freer trade and investment can also enhance other foreign policy goals. The Doha Round was launched shortly after 9/11 because of the view that global poverty is intimately linked to international insecurity and instability. The Doha Round was also intended to remedy the widespread perception that previous rounds of trade negotiations had treated poor nations unfairly by failing to open the very sectors—such as agriculture—whose openness would most likely help the world's poor. Accordingly, it is believed that a successful Doha agreement would enhance the United States' image and promote its interests around the world.

There are three common explanations for why protectionism is on the rise in the United States even though globalization is good for both the U.S. economy and U.S. security interests. None, however, are convincing. The first is that a narrow set of industries, such as agriculture and apparel manufacturing, have been harmed by freer trade and, in response, have lobbied hard to turn lawmakers against liberalization. But the incentives for these industries to oppose globalization have not changed in recent years, and there are also many industries that have benefited from, and thus lobbied for, further liberalization. What is new today is that special-interest protectionists are facing a more receptive audience.

The second explanation is that policymakers and the business community have failed to adequately explain the benefits of freer trade and investment to the public. But in fact, public-opinion data show the opposite: large majorities of Americans acknowledge these broad benefits. If anything, the public seems to understand certain benefits better than ever—for example, that its enjoyment of relatively affordable toys, DVD players, and other products depends on globalization.

Finally, there is the security explanation: that the need to balance economic interests with national security concerns has resulted in a more protectionist stance. This may help explain policy debates on certain issues, such as immigration. But generally, security concerns strengthen rather than weaken the case for further trade and investment liberalization, as long as such liberalization is viewed as fair to the developing world.

The Roots of Protectionism

The fundamental explanation is much simpler: policy is becoming more protectionist because the public is becoming more protectionist, and the public is becoming more protectionist because incomes are stagnating or falling. The integration of the world economy has boosted productivity and wealth creation in the United States and much of the rest of the world. But within many countries, and certainly within the United States, the benefits of this integration have been unevenly distributed—and this fact is increasingly being recognized. Individuals are asking themselves, "Is globalization good for me?" and, in a growing number of cases, arriving at the conclusion that it is not.

This account of rising protectionism depends on two key facts. First, there is a strong link between individuals' labor-market interests and their policy opinions about globalization. Second, in the past several years labor-market outcomes have become worse for many more Americans—and globalization is plausibly part of the reason for this poor performance.

Research on polling data shows that opinions about trade, FDI, and immigration are closely correlated to skill and educational levels. Less skilled Americans—who make up the majority of the U.S. labor force—have long led opposition to open borders. Workers with only high school educations are almost twice as likely to support protectionist policies as workers with college educations are.

This divide in opinion according to skill level reflects the impact that less skilled Americans expect market liberalization to have on their earnings. It also reflects their actual poor real and relative earnings performance in recent decades. It is now well established that income inequality across skill levels has been rising since (depending on the measure) the mid- to late 1970s and that the benefits of productivity gains over this time accrued mainly to higher-skilled workers. For example, from 1966 to 2001, the median pretax inflation-adjusted wage and salary income grew just 11 percent—versus 58 percent for incomes in the 90th percentile and 121 percent for those in the 99th percentile. Forces including skill-biased technological change played a major role in these income trends; the related forces of globalization seem to have played a smaller role—but a role nonetheless.

There are two important points about this link between policy opinions and labor-market skills and performance. One is that it does not simply reflect different understandings of the benefits of globalization. Polling data are very clear here: large majorities of Americans acknowledge the many benefits of open borders—lower prices, greater product diversity, a competitive spur to firms—which are also highlighted by academics, policymakers, and the business community. At the same time, they perceive that along with these benefits, open borders have put pressures on worker earnings.

Second, a worker's specific industry does not appear to drive his or her view of globalization. This is because competition in the domestic labor market extends the pressures of globalization beyond trade- and foreign-investment-exposed industries to the entire economy. If workers in a sector such as automobile manufacturing lose their jobs, they compete for new positions across sectors—and thereby put pressure on pay in the entire economy. What seems to matter most is what kind of worker you are in terms of skill level, rather than what industry you work in.

The protectionist drift also depends on worsening labor-market outcomes over the past several years. By traditional measures, such as employment growth and unemployment rates, the U.S. labor market has been strong of late. Today, with unemployment at 4.5 percent, the United States is at or near full employment. But looking at the number of jobs misses the key change: for several years running, wage and salary growth for all but the very highest earners has been poor, such that U.S. income gains have become extremely skewed.

Of workers in seven educational categories—high school dropout, high school graduate, some college, college graduate, nonprofessional master's, Ph.D., and M.B.A./J.D./M.D.—only those in the last two categories, with doctorates or professional graduate degrees, experienced any growth in mean real money earnings between 2000 and 2005. Workers in these two categories comprised only 3.4 percent of the labor force in 2005, meaning that more than 96 percent of U.S. workers are in educational groups for which average money earnings have fallen. In contrast to in earlier decades, since 2000 even college graduates and those with nonprofessional master's degrees—29 percent of workers in 2005—suffered declines in mean real money earnings.

The astonishing skewness of U.S. income growth is evident in the analysis of other measures as well. The growth in total income reported on tax returns has been extremely concentrated in recent years: the share of national income accounted for by the top one percent of earners reached 21.8 percent in 2005—a level not seen since 1928. In addition to high labor earnings, income growth at the top is being driven by corporate profits, which are at nearly 50-year highs as a share of national income and which accrue mainly to those with high labor earnings. The basic fact is clear: the benefits of strong productivity growth in the past several years have gone largely to a small set of highly skilled, highly compensated workers.

Economists do not yet understand exactly what has caused this skewed pattern of income growth and to what extent globalization itself is implicated, nor do they know how long it will persist. Still, it is plausible that there is a connection. Poor income growth has coincided with the integration into the world economy of China, India, and central and eastern Europe. The IT revolution has meant that certain workers are now facing competition from the overseas outsourcing of jobs in areas such as business services and computer programming. Even if production does not move abroad, increased trade and multinational production can put pressure on incomes by making it easier for firms to substitute foreign workers for domestic ones.

These twin facts—the link between labor-market performance and opinions on globalization and the recent absence of real income growth for so many Americans—explain the recent rise in protectionism. Several polls of U.S. public opinion show an alarming rise in protectionist sentiment over the past several years. For example, an ongoing NBC News/Wall Street Journal poll found that from December 1999 to March 2007, the share of respondents stating that trade agreements have hurt the United States increased by 16 percentage points (to 46 percent) while the "helped" share fell by 11 points (to just 28 percent). A 2000 Gallup poll found that 56 percent of respondents saw trade as an opportunity and 36 percent saw it as a threat; by 2005, the percentages had shifted to 44 percent and 49 percent, respectively. The March 2007 NBC News/Wall Street Journal poll found negative assessments of open borders even among the highly skilled: only 35 percent of respondents with a college or higher degree said they directly benefited from the global economy.

Given the lack of recent real income growth for most Americans, newfound skepticism about globalization is not without cause. Nor is it without effect: the change in public opinion is the impetus for the protectionist drift in policy. Politicians have an incentive to propose and implement protectionist policies because more citizens want them, and protectionist special interests face an audience of policymakers more receptive to their lobbying efforts than at any time in the last two decades.

Inadequate Adjustments

Because the protectionist drift reflects the legitimate concerns of a now very large majority of Americans, the policy debate needs fresh thinking. There is reason to worry even if one does not care about social equity. When most workers do not see themselves as benefiting from the related forces of globalization and technology, the resulting protectionist drift may end up eliminating the gains from globalization for everybody. Current ignorance about the exact causes of the skewed income growth is not reason for inaction. Policymakers may not be able to attack the exact source (or sources) and likely would not want to even if they could identify them, because doing so could reduce or even eliminate the aggregate gains from globalization.

Supporters of globalization face a stark choice: shore up support for an open global system by ensuring that a majority of workers benefit from it or accept that further liberalization is no longer sustainable. Given the aggregate benefits of open borders, the preferable option is clear.

Current policy discussions addressing the distributional consequences of globalization typically focus on the main U.S. government program for addressing the labor-market pressures of globalization—Trade Adjustment Assistance (TAA)—and on investing more in education. These ideas will help but are inadequate for the problem at hand.

The problem with TAA is that it incorrectly presumes that the key issue is transitions across jobs for workers in trade-exposed industries. Established in the Trade Act of 1974 (with a related component connected to the North American Free Trade Agreement), the program aids groups of workers in certain industries who can credibly claim that increased imports have destroyed their jobs or have reduced their work hours and wages. TAA-certified workers can access supports including training, extended unemployment benefits while in full-time training, and job-search and relocation allowances.

In short, TAA is inappropriately designed to address the protectionist drift. The labor-market concern driving this drift is not confined to the problem of how to reemploy particular workers in particular sectors facing import competition. Because the pressures of globalization are spread economy-wide via domestic labor-market competition, there is concern about income and job security among workers employed in all sectors.

Today many are calling for reform and expansion of TAA. For example, President George W. Bush has proposed streamlining the processes of eligibility determination and assistance implementation to facilitate reemployment. This year, TAA is due to be reauthorized by Congress, and many legislators have proposed broadening the number of industries that are TAA-eligible. TAA improvements like these are surely welcome. But they alone cannot arrest the protectionist drift.

The idea behind investing in education is that higher-skilled workers generally earn more and are more likely to directly benefit from economic openness. The problem with this approach, however, is that upgrading skills is a process that takes generations—its effects will come far too late to address today's opposition to globalization. It took 60 years for the United States to boost the share of college graduates in the labor force from six percent (where it was at the end of World War II) to about 33 percent (where it is today). And that required major government programs, such as the GI Bill, and profound socioeconomic changes, such as increased female labor-force participation.

If the United States today undertook the goal of boosting its college-graduate share of the work force to 50 percent, the graduation of that median American worker would, if the rate of past efforts is any indication, not come until about 2047. And even this far-off date might be too optimistic. In the past generation, the rate of increase in the educational attainment of U.S. natives has slowed from its 1960s and 1970s pace, in part because college-completion rates have stalled. Rising income inequality may itself be playing a role here. Since 1988, 74 percent of American students at the 146 top U.S. colleges have come from the highest socioeconomic quartile, compared with just 3 percent from the lowest quartile. Moreover, even college graduates and holders of nonprofessional master's degrees have experienced falling mean real money earnings since 2000. If this trend continues, even completing college will not assuage the concerns behind rising protectionism.

Globalization and Redistribution

Given the limitations of these two reforms and the need to provide a political foundation for engagement with the world economy, the time has come for a New Deal for globalization—one that links trade and investment liberalization to a significant income redistribution that serves to share globalization's gains more widely. Recall that $500 billion is a common estimate of the annual income gain the United States enjoys today from earlier decades of trade and investment liberalization and also of the additional annual income it would enjoy as a result global free trade in goods and services. These aggregate gains, past and prospective, are immense and therefore immensely important to secure. But the imbalance in recent income growth suggests that the number of Americans not directly sharing in these aggregate gains may now be very large.

Truly expanding the political support for open borders requires a radical change in fiscal policy. This does not, however, mean making the personal income tax more progressive, as is often suggested. U.S. taxation of personal income is already quite progressive. Instead, policymakers should remember that workers do not pay only income taxes; they also pay the FICA (Federal Insurance Contributions Act) payroll tax for social insurance. This tax offers the best way to redistribute income.

The payroll tax contains a Social Security portion and a Medicare portion, each of which is paid half by the worker and half by the employer. The overall payroll tax is a flat tax of 15.3 percent on the first $94,200 of gross income for every worker, with an ongoing 2.9 percent flat tax for the Medicare portion beyond that. Because it is a flat-rate tax on a (largely) capped base, it is a regressive tax—that is, it tends to reinforce rather than offset pretax inequality. At $760 billion in 2005, the regressive payroll tax was nearly as big as the progressive income tax ($1.1 trillion). Because it is large and regressive, the payroll tax is an obvious candidate for meaningful income redistribution linked to globalization.

A New Deal for globalization would combine further trade and investment liberalization with eliminating the full payroll tax for all workers earning below the national median. In 2005, the median total money earnings of all workers was $32,140, and there were about 67 million workers at or below this level. Assuming a mean labor income for this group of about $25,000, these 67 million workers would receive a tax cut of about $3,800 each. Because the economic burden of this tax falls largely on workers, this tax cut would be a direct gain in after-tax real income for them. With a total price tag of about $256 billion, the proposal could be paid for by raising the cap of $94,200, raising payroll tax rates (for progressivity, rates could escalate as they do with the income tax), or some combination of the two. This is, of course, only an outline of the needed policy reform, and there would be many implementation details to address. For example, rather than a single on–off point for this tax cut, a phase-in of it (like with the earned-income tax credit) would avoid incentive-distorting jumps in effective tax rates.

This may sound like a radical proposal. But keep in mind the figure of $500 billion: the annual U.S. income gain from trade and investment liberalization to date and the additional U.S. gain a successful Doha Round could deliver. Redistribution on this scale may be required to overcome the labor-market concerns driving the protectionist drift. Determining the right scale and structure of redistribution requires a thoughtful national discussion among all stakeholders. Policymakers must also consider how exactly to link such redistribution to further liberalization. But this should not obscure the essential idea: to be politically viable, efforts for further trade and investment liberalization will need to be explicitly linked to fundamental fiscal reform aimed at distributing globalization's aggregate gains more broadly.

Saving Globalization

Averting a protectionist backlash is in the economic and security interests of the United States. Globalization has generated—and can continue to generate—substantial benefits for the United States and the rest of the world. But realizing those broad benefits will require addressing the legitimate concerns of U.S. voters by instituting a New Deal for globalization.

In many ways, today's protectionist drift is similar to the challenges faced by the architect of the original New Deal. In August 1934, President Franklin Roosevelt declared:

> Those who would measure confidence in this country in the future must look first to the average citizen. . . .

This government intends no injury to honest business. The processes we follow in seeking social justice do not, in adding to general prosperity, take from one and give to another. In this modern world, the spreading out of opportunity ought not to consist of robbing Peter to pay Paul. In other words, we are concerned with more than mere subtraction and addition. We are concerned with multiplication also—multiplication of wealth through cooperative action, wealth in which all can share.

Today, such multiplication will depend on striking a delicate balance—between allowing globally engaged companies to continue to generate large overall gains for the United States and using well-targeted fiscal mechanisms to spread the gains more widely.

Would addressing concerns about income distribution make voters more likely to support open borders? The public-opinion data suggest that the answer is yes. Americans consistently say that they would be more inclined to back trade and investment liberalization if it were linked to more support for those hurt in the process. The policy experience of other countries confirms this point: there is greater support for engagement with the world economy in countries that spend more on programs for dislocated workers.

U.S. policymakers face a clear choice. They can lead the nation down the dangerous path of creeping protectionism. Or they can build a stable foundation for U.S. engagement with the world economy by sharing the gains widely. A New Deal for globalization can ensure that globalization survives.

CHAPTER 4 MIGRATION BRINGS ECONOMIC GAINS *v.* MIGRATION REDUCES CULTURAL COHESION

Migration Brings Economic Gains

Advocate: Philippe LeGrain

Source: "The Case for Immigration," *The International Economy*, Summer 2007: 26–29

Migration Reduces Cultural Cohesion

Advocate: David Goodhart

Source: "Too Diverse?" *Prospect Magazine,* no. 95 (February 2004), http://www.prospect-magazine.co.uk/article_details.php?id=5835

Although the world's governments have greatly liberalized the cross-border flow of goods, services, technology, and financial capital, they continue to tightly restrict the flow of people. Indeed, government restriction on migration is perhaps the feature that most distinguishes contemporary globalization from the "first wave." In the late nineteenth and early twentieth centuries, approximately 60 million people migrated from Europe to Argentina, Australia, Brazil, Canada, and the United States. Most governments restricted inward migration following World War I and have continued to do so ever since.

In spite of government efforts to restrict migration, however, people have been migrating from less to more developed countries in large numbers. According to the International Organization for Migration, some 500,000 people migrated in 1960.[1] The number has grown steadily during the last forty years, and in the 2000–2005 period, the latest period for which data are available, 3.3 million per year moved from developing to developed countries. The re-emergence of substantial migrant flows has kindled a policy debate in the United States and in European countries.

---

[1] International Organization for Migration, *World Migration 2008: Managing Labour Mobility in the Evolving Global Economy* (Geneva: International Organization for Migration, 2008), 36.

MIGRATION BRINGS ECONOMIC GAINS

Proponents of liberalization focus on the economic benefits migration delivers. Foreign-born workers play an important role in their host economies. In the United States' case, they account for 15 percent of all workers and 40 percent of Ph.D. research scientists. They thus contribute to national income and they help raise productivity. Moreover, immigrants typically complement rather than substitute for native workers. That is, immigrants do not take jobs from the local population. Instead, they help the native population produce more.

Philippe LeGrain, a British journalist, develops an argument along these lines. He argues that migration delivers clear economic benefits to the foreign-born workers and the native population. Such potential gains, he suggests, should convince governments to abandon their efforts to limit migration.

MIGRATION REDUCES CULTURAL COHESION

Opposition to migration focuses on its potential negative economic and cultural consequences. Those who focus on possible negative economic consequences argue that immigrants take jobs from natives and push wages down. Those who focus on the cultural consequences voice concerns that the influx of large numbers of people with distinct cultural-linguistic traditions may undermine the social and cultural cohesiveness in the host country with eventual consequences for political cohesion. Examples might include the large North African community in France, the large Pakistani community in England, and the large Turkish population in Germany. The central question in each instance is the extent to which migrants, their children, and their grandchildren and the local population encourage the assimilation that produces a cohesive society.

David Goodhart develops a variant of the cultural consequences argument by focusing on what he asserts is an inherent tension between the twin progressive values of risk sharing and multicultural diversity. Goodhart explores the degree to which migration to Great Britain from its former colonies (as well as migration to other West European societies from developing societies) is reducing the social cohesion required to foster public support for the welfare state. The "progressive dilemma," he argues, is that one value—a diverse multicultural society—might come at the expense of another value—a society in which individuals are willing to pay high taxes to insure each other against the risks associated with a market economy. He concludes that governments must restrict inward migration and encourage assimilation of new immigrants into the local culture—and thereby reduce diversity—to sustain social solidarity.

POINTS **TO PONDER**

1. What, according to LeGrain, are the principal benefits of migration?

2. Think of some other countries to which one can apply Goodhart's argument. What lessons, if any, might one draw from these cases that have relevance to the American case?

3. How do you balance the benefits of migration against the potential costs? Can you think of policy measures that might minimize the risk that migration will have the consequences Goodhart fears?

Philippe Legrain
The Case for Immigration

There is a contradiction at the heart of our globalizing world: while goods, services, and capital move across borders ever more freely, most people cannot. No government except perhaps North Korea's would dream of banning cross-border trade in goods and services, yet it is seen as perfectly normal and reasonable for governments to outlaw the movement across borders of most people who produce goods and services. No wonder illegal immigration is on the rise: most would-be migrants have no other option.

This is perverse. Immigrants are not an invading army: they are mostly people seeking a better life. Many are drawn to rich countries such as the United States by the huge demand for workers to fill the low-end jobs that their increasingly well-educated and comfortable citizens do not want. And just as it is beneficial for people to move from Alabama to California in response to market signals, so too from Mexico to the United States.

Where governments permit it, a global labor market is emerging: international financiers cluster in New York and London, information technology specialists in Silicon Valley, and actors in Hollywood, while multinational companies scatter skilled professionals around the world. Yet rich-country governments endeavor to keep out Mexican construction workers, Filipino care workers, and Congolese cooks, even though they are simply service providers who ply their trade abroad, just as American investment bankers do. And just as it is often cheaper and mutually beneficial to import information technology services from Asia and insurance from Europeans, it often makes sense to import menial services that have to be delivered on the spot, such as cleaning. Policymakers who want products and providers of high-skilled services to move freely but people who provide less-skilled services to stay put are not just hypocrites; they are economically illiterate.

From a global perspective, the potential gains from freer migration are huge. When workers from poor countries move to rich ones, they too can make use of advanced economies' superior capital and technologies, making them much more productive. This makes them—and the world—much better off. Starting from that simple insight, economists calculate that removing immigration controls could more than double the size of the world economy. Even a small relaxation of immigration controls would yield disproportionately big gains.

Yet many people believe that while the world would gain, workers in rich countries would lose out. They fear that foreigners harm the job prospects of local workers, taking their jobs or depressing their wages. Others fret that immigrants will be a burden on the welfare state. Some seem to believe that immigrants somehow simultaneously "steal" jobs and live off welfare.

Governments increasingly accept the case for allowing in highly skilled immigrants. The immigration bill before the Senate would tilt U.S. policy in that direction, establishing a points system that gives preference to university graduates. Such skills-focused points systems are in vogue: Canada and Australia employ one, Britain is introducing one, and other European countries are considering them.

For sure, as the number of university graduates in China, India, and other emerging markets soars in coming decades, it will be increasingly important for the United States to be able to draw on the widest possible pool of talent—not just for foreigners' individual skills and drive, but for their collective diversity.

It is astonishing how often the exceptional individuals who come up with brilliant new ideas happen to be immigrants. Twenty-one of Britain's Nobel Prize winners arrived in the country as refugees. Perhaps this is because immigrants tend to see things differently rather than following the conventional wisdom, perhaps because as outsiders they are more determined to succeed.

Yet most innovation nowadays comes not from individuals, but from groups of talented people sparking off each other—and foreigners with different ideas, perspectives, and experiences add something extra to the mix. If there are ten people sitting around a table trying to come up with a solution to a problem and they all think alike, then they are no better than one. But if they all think differently, then by bouncing ideas off each other they can solve problems better and faster. Research shows that a diverse group of talented individuals can perform better than a like-minded group of geniuses.

Just look at Silicon Valley: Intel, Yahoo!, Google, and eBay were all co-founded by immigrants, many of whom arrived as children. In fact, nearly half of America's venture capital–backed start-ups have immigrant founders. An ever-increasing share of our prosperity comes from companies that solve problems, be they developing new drugs, video games, or pollution-reducing technologies, or providing management advice. That's why, as China catches up, America and Europe need to open up further to foreigners in order to stay ahead.

Diversity also acts as a magnet for talent. Look at London: it is now a global city, with three in ten Londoners born abroad, from all over the world. People are drawn there because it is an exciting, cosmopolitan place. It's not just the huge range of ethnic restaurants and cultural experiences on offer; it's the opportunity to lead a richer life by meeting people from different backgrounds: friends, colleagues, and even a life partner.

Yet it is incorrect to believe that rich countries only need highly skilled immigrants, still less that bureaucrats can second-guess through a points system precisely which people the vast number of businesses in the economy need. America and Europe may increasingly be knowledge-based economies, but they still rely on low-skilled workers too. Every hotel requires not just managers and marketing people, but also receptionists, chambermaids, and waiters. Every hospital requires not just doctors and nurses, but also many more cleaners, cooks, laundry workers, and security staff. Everyone relies on road-sweepers, cabdrivers, and sewage workers.

Many low-skilled jobs cannot readily be mechanized or imported: old people cannot be cared for by a robot or from abroad. And as people get richer, they increasingly pay others to do arduous tasks, such as home improvements, that they once did themselves, freeing up time for more productive work or more enjoyable leisure. As advanced economies create high-skilled jobs, they inevitably create low-skilled ones too.

Critics argue that low-skilled immigration is harmful because the newcomers are poorer and less-educated than Americans. But that is precisely why they are willing to do low-paid, low-skilled jobs that Americans shun. In 1960, over half of American workers older than 25 were high school dropouts: now, only one in ten are. Understandably, high-school graduates aspire to better things, while even those with no qualifications don't want to do certain dirty, difficult, and dangerous jobs. The only way to reconcile aspirations to opportunity for all with the reality of drudgery for some is through immigration.

Fears that immigrants threaten American workers are based on two fallacies: that there is a fixed number of jobs to go around, and that foreign workers are direct substitutes for American ones. Just as women did not deprive men of jobs when they entered the labor force too, foreigners don't cost Americans their jobs—they don't just take jobs; they create them too. When they spend their wages, they boost demand for people who produce the goods and services that they consume; and as they work, they stimulate demand for Americans in complementary lines of work. An influx of Mexican construction workers, for instance, creates new jobs for people selling building materials, as well as for interior designers. Thus, while the number of immigrants has risen sharply over the past twenty years, America's unemployment rate has fallen.

But do some American workers lose out? Hardly any: most actually gain. Why? Because, as critics of immigration are the first to admit, immigrants are different than to Americans, so that they rarely compete directly with them in the labor market: often, they complement their efforts—a foreign child-minder may enable an American nurse to go back to work, where her productivity may be enhanced by hard-working foreign doctors and cleaners—while also stimulating extra capital investment.

Study after study fails to find evidence that immigrants harm American workers. Harvard's George Borjas claims otherwise, but his partial approach is flawed because it neglects the broader complementarities between immigrant labor, native labor, and capital. A recent National Bureau of Economic Research study by Gianmarco Ottaviano and Giovanni Peri finds that the influx of foreign workers between 1990 and 2004 raised the average wage of U.S.-born workers by 2 percent. Nine in ten American workers gained: only one in ten, high-school dropouts, lost slightly, by 1 percent.

Part of the opposition to immigration stems from the belief that it is an inexorable, once-and-for-all movement of permanent settlement. But now that travel is ever cheaper and economic opportunities do not stop at national borders, migration is increasingly temporary when people are allowed to move freely. That is true for globe-trotting businessmen and it is increasingly so for poorer migrants too: Filipino nurses as well as Polish plumbers.

Britain's experience since it opened its borders to the eight much poorer central and eastern European countries which joined the European Union in 2004 is instructive. All 75 million people there could conceivably have moved, but in fact only a small fraction have, and most of those have already left again. Many are, in effect, international commuters, splitting their time between Britain and Poland. Of course, some will end up settling, but most won't. Most migrants do not want to leave home forever: they want to go work abroad for a while to earn enough to buy a house or set up a business back home.

Studies show that most Mexican migrants have similar aspirations. If they could come and go freely, most would move only temporarily. But perversely, U.S. border controls end up making many stay for good, because crossing the border is so risky and costly that once you have got across you tend to stay.

Governments ought to be encouraging such international mobility. It would benefit poor countries as well as rich ones. Already, migrants from poor countries working in rich ones send home much more—$200 billion a year officially, perhaps twice that informally (according to the Global Commission on International Migration)—than the miserly $100 billion that Western governments give in aid. These remittances are not wasted on weapons or siphoned off into Swiss bank accounts; they go straight into the pockets of local people. They pay for food, clean water, and medicines. They enable children to stay in school, fund small businesses, and benefit the local economy more broadly. What's more, when migrants return home, they bring new skills, new ideas, and capital to start new businesses. Africa's first internet cafés were started by migrants returning from Europe.

The World Bank calculates that in countries where remittances account for a large share of the economy (11 percent of GDP [gross domestic product] on average), they slash the poverty rate by a third. Even in countries which receive relatively little (2.2 percent of GDP on average), remittances can cut the poverty rate by nearly a fifth. Since the true level of remittances is much higher than official figures, their impact on poverty is likely to be even greater.

Remittances can also bring broader economic benefits. When countries are hit by a hurricane or earthquake, remittances tend to soar. During the Asian financial crisis a decade ago, Filipino migrants cushioned the blow on the Philippines' economy by sending home extra cash—and their dollar remittances were worth more in devalued Filipino pesos. Developing country governments can even borrow using their country's expected future remittances as collateral. Even the poorest countries, which receive $45 billion in remittances a year, could eventually tap this relatively cheap form of finance, giving them the opportunity of faster growth.

By keeping kids in school, paying for them to see a doctor, and funding new businesses, remittances can boost growth. A study by Paola Guiliano of Harvard and Marta Ruiz-Arranz of the International Monetary Fund finds that in countries with rudimentary financial systems, remittances allow people to invest more and better, and thus raise growth. When remittances increase by one percentage point of GDP, growth rises by 0.2 percentage points.

John Kenneth Galbraith said, "Migration is the oldest action against poverty. It selects those who most want help. It is good for the country to which they go; it helps break the equilibrium of poverty in the country from which they come. What is the perversity in the human soul that causes people to resist so obvious a good?"

Part of the answer is that people tend to focus their fears about economic change on foreigners. Other fears are cultural; more recently, these have [been] mixed up with worries about terrorism. Mostly, this is illogical: Christian Latinos are scarcely likely to be a fifth column of al Qaeda operatives, as Pat Buchanan has suggested. But logic scarcely comes into it. Psychological studies confirm that opposition to immigration tends to stem from an emotional dislike of foreigners. Intelligent critics then construct an elaborate set of seemingly rational arguments to justify their prejudice.

In Who Are We: The Challenges to America's National Identity, Harvard academic Samuel Huntington warns that Latino immigrants are generally poor and therefore a drain on American society, except in Miami, where they are rich and successful, at Americans' expense. Ironically, when he shot to fame by warning about a global "clash of civilizations," he lumped Mexicans and Americans together in a single civilization: now he claims that Latinos in the United States threaten a domestic clash of civilizations. He frets that Latinos have until recently clustered in certain cities and states, and then that they are starting to spread out. Immigrants can't win: they're damned if they do and damned if they don't.

Rich-country governments should not let such nonsense define their policies. Opening up our borders would spread freedom, widen opportunity and enrich the economy, society and culture. That may seem unrealistic, but so too, once, did abolishing slavery or giving women the vote.

David Goodhart

Too Diverse?

Britain in the 1950s was a country stratified by class and region. But in most of its cities, suburbs, towns and villages there was a good chance of predicting the attitudes, even the behavior, of the people living in your immediate neighborhood.

In many parts of Britain today that is no longer true. The country has long since ceased to be Orwell's "family" (albeit with the wrong members in charge). To some people this is a cause of regret and disorientation—a change which they associate with the growing incivility of modern urban life. To others it is a sign of the inevitable, and welcome, march of modernity. After three centuries of homogenization through industrialization, urbanization, nation-building and war, the British have become freer and more varied. Fifty years of peace, wealth and mobility have allowed a greater diversity in lifestyles and values. To this "value diversity" has been added ethnic diversity through two big waves of immigration: first the mainly commonwealth immigration from the West Indies and Asia in the 1950s and 1960s, followed by asylum-driven migrants from Europe, Africa and the greater middle east in the late 1990s.

The diversity, individualism and mobility that characterize developed economies—especially in the era of globalization—mean that more of our lives is spent among strangers. Ever since the invention of agriculture 10,000 years ago, humans have been used to dealing with people from beyond their own extended kin groups. The difference now in a developed country like Britain is that we not only live among stranger citizens but we must share with them. We share public services and parts of our income in the welfare state, we share public spaces in towns and cities where we are squashed together on buses, trains and tubes, and we share in a democratic conversation—filtered by the media—about the collective choices we wish to make. All such acts of sharing are more smoothly and generously negotiated if we can take for granted a limited set of common values and assumptions. But as Britain becomes more diverse that common culture is being eroded.

And therein lies one of the central dilemmas of political life in developed societies: sharing and solidarity can conflict with diversity. This is an especially acute dilemma for progressives who want plenty of both solidarity—high social cohesion and generous welfare paid out of a progressive tax system—and diversity—equal respect for a wide range of peoples, values and ways of life. The tension between the two values is a reminder that serious politics is about trade-offs. . . .

It was the Conservative politician David Willetts who drew my attention to the "progressive dilemma." Speaking at a round table on welfare reform (Prospect, March 1998), he said: "The basis on which you can extract large sums of money in tax and pay it out in benefits is that most people think the recipients are people like themselves, facing difficulties which they themselves could face. If values become more diverse, if lifestyles become more differentiated, then it becomes more difficult to sustain the legitimacy of a universal risk-pooling welfare state. People ask, 'Why should I pay for them when they are doing things I wouldn't do?' This is America versus Sweden. You can have a Swedish welfare state provided that you are a homogeneous society with intensely shared values. In the U.S. you have a very diverse, individualistic society where people feel fewer obligations to fellow citizens. Progressives want diversity but they thereby undermine part of the moral consensus on which a large welfare state rests."

. . . Thinking about the conflict between solidarity and diversity is another way of asking a question as old as human society itself: who is my brother? With whom do I share mutual obligations? The traditional conservative Burkean view is that our affinities ripple out from our families and localities, to the nation and not very far beyond. That view is pitted against a liberal universalist one which sees us in some sense equally obligated to all human beings from Bolton to Burundi—an idea associated with the universalist aspects of Christianity and Islam, with Kantian universalism and with left-wing internationalism. Science is neutral in this dispute, or rather it stands on both sides of the argument. Evolutionary psychology stresses both the universality of most human traits and—through the notion of kin selection and reciprocal altruism—the instinct to favor our own. Social psychologists also argue that the tendency to perceive in-groups and out-groups, however ephemeral, is innate. In any case, Burkeans claim to have common sense on their side. They argue that we feel more comfortable with, and are readier to share with, and sacrifice for, those with whom we have shared histories and similar values. To put it bluntly—most of us prefer our own kind.

The category "own kind" or in-group will set alarm bells ringing in the minds of many readers. So it is worth stressing what preferring our own kind does not mean, even for a Burkean. It does not mean that we are necessarily hostile to other kinds or cannot empathize with outsiders. (There are those who do dislike other kinds but in Britain they seem to be quite a small minority.) In complex societies, most of us belong simultaneously to many in-groups—family, profession, class, hobby, locality, nation; an ability to move with ease between groups is a sign of maturity. An in-group is not, except in the case of families, a natural or biological category and the people who are deemed to belong to it can change quickly, as we saw so disastrously in Bosnia. Certainly, those we include in our in-group could be a pretty diverse crowd, especially in a city like London.

Moreover, modern liberal societies cannot be based on a simple assertion of group identity—the very idea of the rule of law, of equal legal treatment for everyone regardless of religion, wealth, gender or ethnicity, conflicts with it. On the other hand, if you deny the assumption that humans are social, group-based primates with constraints, however imprecise, on their willingness to share, you find yourself having to defend some implausible positions: for example that we should spend as much on development aid as on the NHS [National Health Service], or that Britain should have no immigration controls at all. The implicit "calculus of affinity" in media reporting of disasters is easily mocked—two dead Britons will get the same space as 200 Spaniards or 2,000 Somalis. Yet everyday we make similar calculations in the distribution of our own resources. Even a well-off, liberal-minded Briton who already donates to charities will spend, say, 200 on a child's birthday party, knowing that such money could, in the right hands, save the life of a child in the third world. The extent of our obligation to those to whom we are not connected through either kinship or citizenship is in part a purely private, charitable decision. But it also has policy implications, and not just in the field of development aid. For example, significant NHS resources are spent each year on foreign visitors, especially in London. Many of us might agree in theory that the needs of desperate outsiders are often greater than our own. But we would object if our own parent or child received inferior treatment because of resources consumed by non-citizens.

Is it possible to reconcile these observations about human preferences with our increasingly open, fluid and value-diverse societies? At one level, yes. Our liberal democracies still work fairly well; indeed it is one of the achievements of modernity that people have learned to tolerate and share with people very unlike themselves. (Until the 20th century, today's welfare state would have been considered contrary to human nature.) On the other hand, the logic of solidarity, with its tendency to draw boundaries, and the logic of diversity, with its tendency to cross them, do at times pull apart. Thanks to the erosion of collective norms and identities, in particular of class and nation, and the recent surge of immigration into Europe, this may be such a time.

The modern idea of citizenship goes some way to accommodating the tension between solidarity and diversity. Citizenship is not an ethnic, blood and soil concept but a more abstract political idea—implying equal legal, political and social rights (and duties) for people inhabiting a given national space. But citizenship is not just an abstract idea about rights and duties; for most of us it is something we do not choose but are born into—it arises out of a shared history, shared experiences, and, often, shared suffering; as the American writer Alan Wolfe puts it: "Behind every citizen lies a graveyard."

Both aspects of citizenship imply a notion of mutual obligation. Critics have argued that this idea of national community is anachronistic—swept away by globalization, individualism and migration—but it still has political resonance. When politicians talk about the "British people" they refer not just to a set of individuals with specific rights and duties but to a group of people with a special commitment to one another. Membership in such a community implies acceptance of moral rules, however fuzzy, which underpin the laws and welfare systems of the state.

In the rhetoric of the modern liberal state, the glue of ethnicity ("people who look and talk like us") has been replaced with the glue of values ("people who think and behave like us"). But British values grow, in part, out of a specific history and even geography. Too rapid a change in the make-up of a community not only changes the present; it also, potentially, changes our link with the past. As Bob Rowthorn wrote (Prospect, February 2003), we may lose a sense of responsibility for our own history—the good things and shameful things in it—if too many citizens no longer identify with it.

Is this a problem? Surely Britain in 2004 has become too diverse and complex to give expression to a common culture in the present, let alone the past. Diversity in this context is usually code for ethnic difference. But that is only one part of the diversity story, albeit the easiest to quantify and most emotionally charged. The progressive dilemma is also revealed in the value and generational rifts that emerged with such force in the 1960s. At the Prospect roundtable mentioned above, Patricia Hewitt, now trade secretary, recalled an example of generational conflict from her Leicester constituency. She was canvassing on a council estate when an elderly white couple saw her Labour rosette and one of them said, "We're not voting Labour—you hand taxpayers' money to our daughter." She apparently lived on a nearby estate, with three children all by different fathers, and her parents had cut her off. (Evidence that even close genetic ties do not always produce solidarity.)

Greater diversity can produce real conflicts of values and interests, but it also generates unjustified fears. Exposure to a wider spread of lifestyles, plus more mobility and better education, has helped to combat some of those fears—a trend reinforced by popular culture and the expansion of higher education (graduates are notably more tolerant than non-graduates). There is less overt homophobia, sexism or racism (and much more racial intermarriage) in Britain than 30 years ago and racial discrimination is the most politically sensitive form of unfairness. But 31 percent of people still admit to being racially prejudiced. Researchers such as Isaac Marks at London's Institute of Psychiatry warn that it is not possible to neatly divide the population between a small group of xenophobes and the rest. Feelings of suspicion and hostility towards outsiders are latent in most of us.

The visibility of ethnic difference means that it often overshadows other forms of diversity. Changes in the ethnic composition of a city or neighborhood can come to stand for the wider changes of modern life. Some expressions of racism, especially by old people, can be read as declarations of dismay at the passing of old ways of life (though this makes it no less unpleasant to be on the receiving end). The different appearance of many immigrants is an outward reminder that they are, at least initially, strangers. If welfare states demand that we pay into a common fund on which we can all draw at times of need, it is important that we feel that most people have made the same effort to be self-supporting and will not take advantage. We need to be reassured that strangers, especially those from other countries, have the same idea of reciprocity as we do. Absorbing outsiders into a community worthy of the name takes time.

Negotiating the tension between solidarity and diversity is at the heart of politics. But both left and right have, for different reasons, downplayed the issue. The left is reluctant to acknowledge a conflict between values it cherishes; it is ready to stress the erosion of community from "bad" forms of diversity such as market individualism but not from "good" forms of diversity such as sexual freedom and immigration. And the right, in Britain at least, has sidestepped the conflict, partly because it is less interested in solidarity than the left, but also because it is still trying to prove that it is comfortable with diversity.

But is there any hard evidence that the progressive dilemma actually exists in the real world of political and social choices? In most EU [European Union] states the percentage of GDP [gross domestic product] taken in tax is still at historically high levels, despite the increase in diversity of all kinds. Yet it is also true that Scandinavian countries with the biggest welfare states have been the most socially and ethnically homogeneous states in the west. By the same token the welfare state has always been weaker in the individualistic, ethnically divided U.S. compared with more homogeneous Europe. And the three bursts of welfarist legislation that the U.S. did see—Franklin Roosevelt's New Deal, Harry Truman's Fair Deal and Lyndon Johnson's Great Society—came during the long pause in mass immigration between the first world war and 1968. (They were also, clearly, a response to the depression and two world wars.)

In their 2001 Harvard Institute of Economic Research paper "Why Doesn't the U.S. Have a European-style Welfare State?" Alberto Alesina, Edward Glaeser and Bruce Sacerdote argue that the answer is that too many people at the bottom of the pile in the U.S. are black or Hispanic. Across the U.S. as a whole, 70 percent of the population are non-Hispanic whites—but of those in poverty only 46 percent are non-Hispanic whites. So a disproportionate amount of tax income spent on welfare is going to minorities. The paper also finds that U.S. states that are more ethnically fragmented than average spend less on social services. The authors conclude that Americans think of the poor as members of a different group, whereas Europeans still think of the poor as members of the same group. Robert Putnam, the analyst of social capital, has also found a link between high ethnic mix and low trust in the U.S. There is some British evidence supporting this link too. Researchers at Mori found that the average level of satisfaction with local authorities declines steeply as the extent of ethnic fragmentation increases. Even allowing for the fact that areas of high ethnic mix tend to be poorer, Mori found that ethnic fractionalization still had a substantial negative impact on attitudes to local government.

Finally, Sweden and Denmark may provide a social laboratory for the solidarity/diversity trade-off in the coming years. Starting from similar positions as homogeneous countries with high levels of redistribution, they have taken rather different approaches to immigration over the past few years. Although both countries place great stress on integrating outsiders, Sweden has adopted a moderately multicultural outlook. It has also adapted its economy somewhat, reducing job protection for older native males in order to create more low-wage jobs for immigrants in the public sector. About 12 percent of Swedes are now foreign-born and it is expected that by 2015 about 25 percent of under-18s will be either foreign-born or the children of the foreign-born. This is a radical change and Sweden is adapting to it rather well (the first clips of mourning Swedes after Anna Lindh's murder were of crying immigrants expressing their sorrow in perfect Swedish). But not all Swedes are happy about it.

Denmark has a more restrictive and "nativist" approach to immigration. Only 6 percent of the population is foreign-born and native Danes enjoy superior welfare benefits to incomers. If the solidarity/diversity trade-off is a real one and current trends continue, then one would expect in, say, 20 years' time that Sweden will have a less redistributive welfare state than Denmark; or rather that Denmark will have a more developed two-tier welfare state with higher benefits for insiders, while Sweden will have a universal but less generous system.

What are the main objections, at least from the left, to this argument about solidarity and diversity? Multiculturalists stress Britain's multiple diversities, of class and region, which preceded recent waves of immigration. They also argue that all humans share similar needs and a common interest in ensuring they are met with minimum conflict; this, they say, can now be done through human rights laws. And hostility to diversity, they conclude, is usually a form of "false consciousness."

Critics of the dilemma also say, rightly, that the moral norms underpinning a community need not be hard for outsiders to comply with: broad common standards of right and wrong, some agreement on the nature of marriage and the family, respect for law, and some consensus about the role of religion in public life. Moreover, they add, there are places such as Canada (even Australia) which are happily combining European-style welfare with an officially multicultural politics. London, too, has U.S. levels of ethnic diversity but is the most left-wing part of Britain. . . .

A further point made by the multiculturalists is more telling. They argue that a single national story is not a sound base for a common culture because it has always been contested by class, region and religion. In Britain, the left traces democracy back to the peasants' revolt, the right back to Magna Carta, and so on. But while that is true, it is also the case that these different stories refer to a shared history. This does not imply a single narrative or national identity any more than a husband and wife will describe their married life together in the same way. Nor does it mean that the stress on the binding force of a shared history (or historical institutions like parliament) condemns immigrants to a second-class citizenship. Newcomers can and should adopt the history of their new country as well as, over time, contributing to it—moving from immigrant "them" to citizen "us." Helpfully, Britain's story includes, through empire, the story of many of our immigrant groups—empire soldiers, for example, fought in many of the wars that created modern Britain.

I would add a further qualification to the progressive dilemma. Attitudes to welfare have, for many people, become more instrumental: I pay so much in, the state gives me this in return. As we grow richer the ties that used to bind workers together in a risk-pooling welfare state (first locally, later nationally) have loosened—"generosity" is more abstract and compulsory, a matter of enlightened self-interest rather than mutual obligation. Moreover, welfare is less redistributive than most people imagine—most of the tax paid out by citizens comes back to them in one form or another so the amount of the average person's income going to someone they might consider undeserving is small. This, however, does little to allay anxieties based on perceptions rather than fiscal truths. And poor whites, who have relatively little, are more likely to resent even small transfers compared with those on higher incomes.

Despite these qualifications it still seems to me that those who value solidarity should take care that it is not eroded by a refusal to acknowledge the constraints upon it. The politician who has recently laid most stress on those constraints, especially in relation to immigration, is the home secretary, David Blunkett. He has spoken about the need for more integration of some immigrant communities—especially Muslim ones—while continuing to welcome high levels of net immigration into Britain of over 150,000 a year.

Supporters of large-scale immigration now focus on the quantifiable economic benefits, appealing to the self-interest rather than the idealism of the host population. While it is true that some immigration is beneficial—neither the NHS nor the building industry could survive without it—many of the claimed benefits of mass immigration are challenged by economists such as Adair Turner and Richard Layard. . . .

But large-scale immigration, especially if it happens rapidly, is not just about economics; it is about those less tangible things to do with identity and mutual obligation—which have been eroded from other directions too. It can also create real—as opposed to just imagined—conflicts of interest. One example is the immigration-related struggles over public housing in many of Britain's big cities in the 1970s and 1980s. In places like London's east end the right to a decent council house had always been regarded as part of the inheritance of the respectable working class. When immigrants began to arrive in the 1960s they did not have the contacts to get on the housing list and so often ended up in low quality private housing. Many people saw the injustice of this and decided to change the rules: henceforth the criterion of universal need came to supplant good contacts. So if a Bangladeshi couple with children were in poor accommodation they would qualify for a certain number of housing points, allowing them to jump ahead of young local white couples who had been on the list for years. This was, of course, unpopular with many whites. Similar clashes between group based notions of justice and universally applied human rights are unavoidable in welfare states with increasingly diverse people.

The "thickest" solidarities are now often found among ethnic minority groups themselves in response to real or perceived discrimination. This can be another source of resentment for poor whites who look on enviously from their own fragmented neighborhoods as minorities recreate some of the mutual support and sense of community that was once a feature of British working-class life. Paradoxically, it may be this erosion of feelings of mutuality among the white majority in Britain that has made it easier to absorb minorities. The degree of antagonism between groups is proportional to the degree of co-operation within groups. Relative to the other big European nations, the British sense of national culture and solidarity has arguably been rather weak—diluted by class, empire, the four different nations within the state, the north–south divide, and even the long shadow of American culture. That weakness of national solidarity, exemplified by the "stand-off-ishness" of suburban England, may have created a bulwark against extreme nationalism. We are more tolerant than, say, France because we don't care enough about each other to resent the arrival of the other.

When solidarity and diversity pull against each other, which side should public policy favor? Diversity can increasingly look after itself—the underlying drift of social and economic development favors it. Solidarity, on the other hand, thrives at times of adversity, hence its high point just after the second world war and its steady decline ever since as affluence, mobility, value diversity and (in some areas) immigration have loosened the ties of a common culture. Public policy should therefore tend to favor solidarity in four broad areas.

Immigration and Asylum

About 9 percent of British residents are now from ethnic minorities, rising to almost one third in London. On current trends about one fifth of the population will come from an ethnic minority by 2050, albeit many of them fourth or fifth generation. Thanks to the race riots in northern English towns in 2001, the fear of radical Islam after 9/11, and anxieties about the rise in asylum-led immigration from the mid-1990s (exacerbated by the popular press), immigration has shot up the list of voter concerns, and according to Mori 56 percent of people (including 90 percent of poor whites and even a large minority of immigrants) now believe there are too many immigrants in Britain. . . .

Immigrants come in all shapes and sizes. From the American banker or Indian software engineer to the Somali asylum seeker—from the most desirable to the most burdensome, at least in the short term. Immigrants who plan to stay should be encouraged to become Britons as far as that is compatible with holding on to some core aspects of their own culture. In return for learning the language, getting a job and paying taxes, and abiding by the laws and norms of the host society, immigrants must be given a stake in the system and incentives to become good citizens. . . . Immigrants from the same place are bound to want to congregate together but policy should try to prevent that consolidating into segregation across all the main areas of life: residence, school, workplace, church. In any case, the laissez-faire approach of the postwar period in which ethnic minority citizens were not encouraged to join the common culture (although many did) should be buried. Citizenship ceremonies, language lessons and the mentoring of new citizens should help to create a British version of the old U.S. melting pot. This third way on identity can be distinguished from the coercive assimilationism of the nationalist right, which rejects any element of foreign culture, and from multiculturalism, which rejects a common culture. . . .

Welfare Policy

A generous welfare state is not compatible with open borders and possibly not even with U.S.-style mass immigration. Europe is not America. One of the reasons for the fragmentation and individualism of American life is that it is a vast country. In Europe, with its much higher population density and planning controls, the rules have to be different. We are condemned to share—the rich cannot ignore the poor, the indigenous cannot ignore the immigrant—but that does not mean people are always happy to share. A universal, human rights–based approach to welfare ignores the fact that the rights claimed by one group do not automatically generate the obligation to accept them, or pay for them, on the part of another group—as we saw with the elderly couple in Leicester. If we want high tax and redistribution, especially with the extra welfare demands of an aging population, then in a world of stranger citizens taxpayers need reassurance that their money is being spent on people for whose circumstances they would have some sympathy. For that reason, welfare should become more overtly conditional. The rules must be transparent and blind to ethnicity, religion, sexuality and so on, but not blind to behavior. People who consistently break the rules of civilized behavior should not receive unconditional benefits. . . .

Culture

Good societies need places like London and New York as well as the more homogeneous, stable, small and medium-size towns of middle Britain or the American midwest. But the emphasis, in culture and the media, should be on maintaining a single national conversation at a time when the viewing and listening public is becoming more fragmented. In Britain, that means strong support for the "social glue" role of the BBC. (The glue once provided by religion no longer works, and in any case cannot include immigrants of different faiths.) The teaching of multi-ethnic citizenship in schools is a welcome step. But too many children leave school with no sense of the broad sweep of their national history. The teaching of British history, and in particular the history of the empire and of subsequent immigration into Britain, should be a central part of the school curriculum. At the same time, immigrants should be encouraged to become part of the British "we," even while bringing their own very different perspective on its formation.

Politics and Language

Multiculturalists argue that the binding power of the liberal nation state has been eroded from within by value diversity and from without by the arrival of immigrant communities with other loyalties. But the nation state remains irreplaceable as the site for democratic participation and it is hard to imagine how else one can organize welfare states and redistribution except through national tax and public spending. Moreover, since the arrival of immigrant groups from non-liberal or illiberal cultures it has become clear that to remain liberal the state may have to prescribe a clearer hierarchy of values. The U.S. has tried to resolve the tension between liberalism and pluralism by developing a powerful national myth. Even if this were desirable in Britain, it is probably not possible to emulate. Indeed, the idea of fostering a common culture, in any strong sense, may no longer be possible either. One only has to try listing what the elements of a common culture might be to realize how hard it would be to legislate for. That does not mean that the idea must be abandoned; rather, it should inform public policy as an underlying assumption rather than a set of policies. Immigration and welfare policies, for example, should be designed to reduce the fear of free riding, and the symbolic aspects of citizenship should be reinforced; they matter more in a society when tacit understandings and solidarities can no longer be taken for granted. Why not, for example, a British national holiday or a state of the union address?

Lifestyle diversity and high immigration bring cultural and economic dynamism but can erode feelings of mutual obligation, reducing willingness to pay tax and even encouraging a retreat from the public domain. In the decades ahead European politics itself may start to shift on this axis, with left and right being eclipsed by value-based culture wars and movements for and against diversity. Social democratic parties risk being torn apart in such circumstances, partly on class lines: recent British Social Attitudes reports have made clear the middle class and the working class increasingly converge on issues of tax and economic management, but diverge on diversity issues.

The anxieties triggered by the asylum seeker inflow into Britain now seem to be fading. But they are not just a media invention; a sharp economic downturn or a big inflow of east European workers after EU enlargement might easily call them up again. The progressive centre needs to think more clearly about these issues to avoid being engulfed by them. And to that end it must try to develop a new language in which to address the anxieties, one that transcends the thin and abstract language of universal rights on the one hand and the defensive, nativist language of group identity on the other. Too often the language of liberal universalism that dominates public debate ignores the real affinities of place and people. These affinities are not obstacles to be overcome on the road to the good society; they are one of its foundation stones. People will always favor their own families and communities; it is the task of a realistic liberalism to strive for a definition of community that is wide enough to include people from many different backgrounds, without being so wide as to become meaningless.

CHAPTER 5 FREE TRADE AGREEMENTS ARE STEPPING-STONES v. FREE TRADE AGREEMENTS ARE STUMBLING BLOCKS

Free Trade Agreements Are Stepping-Stones toward Global Free Trade

Advocate: Daniel T. Griswold

Source: Free-Trade Agreements: Steppingstones to a More Open World, Trade Briefing Paper #18 (Washington, DC: CATO Institute, July 10, 2003)

Free Trade Agreements Are Stumbling Blocks toward Global Free Trade

Advocate: Jagdish Bhagwati

Source: "Why PTAs Are a Pox on the World Trading System," in *Termites in the Trading System: How Preferential Agreements Undermine Free Trade* (New York: Oxford University Press, 2008), 49–88

The last twenty years have seen an explosion of preferential trade agreements (PTAs). PTAs, sometimes referred to as regional trade agreements, are trade agreements that discriminate between members and nonmembers. PTAs come in two basic forms. In a free trade agreement (FTA), governments eliminate tariffs on goods entering their markets from their FTA partners, but each member retains independent tariffs on goods entering from non–FTA members. In a customs union, like the European Union, member governments combine an FTA with a common external tariff for goods entering the union from nonmembers. Although PTAs have been part of the global trade system throughout the postwar period, the number of such agreements accelerated rapidly during the 1990s. Today, approximately 180 PTAs are in force, and all World Trade Organization (WTO) members except Mongolia belong to at least one PTA.[1]

The proliferation of PTAs has thus generated debate concerning their impact on the multilateral trade system. Article 24 of the General Agreement on Tariffs and Trade gives governments the right to create PTAs, so the central

---

[1]World Trade Organization, "Regionalism: Friends or Rivals?" http://www.wto.org/english/theWTO_e/whatis_e/tif_e/bey1_e.htm.

issue is not really about whether PTAs are consistent with WTO obligations. Instead, the debate focuses on whether PTAs, in spite of their seeming trade-liberalizing consequences, are stepping-stones or stumbling blocks: Do they bring the world closer to or further from free trade?

FREE TRADE AGREEMENTS ARE STEPPING-STONES TOWARD GLOBAL FREE TRADE

Proponents argue that PTAs are stepping-stones to global free trade. Liberal-izing trade within the WTO is difficult because negotiations must produce agree-ments that satisfy more than 150 governments. In this context, a strategy based on PTAs might gradually lead to global free trade. Each successive PTA will eliminate tariffs on trade between some countries. Each PTA that governments negotiate will exert a gravitational pull that attracts new members. Eventually, the global network of PTAs will eliminate tariffs between most countries. Govern-ments thus achieve via PTAs what they cannot achieve as readily via multilateral negotiations within the WTO.

Daniel Griswold, an American economist, develops an argument along these lines. Griswold supports the American policy of negotiating FTAs as a second-best alternative to multilateral negotiations. He recognizes the legal and economic complexities that characterize PTAs: Are they consistent with WTO rules, and do they divert more trade than they create? Yet he argues that on balance the careful construction of FTAs is a useful policy tool that can advance American interests and promote gradual movement toward global free trade.

FREE TRADE AGREEMENTS ARE STUMBLING BLOCKS TOWARD GLOBAL FREE TRADE

Critics of PTAs argue that on balance the recent proliferation of such arrange-ments constitutes a real threat to the global multilateral trade system. On the one hand, critics argue that the logical evolution of a system based on PTAs is to three rival trade blocs, one based in Europe, one based in the Americas, and one based in Asia. These rivals would then engage in trade wars. One bloc might raise tariffs on imports from outside to protect local producers. The other blocs would respond by raising tariffs in return. The resulting trade wars would progressively reduce trade between the blocs and thus push the world toward a regional rather than a multilateral and global trade organization. And even if this worst case scenario does not arise, the negotiation of PTAs necessarily reduces the attention paid to the multilateral WTO. Consequently, PTAs gradually, even if unintentionally, erode support for the WTO-based trade system.

Jagdish Bhagwati is perhaps the most vocal critic of the contemporary pro-liferation of PTAs. In the extract presented here, Bhagwati criticizes PTAs on three grounds. First, he asserts that the resulting trade diversion is much larger than commonly recognized. Second, he claims that the proliferation of PTAs has created an extraordinarily complex network of rules that make it impossible *ex ante* to determine which tariff rates apply to a particular product. Finally, PTAs enable the United States to use its power to extract concessions from smaller countries that it could not otherwise obtain. This power asymmetry creates the opportunity to use PTAs to establish "trade unrelated rules" such as common labor and environmental standards and protection of property rights.

POINTS TO PONDER

1. Does the United States, as a hegemon, have a responsibility to pursue liberalization exclusively through the multilateral system?

2. Which of the following do you believe more likely: The threat to liberalize through PTAs will spur WTO negotiations to successful conclusion, or the emergence of PTAs will cause governments to gradually place less emphasis on the WTO?

3. Which do you consider more worrisome: a world in which governments liberalize trade through PTAs rather than the WTO or a world in which they eschew PTAs but are unable to make progress within the WTO? Justify your selection.

Daniel T. Griswold

Free-Trade Agreements:
Steppingstones to a More Open World

Introduction

. . . Since final passage of trade promotion authority in 2002, the Bush administration has launched an aggressive campaign to negotiate bilateral and regional free-trade agreements (FTAs). . . . Those agreements already negotiated or in the pipeline are sure to spark the usual debate about free trade versus fair trade, environmental standards and working conditions in poor countries, jobs and wages in the United States, and the other issues that inevitably swirl around any trade agreement before Congress.[1] But bilateral and regional trade agreements also raise a peculiar set of policy issues, economic and noneconomic alike, that are generally neglected when deals are debated and voted on.

Even for supporters of trade expansion, not every bilateral and regional free-trade agreement proposed is necessarily good economic policy. Despite the name, free-trade agreements do not always promote more trade, nor do they necessarily leave parties to the agreement or the rest of the world better off. Beyond the economic ambiguities of FTAs are a number of important strategic and foreign policy considerations that cannot be ignored.

This paper examines the merits of negotiating free-trade agreements. It analyzes both the economic and noneconomic implications of FTAs, weighs the costs and benefits of the specific agreements put forward by the Bush administration in light of those implications, and proposes guidelines for future negotiations to maximize the benefits and minimize the costs to both the U.S. economy and our broader national interests.

On balance, . . . bilateral and regional agreements . . . further our national interests. If crafted properly, those agreements would strengthen the U.S. economy by injecting new import competition into domestic markets and opening markets abroad more widely to U.S. exports. More important, they would encourage economic reform abroad and cement economic and foreign policy ties between the United States and key allies.

The Peculiarities of FTAs

For anyone who supports free trade, support for free-trade agreements would at first glance seem to be automatic. Such agreements by definition lower barriers to trade between participants, and lowering or eliminating barriers altogether has been the aim of the whole trade liberalization movement. Yet regional and bilateral trade agreements raise legal and economic questions that should be addressed.

Departing from Multilateral Trade

FTAs are an exception to the basic legal principle of nondiscrimination in international trade. Article III of the basic charter [of] the World Trade Organization ([WTO;] the General Agreement on Tariffs and Trade [GATT] 1947 as amended by the 1994 Uruguay Round Agreement) declares as a fundamental principle that market access should be extended to all members on a most-favored-nation, or nondiscriminatory, basis. Specifically, "any advantage, favor, privilege or immunity granted by any contracting party to any product originating in or destined for any other country shall be accorded immediately and unconditionally to the like product originating in or destined for the territories of all other contracting parties."[2]

Of course, FTAs explicitly deviate from that principle. They grant an advantage (lower or zero tariffs) to parties to an agreement that are not granted to other members of the WTO that are not parties to the agreement. But free-trade agreements and customs unions, when properly crafted, are consistent with GATT rules.

When the GATT was originally signed in 1947, its founding members carved out an exception for free-trade areas. Article XXIV of the GATT allows customs unions or free-trade agreements between members,[3] recognizing "the desirability of increasing freedom of trade by the development, through voluntary agreements, of closer integration between the economies of the countries [party] to such agreements."[4] Such agreements are allowed provided they (1) do not result in higher trade barriers overall for WTO members outside the agreement,[5] (2) eliminate "duties and other restrictive regulations of commerce" on "substantially all the trade between the constituent territories . . . in products originating in such territories,"[6] and (3) do so "within a reasonable length of time."[7] Article XXIV can be waived entirely by a two-thirds vote of WTO members.[8]

The most obvious exception under Article XXIV has been the European Union, which began in the 1950s as the six-member European Economic Community. Other well-known FTAs or customs unions among WTO members are the European Free Trade Association, the North American Free Trade Agreement, the Southern Common Market, the Association of Southeast Asian Nations Free Trade Area, and the Common Market of Eastern and Southern Africa.

In fact, free-trade agreements have been proliferating among WTO members. Today more than 150 such agreements are in effect, and the trend has been accelerating in the last decade. In the first 46 years of the GATT, between 1948 and 1994, 124 such agreements were signed (many of which have since expired), an average of 2.7 per year. Since 1995 the WTO has been notified of 130 such agreements, an average of more than 15 per year.[9] Today an estimated 43 percent of international trade occurs under free-trade agreements, and that share would reach 55 percent if agreements currently being negotiated worldwide were to be implemented.[10]

Despite Article I, free-trade agreements are a legal fact of life in international trade. More and more WTO members are choosing to negotiate FTAs. The question for U.S. trade policy is whether we should join or resist the trend.

The Messy Economics of FTAs

The economics of FTAs is more ambiguous than the legalities. Even though FTAs by definition result in lower trade barriers between member countries, they do not necessarily result in economic gains for all members or the world as a whole.

Economists have been investigating this phenomenon since 1950, when Jacob Viner published his seminal study, *The Customs Union Issue*.[11] Viner noted that customs unions can promote new trade among members, but they can also divert trade from more efficient producers outside the agreement.

If signed with a low-cost foreign producer, an agreement can result in *trade creation* by allowing the low-cost producer to enter the domestic market tariff free, reducing domestic prices, and displacing higher-cost *domestic* producers. But if signed with a relatively high-cost foreign producer, an agreement can result merely in *trade diversion* by allowing the higher-cost importer to displace lower-cost *foreign* importers simply because producers in the new FTA partner can import tariff free. As Viner concluded, customs unions are likely to yield more economic benefit than harm when "they are between sizeable countries which practice substantial protection of substantially similar [that is, competing] industries."[12]

To maximize trade creation, FTAs should unleash real competition in previously protected markets. From an economic perspective, the essential purpose and principal payoff of international trade is expanded competition within the domestic economy and expanded markets abroad for domestic producers. Increased import competition results in lower prices for consuming households and businesses, more product choice, higher quality, and increased innovation. By stimulating more efficient production, import competition increases the productivity of workers, real wages, living standards, and the long-run growth of the economy.

If an FTA does not result in lower prices for the importing country but merely reshuffles imports from the rest of the world to FTA partners, the importing country can suffer a welfare loss. Its government loses tariff revenue, but its consumers do not reap any gain from lower prices. In effect, the importing country's treasury subsidizes less efficient production in the partner country. If global prices outside the FTA fall because of the diverted demand, then the rest of the world loses from lost producer surplus.

To minimize trade diversion, the best FTAs allow a large and competitive foreign producer to displace domestic producers in a large and protected domestic market, thus delivering lower prices and higher real incomes to workers and families. The worst allow less competitive foreign producers to replace more competitive foreign producers in a large and protected domestic market, costing the treasury tariff revenue without delivering lower domestic prices or more efficient domestic production.

Free-trade economists argue among themselves about whether trade creation or trade diversion usually predominates under free-trade agreements. Settling that dispute definitively is beyond the scope of this paper.[13] But we do know that the evidence is mixed and that the short-term, static economic impact of a free-trade agreement is only one factor in deciding whether a particular FTA meets the test of good public policy. The possibility of trade diversion is not sufficient reason to reject the Bush administration's policy of pursuing FTAs.

How FTAs Advance Trade Liberalization

Even if trade diversion occurs, free-trade agreements can advance the goals of expanding free markets, individual liberty, and more peaceful cooperation among nations. In addition to their short-term economic effects, free-trade agreements can advance American interests in several ways.

A Safety Valve for the Multilateral System

One, FTAs provide an important safety valve if multilateral negotiations become stuck—an all-too-real possibility. Multilateral negotiations through the GATT and now the WTO can be long, tortuous, and uncertain. Since the Kennedy Round concluded in 1967, only two other comprehensive multilateral agreements have been reached—the Tokyo Round Agreement in 1979 and the Uruguay Round Agreement in 1994. And because of the need for consensus, it takes only one of the 146 nations in the WTO to scuttle a new agreement.

To cite one plausible scenario, the French government could prevent completion of a Doha Round Agreement because of its long-standing objections to liberalization of agricultural trade. Negotiators have already missed a March 31, 2003, deadline for preliminary agreements on agriculture, and doubt is widespread that the round will be concluded by 2005 as agreed in the 2001 agreement that launched it. The Uruguay Round, it should be remembered, almost foundered on the subject of agriculture. Given the history of multilateral negotiations, it would be unwise to put all of our tradable eggs in the Doha Round basket.

FTAs provide institutional competition to keep multilateral talks on track. If other WTO members become intransigent, the United States should have the option of pursuing agreements with a "coalition of the willing" in pursuit of trade liberalization. Negotiating FTAs, or at least retaining the option to do so, can send a signal to other WTO members that, if they are unwilling to negotiate seriously to reduce trade barriers, we retain the right to find bilateral and regional partners who will. Knowing that WTO members, including the United States, can pursue FTAs outside the multilateral process can focus the minds and wills of negotiators to reach an agreement.

Fears that FTAs could divert attention from the multilateral track are unfounded. Most WTO members that have pursued regional and bilateral FTAs have not abandoned their commitment to multilateral negotiations. The U.S. government signed agreements with Israel, Canada, and Mexico during the Uruguay Round negotiations from 1986 to 1994 without reducing its commitment to a final multilateral agreement. And there is no evidence that pursuit of FTAs today has distracted the Bush administration from the ongoing Doha Round of WTO negotiations. Indeed, U.S. Trade Representative Robert Zoellick has been leading the charge in the Doha Round with aggressive proposals to liberalize global trade in manufactured goods, agricultural products, and services.

A Level Playing Field for U.S. Exporters

Two, FTAs can level the playing field for U.S. exporters who have been put at a disadvantage by free-trade agreements that do not include the United States. The United States is party to only 3 of the 150 or so FTAs currently in force around the world—NAFTA [North American Free Trade Agreement] and bilateral agreements with Israel and Jordan. Even though American producers may be the most efficient in the world in a certain sector, our exporters may not be able to overcome the advantage of rival foreign producers who can export tariff free to countries with which their governments have signed an FTA.

In Chile, for example, U.S. exporters encounter a uniform 6 percent tariff. Competing exporters in the European Union, Canada, and Brazil, in contrast, sell duty-free in the same market because their governments have signed free-trade agreements with Chile. According to the National Association of Manufacturers, U.S. exporters have lost market share in Chile since its government began to aggressively pursue free-trade agreements with its non-U.S. trading partners in 1997. Especially hard-hit by the tariff differential have been U.S. exports to Chile of wheat, soybeans, corn, paper products, plastics, fertilizers, paints and dyes, and heating and construction equipment.[14] All those sectors have seen their market share drop significantly in the absence of a U.S.–Chile free-trade agreement.

Institutionalizing Reforms Abroad

Three, FTAs can help less-developed countries lock in and institutionalize ongoing economic reforms. A signed agreement prevents nations from backsliding in times of economic or political duress. Agreements assure foreign investors that reforms mark a permanent commitment to liberalization. For example, when Mexico suffered its peso crisis in 1994–95, its NAFTA commitments kept its market open to U.S. exports. The assurance of an FTA also works the other way, guaranteeing that exporters in the partner country will enjoy duty-free access to the large American market. By signing an FTA with the United States, less-developed countries signal to the rest of the world that they are serious about embracing global competition. That signal, combined with access to the U.S. market, can help to attract foreign investment and spur faster development.

Blazing a Trail for Broader Negotiations

Four, FTAs can provide useful templates for broader negotiations. As the members of the WTO grow in number and diversity, reaching consensus among all 146 members becomes more difficult. Negotiators can be forced to consider only the lowest common denominator acceptable to all members. Negotiating with only one country or a small group of like-minded countries can allow more meaningful liberalization in areas such as sanitary and phytosanitary (i.e., animal and plant) regulations, technical barriers to trade, service trade and investment, electronic commerce, customs facilitation, labor and environmental standards, dispute settlement, and market access for politically sensitive sectors.

Those agreements, in turn, can blaze a trail for wider regional and multilateral negotiations. The U.S.–Chile FTA provides an example of how to incorporate labor and environmental standards into the text of an agreement without threatening to hold trade hostage to rich-country demands for higher standards in less-developed countries. FTAs can provide creative solutions to sticky political problems that can then be adapted in other agreements.

Internal Competition and Integration

Five, FTAs can spur internal reform and consolidation within member states, enhancing economic growth and support for more liberalization. By encouraging regional integration, FTAs hasten the consolidation of production within the FTA, increase economies of scale, and create a more integrated production process. Consolidation may be most pronounced in more heavily protected service sectors such as telecommunications, financial services, and transportation. More efficient industries and infrastructure can yield dynamic gains year after year, boosting growth, investment, and demand for imports from FTA partners as well as the rest of the world.

For all those reasons, the Bush administration's agenda of negotiating free-trade agreements is worth pursuing. Under the right conditions, FTAs can inject new competition into our domestic economy, lowering prices for consumers and shifting factors of production to more efficient uses, while leveling the playing field for U.S. exporters. Beyond those immediate benefits, FTAs can provide institutional competition for multilateral talks, spurring integration among FTA countries and liberalization abroad and blazing a trail through difficult areas for broader negotiations in the future. As a foreign policy tool, FTAs can cement ties with allies and encourage countries to stay on the trail of political and economic reform.

Conclusion

As a tool for expanding freedom and prosperity, regional and bilateral free-trade agreements are useful if less than ideal. They complicate the international trading system by deviating from the most-favored-nation principle of nondiscrimination, and they can blunt the benefits of international trade by diverting it from the most efficient foreign producers to those that are favored but less efficient. But FTAs can produce compensating benefits by opening domestic markets to fresh competition, encouraging economic liberalization abroad, cementing important foreign policy and security ties, integrating regional economies, opening markets to U.S. exports, and providing healthy institutional competition for multilateral negotiations.

To maximize the economic benefits of free-trade agreements, the U.S. government should focus its efforts on negotiations with countries that provide new opportunities for U.S. exporters and whose producers would be most likely to enhance competition in our own market. That approach requires that U.S. negotiators not duck politically sensitive sectors through long phase-in periods for or exemptions from liberalization. Instead, they should tout the immediate liberalization of those sectors as offering the best opportunities to reap the benefits of trade.

As a broader foreign policy tool, free-trade agreements should reward and solidify market and political reform abroad. If FTA partners are not major export markets or significant producers of goods that compete in our domestic market, they should be moving decisively toward free markets and representative government. They should be reform leaders in regions of the world where models of successful reform are most needed. In this way, free-trade agreements can serve as carrots to encourage the spread of political and economic freedom abroad.

Despite their peculiarities and incremental nature, free-trade agreements can serve the cause of freedom and development by breaking down barriers to trade between nations. If crafted according to sound principles, free-trade agreements can serve America's economic and foreign policy interests.

ENDNOTES

1. For articles and studies on those more general trade issues, see previous materials published by the Cato Institute's Center for Trade Policy Studies available at www.freetrade.org.
2. General Agreement on Tariffs and Trade 1947, Part I, Article I, Section 1, www .wto.org/english/docs_e/legal_e/gatt47_01_e.htm.
3. Members of a customs union adopt a common external trade policy with uniform tariffs applying to imports of all members. Members of a free-trade agreement retain independent external trade policies while eliminating barriers among themselves.
4. General Agreement on Tariffs and Trade 1947, Part III, Article XXIV, Section 4.
5. Ibid., Part III, Article XXIV, Section 5 (a) and (b).
6. Ibid., Part III, Article XXIV, Section 8(a)i.
7. Ibid., Part III, Article XXIV, Section 5(c).
8. Ibid., Part III, Article XXIV, Section 10.
9. World Trade Organization, "Regional Trade Agreements: Facts and Figures," www.wto.org/english/tratop_e/region_e/regfac_e.htm.
10. Organization for Economic Cooperation and Development, "Regional Trade Agreements and the Multilateral Trading System," November 20, 2002, p. 12.
11. Jacob Viner, *The Customs Union Issue* (New York: Carnegie Endowment for International Peace, 1950).
12. Ibid., p. 135.
13. For a favorable assessment of free-trade agreements, see Robert Z. Lawrence, "Emerging Regional Arrangements: Building Blocks or Stumbling Blocks?" in *International Political Economy: Perspectives on Global Power and Wealth,* ed. Jeffry A. Frieden and David A. Lake, 3d ed. (New York: Routledge, 1995), pp. 407–15; and Lawrence H. Summers, "Regionalism and the World Trading System," in *Trading Blocs: Alternative Approaches to Analyzing Preferential Trade Agreements,* ed. Jagdish Bhagwati, Pravin Krishna, and Arvind Panagariya (Cambridge, Mass.: MIT Press, 1999), pp. 561–66. For a negative assessment, see Jagdish Bhagwati and Arvind Panagariya, *The Economics of Preferential Trade Agreements* (Washington: AEI Press, 1996), especially pp. 1–78.
14. National Association of Manufacturers, "Absence of Chilean Trade Agreement Costing U.S. over $1 Billion per Year," Washington, February 4, 2003, www .nam.org/Docs/ITIA/25837_ABSENCEOFCHILEANTRADEAGREE MENT.pdf.

Jagdish Bhagwati

Why PTAs Are a Pox on the World Trading System

The worries over PTAs [preferential trade agreements] have increased dramatically in the past two decades as PTAs have proliferated. What exactly are the downsides of this phenomenon, which has gathered speed and become an addiction of the politicians, even as economists (with few exceptions) have expressed alarm at the development? What exactly are they worried about?

Trade Diversion

The traditional objection to PTAs was simply that . . . they could divert trade from the cost-efficient nonmember countries to the relatively inefficient member countries. The reason, of course, is that the nonmembers continue to pay the pre-PTA tariffs, whereas the higher cost member countries no longer have to.

It is easy to see that such a shift in production to a higher cost member country must sabotage the efficient allocation among countries and thus undermine what economists call "world welfare," or, in more palatable language, "cosmopolitan advantage." Recall that Jacob Viner was the first to draw attention to the possibility of trade diversion arising with discriminatory reduction of trade barriers in PTAs. He had focused mainly on PTAs' impact on cosmopolitan advantage, but it was pretty obvious to economists that such trade discrimination could hurt the liberalizing country itself. Why? Because when a country (call it the "home" country) shifts to a higher cost within-the-PTA supplier, it is buying its imports more expensively, incurring what economists call a "terms of trade" loss.

Trade diversion is not a slam-dunk argument against PTAs, for offsetting the loss from trade diversion can be a gain if trade creation takes place. Trade may grow because consumers in the home country now pay lower prices in their own markets; the higher cost supply from the member country is still cheaper than what the domestic consumers had to pay before the PTA was formed. Again, the import-competing producers in the home country will reduce their own inefficient production as the domestic price of imports falls after the PTA comes into operation; this also leads to welfare-enhancing trade creation. Therefore, whether a specific trade-diverting PTA brings loss or gain to a country depends on the relative strengths of the trade diversion and trade creation effects.[1]

The really important implication of the "trade diversion" analysis, however, was that informed economists could no longer pretend that it did not matter how one liberalized trade, that preferential trade liberalization was possibly a two-edged sword on which one could impale oneself. Thus, when some policy makers said that all trade liberalization was good, whether it was through bilateralism, plurilateralism, or multilateralism, they were really flying in the face of science. . . .

As it happens, the proponents of PTAs are too complacent about the phenomenon of trade diversion. Consider seven principal arguments.

1. There is evidence of fierce competition in many products and sectors today, with few managing to escape with "thick" margins of competitive advantage that provide comforting buffers against loss of comparative advantage.[2] Thus, even small tariffs are compatible with trade diversion as tariffs are removed from members of a PTA while they remain in place on nonmembers.

2. The thinness of comparative advantage also implies that today we have what I have called kaleidoscopic comparative advantage, or what in jargon we economists call "knife-edge" comparative advantage. Countries can easily lose comparative advantage to some "close" rivals, who may be from any number of foreign suppliers. So even if preferences today do not lead to trade diversion, the menu of products where you develop comparative advantage in a world of volatility and rapidly shifting comparative advantage will be forever changing, and any given preferences may lead to trade diversion in the near future, if not today.

3. While Article 24 requires that the external tariffs not be raised when the PTA is formed so as not to harm nonmembers,[3] the fact is that they can be raised when the external (MFN [most favored nation]) tariffs are bound at higher levels than the actual tariffs. In these cases, a member of the PTA is free to raise the external MFN tariffs up to the bound levels, whereas typically the scheduled tariff reductions in the PTA, when a hegemonic power is involved, will be hard to suspend.[4] This is in fact what happened during the Mexican peso crisis of 1994, when external tariffs were raised on 502 items from 20 percent or less to as much as 35 percent, while the NAFTA [North American Free Trade Agreement]-defined reductions in Mexican tariffs on U.S. and Canadian goods continued. So the prospect of trade diversion actually increased, despite the intent of those who drafted Article 24.

4. Article 24 freezes only external tariffs when the PTA is formed, with no increase in the external tariff allowed. But it does not address the modern reality that "administered protection" (i.e., antidumping and other actions by the executive) . . . can be used and abused more or less freely

in practice. Once you take into account the fact that trade barriers can take the form of antidumping measures, . . . initially welfare-enhancing trade creation can be transformed into harmful trade diversion through antidumping actions taken against nonmembers. . . .

5. There is plenty of evidence that trade diversion can occur through content requirements placed on member countries to establish "origin" so as to qualify for the preferential duties. . . . To qualify for the preferential tariffs in PTAs that include the United States, one must satisfy requirements such as that the imports of raw materials and components . . . come from the United States. For example, if apparel exports to the United States are accorded preferential tariffs, they must be made with U.S. textiles. This naturally diverts trade in textiles from efficient nonmember suppliers to inefficient U.S. textile producers.

6. Many analysts do not understand the distinction between trade diversion and trade creation and simply take all trade increase as welfare-enhancing. However, some recent analysts who are familiar with the phenomenon of trade diversion have tried to estimate it using what is called the "gravity model." Dating back some decades, this equation simply explains trade between two countries as a function of income and distance. Adapting this simple equation to their use, the economists Jeffrey Frankel and Shang-Jin Wei, who pioneered the use of gravity analysis to estimate trade creation and trade diversion, estimated total bilateral trade between any pair of countries as a function of their income and per capita incomes, with bilateral distance accounted for by statistical procedures.[5] If the countries belonged to, say, the Western hemisphere and they traded more with each other than with a random pair of countries located outside the region, that would mean that the PTA between countries in the Western hemisphere had led to trade creation. . . . The real problem with the analysis is that more trade between partners in a PTA can take place with *both* trade creation and trade diversion, so that one simply cannot infer trade creation alone from this procedure. Hence, the recent estimates based on gravity equations . . . which sometimes (but not always) suggest that PTAs in practice have led to more trade creation than diversion, cannot be treated as reliable guides to the problem of determining whether or not a PTA has led to trade diversion.[6]

7. Several economists have suggested that we need not worry about trade diversion and that beneficial effects will prevail if PTAs are undertaken with "natural trading partners." The initial proponents of this idea, Paul Wonnacott and Mark Lutz, declared creation is likely to be great and trade diversion small if the prospective members of an FTA [free trade agreement] are "natural trading partner."[7] One criterion proposed for

saying that PTA partners are natural trading partners is the volume of trade already between them; the other is geographic proximity. Neither really works.[8]

. . . There is no evidence that pairs of contiguous countries or countries with common borders have larger volumes of trade with each other than do pairs that are not so situated, or that trade volumes of pairs of countries arranged by distance between the countries in the pair will also show distance to be inversely related to trade volumes.[9] . . .

The "Spaghetti Bowl": A Systemic Concern

. . . The systemic problem from discriminatory trade liberalization under PTAs arises in two ways. First, when a country enters into multiple FTAs, it is evident that the same commodity will be subjected to different tariff rates if, as is almost always the case, the trajectories of tariff reduction vary for different FTAs. Second, and much more important, is the . . . fact that . . . tariffs on specific commodities must depend on where a product . . . originates (requiring inherently arbitrary "rules of origin").

With PTAs proliferating, the trading system can then be expected to become chaotic. Crisscrossing PTAs, where a nation had multiple PTAs with other nations, each of which then had its own PTAs with yet other nations, was inevitable. Indeed, if one only mapped the phenomenon, it would remind one of a child scrawling a number of chaotic lines on a sketch pad. . . .

. . . Crisscrossing PTAs, causing in turn the mish-mash of preferential trade barriers, prompted me to christen them the "spaghetti bowl" phenomenon and problem. . . . The phrase has caught on famously. . . . Then again, in the Far East, and in the context of Asian PTAs, it is now referred to as the "noodle bowl," and each PTA that contributes to the chaos is called a "noodle."[10] Of course, Marco Polo is reputed to have brought noodles, eaten since the Han Dynasty, back from China, giving us the Italian spaghetti. So perhaps this Asian shift of terminology from spaghetti to noodles is only a matter of extended reciprocity spanning two millennia.

The chaos resulting from arbitrary rules of origin, designed to establish which product is whose—what I have called the "who is whose" question . . . would be considerable even if the rules of origin were unique and uniformly applied. Typical rules of origin require what are called "substantial transformation" tests to decide whether a product is eligible for the preferential tariff rate. Thus, if a Canadian product is to be certified as eligible for NAFTA preferential tariffs when entering the U.S. market, and it uses imported components or raw materials (e.g., Honda in Canada uses steel that may be imported), the product must generally satisfy one of the following criteria:

1. A change in tariff classification: Under the Harmonized System of Tariffs [HST] (which is also used for other purposes such as trade negotiations, according to transformation by HST categories, at an agreed level of product classification), of the imported component into the final product; or
2. Value content: The domestic content must be no less than a certain proportion of the value of the final product.[11]

But it is immediately obvious that, even when such common rules are imposed, there are impossible ambiguities in application that lead to chaos. Thus, if Canada imports and also produces steel ingots, how do we decide what imports went into the production of Toyota transplants in Canada? Do we apply the required domestic component value to NAFTA, or to Canadian production alone? Even if that were settled, there is the problem that Japanese steel ingots may have used iron ore from the United States and chemicals from Canada; these in turn may have used components from non-NAFTA sources, in an endless regress as one goes back into the product chain. The mind reels as one contemplates the level of ambiguity and the scope for skullduggery and corruption at every stage.

In fact, in the modern age, where multinationals source components from around the world and trade has expanded among many countries, it is a . . . folly to run your trade policy on the basis of preferences. . . . There are in fact numerous cases where such questions have led to disputes that come for resolution before . . . dispute settlement panels. In a classic case, the U.S. Customs Service refused to certify Hondas produced in Ontario, Canada, as "North American," and hence eligible for duty-free exports from Canada to the United States, on the grounds that . . . Canadian Hondas did not meet the local content requirement of more than 50 percent imposed by the Canada–U.S. Free Trade Agreement (CUFTA). Honda countered that its estimates showed that they did. There is no sure-fire, analytically respectable way to determine the truth in such a case: it all boils down to who has greater stamina and whether Honda is willing to put moneys into legal costs.

But the reality also is far more complex than even this neat but sorry situation. For, in practice, the rules of origin vary between members and nonmembers, across different FTAs by the same country, and across different products within each FTA. For instance, the United States generally applies the substantial transformation test to nonmembers, but, as in the Honda case, it uses the value content test for members of CUFTA and other bilaterals.

Again, in nearly all FTAs worldwide, the rules of origin vary by product. The reason, of course, is that while trade is being freed in these products for imports from member countries, the ability to exploit this opportunity is being undercut by imposing cost-raising rules of origin as required by the specific products. In short, the rules of origin . . . vary as necessary to . . . offset . . . the freeing of trade. They take away with one hand what they give with the other. . . .

In fact, the insertion of these extensive product-specific rules of origin, with their deleterious effect on cross-sector uniformity of protection, creates massive treaties that have prompted cynical comments, such as "If NAFTA was really about free trade, you would need only one page, not a document hundreds of pages long." I have seen the NAFTA treaty volume, or I think I have. In some of my debates with the foe of the WTO [World Trade Organization] and free trade Lori Wallach, an articulate and assertive chief of the trade policy division at Ralph Nader's NGO [nongovernmental organization], Public Citizen, she would often carry a fat volume, plonk it down on the table, and announce that it was the NAFTA treaty. Her point was the only one that I wholeheartedly agreed with: that the treaty's bulk reflected the fact that it was freighted with numerous rules of origin and the intrusion of several extraneous issues that had nothing to do with the freeing of trade. . . .

The complexity that the spaghetti bowls create for international trade causes distortions in trade and investment. Much energy and many resources must be expended to discover the optimal sourcing of large numbers of components with a view to minimizing the cost of manufacture plus transportation and the differential tariffs and charges levied by origin.[12]

. . . The Hong Kong businessman Victor Fung has written eloquently . . . about the distortions and costs imposed on businesses by the spaghetti bowls:

> Bilateralism distorts the flow of goods, throws up barriers, creates friction, reduces flexibility and raises prices. In structuring the supply chain, every country of origin rule and every bilateral deal [have] to be tacked on as an additional consideration, thus constraining companies in optimizing production globally. In each new bilateral agreement, considerations relating to "rules of origin" multiply and become more complex. . . .[13]

As Fung notes, these problems and costs created by the spaghetti bowl are particularly onerous for small enterprises. But they are appallingly difficult for the poorer countries. . . . Because of the spaghetti bowl, and because hegemonic powers use PTAs to impose a host of expensive trade-unrelated demands on the poor-country partners in PTAs that reflect lobbying demands in the hegemon, PTAs are a particularly unattractive trade option for the poor countries relative to multilateralism.

Trade-Unrelated Issues: Turning the Trade Game into a Shell Game

When poor countries enter into PTAs with one another . . . the agreements almost always address trade liberalization. But when they enter into PTAs with . . . the United States and often the European Union, the lobbies in the hegemon countries insist on inserting into the agreements a number of "trade-unrelated" demands on the poor countries. How and why?

First, the lobbies that wish to advance their trade-unrelated agendas by incorporating them into trade treaties and institutions typically mislead by claiming that their agendas are "trade-related." Thus, intellectual property protection has to do with collecting royalties, not with trade. . . . By inserting the phrase "trade-related" into the agreement on trade-related intellectual property (TRIPs), the pharmaceutical and software lobbies managed to get the U.S. trade representative at the Uruguay Round to get the issue into the newly formed WTO in 1995. . . . The process by which trade-unrelated issues are turned into trade-related matters is a cynical one and an inversion of the truth. In fact, when the phrase "trade-related" is used, you can be sure that the issue is trade-unrelated. . . .

Second, it is noteworthy that the PTAs among the poor countries are almost never characterized by the inclusion of such trade-unrelated issues. They concentrate exclusively on trade liberalization. It is only when the hegemonic powers, especially the United States and occasionally the European Union, are involved that one finds the inclusion of such extraneous matters. When important developing countries such as India and Brazil refuse to accommodate these demands and insist on keeping trade negotiations free from such extraneous issues, the reaction is frequently to dismiss these objections as "rejectionist." When President Lula of Brazil refused to extend the proposed Free Trade Agreement of the Americas (FTAA) to include these lobby-driven issues, Washington lobbies and the U.S. trade representative condemned Brazil as embracing an FTAA Lite. . . .

Third, it has become customary to pretend that these trade-unrelated conditions are being imposed "in your interest," that they are really "good for you." Thus, when the software and pharmaceutical industries were advocating intellectual property protection (IPP) during the Uruguay Round, the U.S. trade representative claimed the existence of a study, seen by no one I know, in which benefits had been empirically established for countries moving to adopt IPP. Not content with such propaganda, U.S. legislators also enacted, as part of the 1988 Omnibus Trade and Competitiveness Act, . . . Section 301 which would legitimate the use of retaliatory tariffs against countries that the United States unilaterally decided were indulging in "unreasonable practices." Part of this legislation was specifically aimed at countries that did not provide intellectual property protection. It was a unilateral measure that had no legitimacy since these countries had not entered into any treaty or even an agreement to adopt such protection.[14]

Finally, the U.S. trade representative made it clear during the negotiations in the Uruguay Round that IPP had to be included in the new WTO if the Uruguay Round was to be concluded. It was a position that all other producers of intellectual property signed on to as in their interest, while pretending publicly that it was also in the interest of the poorer nations themselves, even if they were not producers of intellectual property. Having managed to get TRIPs inserted thus into the WTO, in violation of the fact that royalty collection is not a trade isssue, the IPP lobby proceeded to use PTAs to advance their agendas beyond what the multilateral negotiations had yielded. . . .

[Negotiations for an FTA with the Southern Africa Customs Union (SACU) sought] IPP in excess of those agreed to, under de jure and de facto duress in the first instance, at the WTO under the TRIPs agreement. The SACU countries were to be asked to agree on IPP standards "similar to that found in U.S. law" and that exceeded standards agreed to under the TRIPs agreement.[15]

The problem of inclusion of labor and domestic environmental standards in trade treaties is [even] more complex. . . . These are what Robert Hudec and I have called "values-related" demands.[16] . . . Because these demands are "values-based" (e.g., that workers deserve adequate labor standards), it is also easy to present the hegemonic countries' self-serving demands (motivated by the desire to moderate foreign competition) as if they are really demands made for altruistic reasons aimed at benefiting foreign workers. There are in fact a number of bad arguments for bringing these trade-unrelated issues into trade treaties, in one form or another. Such arguments have been floating around for years in the rich-country public domain; they are not compelling and should be rejected.

Take domestic environmental standards (as distinct from international standards, such as to reduce global warming, which involves all nations, or to reduce acid rain, which involves two or more but not all nations).[17] Why does it matter what a producer of steel in Brazil pays by way of a pollution tax for dumping carcinogens in a lake in Brazil that probably no one in the United States has even heard of? . . . Yet if your competitor in Country A pays a lower tax rate than you do, your lobby will insist that this amounts to "unfair trade" and will demand that before trade is freed, Country A must impose an identical burden on your rival.

This sounds reasonable until you spend some time thinking seriously about it. What the pollution tax rate should be (relative to yours) for your foreign rival in your industry cannot be determined except in the total context of the two countries' endowments and preferences. Thus, for instance, even if Mexico and the United States have an identical absolute preference for doing something for the environment, Mexico may have worse water and better air than the United States. . . . So it may make perfect sense for Mexico to worry about polluted water and for the United States to worry about polluted air. Correspondingly, it would make perfect sense for Mexico to have higher pollution taxes for industries generating water pollution than the United States does, and for the United States to have higher taxes for industries generating air rather than water pollution. To insist then that . . . pollution taxes be equalized for each industry everywhere is to ignore this elementary piece of logic. Even so, it is the principal driver of demands that domestic environmental standards must be forced via trade treaties and institutions to be identical across countries for the same industry.

When it comes to labor standards, the rationale for legitimate cross-country diversity, reflecting different stages of development and differential economic contexts, is equally pertinent. Generally speaking, countries will have different sequences by which they approach . . . labor standards, as well as different needs and capabilities. For example, the AFL-CIO has insisted on inclusion of labor standards in trade treaties, given its huge concern that competition from the poor countries is hurting U.S. workers' wages and threatens their hard-won standards, and bringing foreign countries' labor standards to the level of those in the United States has often been their desire. Yet many have asked: What is so sacrosanct about the labor standards of the United States, where workers' right to strike is badly crippled by half-century-old restrictions, and where the net result has been that union membership has shrunk steadily to almost a tenth of the labor force? It is truly ironic if U.S. labor standards are to be the gold standard for its trading partners.

As it happens, . . . the PTA negotiators of the United States with the developing countries initially settled—on the principle of "getting a foot in the door"—for enacting, despite Mexican hesitations, an agreement in an annex to the NAFTA treaty: that each country would enforce its own standards.[18] This agreement was then moved to the main text in the PTAs with Jordan and Morocco. In . . . PTAs with Peru and Colombia, the U.S. legislators have sought to raise the standards. . . .

But it is pretty clear that, no matter how flawed are the demands to include labor and domestic environmental issues in trade treaties, PTAs with weaker nations offer the best way of getting these demands accepted. And every lobby in Washington, D.C., is playing this game, regardless of the interests of these partner nations themselves. Thus, when the PTAs with Chile and Singapore were being negotiated, the U.S. position was that the use of capital account controls during financial crises ought to be proscribed. This ideological position, favorable to the interests of our financial lobbies, was at variance with even the IMF's [International Monetary Fund's] latest thinking. . . .

Astonishingly, the Australia–U.S. Free Trade Agreement was also witness to lobbying to get Australia's medicine policy, much admired in many circles, changed under pressure from the pharmaceutical lobby in the United States. Entering into force on January 1, 2005, the FTA has been much criticized within Australia. It contains many intellectual property provisions and others related to altering pharmaceutical regulation and public health policy in Australia, as embodied in its Pharmaceutical Benefits Scheme, which had been designed with a view to ensuring equitable and affordable access to essential medicine.[19]

While the PTAs are clearly being used by lobbies in the United States and, to a lesser degree, by the European Union to secure their agendas in one-on-one negotiations with weak nations, one must also entertain the thought that the aim of these lobbies is surely more ambitious. What they cannot secure immediately at the WTO, because the developing countries are there in greater numbers and can resist the pressure from the hegemonic powers by the sheer force of their numbers and some ability and willingness to take concerted stands in their own interest, the hegemonic powers can hope to secure by breaking away the developing countries one by one through the PTAs. Thus, if a developing country has signed a PTA with the United States that includes labor standards provisions, that country is unlikely to say at the WTO: We will not have labor standards at the WTO. This is in fact a strategy of "divide and conquer." The United States can be interpreted as playing this strategic game, hoping to get its lobbies' agendas on to the WTO by using the PTAs as a mechanism by which the opposition to these lobbies' agendas is steadily eroded at the WTO. Charles Kindleberger wrote about "altruistic hegemons" providing leadership for the world trading system; here we have the strategic behavior of what I have called a "selfish hegemon."[20]

Are PTAs Building Blocks or Stumbling Blocks to Multilateral Free Trade?

Recall that the original embrace of PTAs by the United States in the early 1980s was a result of frustration with the inability to get multilateral talks started under GATT [General Agreement on Tariffs and Trade] auspices. Once the Uruguay Round was launched, the United States should have reverted to its traditional "multilateralism only" doctrine that it adhered to for over 30 years. But it did not. In fact, its leadership, mainly Secretary of State Baker and his deputy, Robert Zoellick, decided that the United States should do both. Their argument was that PTAs would . . . serve as "building blocks" toward multilateral freeing of trade, that the two trade policies were complementary. . . . They would soon call it the theory of "competitive liberalization."

As Zoellick put it eloquently in 2003:

> When the Bush administration set out to revitalize America's trade agenda almost three years ago, we outlined our plans

clearly and openly: We would pursue a strategy of "competitive liberalization" to advance free trade globally, regionally, and bilaterally. By moving forward simultaneously on multiple fronts the United States can overcome or bypass obstacles; exert maximum leverage for openness, *target the needs of developing countries,* especially the most committed to economic and political reforms; establish models of success, especially in cutting-edge areas; strengthen America's ties with all regions within a global economy; and create a fresh political dynamic by putting free trade on the offensive.[21]

Zoellick thus argued that the United States would use the FTAs to advance a number of trade-unrelated objectives, and (astonishingly) that these issues were in fact addressing the "needs of developing countries," when in fact (as discussed earlier) they were being imposed by the United States as a precondition to signing an FTA with [the developing country]. In addition, Zoellick and his U.S. trade representative deputies also claimed that such initiatives would prompt other countries to seek trade liberalization, first in the shape of FTAs with the United States, and second, by embracing the multilateral system and negotiations at the WTO.

The former is surely an exaggerated claim, at best. While preferences are a wasting asset as MFN tariffs come down over time, the willingness of the United States to sign more FTAs implies that the preferences earned by signing an FTA with the United States are also a wasting asset, insofar as your close rivals may also join an FTA. Simon Evenett and Michael Meier in fact find far too few public statements by policy makers worldwide to the effect that they would like an FTA with the United States because their rivals have one.[22]

. . . The . . . claim that . . . FTAs . . . advance WTO negotiations is even more problematic. Fred Bergsten, a prominent trade expert in Washington, D.C., is a leading exponent of this view. His principal claim of a positive link between PTAs and multilateral trade negotiations is the assertion that the Uruguay Round was brought to a close because the APEC [Asia-Pacific Economic Cooperation] Summit in Seattle in November 1993 was used by the United States to threaten the recalcitrant European Union [EU] that if the EU did not close the Round, the United States would have a competing alternative: APEC liberalization. I have asked many European trade officials about his claim, and they simply laugh at it. . . . Surely, everyone could see that there was not the slightest chance that APEC, with its many disparate economies and political differences, would turn into an FTA. . . .

The implausibility of the benign Bergsten argument leaves one with a whole range of arguments that suggest instead that the effect of PTAs on the multilateral trade negotiations is malign. . . .

1. Consider that a dollar's worth of lobbying on opening up Mexico under a PTA will get the Mexican market opened to you. But if you spend the same dollar in Geneva, opening up the Mexican market on an MFN basis, your benefit will be diluted by the "free riders," your rivals from EU, Japan, and elsewhere who have not spent any money to open the Mexican market. So you will spend the dollar on PTAs, not on MTN [multilateral trade negation].

2. Although there are any number of routine bureaucrats available to negotiate trade deals, the supply of skilled bureaucrats is always limited. If PTAs are being pursued simultaneously with MTN, you can be sure that the talented bureaucrats' attention will be split, at best. I saw this in Seattle in November 1999 when the WTO meeting erupted under protests. U.S. Trade Representative Charlene Barshefsky arrived just in time, after long trade negotiations with China: her eye was not on the WTO ball.

3. Politicians often equate all kinds of trade deals, so if you nail down a PTA, no matter how negligible in trade volume, that is a feather in your cap. In fact, I was once at a Bureau of Labor function to honor a bureaucrat whom U.S. Trade Representative Mickey Kantor congratulated for participating in negotiations of over 250 trade deals. Of these, one was the Uruguay Round, another was NAFTA (much less important and, in fact, arguably even a mistake), and the rest were trade-restricting, quota-setting textiles deals under the Multi-Fiber Arrangement!

4. Lobbies provide the foot soldiers in the battles to open trade, and I have already documented that several lobbies with trade-unrelated causes also find PTAs, where weak countries can be intimidated into making concessions, a more agreeable way to go. These lobbies use the PTAs to provide templates—"Ah, we now have our agenda accepted as a part of trade liberalization, and that is the way it will be for other PTAs from now on"—and to steadily encircle the WTO to push their agendas. Aside from the AFL-CIO, few groups are spending as much time and money on Doha as on the PTAs with Peru and Colombia.

5. In the United States, given the general anxiety over trade, it has been a mistake to ask politicians (especially Democrats who have unions among their constituents) to repeatedly spend their limited pro-trade political capital on a succession of trivial PTAs, leading to "trade fatigue" that afflicts then the Doha Round as well.

6. Finally, recent empirical analysis by Nuno Limao, using tariff reduction data during the most recent MTN, demonstrates that PTAs by

the United States were a stumbling block to multilateral trade liberalization.[23] The adverse effect operates through the mechanism that the hegemon maintains higher multilateral tariffs on products imported from the preferential trade partner relative to those on similar products imported from the rest of the world. These higher MFN tariffs act virtually as bargaining chips to be used in negotiating PTAs, because the value of the preference increases the higher the MFN tariff is. This provides an incentive not to reduce MFN tariffs relative to the situation where PTAS were not permitted.

It is hard indeed to contemplate the consequences of PTAs with equanimity. The most important item on our policy agenda has to be to devise an appropriate response to their spread and the damage they impose on the multilateral trading system.

ENDNOTES

1. This analysis of trade diversion and creation is in a simplified framework, designed to convey the essence of the trade-diversion issues raised by PTAs. For a theoretically tight treatment, the reader is referred to the extended analysis by Panagariya and me in Bhagwati, Krishna, and Panagariya, *Trading Blocs,* chapter 2.

2. I have discussed the reasons for this phenomenon and its consequence for coping with globalization in my book, *In Defense of Globalization* (New York: Oxford University Press, 2007), afterword.

3. This restriction is compatible with trade diversion even when the external terms of trade are inflexible and the damage is to the member rather than the nonmember countries. But the nonmember countries also can be hurt when the terms of trade are variable. The empirical evidence of such nonmember terms-of-trade effects is provided in W. Chang and Alan Winters, "How Regional Blocs Affect Excluded Countries: The Price Effects of MERCOSUR," *American Economic Review* 92, no. 4 (2001). Recent theoretical work by Masahiro Endoh, Koichi Hamada, and Koji Shimomura, "Can a Preferential Trade Agreement Benefit Neighbor Countries without Compensating Them?" unpublished manuscript, Yale University, December 2007, demonstrates in fact that PTAs, unless accompanied by tariff concessions or compensatory transfers, will generally speaking hurt nonmember countries under reasonable restrictions.

4. As Petros Mavroidis has reminded me, when PTAs are formed under Article 24, the members of the PTA are free to raise their external tariffs from the applied levels to the higher bound levels. So the discipline on external tariffs essentially does not operate when the bound levels are higher than the applied tariffs, which is almost always the case, though in varying degrees for different countries.

5. In technical terms, the Frankel–Wei estimating equation uses dummy variables that take a value of 1 if both countries are in Western Europe and zero

otherwise. I am grateful to Arvind Panagariya, who took me through the statistical procedures and their rather drastic limitations, in both the original Frankel–Wei analysis and its later variants by themselves, Gary Hufbauer, and others.

6. Some economists have posed the question of the welfare effects directly by using computable general equilibrium (CGE) models to compare the welfare outcomes under different trade policies, such as multilateral free trade under the Doha Round and current and potential preferential trade agreements. Using the Michigan CGE model of world production and trade developed by Robert Stern, Alan Deardorff, and Drusilla Brown, the economists Kozo Kiyota and Stern have calculated that the gains under multilateral trade liberalization dominate significantly those from a policy of PTAs.

7. Paul Wonnacott and Mark Lutz, "Is There a Case for Free Trade Areas?," in Jeffrey Schott, ed., *Free Trade Areas and U.S. Trade Policy* (Washington D.C.: Institute for International Economics, 1989).

8. The following discussion draws on the far more thorough analysis of the "natural trading partner" hypothesis by Panagariya and me in Bhagwati, Krishna, and Panagariya, *Trading Blocs,* chapter 2.

9. This would generally be true, I am sure, even if one were to take the measure just for one individual country with every other country instead of pooling all possible pairs together. I might add that the gravity equation that shows distance to matter for the volume of trade is taking only a "partial derivative," so to speak, with regard to distance; the discussion in the text relates instead, as is proper in the matter of the equation of the "volume of trade" and "geographical proximity" by Krugman and Summers, simply to the relationship between distance and observed trade volumes.

10. The phrase was introduced by President Haruhiko Kuroda of the Asian Development Bank in July 2006 in a speech delivered to the Jeju Summer Forum in South Korea.

11. There can also be some technical requirements for eligibility, such as meeting certain technical standards on safety, but it is obviously rare for such requirements to be imposed differentially against members of the FTA and not against nonmembers.

12. Sometimes the cost of establishing origin is so high for a firm that it decides instead to forgo the process and to pay the MFN tariff. It is not clear how significant this "opting out" is, however.

13. Victor Fung, "Bilateral Deals Destroy Global Trade," *Financial Times,* November 3, 2005.

14. For an analysis of 301 legislation, and the dangers it posed for the world trading system, see Jagdish Bhagwati and Hugh Patrick, eds., *Aggressive Unilateralism* (Ann Arbor: University of Michigan Press, 1991), especially the chapters by Robert Hudec and by me.

15. See Jonathan Berger and Achal Prabhala, "Assessing the Impact of TRIPs–Plus Rules in the Proposed U.S.–SACU Free Trade Agreement," Working Paper, preliminary draft, Center for Applied Legal Studies, University of Witwatersrand, Johannesburg, South Africa, February 2005.

16. There is a huge literature on this subject, which includes several of my writings in the past fifteen years in places as diverse as the *American Journal of International Law* and two substantial volumes based on a research project involving several of the leading international economists and trade jurists today: Jagdish Bhagwati and Robert Hudec, eds., *Fair Trade and Harmonization: Prerequisites for Free Trade?* (Cambridge, Mass.: MIT Press, 1996). See, in particular, the extensive analytical discussion of the issues involved in Bhagwati and T.N. Srinivasan, "Trade and the Environment: Does Environmental Diversity Detract from the Case for Free Trade?" chapter 4 of Vol. I.

17. International pollution raises a different set of analytical issues than domestic pollution and is usually negotiated in self-standing treaties, such as Kyoto on global warming and the Montreal Protocol on the ozone layer. There are implications for the WTO, for sure, but these have little to do with the question of PTAs versus multilateralism. For instance, see Jagdish Bhagwati and Petros Mavroidis, "Is Action against U.S. Exports for Failure to Sign Kyoto Protocol WTO–Legal?" *World Trade Review* 6, no. 2 (2007): 299–310; and Bhagwati and Srinivasan, "Trade and the Environment: Does Environmental Diversity Detract from the Case for Free Trade?"

18. This sounds innocuous but is not. Often, legislation is not expected to be enforced. For that reason, it is often pitched high, with minimum wages, for example, being defined at sumptuous levels that no one expects to pay. Again, laws are left on the books because taking them off would be politically difficult, but no one expects them to be enforced. Thus, there are still laws against adultery in some states, but President Clinton can confidently expect to go to these states without being handcuffed and produced in court because the laws are dormant. Asking developing countries, with their low enforcement ability besides, to enforce their own laws on labor standards is therefore either naive or cynical.

19. Among numerous articles on the subject, I found the following most informative: Thomas Faunce, Evan Doran, David Henry, Peter Drahos, Andrew Searles, Brita Pekarsky, Warwick Neville, and Andrew Searles, "Assessing the Impact of the Australia–United States Free Trade Agreement on Australian and Global Medicines Policy," *Globalization and Health* 15 (2005): 1–10.

20. The phrase and idea of a "selfish hegemon" was introduced by me in "Threats to the World Trading System: Income Distribution and the Selfish Hegemon," *Journal of International Affairs* 48 (1994): 279–285.

21. Cited in Evenett and Meier, "An Interim Assessment of the U.S. Trade Policy of 'Competitive Liberalization,'" emphasis added. It is from a report by the U.S. General Accounting Office on international trade, January 2004. Other such pronouncements by Zoellick are on record as well. Perhaps the most remarkable one is from Zoellick's Op Ed piece, "Our Credo: Free Trade and Competition," *Wall Street Journal,* July 10, 2003: "FTAs break new ground—they establish prototypes for liberalization in areas such as services, e-commerce, intellectual property for knowledge societies, transparency in government regulation, and better enforcement of labor and environmental protections."

22. Perhaps the most dramatic such statements are from New Zealand vis-à-vis the Australia–U.S. FTA and the plaintive worries of Colombia, struggling to get its FTA with the United States, over the fact that Peru has gotten ahead in the queue.

23. Nuno Limao, "Preferential Trade Agreements as Stumbling Blocks for Multilateral Trade Liberalization: Evidence for the U.S.", *American Economic Review* 96, no. 3 (June 2006), 896–914. This paper's brilliant empirical analysis nicely complements the theoretical analyses such as those of Phil Levy and Pravin Krishna . . . on the question of the dynamic time-path issues concerning PTAs.

CHAPTER 6 RESTRICT TRADE TO REDUCE GREENHOUSE GASES v. DON'T RESTRICT TRADE TO SUPPORT CLIMATE CHANGE GOALS

Restrict Trade to Reduce Greenhouse Gases

Advocate: Jeffrey A. Frankel

Source: "Addressing the Leakage/Competitiveness Issue in Climate Change Policy Proposals," *Brookings Trade Forum,* 2008/09: 69–82

Don't Restrict Trade to Support Climate Change Goals

Advocate: Jason E. Bordoff

Source: "International Trade Law and the Economics of Climate Policy," *Brookings Trade Forum,* 2008/09: 35–59

Efforts to craft a fully inclusive global climate change regime have been stymied by distributive conflict between China and India on the one hand and the United States on the other. Governments of developing countries have called for a climate change regime that rests on the principle of "common but differentiated responsibilities." Under this principle, the United States and the European Union (EU) would accept enforceable commitments for greenhouse gas reduction, but China, India, and other developing countries would not. The rationale for differentiated obligations rests on the recognition that current climate change is a problem created by the United States and the EU.

Policy makers in the United States have argued that in the absence of binding commitments to reduce emissions in China and India, any reductions that occur in the United States and the EU will be offset by rising emissions elsewhere. As a result of such leakage, the regime's impact on climate change will be negligible. Moreover, U.S. policy makers argue that a regime based on differentiated responsibilities creates a competitive disadvantage for U.S. business. Production costs in countries with ambitious emissions targets rise relative to costs in countries that have no emissions targets. Firms in regulated economies will thus face a regulatory disadvantage at home and in foreign markets.

BORDER ADJUSTMENTS ARE CONSISTENT WITH WTO RULES AND GOOD PUBLIC POLICY

One possible solution to the leakage and competitiveness issues generated by the asymmetric obligations is to allow the U.S. and European governments to employ border adjustments, which are tariffs levied on carbon-intensive goods imported from countries that lack effective climate change regimes. By raising the cost of foreign goods in the local markets, border adjustments will reduce leakage and mitigate the competitiveness issues that arise from differentiated regulatory burdens. Of course, one possible downside to border adjustments is that they may be inconsistent with the World Trade Organization (WTO) rules.

Jeffrey Frankel, a professor of economics at Harvard University's John F. Kennedy School, argues that border adjustments offer a useful and productive instrument to address the leakage and competitive consequences of the asymmetric obligations. Moreover, he asserts that border adjustments adopted in pursuit of environmental objectives are most likely fully consistent with WTO rules. He worries, however, that governments will be tempted to use border adjustments in ways that undermine their adherence to WTO norms. Consequently, he calls for the construction of a multilateral regime that would oversee the use of border adjustments.

BORDER ADJUSTMENTS ARE INCONSISTENT WITH WTO RULES AND BAD PUBLIC POLICY

The use of border adjustments to support climate change goals is controversial, however. Some analysts argue that governments should design new instruments to achieve their environmental objectives rather than restrict trade to do so. They worry that allowing border adjustments in support of climate change goals opens the door to disguised protectionism that will quickly unravel the achievements realized under the WTO.

Jason Bordoff, a policy director at the Hamilton Project, argues that the costs of border adjustments are greater than the expected benefits. Border adjustments are unlikely to do much to reduce leakage or redress the competitiveness consequences of emission-reduction legislation. On the other hand, Bordoff argues that border adjustments are quite costly. In particular, he argues that border adjustments are unlikely to be compatible with WTO rules and thus generate rising protectionism and a weakening of WTO norms. Because the potential costs are greater than the expected benefits, Bordoff concludes that border adjustments are bad policy.

POINTS **TO PONDER**

1. What is a process and production method (PPM)? Why do you think governments agreed to rules that prohibit differentiating between goods based on PPMs? Do you think this is sound policy generally? Why or why not?

2. Although the WTO's dispute settlement mechanism has not yet heard a case concerning greenhouse gases, it has considered other environmental disputes. Which of these other disputes seem most directly relevant to the issues posed by border adjustments in support of greenhouse gas reductions?

3. How do you think governments should manage the relationship between environmental objectives and international trade?

Jeffrey A. Frankel

Addressing the Leakage/ Competitiveness Issue in Climate Change Policy Proposals

Of all the daunting obstacles faced by the effort to combat global climate change, the problem of leakage was perhaps the last to gain serious attention from policy-makers. Assume that a core of rich countries is able to agree for the remainder of the century on a path of targets for emissions of greenhouse gases (GHGs), following the lead of the Kyoto Protocol, or to agree on other measures to cut back on emissions and that the path is aggressive enough at face value to go some way toward achieving the GHG concentration goals that environmental scientists say are necessary. Will global emissions in fact be reduced? Even under the business-as-usual scenario—that is, the path along which technical experts forecast that countries' emissions would increase in the absence of a climate change agreement—most emissions growth was expected to come from China and other developing countries. If these nations are not included in a system of binding commitments, global emissions will continue their rapid growth. But the problem is worse than that. Leakage means that emissions in the nonparticipating countries would actually rise above where they would otherwise be, thus working to undo the environmental benefits of the rich countries' measures. Furthermore, not wanting to lose "competitiveness" and pay economic costs for minor environmental benefits, the rich countries could lose heart and the entire effort could unravel. Thus, it is important to find ways to address concerns about competitiveness and leakage, but without undue damage to the world trading system.

Developing Countries, Leakage, and Competitiveness

We need the developing countries inside the emissions control program, for several reasons.[1] As noted, these countries will be the source of the big increases in GHG emissions in coming years, according to the business-as-usual path. China, India, and other developing countries will represent up to two-thirds of global carbon dioxide emissions over the course of this century, vastly exceeding the expected contribution of countries belonging to the Organization for Economic Cooperation and Development of roughly one-quarter of global emissions. Without the participation of major developing countries, emissions abatement by industrial countries will not do much to mitigate global climate change.

If a quantitative international regime is implemented without the developing countries, their emissions are likely to rise even faster than the business-as-usual path, due to the problem of leakage. Leakage of emissions could come about through several channels. First, the output of energy-intensive industries could relocate from countries with emissions commitments to countries without. This could happen either if firms in these sectors relocate their plants to unregulated countries, or if firms in these sectors shrink in the regulated countries while their competitors in the unregulated countries expand. A particularly alarming danger is that a plant in a poor, unregulated country might use dirty technologies and thus emit more than a plant producing the same output would have in a high-standard, rich, regulated country, so that aggregate world emissions would actually go up rather than down!

Another channel of leakage runs via world energy prices. If participating countries succeed in cutting back their consumption of coal and oil, the high-carbon fossil fuels, demand will fall and the prices of these fuels will fall on world markets (other things equal). This is equally true if the initial policy is a carbon tax that raises the price to rich-country consumers as if it comes via other measures. Nonparticipating countries would naturally respond to declines in world oil and coal prices by increasing consumption.

Estimates vary regarding the damage in tons of increased GHG emissions from developing countries for every ton abated in an industrial country. But an authoritative survey concludes "Leakage rates in the range 5 to 20 per cent are common."[2]

Even more salient politically than leakage is the related issue of competitiveness: American industries that are particularly intensive in energy or otherwise GHG-generating activities will be at a competitive disadvantage to firms in the same industries operating in nonregulated countries.[3] Such sectors as aluminum, cement, glass, paper, chemicals, iron, and steel will point to real costs in terms of lost output, profits, and employment.[4] They will seek protection and are likely to get it.

The policy response to fears of leakage and competitiveness can take a variety of forms. *Tariffs* on imports of goods from producers who do not operate under emission regulations are perhaps the most straightforward, except that ascertaining carbon content is difficult. *Border tax adjustments* apply not just to import tariffs alone but to a combination of import tariffs and export subsidies. Broader phrases such as *trade controls*, import penalties, *or carbon-equalization measures* include the option—likely to be adopted in practice—of requiring importers to buy emission permits or "international reserve allowances." For economists, such *importer permit requirements* are precisely equivalent to import tariffs—the cost of the permit is the same as the tariff rate. Others would not so readily make this connection, however. International law may well defy economic logic by treating import tariffs as impermissible but permit requirements for imports as acceptable.[5] *Trade sanctions* go beyond trade controls: while the latter fall only on environmentally relevant sectors, the former target products that are arbitrary and unrelated to the non-compliant act, in an effort to induce compliance.[6]

The Possible Application of Trade Barriers by the United States

Of the twelve market-based climate change bills introduced in the 110th Congress, almost half called for some sort of border adjustments. Some would have featured a tax to be applied to fossil fuel imports. . . . Others would have required that energy-intensive imports surrender permits corresponding to the carbon emissions embodied in them.[7] The Bingaman–Specter Low Carbon Economy Act of 2007 would have provided that "if other countries are deemed to be making inadequate efforts [in reducing global GHG emissions], starting in 2020 the president could require importers from such countries to submit special emission allowances (from a separate reserve pool) to cover the carbon content of certain products.". . . These requirements are equivalent to a tax on the covered imports. The two major presidential candidates in the 2008 U.S. election campaign apparently supported some version of these bills, including import penalties in the name of safeguarding competitiveness vis-à-vis developing countries. . . .

The Possible Application of Trade Barriers by the EU

It is possible that many in Washington do not realize that the United States is likely to be the victim of legal sanctions before it is the wielder of them. In Europe, firms have already entered the first Kyoto budget period of binding emission limits, competitiveness concerns are well advanced, and the nonparticipating United States is an obvious target of resentment.[8]

After the United States failed to ratify Kyoto, European parliamentarians in 2005, and French Prime minister Dominique de Villepin in 2006, proposed a "Kyoto carbon tax" or "green tax" against imports from the United States.[9] The European Commission had to make a decision on the issue in January 2008, when the European Union [EU] determined its emission targets for the post-Kyoto period. In preparation for this decision, French president Nicolas Sarkozy warned:

> If large economics of the world do not engage in binding commitments to reduce emissions, European industry will have incentives to relocate to such countries. . . . The introduction of a parallel mechanism for border compensation against imports from countries that refuse to commit to binding reductions therefore appears essential, whether in the form of a tax adjustment or

an obligation to buy permits by importers. This mechanism is in any case necessary in order to induce those countries to agree on such a commitment.[10]

. . . In the event, the EU Commission instead included this provision in its directive:

> Energy-intensive industries which are determined to be exposed to significant risk of carbon leakage could receive a higher amount of free allocation or an effective carbon equalization system could be introduced with a view to putting EU and non-EU producers on a comparable footing. Such a system could apply to importers of goods requirements similar to those applicable to installations within the EU, by requiring the surrender of allowances."[11]. . .

Would Trade Controls or Sanctions Be Compatible with the WTO?

Would measures that are directed against carbon dioxide emissions in other countries, as embodied in electricity or in goods produced with it, be acceptable under international law? Not many years ago, most international experts would have said that import barriers against carbon-intensive goods, whether tariffs or quantitative restrictions, would necessarily violate international agreements. Under the General Agreement on Tariffs and Trade (GATT), although countries could use import barriers to protect themselves against environmental damage that would otherwise occur within their own borders, they could not use import barriers in efforts to affect how goods are produced in foreign countries, so-called process and production methods (PPMs). A notorious example was the GATT ruling against U.S. barriers to imports of tuna from dolphin-unfriendly Mexican fishermen. But things have changed.

The World Trade Organization (WTO) came into existence, succeeding the GATT, at roughly the same time as the Kyoto Protocol. The drafters of each treaty showed more consideration for the other than do the rank and file among environmentalists and free traders, respectively. The WTO regime is more respectful of the environment than was its predecessor, Article XX allows exceptions to Articles I and III for purposes of health and conservation. The Preamble to the 1995 Marrakech Agreement establishing the WTO seeks "to protect and preserve the environment"; and the 2001 Doha Communiqué that sought to start a new round of negotiations declares: "The aims of . . . open and non-discriminatory trading system, and acting for the protection of the environment . . . must be mutually supportive." The Kyoto Protocol text is equally solicitous of the trade regime. It says that the parties should "strive to implement policies and measures . . . to minimize adverse effects . . . on international trade." The United Nations Framework Convention on Climate Change features similar language.

GHG emissions are PPMs. Is this an obstacle to the application measures against them at the border? I do not see why it has to be. Three precedents can be cited: sea turtles in the Indian Ocean, ozone in the stratosphere, and tires in Brazil.

The true import of a 1998 WTO panel decision on the shrimp–turtle case was missed by almost everyone. The big significance was a pathbreaking ruling that environmental measures can target not only exported products (Article XX) but also partners' PPMs—subject, as always, to nondiscrimination (Articles I and III). The United States was in the end able to seek to protect turtles in the Indian Ocean, provided it did so without discrimination against Asian fishermen. Environmentalists failed to notice or consolidate the PPM precedent, and to the contrary were misguidedly up in arms over this case.[12]

Another important precedent was the Montreal Protocol on stratospheric ozone depletion, which contained trade controls. The controls had two motivations.[13] The first was to encourage countries to join. And the second, if major countries had remained outside, was to minimize leakage, the migration of the banned substances to nonparticipating countries. In the event, the first worked, so the second was not needed.

In case there is any doubt that Article XX, which uses the phrase "health and conservation," also applies to environmental concerns such as climate change, a third precedent is relevant. In 2007, a new WTO Appellate Body decision regarding Brazilian restrictions on imports of retreaded tires confirmed the applicability of Article XX(b): Rulings "accord considerable flexibility to WTO Member governments when they take trade-restrictive measures to protect life or health . . . [and] apply equally to issues related to trade and environmental protection, . . . including measures taken to combat global warming."[14]

These three examples go a long way toward establishing the legitimacy of trade measures against PPMs. Many trade experts, both economists and international lawyers, are not yet convinced[15]—let alone representatives of India and other developing countries. I personally have come to believe that the Kyoto Protocol could have followed the Montreal Protocol by incorporating well-designed trade controls aimed at nonparticipants. One aspect that strengthens the applicability of the precedent is that we are not talking about targeting practices in other countries that harm solely the local environment, where the country can make the case that this is nobody else's business. The depletion of the stratospheric ozone and the endangerment of sea turtles are global externalities. (It helped that these are turtles that migrate globally.) So is climate change from GHG emissions. A ton of carbon emitted into the atmosphere hurts all residents of the planet. . . .

The Big Danger

Just because a government measure is given an environmental label does not necessarily mean that it is motivated primarily—or even at all—by bona fide environmental objectives. To see the point, one has only to look at the massive mistake of American subsidies of biofuels (and protection against competing imports from Brazil). If each country on its own imposes border penalties on imports in whatever way suits national politics, they will be poorly targeted, discriminatory, and often disguisedly protectionist. When reading the language in the U.S. congressional bills or the EU decision, it is not hard to imagine that special interests could take over for protectionist purposes the process whereby each government decides whether other countries are doing their share or what foreign competitors merit penalties.[16] Thus the competitiveness provisions will indeed run afoul of the WTO, and they will deserve to.

It is important who makes the determinations regarding what countries are abiding by carbon-reduction commitments, what entity can retaliate against the noncompliers, what sectors are fair game, what sort of barriers are appropriate, and when a target country has moved into compliance so that it is time to remove the penalty. One policy conclusion is that these decisions should be delegated to independent panels of experts rather than made by politicians.

The most important policy conclusion is that we need a multilateral regime to guide such measures. Ideally, such a regime would be negotiated along with a successor to the Kyoto Protocol that sets targets for future periods and brings the United States and developing countries inside. But if that negotiation process takes too long, it might be useful in the shorter run for the United States to enter into negotiations with the European Union to harmonize guidelines for border penalties, ideally in informal association with the secretariats of the UNFCCC [United Nations Framework Convention on Climate Change] and the WTO.[17]

Why Take Multilateralism Seriously?

"Why should WTO obligations be taken seriously?" some may ask. There are three possible answers, based on considerations of international citizenship, good policy, and realpolitik.

First, with regard to international citizenship, one question is whether the United States wants to continue the drift of the recent past in the general direction of international rogue country status or rather return to the highly successful postwar strategy of adherence to international law and full membership in—indeed, leadership of—multilateral institutions. The latter course does not mean routinely subordinating U.S. law, let alone American interests, to international law. There will be cases where the United States wants to go its own way. But the effort on climate change should surely not be one of these cases. Among other reasons is the fact that GHG emissions are inherently a global externality. No single country can address the problem on its own, due to the free rider problem. Although there is a role for unilateral actions on climate change—for example, by the United States, as part of a short-term effort to demonstrate seriousness of purpose and begin to catch up with the record of the Europeans—in the long term, multilateral action offers the only hope of addressing the problem. The multilateral institutions are already in place—specifically, the UNFCCC; its child, the Kyoto Protocol; and the WTO—and they were predominantly created under U.S. leadership.

Second, the basic designs and operations of these institutions happen to be relatively sensible, taking political realities as given. They are more sensible than most critics of the international institutions and their alleged violations of national sovereignty believe. This applies whether the critics are on the left or right, and whether their main concern is the environment or the economy.[18] One can place very heavy weight on economic goals and yet realize the desirability of addressing externalities, minimizing leakage, dealing with competitiveness concerns, and so forth. One can place very heavy weight on environmental goals and yet realize the virtues of market mechanisms, nondiscrimination, reciprocity, addressing international externalities *cooperatively*, preventing special interests from hijacking environmental language for their own financial gain, and so forth.

The third reason why the United States should be prepared to . . . move in the direction of multilateral coordination of guidelines for such measures comes from hardheaded self interest: a desire to avoid being the victim of emulation or retaliation. Section 6006 of Lieberman–Warner does not envision these measures going into effect until 2020.[19] This is as it should be, because any such bill must give the United States time to start playing the game before it can presume to punish other players for infractions. But the EU language could be translated into penalties against U.S. products any day. The EU members are far from the only governments that could claim to have taken stronger climate change policies than the United States.[20] It is in the American interest to have any border penalties governed by a sensible system of multilateral guidelines. The European Union might welcome U.S. participation in joint negotiations to agree on guidelines, as part of a process of negotiations over the Kyoto successor regime.

The argument is stronger than the historical examples of U.S. import barriers leading to subsequent emulation and retaliation that comes back to hit American exports (the Smoot Hawley tariff in 1930, antidumping cases in the 1980s, . . .). Here the United States has an opportunity to influence others' barriers against its goods ten years before it would be putting up barriers against theirs.

Concluding Recommendations

Both the economics and the law are complicated. The issues need further study. Nevertheless, this chapter offers a central message: border measures to address leakage need not necessarily violate WTO law or sensible trade principles, but . . . there is a very great danger in practice that they will.

I conclude with several subjective judgments as to principles that could guide a country's border measures if its goal were indeed to reduce leakage and to avoid artificially tilting the playing field toward carbon-intensive imports from nonparticipating countries or damaging the world trading system, especially if it is viewed as politically necessary to do something to address competitiveness concerns. I classify characteristics of possible border measures into three categories, which I will name by color (for lack of better labels):

—The "white" category: those that seem to me reasonable and appropriate.[21]
—The "black" category: those that seem to me very dangerous, in that they are likely to become an excuse for protectionism.
—The "gray" category: those that fall in between.

The white (appropriate) border measures could be either tariffs or (equivalently) a requirement for importers to surrender tradable permits. These principles include:

—Measures should follow some multilaterally agreed-to set of guidelines among countries participating in the emission targets of the Kyoto Protocol and/or its successors.
—Judgments as to findings of fact—which countries are complying or not, which industries are involved and what is their carbon content, which countries are entitled to respond with border measures, and the nature of the response—should be made by independent panels of experts.
—Measures should only be applied by countries that are reducing their emissions in line with the Kyoto Protocol and/or its successors, against countries that are not, either due to refusal to join or to failure to comply.
—Border tax adjustments should target only imported fossil fuels, and a half dozen of the most energy-intensive major import-competing industries: aluminum, cement, steel, paper, and glass, and perhaps iron and chemicals.

The black (inappropriate) border measures include:

—Unilateral measures applied by countries that are not participating in the Kyoto Protocol or its successors.
—Calculations of carbon content of imports by formulas that presume firms necessarily use the same production processes as domestic competitors.[22]

—Judgments as to findings of fact that are made by politicians, who are vulnerable to political pressure from interest groups for special protection.

—Unilateral measures that seek to sanction an entire country, rather than targeting narrowly defined energy-intensive sectors.

—Import barriers against products that are further removed from the carbon-intensive activity, such as firms that use inputs that are produced in an energy-intensive process.

—Subsidies—whether in the form of money or extra permit allocations—to domestic sectors that are considered to have been put at a competitive disadvantage.

The gray (intermediate) measures include:

—Unilateral measures that are applied in the interim before there has been time for multilateral negotiation over a set of guidelines for border measures.

—The import penalties might follow the form of existing legislation on countervailing duties.

The author would like to acknowledge useful input from Joe Aldy, Lael Brainard, Thomas Brewer, Steven Charnovitz, Iuan Delgado, and Gary Sampson. He would further like to thank for support the Sustainability Science Program, funded by the Italian Ministry for Environment, Land and Sea, at the Center for International Development at Harvard University.

ENDNOTES

1. An additional reason we need developing countries inside the cap-and-trade system is to give the United States and other industrial countries the opportunity to buy relatively low-cost emissions abatement from developing countries, which is crucial to keep low the economic cost of achieving any given goal in terms of concentrations. This would increase the probability that industrial countries comply with the system of international emissions commitments. Elaboration is available from Aldy and Frankel (2004), Frankel (1998, 2005c, 2007). Seidman and Lewis (2009), and many other sources.

2. Intergovernmental Panel on Climate Change (2001, chap. 8.3.2 3. pp.536–44). In chapter 2, Bordoff reports studies' estimates in the range of 8 to 11 percent, including an estimate from McKibbin and others (1999) that leakage, if the United States adopted its Kyoto Protocol target unilaterally, would have been 10 percent. Ho, Morgenstern, and Shih (2008) also find that the imposition of a price on carbon in the United States would produce substantial leakage for some industries, especially in the short run; they conclude that petrochemicals and cement are the most adversely impacted, followed by iron and steel, aluminum, and lime products. Demailly and Quirion (2008a) and Reinaud (2008) do not find large leakage effects from the first stage of the EU Emissions Trading

System; but this tells us little about the next, much more serious, stage. I cannot help feeling that all these studies may underestimate some long-run general equilibrium effects.

3. It is not meaningful to talk about an adverse effect on the competitiveness of the American economy in the aggregate. Those sectors *low* in carbon intensity would in theory *benefit* from an increase in taxation of carbon relative to everything else. This theoretical point is admittedly not very intuitive. Far more likely to resonate publicly is the example that producers of renewable energy, and of the equipment that they use, would benefit from higher fossil fuel prices.

4. Houser and others (2008).

5. Pauwelyn (2007) and Fischer and Fox (2009).

6. They are used multilaterally only by the WTO [World Trade Organization] and United Nations Security Council, and are not currently under consideration as a mechanism for addressing climate change (Charnovitz 2003b, page 156). Pauwelyn (2007 compares some of these options more carefully, from a legal standpoint. Fischer and Fox (2009) compare four of them from an economic standpoint: import tax alone, export rebate alone, full border adjustment, and domestic production rebate; Hufbauer, Charnovitz, and Kim (2009, Chapter 3) are more exhaustive still.

7. Hufbauer, Charnovitz, and Kim (2009, Table 1.A.2). . . .

8. Bierman and Brohm (2005); Bhagwati and Mavroidis (2007); National Board of Trade, Government of Sweden (2004). Recent papers that compare the various options for border measures in a European context include Alexeeva-Talebi, Loschel, and Mennel (2008), Demailly anti Quiron (2009), and Reinaud (2008).

9. Beattie (2008): "Mandelson Rejects C02 Border Tax," EurActiv.com, December l 8, 2006.

10. Letter to EU Commission President José Manuel Borroso, January 2008.

11. The source for this is paragraph 13 of the "Directive of the European Parliament and of the Council Amending Directive 2003/87/EC so as to Improve and Extend the EU Greenhouse Gas Emissions Allowance Trading System," January 2008. . . .

12. For a full explanation of the legal issues, see Charnovitz (2003). Also see Bhagwati and Mavroidis (2007), Charnovitz and Weinstein (2001); Deal (2008); and Weinstein (2001).

13. Brack (1996).

14. From a personal communication with Brendan McGivern, December 12, 2007.

15. Some experts believe that even multilateral trade penalties against nonmembers might not be permissible under the WTO. See Sampson (2000, 87). . . .

16. The congressional language imposing penalties on imports from countries that do not tax carbon was apparently influenced by the International Brotherhood of Electrical Workers, which regularly lobbies for protection of American workers from foreign competition; see Beattie (2008). Simultaneously, the European Trade Union Confederation urged the EU Commission to tax imports from countries refusing to reduce emissions. See *Wall Street Journal* (2008).

17. Sampson (1999).

18. I have addressed elsewhere other ways by which the climate regime (Kyoto) could come into conflict with the trade regime (WTO) and the more

general questions of whether free trade and environmental protection need be in conflict—Frankel (2004, 2005a, 2005c).

19. The Boxer–Lieberman–Warner substitute version (S 3036), voted on in June 2008, moved the starting date for border adjustments forward to 2014.

20. Even China has apparently enacted efficiency standards on automobiles, refrigerators, and air conditioners that exceed regulations in the United States. How will Americans react if China puts justified penalties on imports from the United States?

21. Hufbauer, Charnovitz, and Kim (2009, Chapter 5) call this category "the green space" and present a list of desirable attributes, which is more authoritative than the one I had drawn up, at least from a legal standpoint. Green is the more familiar color, but I had thought to avoid it because of possible confusion with the "green box" of the WTO's Agreement on Agriculture.

22. In the Venezuelan reformulated gasoline case, the WTO panel ruled that the United States should have allowed for differences in foreign firms' production processes. Venezuela successfully claimed that U.S. law violated national treatment—that is, discriminated in favor of domestic producers with regard to whether refineries were allowed to use individual composition baselines when measuring pollution reduction. Pauwelyn (2007) proposes that if the foreign producer does not voluntarily provide the information needed to calculate carbon content, then as a back-up the U.S. Customs Bureau assign imports an implicit carbon content based on the production techniques that are dominant in the United States.

REFERENCES

Aldy, Joseph, and Jeffrey Frankel. 2004. "Designing a Regime of Emission Commitments for Developing Countries That Is Cost-Effective and Equitable." Paper written for conference on G20 Leaders and Climate Change, Council on Foreign Relations, New York, September 20–21.

Aldy. J. E., and W. A. Pizer. 2008. *Issues in the Design of U.S. Climate Change Policy.* RFF Discussion Paper 08-20. Washington: Resources for the Future.

Aldy, J.E., and W.A. Pizer. 2009. *The Competitiveness Impacts of Climate Change Mitigation Policies.* Arlington, VA: Pew Center on Global Climate Change, May.

Aldy, Joseph, Scott Barrett, and Robert Stavins, 2003. "Thirteen Plus One: A Comparison of Global Climate Architectures." *Climate Policy* 3, no. 4: 373–97.

Alexeeva-Talebi. Victoria, Andreas Loschel, and Tim Mennel. 2008. "Climate Policy and the Problem of Competitiveness: Border Tax Adjustments or Integrated Emissions Trading?" Discussion Paper 08–061. Zentrum fur Europaische Wirtschaftsforschung GmbH. Mannheim, Germany.

Beattie, Alan. 2008, "Green Barricade: Trade Faces a New Test as Carbon Taxes Go Global." *Financial Times,* January 24.

Bhagwati, Jagdish, and Petros C. Mavroidis. 2007. "Is Action Against U.S. Exports for Failure to Sign the Kyoto Protocol WTO Legal?" *World Trade Review* 6: 299–310.

Bierman, Frank, and Rainer Brohm. 2005. "Implementing the Kyoto Protocol without the United States: The Strategic Role of Energy Tax Adjustments at the Border." *Climate Policy* 4, no. 3: 289–302 .

Brack. D. 1996. *International Trade and the Montreal Protocol.* London: Royal Institute of International Affairs and Earthscan Publications.

Charnovitz, Steven. 2003a. "The Law of Environmental 'PPMs' in the WTO: Debunking the Myth of Illegality," *Yale Journal of International Law* 27, no. 1: 59–110.

———. 2003b. "Trade and Climate: Potential Conflicts and Synergies." In *Beyond Kyoto: Advancing the International Effort against Climate Change.* Washington: Pew Center on Global Climate Change.

Charnovitz, Steven, and Michael Weinstein. 2001. "The Greening of the WTO." *Foreign Affairs* 80, no. 6: 147–56.

Cosbey, Aaron, Sergio Saba, and Lucas Assuncao. 2003. "Options on Kyoto under WTO Rules." In *Implications, Including for Development, of the Interface between Environment and Trade Policies for Oil-Exporting Countries.* New York: United Nations.

Deal, Timothy. 2008. *WTO Rules and Procedures and Their Implication for the Kyoto Protocol.* New York: United States Council for International Business.

Demailly., D., and P. Quirion. 2008a. "European Emission Trading Schemes and Competitiveness: A Case Study on the Iron and Steel Industry." *Energy Economics* 30: 2009–2027.

———. 2009. "Leakage from Climate Polices and Border Tax Adjustment: Lessons from a Geographic Model of the Cement Industry." In *The Design of Climate Policy,* ed. R. Guesnerie and H. Tulkens. MIT Press.

Ederington., J. J. Minier, and A. Levinson. 2005. "Footloose and Pollution-Free." *Review of Economics and Statistics* 87, no. 1: 92–99.

Fischer. Carolyn, and Alan Fox. 2009. "Comparing Policies to Combat Emissions Leakage: Border Tax Adjustment versus Rebates," RFF Discussion Paper 09-02. Washington: Resources for the Future.

Frankel. Jeffrey. 1998. "The Kyoto Agreement on Global Climate Change: The Administration Economic Analysis, Remarks to the NBER Conference on Tax Policy and the Economy." Oct. 20 (http://ksghome.harvard.edu/~jfrankel/speechs&testimony.htm [May 2009]).

———. 2004. "Kyoto and Geneva: Linkage of the Climate Change Regime and the Trade Regime." Paper presented at Broadening Climate Discussion: The Linkage of Climate Change to Other Policy Areas, conference sponsored by Fondazione Eni Enrico Mattei and Massachusetts Institute of Technology. Venice, June.

———. 2005a. "Climate and Trade: Links between the Kyoto Protocol and WTO." *Environment* 47, no. 7: 8–19.

———. 2005b. "The Environment and Globalization," In *Globalization: What's New,* ed. Michael Weinstein. New York: Columbia University Press.

———. 2005c. "You're Getting Warmer: The Most Feasible Path for Addressing Global Climate Change Does Run Through Kyoto." In *Trade and Environment: Theory and Policy in the Context of EU Enlargement and Transition Economies,* ed. John Maxwell and Rafael Reuveny. Cheltenham, U.K.: Edward Elgar.

———.2007. "Formulas for Quantitative Emission Targets." In *Architectures for Agreement: Addressing Global Climate Change in the Post Kyoto World,* ed. Joseph E. Aldy and Robert Stavins. New York: Cambridge University Press.

Frankel, Jeffrey, and Andrew Rose. 2005. "Is Trade Good or Bad for the Environment? Sorting out the Causality." *Review of Economics and Statistics* 87, no. 1: 85–91.

Ho, Mun, Richard Morgenstern, and Jhih-Shyang Shih. 2008. "Impact of Carbon Price Policies on U.S. Industry." RFF Discussion Paper 09–37. Washington: Resources for the Future.

Houser, Trevor, Rob Bradley, Britt Childs, Jacob Werksman, and Robert Heilmayr. 2008. *Leveling the Carbon Playing Field: International Competition and US Climate Policy Design.* Washington: Peterson Institute for International Economics.

Hufbauer, Gary. Steve Charnovitz, and Jisun Kim. 2009. *Global Warning and the World Trading System.* Washington: Peterson Institute for International Economics.

Intergovernmental Panel on Climate Change. 2001. *Third Assessment Report: Climate Change 2001,* ed. Working Group III. Geneva.

McKibbin, W., M. Ross, R. Shackleton, and P. Wilcoxen. 1999. *Emissions Trading, Capital Flows and the Kyoto Protocol.* Discussion Paper in International Economics 144. Brookings.

National Board of Trade (Kommerskollegium), Government of Sweden. 2004. *Climate and Trade Rides: Harmony or Conflict?*

Pauwelyn, Joost. 2007. "U.S. Federal Climate Policy and Competitiveness Concerns: The Limits and Options of International Trade Law," Nicholas Institute for Environmental Policy Solutions Working Paper 0702. Duke University.

Reinaud, Julia. 2008. "Issues Behind Competitiveness and Carbon Leakage – Focus on Heavy Industry." IEA Information Paper. International Energy Agency: Paris.

Sampson, Gary. 1999. "WTO Rules and Climate Change: The Need for Policy Coherence." In *Global Climate Governance: A Report on the Inter-Linkages between the Kyoto Protocol and Other Multilateral Regimes,* ed. Bradnee Chambers. United Nations University.

———. 2000. *Trade, Environment and the WTO: The Post-Seattle Agenda.* Policy Essay 27. Washington: Overseas Development Council.

Seidman, Laurence, and Kenneth Lewis. 2009. "Compensation and Contributions under an International Carbon Treaty." *Journal of Policy Modeling* 31, no. 3: 341–350.

Slater, J. 2008. "Climate Change: Competitiveness Concerns and Prospects for Engaging Developing Countries." Testimony before the Energy and Air Subcommittee. Energy, and Commerce Committee, U.S. House of Representatives, March 5.

U.S. Energy Information Administration. 2006. *Energy Market Impacts of Alternative Greenhouse Gas Intensity Reduction Goals.* Report SR/OIAl-72006-01. U.S. Department of Energy.

———. 2007. *Emissions of Greenhouse Gases in the United States 2006.* Report DOE/EIA-0573(2006). U.S. Department of Energy.

———. 2008. *Energy Market and Economic Impacts of S. 2101. the Lieberman-Warner Climate Security Act of 2007.* Report DOE/EIA-SR/OIAF/2008-01. U.S. Department of Energy.

Wall Street Journal. 2008. "Unions Back Carbon Tax on Big Polluting Nations." January 16.

Webster, D. G. 2008. *Adaptive Governance: Dynamics of Atlantic Fisheries Management*, MIT Press.

Weinstein, M. 2001. "Greens and Globalization: Declaring Defeat in the Face of Victory." *New York Times*. April 22.

Jason E. Bordoff

International Trade Law and the Economics of Climate Policy: Evaluating the Legality and Effectiveness of Proposals to Address Competitiveness and Leakage Concerns

There is a growing consensus that a market mechanism that puts a price on carbon, such as a cap-and-trade system or a carbon tax, should be at the heart of the most flexible and cost-effective way to address climate change.[1] Ideally, such an approach would be adopted as part of a multilateral agreement. The reason is that carbon is a global pollutant, so a ton of carbon emitted in Beijing contributes to climate change just as much as a ton of carbon emitted in New York. This tragedy-of-the-commons nature of climate change raises concerns that any unilateral effort by the United States to put a price on carbon could disadvantage U.S. industrial firms or undermine the measure's environmental objective. These two concerns, in effect flip sides of the same coin, are referred to as "competitiveness" and "leakage," respectively. The competitiveness concern is that U.S. products—particularly carbon-intensive ones like steel, cement, chemicals, glass, and paper—will be at a competitive disadvantage relative to foreign-made goods if the United States unilaterally imposes a carbon price policy and thus raises production costs for U.S. firms.[2]

The second, related concern—emissions leakage—occurs when a policy that raises the price of carbon-intensive domestic goods causes domestic production to shift abroad and domestic consumption to shift to more carbon-intensive imports, thus undermining the policy's effect on reducing global levels of greenhouse gases (GHGs). Leakage also may occur as a result of reduced domestic demand for fossil fuel products, which depresses fuel prices in the global market and thus results in increased consumption.

An often-proposed response to the related concerns about competitiveness and leakage, which indeed has been incorporated into the leading cap-and-trade legislation, is to level the carbon playing field and encourage developing countries to adopt climate change policies by imposing a border adjustment that puts a price on the carbon contained in imports from countries without similarly stringent climate policies. Under a cap-and-trade system, this border measure could take the form of a requirement that importers from countries without comparable emissions reduction policies purchase emissions allowances to cover the carbon content of their products (or, alternatively, pay a tax equal to the allowance price). In theory, U.S. exporters might also be provided with allowances as rebates for the price of the embedded carbon in their products (though no proposal today calls for this).

Though perhaps sound in theory, the wisdom of leveling the carbon playing field by imposing border adjustments is more debatable when the expected benefits are weighed against the potential harms. The second section of this chapter briefly outlines these benefits and harms, and finds that one of the oft-cited benefits (and one that is most relevant under international law)—the reduction in GHG emissions—is likely to be quite small. To help fully explain the expected costs, and thus better compare them with the expected benefits of competitiveness and leakage prevention measures, the third section then analyzes one particular concern regarding the compatibility with World Trade Organization's (WTO's) law of border adjustments. . . . [T]he section identifies several ways in which a border adjustment might not be compliant with WTO law. Viewing border adjustments through the lens of WTO law also raises broader questions about the wisdom of imposing border adjustments as a policy matter. . . .

The Expected Benefits and Harms of Border Adjustments

Weighing the expected benefits of border adjustments against the expected harms raises doubts about the wisdom and effectiveness of such measures. As to the expected benefits, there are at least three. First, the environmental benefit of border adjustments would be to avoid some of the increase in foreign emissions that would otherwise occur in response to a unilateral U.S. climate policy. This potential increase in foreign emissions (that is, leakage) is small, however. Though estimates vary, most suggest that roughly 10 percent of the reduction in U.S. emissions will be replaced by increases in foreign emissions.[3] Most U.S. emissions occur in nontradable sectors, such as transport and residential housing. Further, some firms use little energy relative to other factors that may be more important in determining the location of trade.[4] Even in carbon-intensive sectors, it is estimated that production will decline in response to a carbon price more because of a reduction in domestic consumption than because of a shift to imports or the offshoring of production.[5]

More important, according to a recent analysis by the U.S. Environmental Protection Agency, a border adjustment on carbon-intensive manufactured imports . . . would reduce that 10 percent by only about half a percentage point because it (1) ignores production leakage due to export competitiveness, (2) applies only to a subset of imports, and (3) does not address the increased global demand for fossil fuels in response to the lower prices that reductions in the U.S. quantity demanded will have.[6]. . .

Even if border adjustments do little to reduce emissions leakage, some argue that they can enhance the overall environmental utility of a cap-and-trade regime by achieving greater global GHG reductions in [other] ways. . . . [B]order adjustments [may] induce developing countries to reduce their own emissions so as to avoid the border charge. Given that China alone is expected to account for 47 percent of the growth in GHG emissions over the next twenty-five years,[7] engaging emerging economies in efforts to address climate change is critically important. Yet only a very small fraction of carbon-intensive products made in China are exported to the United States, so a border adjustment in the United States would be a small stick with which to pressure China to implement more costly low-carbon production processes. . . . Moreover, even if border adjustments were successful in reducing emissions in carbon-intensive industries, they would do nothing to reduce the three-quarters of Chinese emissions that come from other sources.[8] . . .

The second potential benefit of a border adjustment is that it can protect certain industries by leveling the carbon playing field. . . . The Environmental Protection Agency, for example, estimates that U.S. imports from Annex II countries—those not subject to the Kyoto Protocol caps—would be roughly 12 percent higher in 2050 without a border adjustment than they would be with one.[9] To some extent, the benefits to U.S. carbon-intensive manufacturers may be limited by the fact that many of the carbon-intensive imports to the United States come from Annex I countries—those that . . . are already part of the Kyoto Protocol and thus would likely be exempt from most border adjustment proposals.[10] Indeed, Canada is the largest source of imports in all carbon-intensive industries except one, with Europe and Russia not far behind.[11] . . . [T]he competitiveness benefit may still be considerable because the sectors in which roughly two-thirds of U.S. imports come from Annex II countries (chemicals and cement) are also among the carbon-intensive sectors that comprise the largest shares of U.S. gross domestic product (GDP) and employment.[12] Moreover, the growth rates for imports in these sectors have been more rapid than for imports in other carbon-intensive sectors.[13]

Third, as a political matter, border adjustments also may have the benefit of helping to secure passage of a cap-and-trade bill in the U.S. Congress (where some measure to address adverse effects on domestic industry likely will be necessary). They might also encourage other developed nations to adopt similar policies, which might do more to induce developing countries to negotiate an international agreement.

Against these expected benefits need to be weighed at least three expected costs of border adjustments. First there is a risk that the border adjustment system could be abused for purely protectionist reasons by U.S. firms facing growing global competitive pressures. Second, there is a risk that border adjustments could lead to retaliatory tit-for-tat trade wars, particularly with developing nations, which may believe that developed nations bear a greater responsibility for curbing climate change. . . . Finally, there is a risk that a border adjustment would be illegal under WTO law, . . . which could potentially lead the WTO to authorize retaliatory tariffs.

Evaluating Border Adjustments under WTO Law . . .

There are three steps in the analysis of whether a border adjustment is consistent with WTO law. First, is the border adjustment consistent with WTO market access commitments? If so, is it also consistent with the nondiscrimination obligations under the WTO? If not, is it permissible nonetheless under one of the exceptions provided for under GATT Article XX?[14]

As to the first question, . . . [a] border adjustment that applies to imports the same requirements imposed on domestic products is generally permissible . . . assuming it does not violate national treatment or most-favored-nation treatment obligations. . . . Assuming the border adjustment is imposed as part of an overall domestic cap-and-trade system, therefore, the WTO may well view it as a border-enforced internal measure. [T]he focus of this analysis, therefore, is on the second and third questions regarding whether the measure is discriminatory or falls under an environmental exception. . . .

Nondiscrimination Obligations

Even if a border adjustment is accepted as a permissible border-enforcement of an internal measure, the border adjustment must . . . not violate Article III's "national treatment" obligation by discriminating against imports or Article I's "most-favored-nation" obligation by discriminating among importing nations. . . .

NATIONAL TREATMENT

Article III:4 requires that the United States accord to imported products "treatment *no less favorable* than that accorded to *like* products of national origin in respect of all laws, regulations and requirements affecting their internal sale, offering for sale, purchase, transportation, distribution or use" (emphasis added). . . .

. . . In the case of climate change border adjustments, however, this seemingly straightforward principle proves exceptionally difficult to put into effect. . . .

The Appellate Body has explained that whether two products are "like" under Article III:4 is to be determined by whether they are in a "competitive relationship,"[15] and thus a basic industrial product like steel would most likely be considered "like" other steel, even if they were produced in ways that emitted different amounts of carbon. An importer of more carbon-intensive steel might thus challenge a border adjustment . . . by claiming its "like" product was being treated less favorably. If the U.S. regulation instead imposed an allowance requirement equal to that paid by U.S. manufacturers regardless of carbon content (for example, a charge per unit of steel imported), low-carbon producers (such as those in nations that rely more heavily on nuclear or natural gas) would likely object on the grounds that their products were being treated less favorably.

The United States might respond that high-carbon steel is not "like" lower-carbon steel because one contributes more than the other to climate change. Generally speaking, the interpretation of "like" products does not permit differentiation based on the way a product is made (so-called process and production methods, or PPMs), but rather only on the product's physical characteristics.[16] . . . Given that steel created in a climate-friendly way is physically indistinguishable from steel created in a climate-unfriendly way, GATT jurisprudence suggests that a measure that distinguishes like products based on how much carbon was emitted in their creation might not fall within the scope of Article III.[17] . . .

Even if a border adjustment were found not to discriminate between like products, importers would need to pay the same price per ton of carbon emitted as domestic producers (through the purchase of allowances in a market) to be treated "no less favorably." The problem, however, is that it can be difficult to agree on what price U.S. manufacturers paid to emit a ton of carbon under a domestic cap-and-trade scheme. . . .

Finally, even if the right price could be determined, that carbon price would need to be imposed as a border adjustment *based on the carbon content of the import*, which can be exceptionally complicated to determine. Foreign manufacturers asked to provide detailed carbon content information may be unwilling to do so, or even unable given increasingly disaggregated global supply chains for production.[18] . . .

MOST-FAVORED-NATION TREATMENT

. . . [A] border adjustment must satisfy . . . Article I's "most-favored-nation" requirement, which prohibits discrimination between WTO members. Border adjustment proposals typically only apply to imports from countries that do not have a comparably effective climate policy already in place. . . . Yet such an approach would seem to violate Article I because it would be treating two "like" products differently depending on their origin. The United States might argue that the treatment is nondiscriminatory because the restriction is based not on origin but on conditions of production that apply equally to all nations, and that the treatment differs only because the objective of mitigating climate change is being met differently in different places.[19] Even supporters of border adjustments, however, recognize that such a claim would face difficulty.[20] . . .

Moreover, even if the WTO permitted differential treatment, it would be very difficult to determine which countries have comparably effective climate policies in a way that did not give rise to discrimination claims. The European Union's cap-and-trade system, for example, covers only half the economy. Many EU member countries that impose carbon taxes have exempted energy-intensive industries.[21] Moreover, other nations (like Japan) might eschew market mechanisms altogether in favor of command-and-control regulations. It is also possible to envision ways in which governments could modify their tax systems—effectively doing a corporate tax swap—that would have little or no effect on emissions but would satisfy an assessment of comparable climate policy burdens. For example, a government could cut excise taxes on fossil fuels while imposing a carbon tax. The after-tax cost of using fossil fuels by, say, steel firms would be unchanged, but the country could argue that it has implemented a climate policy comparable to that of the United States. In theory, rather than divide countries into two groups—those with and without comparably effective climate policies—all importers might be required to pay the difference between the U.S. market price for allowances and whatever carbon price they paid in their home country. As an administrative matter, however, such an approach would be massively complex and likely unworkable. . . .

Article XX Exceptions

. . . [T]here is reason to believe that a border adjustment . . . would then be permissible only if it satisfied one of the environmental exceptions in Article XX of the GATT and then, if it did, whether it was also consistent with the introductory paragraph ("chapeau") of Article XX.

The most relevant exceptions are found in Article XX(g) . . . [which] applies to measures "relating to the conservation of exhaustible natural resources if such measures are made effective in conjunction with restrictions on domestic production or consumption." . . .

. . . There are three parts to the Article XX(g) analysis, two of which should be satisfied without much difficulty. A low-carbon atmosphere, necessary to avoid catastrophic climate change, should be viewed as an "exhaustible natural resource"; although carbon only stays in the atmosphere for around a hundred years, the WTO has previously found that clean air is a resource capable of depletion even if it is renewable.[22] A border adjustment would also be "made effective in conjunction with restrictions on domestic production or consumption" if it is part of an overall U.S. cap-and-trade bill.

A more difficult question is whether a border adjustment is "related to" the goal of mitigating climate change. GATT panels have interpreted "relating to" to mean "primarily aimed at" conservation.[23] In *US–Gasoline*, the

Appellate Body found the disputed measure satisfied XX(g) because it had a "substantial relationship" to the conservation of clean air.[24] In *US–Shrimp,* XX(g) was satisfied because the import ban on shrimp harvested without devices to avoid harming turtles while fishing demonstrated a "means and ends relationship" that was "close and real" with the goal of protecting endangered turtles.[25] It is less clear whether a border adjustment would satisfy the test of being primarily . . . related to the goal of reducing GHG emissions when estimates suggest the policy might do little to reduce leakage. . . .

. . . Even if a border adjustment satisfies XX(g), it must also be justified under the "chapeau," or opening clause, to Article XX. . . .The chapeau requires that "measures are not applied in a manner which would constitute a means of arbitrary or unjustifiable discrimination between countries where the same conditions prevail, or a disguised restriction on international trade." . . . Several of the leading environmental cases under the WTO have turned on the standards set forth in the chapeau. In *US–Gasoline, US–Shrimp,* and most recently *Brazil–Tyres,* for example, the Appellate Body found the offending measure to be provisionally justified by . . . either XX(g) or XX(b) . . . but then found the measure violated the chapeau of Article XX.

The Appellate Body has explained that whether the application of a measure violates the chapeau "should focus on the cause or rationale given for the discrimination."[26] As a theoretical matter, a full border adjustment . . . based on the carbon-intensity of an import has a plausible rationale consistent with XX(g), namely, to minimize carbon leakage that can undermine the effectiveness of a U.S. cap-and-trade system in lowering GHG emissions. Moreover, excluding nations with comparably effective climate policies from the scheme also has a defensible environmental rationale, which is that those nations are already taking measures to reduce carbon emissions and thus leakage to them should be of minimal concern.

At the same time, the chapeau addresses the "detailed operating provisions" of the measure at issue and how it is "actually applied."[27] When consideration is given to the administrative complexities and likely implementation, there are [many] possible reasons why a border adjustment, depending on how it is designed, may violate the chapeau.

First, as discussed above, a border adjustment on carbon-intensive manufactured goods from countries that have not taken comparably effective action to address climate change, as commonly proposed today, would do little to reduce overall leakage and have little environmental benefit. . . .

Second, the measure likely will have to permit importers to demonstrate how much carbon they emitted individually and pay for allowances on that basis. The current provision in the Lieberman–Warner Bill, for example, does not do that. Rather, it prescribes a particular formula used to determine the allowance requirement for a category of covered goods in a covered foreign country.[28] Manufacturers in that category would thus have the same allowance requirement regardless how much carbon each actually emitted in production. Such a provision may be ruled arbitrary and unjustifiable discrimination. . . .

Third, the United States cannot require an exporting country to implement a market mechanism, but it must allow flexibility for nations to pursue other approaches "comparable in effectiveness."[29] The Appellate Body has interpreted "arbitrary or unjustifiable discrimination" to preclude requiring essentially the same program as the United States puts in place to address climate change.[30] As a practical matter, this may significantly mute the impact of border adjustments. . . .

Fourth, the U.S. program must take "into consideration different conditions which may occur" in different countries.[31] Failure to do so may constitute "arbitrary discrimination," according to the Appellate Body.[32] In that regard, the WTO might consider the relevance of developed countries' greater historical responsibility for cumulative carbon emissions and higher current emissions per capita. In that case, there is a possibility the WTO would find that even a border adjustment applied equally to domestic and imported goods is non-compliant.

Fifth . . . , the Appellate Body's interpretation of the chapeau requires that . . . the United States must engage in "serious, across-the-board negotiations" with other nations that might be subject to the border adjustments.[33] . . . If the United States were not to undertake such negotiations, or the WTO were to view the efforts as insufficiently "serious," that might lead to a finding that the border adjustment is arbitrary and discriminatory.[34]

The Alternative of Free Allocation

Questions about the WTO legality of border adjustments, combined with concerns about tit-for-tat trade retaliation and their small impact on reducing leakage, may caution against their use. Yet, as a practical matter, some measures may be necessary in a U.S. cap-and-trade law to address potential adverse effects on domestic manufacturers. In response to this political imperative, some have proposed compensating adversely affected sectors in the United States through the free allocation of emission allowances.[35] . . .

Under the WTO Agreement on Subsidies and Countervailing Measures, free allocation would be a subsidy subject to remedies under the agreement if it (1) were a "financial contribution" by the government, (2) conferred a "benefit," and (3) were "specific" to certain industries or sectors.[36] If these elements are satisfied, the subsidy may be inconsistent with WTO law if it also causes adverse effects to other WTO members.[37]

First, free allocation of allowances should be considered a financial contribution, which is defined, among other ways, as the "direct transfer of funds, such as grants, loans and equity infusions."[38] Though it might be argued that free allowances do not constitute the "direct transfer of funds," they are "functionally equivalent to distributing cash," according to the Congressional Budget Office (CBO), because allowances can be sold for monetary value in a liquid secondary market, created and enforced by the government.[39] . . .

Second, if free allowances are a "direct transfer of funds" qualifying as a financial contribution by the government, it should be readily agreed that they also confer a benefit. "If a government gives a sum of money to a company, it seems clear that this financial contribution would generally confer a benefit."[40]

Third, a subsidy is "specific" when it is provided to a specific industry or enterprise but not when it is widely available within an economy.[41] To the extent free allowances are targeted at specifically defined sectors adversely affected by a carbon price, they would likely be considered specific. Conversely, if all allowances were distributed based on objective criteria, like historical emissions, it would be harder to prove that the subsidies were specific.[42] Even if a subsidy is de jure nonspecific, however, it can still be de facto specific if, for example, certain enterprises benefit disproportionately.[43]

Finally, for the program to be an "actionable" subsidy, it must cause "adverse effects" to the interests of another WTO member.[44] The most likely way in which free allocation may be found to do so would be if it caused "serious prejudice," notably because the "subsidy displaces or impedes imports of a like product of another Member in the market of the subsidizing Member."[45]

Although free allocation may appear, at first glance, to harm other WTO members by reducing costs for domestic producers, in fact free allocation should not change a firm's pricing and output decisions, and thus foreign firms should not see their sales reduced by artificially suppressed prices for U.S. goods. As discussed above, free allocation of allowances does *not* exempt firms from the carbon price signal created by a cap-and-trade system. Rather, it is a transfer of resources from the government to the recipients. Even if firms receive allowances for free, they will still pass along the opportunity cost of using those allowances to their customers in the form of higher prices.[46] Indeed, in Europe, which gave allowances away for free, consumers still saw electricity prices rise and fall with the market value of allowances, while firms reaped windfall profits. As prices increase, demand falls, and the firm's output is reduced accordingly.[47] How much output is reduced should not differ depending on whether allowances are auctioned or freely distributed. Firms set prices based on market forces, such as marginal costs and demand, that do not change even if firms receive a cash transfer from the government. This economic effect of free allocation is particularly important to recognize in considering how to protect U.S. industry, because free allocation will increase firms' profits, which ultimately accrue to shareholders, but will *not* prevent production declines and concomitant job tosses in affected sectors.[48] Free allocation thus may not adversely affect other WTO members or be illegal under WTO law–though precisely because it would be *ineffective* in protecting U.S. industries or workers (though it would compensate shareholders). Even if output and pricing decisions are unchanged, however, WTO members may claim they suffered "serious prejudice" if free allocation provides firms with resources to invest in research and development (R&D) or new products, prevents exit from the market, or has other indirect benefits.

It is worth noting that whether free allocation has adverse effects on importers may depend on the formula used for the allocation and updating of allowances. For example, "output-based allocation," which some analysts have proposed,[49] *would* affect the pricing and output decisions of firms.[50] This approach would be the functional equivalent of auctioning off allowances and then using the revenue to subsidize production. Indeed, some proposals on Capitol Hill make this explicit, rebating firms in cash for the average carbon costs (from the purchase of allowances and higher electricity prices) associated with output in their sector—thus preserving some incentive to reduce energy intensity relative to the sector average. With output-based allocation or rebating, output would thus be reduced less than would be the case absent the production subsidy—thereby giving rise to claims of "serious prejudice" by other WTO members.[51] In short, the more effective free allocation is in protecting employment and output in adversely affected sectors, the more likely it may be to violate WTO law. If free allocation were found to be a subsidy inconsistent with WTO law, the adversely affected WTO member might seek the right to retaliate against U.S. products imported to that country if the free allocation were not removed.[52]

In response to a claim by a WTO member that free allocation constituted an illegal subsidy, the United States might respond in its defense that the WTO Agreement on Subsidies and Countervailing Measures permits certain environmental adaptation subsidies, and that free allocation of permits falls within that provision as a subsidy to help manufacturers adjust to the effects of climate policy.[53] Although this provision expired in 2000, the United States might argue that the environmental exceptions to which negotiators agreed in 1995 are still justified today. Yet even if the WTO were to agree that the environmental exceptions existed notwithstanding their expiration, free allocation of permits is unlikely to fall within the narrow scope of the exceptions. The subsidy must provide "assistance to promote adaptation of existing facilities to new environmental requirements imposed by law and/or regulations which result in greater constraints and financial burden on firms,"[54] but free allocation is a cash transfer that firms may use to "green" their facilities or may invest in other more profitable ventures or may distribute as profits to shareholders. Further, environmental adaptation subsidies must be a one-time subsidy,[55] whereas free allocation is likely to take place annually. The subsidies must be limited to 20 percent of the adaptation costs, yet most proposals to compensate carbon-intensive sectors propose much larger subsidies.[56] The subsidies also must be "directly linked to and proportionate to a firm's planned reduction of nuisances and pollution," but, as noted, free allocation is effectively a cash transfer that creates no obligation to invest in cleaner production. Fundamentally, the problem is that the provision for environmental adaptation subsidies was written to address the costs of complying with command-and-control regulations, like improved pollution and efficiency standards, but is inapposite to a market mechanism like a carbon price created by a cap-and-trade regime.

Conclusion

. . . [T]he consistency of border adjustments with WTO law is in doubt and may come down to whether the WTO panel finds the measure to be a genuine effort to protect the environment or a form of stealth protectionism. . . . In short, the expected environmental benefit of border adjustments for carbon-intensive manufactured goods is likely to be quite small compared with the trade and WTO risks they pose. . . .

Ultimately, all the problems and challenges associated with measures to address competitiveness and leakage reinforce the truly global nature of climate change and the limited ability of any one country to address it unilaterally. International engagement is thus critical to mitigate climate change, and a new post–Kyoto Protocol international architecture will be needed in this regard.[57] Achieving this goal is complicated, however, by considerations of economic efficiency, which requires low-cost abatement in the developing world, and distributional equity, which demands action from rich nations historically responsible for emitting GHGs. Until a truly international approach is adopted, it is critical that the United States, at long last, show real leadership and adopt serious unilateral measures to curb GHG emissions, while high-income countries take collective steps to assist the rest of the world in reducing its emissions.

For helpful comments and discussion, the author would like to thank Joseph Aldy, Joel Beauvais, Steven Charnovitz, Manasi Deshpande, Elliot Diringer, Douglas Elmendorf, Andrew Guzman, Michael Levi, Bryan Mignone, Robert Novick, Warren Payne, Billy Pizer, Andrew Shoyer, Timothy Taylor, and Mark Wu. He especially thanks Pascal Noel for exceptionally valuable research assistance. Leandra English and Julie Anderson also provided helpful editorial assistance.

ENDNOTES

1. For a detailed discussion about why a market mechanism is preferable to alternative approaches, see Furman and others (2007).

2. A recent study by the Peterson Institute identifies the following carbon-intensive manufacturing industries that compete with foreign producers: ferrous metals (iron and steel), nonferrous metals (aluminum and copper), nonmetal mineral products (cement and glass), paper and pulp, and basic chemicals. See Houser and others (2008). The Lieberman–Warner Bill specifically names "iron, steel, aluminum, cement, bulk glass, or paper" as "primary products," though it permits the administrator to include "any other manufactured product that is sold in bulk for purposes of further manufacture" and generates significant greenhouse gas (GHG) emissions during production. America's Climate Security Act of 2007, S 2191, 110th Cong.[hereafter ACSA], Sec, 6001 (10). Unless otherwise noted, references to Lieberman–Warner throughout do not reflect revisions in the manager's substitute amendment, released May 21, 2008 (http://epw. senate.gov/public/index.cfm?FuseAction=Files.View&FileStore_id=aaf57ba9-ee98-4204-882a-Ide307ecdb4d [October 2008]).

3. The Environmental Protection Agency [EPA] estimates U.S. emissions leakage rates under Lieberman–Warner of approximately 11 percent in 2030 and 8 percent in 2050. "EPA Analysis of the Lieberman–Warner Climate Security Act of 2008 S 2191 in 110th Congress, March 14, 2008" [hereafter EPA Analysis S 2191], 84 (www.epa.gov/climatechange/downloads/s2191_EPA_ Analysis.pdf [February 2009]). Paltsev (2001) estimates leakage rates of 10.5 percent from Annex I countries under their Kyoto caps, though he estimates U.S. leakage rates (under never-ratified Kyoto targets) of only 5.5 percent. McKibbin and others (1999) estimated in 1999 that if the U.S. unilaterally adopted Kyoto targets, leakage rates would be roughly 10 percent in 2010. The Intergovernmental Panel on Climate Change (2001) surveys a number of multi-regional leakage estimates, finding a range of 5 to 20 percent.

4. For example, energy costs in most manufacturing industries are less than 2 percent of total costs; Morgenstern and others (2007).

5. Aldy and Pizer (2008).

6. EPA Analysis S 2191, 84. In a scenario where Annex II countries take no action on their own but the United States unilaterally adopts an emissions reduction policy, the international Reserve Allowance Requirement in the Lieberman–Warner Climate Security Act reduces leakage from 361 metric tons of carbon dioxide equivalent (MtCO2e) to 350 MtCO2e in 2030 (or from 11.6 percent of U.S. reductions to 11 percent) and from 412 MtCO2e to 385 MtCO2e in 2050 (or from 8.2 percent of U.S. reductions to 7.6 percent). The EPA's ADAGE model does not allow it to break out how much of the emissions leakage is from each of these various sources. In his paper measuring the emissions leakage from implementing the Kyoto Protocol, however. Paltsev (2001. 68 n. 4) finds that leakage from Annex I demand reductions, which lead to reduced world prices and thus increased Annex II consumption, accounts for about one-quarter of total leakage. It is important to note that the manager's substitute amendment to Lieberman–Warner expands the definition of "covered products"

to include not only primary carbon-intensive goods but also manufactured goods for consumption that generate a substantial quantity of direct and indirect GHG emissions, Sec. 1311(7) and (14). Even if such broader coverage did more to reduce leakage, it could create enormous administrative challenges. For most downstream goods, however, a carbon price is likely to be a small enough component of total cost that a border adjustment would do little to change trade flows. . . .

7. Author's calculations, based on DOE (2008). . . .

8. This estimate is based on personal communication with Trevor Houser, Peterson Institute for International Economics, July 14, 2008. . . .

9. EPA Analysis S 2191, 85. See also Morgenstern and others (2007).

10. Annex I countries account for 54 percent of U.S. steel imports, 78 percent of aluminum imports, 34 percent of chemicals imports, 87 percent of paper imports, and 35 percent of cement imports. See Houser and others (2008, 44). To be sure, some Annex I countries like Canada may fail to meet their targets and thus may not be judged to have taken comparably effective measures, even though they are subject to the Kyoto Protocol's caps.

11. Houser and others (2008, 44). Note that to the extent products from these countries already internalize a carbon price, U.S. products may be viewed as receiving a subsidy by emitting carbon without paying such costs. See Stiglitz (2006a, 2006b).

12. Houser and others (2008, 11). Chemicals and cement make up 1.68 and 0.43 percent, respectively, of U.S. GDP and 0.65 and 0.38 percent, respectively, of employment. Paper has roughly equal shares to cement: 0.44 percent of GDP and 0.36 percent of employment. Steel and aluminum make up only 0.29 and 0.20 percent, respectively, of GDP and 0.19 and 0.11 percent, respectively, of employment. Houser and others (2008, Table 1.2).

13. Houser and others (2008, 46, figure 3.3). . . .

14. Other exceptions also exist, such as GATT Article XXI's security exceptions, though only Article XX is likely to be relevant for the purposes of border adjustments. . . .

15. WTO, *Appellate Body Report on European Communities: Measures Affecting Asbestos and Asbestos-Containing Products*, WT/DS135/AB/R, March 12, 2001 [hereafter *EC–Asbestos*], paragraph 99.

16. Matsushita, Schoenbaum, and Mavroidis (2003,163); Hudec (2000, 187, 191). . . .

17. Bhagwati and Mavroidis (2007). . . .

18. See Krugman (2008). As difficult as it is to determine the carbon content of carbon-intensive manufactured goods, it is vastly more complicated to do so for manufactured goods for consumption made from those carbon-intensive primary goods, as required in the Manager's substitute amendment to Lieberman–Warner, Sec. 1311 (7) and (14). . . .

19. In the Canada–Automobiles decision, for example, the panel suggested that origin-neutral criteria might be permissible under Article I. WTO, *Appellate Body Report on Canada: Certain Measures Affecting the Automotive Industry*, WT/DS139/AB/R, WT/DS142/AB/R, February 11, 2000 [hereafter

Canada–Automobiles), paragraphs 3.22–3.24. But see WTO, *Panel Report on Indonesia: Certain Measures Affecting the Automobile Industry*, WT/DS54, 59 and 64/R, July 23, 1998, paragraph 14.143, ruling that "GATT case law is clear to the effect that any . . . advantage [here tax and customs benefits] cannot be made conditional on any criteria that is not related to the imported product itself."

20. Memorandum from Andrew W. Shoyer. "WTO Background Analysis of International Provisions of U.S. Climate Change Legislation," February 28, 2008 (http://energycommerce.house.gov/cmte_mtgs/110-eaq-hrg.030508.Morris-testimony.pdf [February 2009]). . . .

21. World Bank (2008, 24). . . .

22. *US–Gasoline AB*, 14. WTO, *Appellate Body Report on United States: Standards for Reformulated and Conventional Gasoline*, WT/DS2/AB/R, May 20, 1996 [hereafter *US-gasoline AB*], 13–22.

23. *US–Gasoline AB*, 18—19; GATT, *Panel Report on Canada: Measures Affecting Exports of Unprocessed Herring and Salmon*, L/6268, BISD) 35S/98, March 22, 1988, paragraphs 4.5–4.6.

24. *US–Gasoline AB*, 19.

25. *US–Shrimp AB*, 141. . . .

26. *Brazil–Tyres AB*, 246.

27. *US–Shrimp AB*, 160. . . .

28. ACSA, Title VI, Sec. 6001(d).

29. *US–Shrimp*, Article 21.5 AB. 137–44. It is also worth noting that a trade mechanism that requires comparability in form as well as burden runs counter to the *Framework Convention* on Climate Change and the Kyoto Protocol, which *provides* discretion to countries on how they implement their climate change policy goals.

30. *US–Shrimp*, Article 21.5 AB, 144.

31. *US–Shrimp*, Article 21.5 AB, 164.

32. *US–Shrimp*, Article 21.5 AB, 164, 165, 177.

33. *US–Shrimp*, Article 21.5 AB, 166–71.

34. Efforts to undertake "serious, across-the-board negotiations" before the imposition of a border adjustment may be complicated by the most recent Senate climate change bill's reduction from eight years to two years the delay between the start of the domestic cap-and-trade program and the start of the international allowance program. Sec. 1315.

35. See, for example, Pew Center on Global Climate Change (2008).

36. WTO, "Agreement on Subsidies and Countervailing Measures," Articles 1.1, 1.2.

37. WTO, "Agreement on Subsidies and Countervailing Measures," Article 5. In addition to being an "actionable" subsidy if it causes adverse effects, a claim might also be made that it constitutes a "prohibited" export-contingent subsidy, which is forbidden per se. World Trade Organization, "Agreement on Subsidies and Countervailing Measures," Article 3. Though a subsidy may he prohibited if it is contingent de facto or de jure on export (*Appellate Body Report on Canada: Measures Affecting the Export of Civilian Aircraft*. WT/DS70/AB/R, August 2, 1999, Paragraph 167), export orientation alone is not enough; the subsidy must be "in fact tied to actual or anticipated exportation

or export earnings." World Trade Organization, "Agreement on Subsidies and Countervailing Measures," n. 4. Free allocation to carbon-intensive industries is unlikely to meet that test.

38. WTO, "Agreement on Subsidies and Countervailing Measures," Article 1.1 (a) (1)(i).
39. Congressional Budget Office (2007a). . . .
40. Van den Bossche (2005, 557).
41. WTO, "Agreement on Subsidies and Countervailing Measures," Article 2.
42. WTO, "Agreement on Subsidies and Countervailing Measures," n. 2.
43. WTO, "Agreement on Subsidies and Countervailing Measures." Article 2.1(c).
44. WTO, "Agreement on Subsidies and Countervailing Measures," Article 5.
45. WTO, "Agreement on Subsidies and Countervailing Measures," Article 6.3(a).
46. See Congressional Budget office (2007b, 1; 2003).
47. For estimates of output reductions from a carbon charge, see Morgenstern and others (2007).
48. See, for example, Orszag (2008): "Because the additional profits from the allowances' value would not depend on how much a company produced, such profits would be unlikely to prevent the declines in production and resulting job losses that the price increases (and resulting drop in demand) would engender."
49. Fischer and Fox (2004); Fischer, Hoffmann, and Yoshino (2002). Under output-based allocation, a certain number of allowances are allocated to certain sectors, and within each sector each firm would receive a number of permits proportional to its share of the sector's output.
50. In addition to the legal issues, by not allowing the carbon price signal to be passed through in the form of higher prices, output-based allocation is a less-efficient way to reduce emissions because it reduces conservation incentives and instead increases reliance on lowering energy intensity. Conversely, its proponents argue that output-based allocation would reduce leakage, mitigate adverse effects on employment in the affected sector, and reduce negative effects on the real wage by mitigating price increases of energy-intensive goods.
51. In its defense, the United States might argue that output-based allocation is not a *net* subsidy once the impact of the cap-and-trade system is considered, so importers are not adversely affected relative to the business-as-usual scenario of no U.S. climate change regulation. In response, the complaining WTO member might make two points. First, it is theoretically possible for firms to receive a net subsidy under output-based allocation if the sector-level allocations are based on historical emissions shares but, a given sector or subsector does relatively more than others to reduce emissions. Second, the member might argue that the measure being disputed as an actionable subsidy is not the U.S. climate regulation (including the allocation method), but rather output-based allocation itself. Under a cap-and-trade system, the economy as a whole would face higher costs from the domestic climate regulation, but output-based allocation would be a way to offset part of those costs for a certain subset of industries–in a way that induces higher output and thus might harm importers. In that way, exempting certain sectors from regulatory costs (and concomitant GHG reductions) that would otherwise exist may be viewed by the WTO as similar to "forgoing" revenue "otherwise due," which is a financial contribution under Article I of the

"Agreement on Subsidies and Countervailing Measures." When a regulation applies to the entire economy, but only certain sectors receive a subsidy that mutes the regulation's impact, the WTO may find that the benchmark against which to evaluate whether a member has been adversely affected is the absence of the disputed method of allocation, not the absence of the entire regulatory program.

52. WTO, "Agreement on Subsidies and Countervailing Measures," Articles 10–11. In addition, the affected foreign industry might consider bringing a countervailing duty case under its domestic trade laws.

53. WTO, "Agreement on Subsidies and Countervailing Measures," Article 8.2(c).

54. WTO, "Agreement on Subsidies and Countervailing Measures," Article 8.2(c).

55. WTO, "Agreement on Subsidies and Countervailing Measures," Article 8.2(c)(i).

56. Several studies, for example, found that free distribution of around 20 percent of allowances would be sufficient to compensate primary energy producers and electric power generators. See Smith, Ross, and Montgomery (2002); Burtraw and Palmer (2006); and Burtraw and others (2002). A subsidy of 20 percent of total costs would thus require free allocation of only 4 percent of allowances, whereas Lieberman–Warner proposed freely allocating about 30 percent of all allowances each year in its first ten years to owners of manufacturing, fossil fuel–fired electricity generators, petroleum refiners, and natural gas processors.

57. See generally, Ally and Stavins (2007); and Stern and William Antholis (2007).

REFERENCES

Aldy, Joseph E., and William A. Pizer. 2008. *Competitiveness Impacts of Climate Change Mitigation Policies*. RFF Discussion Paper 08-21. Washington: Resources for the Future.

Aldy, Joseph E., and Robert N. Stavins, 2007. *Architectures for Agreement: Addressing Global Climate Change in the Post-Kyoto World*. Washington: Resources for the Future.

Bhagwati, Jagdish, and Petros C. Mavroidis. 2007. 'Is Action against US Exports for Failure to Sign Kyoto Protocol WTO-Legal?" *World Trade Review*, 6: 299–310.

Bradford, Scott C., Paul L. E. Grieco, and Gary Clyde Hufbauer. 2005. "The Payoff to America from Global Integration." In *The United States and the World Economy: Foreign Economic Policy for the Next Decade*, ed. C. Fred Bergsten. Washington: Peterson Institute for International Economics.

Burtraw, Dallas, and Karen Palmer. 2006. "Compensation Rules for Climate Policy in the Electricity Sector." Paper presented at National Bureau of Economic Research Summer Institute, Workshop on Public Policy and the Environment, Cambridge, Mass.

Burtraw, Dallas. Karen Palmer, Ranjit Bharvirkar, and Anthony Paul. 2002. "The Effect on Asset Values of the Allocation of Carbon Dioxide Emission Allowances." *Electricity Journal* 15, no. 5: 51–62.

Charnovitz, Steven. 2002. "The Law of Environmental 'PPMs' in the WTO: Debunking the Myth of Illegality." *Yale Journal of International Law* 27, no. 59: 97.

———. 2003. *Trade and Climate: Potential Conflict and Synergies in Beyond Kyoto: Advancing the International Effort against Climate Change*. Washington: Pew Center on Global Climate Change.

Congressional Budget Office. 2003. *Shifting the Burden of a Cap-and-Trade Program*. Washington.

———. 2007a. "Cost Estimate, S. 2191: America's Climate Security Act of 2007" (www.cbo.gov/ftpdocs/91xx/doc9121/s2191_EPW_Amendment.pdf [March 2009]).

———. 2007b. *Trade-Offs in Allocating Allowances for CO2 Emissions*. Washington.

DOE (U.S. Department of Energy). 2008. *International Energy Outlook 2008*. Report DOE/EIA-0484(2008).

Fischer, Carolyn, and Alan Fox. 2004. *Output-Based Allocations of Emissions Permits: Efficiency and Distributional Effects in a General Equilibrium Setting with Taxes and Trade*. RFF Discussion Paper 04–37. Washington: Resources for the Future.

Fischer, Carolyn, Sandra Hoffmann, and Yutaka Yoshino. 2002. *Multilateral Trade Agreements and Market-Based Environmental Policies*. RFF Discussion Paper 02-28. Washington: Resources for the Future.

Furman, Jason, Jason Bordoff, Manasi Deshpande, and Pascal Noel. 2007. *An Economic Strategy to Address Climate Change and Promote Energy Security*. Hamilton Project Strategy Paper. Brookings.

Houser, Trevor, Rob Bradley, Britt Childs, Jacob Werksman, and Robert Heitmayr. 2008. *Leveling the Carbon Playing Field: International Competition and US Climate Policy Design*. Washington: Peterson Institute for International Economics.

Hudec, Robert E. 2000. "The Product-Process Doctrine in GATT/WTO Jurisprudence." *In New Directions in International Economic Law: Essays in Honour of John H. Jackson*, ed., Marco Bronckcrs and Reinhard Quick. Boston: Kluwer.

Intergovernmental Panel on Climate Change. 2001. *Climate Change 2001: Mitigation: Summary for Policymakers*. Geneva.

Ismer. R., and K. Neuhoff. 2004. *Border Tax Adjustments: A Feasible Way to Address Nonparticipation in Emission Trading*. Cambridge Working Paper in Economics 0409, Cambridge University (http://ideas.repec.org/p/cam/camdae/0409.html [February 2009]).

Kopp, Raymond J. 2007. *Allowance Allocation*. Washington: Resources for the Future.

Krugman. Paul. 2008. "Trade and Wages Reconsidered." *Brookings Papers on Economic Activity*, ed. Douglas Elmendorf, N. Gregory Mankiw, and Lawrence Summers. Spring. 103–54.

Matsushita, Mitsuo, Thomas J. Schoenbaum. and Petros C. Mavroidis. 2003. *The World Trade Organization: Law, Practice, and Policy*. Oxford University Press.

McKibbin, Warwick J., M. Ross. R. Shackjeton, and P. Wilcoxen. 1999. Washington, DC. *Emissions Trading, Capital Flows and the Kyoto Protocol*. Discussion Paper in International Economics 144. Brookings.

Morgenstern, Richard D., Joseph E. Aldy, Evan M. Herrnstadt, Mun Ho, and William A. Pizer. 2007. *Competitiveness Impacts of Carbon Dioxide Pricing Policies on Manufacturing*. RFF issue Brief 7. Washington: Resources for the Future.

Morris, Michael G., and Edwin D. Hill. 2007. "Commentary: Trade in the Key to Climate Change." *Energy Daily*, February 20.

Orszag, Peter R. 2008. "Implications of a Cap-and-Trade Program for Carbon Dioxide Emissions, Testimony before the Senate Finance Committee," April 24 (www.cbo.gov/ftpdocs/91xx/doc9134/04-24-Cap_Trade_Teslimony.I.I.shtml [May 2008]).

Paltsev, Sergey V. 2001. "The Kyoto Protocol: Regional and Sectoral Contributions to the Carbon Leakage." *Energy Journal* 22, no. 4: 53–79.

Pauwelyn, Joost. 2007. *U.S. Federal Climate Policy and Competitiveness Concerns: The Limits and Options of International Trade Law*. Nicholas Institute for Environmental Policy Solutions Working Paper 0702. Durham, N.C.: Duke University.

Pew Center on Global Climate Change. 2008. "Response of the Pew Center on Global Climate Change to Climate Change Legislation Design White Paper: Competitiveness Concerns/Engaging Developing Countries"(www.pewclimate.org/docUploads/Pew%20Center%20on%t20Competitiveness-Developing%20Countries-FINAL.pdf [May 2008]).

Pew Research Center. 2008. "Obama's Image Slips, His Lead Over Clinton Disappears: Public Support for Free Trade Declines" (http://peoplepress.org/reports/display.php3?PageID=1295 [May 2008]).

Rosen, Daniel H., and Trevor Houser. 2007. *China Energy: A Guide for the Perplexed*. Washington: Center for Strategic and International Studies and Peterson Institute for International Economics.

Smith, Anne E., Martin T. Ross, and W. David Montgomery. 2002. *Implications for Trading Implementation Design for Equity-Efficiency Trade-Offs in Carbon Permit Allocations*. Washington: Charles River Associates.

Stern, Todd, and William Antholis. 2007. "A Changing Climate: The Road Ahead for the United States." *Washington Quarterly*, Winter 2007–8, 175–88.

Stiglitz, Joseph E. 2006a. *Making Globalization Work*. New York: W. W. Norton.

———. 2006b. "A New Agenda for Global Warming." *Economists' Voice* 3, no. 7, article 3.

Van den Bossche, Peter. 2005. *The law and Policy of the World Trade Organization*. New York: Cambridge University Press.

World Bank. 2008. *International Trade and Climate Change: Economic, Legal, and Institutional Perspectives*. Washington DC: World Bank.

World Resources Institute. 2008. "Climate Analysis Indicators Tool" (http://cait.wri.org [March 2009]).

PART III

MULTINATIONAL CORPORATIONS

Multinational corporations (MNCs) have always been highly controversial. MNCs are firms with production facilities in two or more countries. Corporations of this type have been part of the global economy from the early days of the British Empire, but the number of such firms operating in the global economy has grown rapidly during the last twenty-five years. Almost 80,000 MNCs are active today, up sharply from the 18,000 active in the late 1980s. MNCs spark controversy, in part, because they are very large actors that extend managerial control across national borders. MNCs, therefore, are vehicles through which foreign residents acquire the ability to make decisions about local resource use.

Chapter 7 examines the debate over whether MNCs create "sweatshops" in developing societies. The growth of MNC investment in manufacturing activities in developing societies has generated substantial concern about how MNCs treat workers in the factories they build. Such concern has focused on how much MNCs pay their developing-country workers and on the safety of the conditions in the factories. Paul Krugman argues that much of this concern is misplaced. The jobs that MNCs provide are better than the other jobs available to developing-country residents. Krugman suggests that trying to raise standards will merely reduce MNC investment in developing countries, thereby reducing the number of jobs created. John Miller counters Krugman. He argues that even if current MNC jobs are better than the alternatives, the jobs still can be made safer and be made to pay more. Doing so will not reduce investment by MNCs in developing countries.

Chapter 8 explores the impact of MNCs on national labor and environmental regulations. A concern commonly voiced is that MNCs will invest heavily in countries with lax regulatory standards and invest little in countries with more stringent regulations. Debora Spar and David Yoffie argue that the ability to invest where regulatory regimes are weakest creates a "race to the bottom" wherein governments relax regulations to attract investment. Daniel Drezner argues that fears of such dynamics are baseless. There is no evidence, he argues, that MNCs make decisions about where to invest based on regulatory regimes. Nor, he argues, is there evidence that governments relax standards to attract investment. Instead, he claims that the race to the bottom is merely a useful myth for proponents and opponents of globalization.

Chapter 9 focuses on a relatively new debate over sovereign wealth funds (SWFs). SWFs are not MNCs; they are state-owned investment funds. But SWFs raise many of the same concerns as MNCs. As Gal Luft argues, SWFs transfer control over domestic productive assets to foreigners. Moreover, foreign control rests in state hands and thus SWFs can be used to achieve political rather than economic objectives. Edwin Truman argues that concerns about SWFs becoming instruments for political influence are overstated. Instead, the dangers of SWFs rest in their relatively opaque decision-making process.

CHAPTER 7 SWEATSHOP REGULATION IS COUNTERPRODUCTIVE *v.* GOVERNMENTS MUST REGULATE SWEATSHOPS

Sweatshop Regulation Is Counterproductive

Advocate: Paul Krugman

Source: "In Praise of Cheap Labor: Bad Jobs at Bad Wages Are Better than No Jobs at All," *Slate,* March 27, 1997, http://www.slate.com/id/1918

Governments Must Regulate Sweatshops

Advocate: John Miller

Source: "Why Economists Are Wrong about Sweatshops and the Antisweatshop Movement," *Challenge* 46 (January/February 2003): 93–122

As Western multinational corporations (MNCs) move manufacturing production to developing countries, they face mounting criticism about working conditions in the factories they establish there. MNCs are often accused of running "sweatshops." Although there is disagreement about what constitutes a sweatshop, an acceptable definition might be a manufacturing facility that requires its workers to work long hours for low wages, often in unsafe conditions. Though we lack extensive and systematic research to determine the prevalence of such factories, considerable evidence documents such practices in the footwear, apparel, toys, and sporting goods industries. They seem also to be more common in locally owned firms than in MNC-owned subsidiaries.

The emergence of sweatshops in developing societies has generated substantial discussion and debate about whether and how governments should respond. Two questions are central. The first question is whether governments should create a set of global labor regulations to reduce the incidence of sweatshops. The question of whether regulations are necessary is tightly linked to the kind of regulation contemplated. Is it a matter of broad human rights principles, or should governments craft very specific rules that regulate wages and workplace practices? The second question is where to pursue such regulations. Should global labor standards remain the exclusive purview of the International Labor Organization (ILO), or should governments make labor standards an integral part of the World Trade Organization (WTO)?

SWEATSHOP REGULATION IS COUNTERPRODUCTIVE

Governments of developing countries are among the most vocal opponents of global labor standards. They oppose such regulation for two primary reasons. First, they argue that current wages and workplace conditions reflect their underlying comparative advantage in low-skill labor. Global standards that raise the cost of labor in developing societies, therefore, make it more difficult for developing countries to capitalize on their current comparative advantage. Moreover, governments of developing countries believe that Western efforts to bring labor standards into the WTO reflect protectionist orientations. As Martin Khor, the director of Third World Network, has argued, "developing countries fear that the objectives of the northern governments that back [global labor standards] are . . . to protect jobs in the North by reducing the low-cost incentive that attracts global corporations to developing societies."[1]

Paul Krugman develops this line of argument in detail. He suggests that rather than lamenting these factories, we should recognize that they represent a positive step on the path of economic development. Working in such factories may not be pleasant, and the wages may not be high by Western standards, but the jobs available in these factories are better than any of the available alternatives. Moreover, sweatshop conditions will gradually disappear as developing countries transition from low-skill, labor-intensive industries to higher-skill types of production. In this context, implementing standards via the WTO will be counterproductive.

GOVERNMENTS MUST REGULATE SWEATSHOPS

Northern labor unions have been among the greatest advocates of international labor regulation. They wish to expand global labor regulations beyond the four core standards currently embodied in the ILO's Declaration on the Fundamental Principles and Rights at Work. These core labor standards require governments to respect and promote principles and rights in four categories: freedom of association and collective bargaining, elimination of compulsory labor, elimination of child labor, and elimination of discrimination in the workplace. Many in the antisweatshop movement would like to expand these core standards to include minimum pay and workplace safety regulations. Advocates of regulation have also sought to make core labor standards an integral part of the WTO in order to compensate for the ILO's lack of enforcement capability. The WTO could enforce compliance through its dispute settlement mechanism. Governments would gain the right to suspend tariff concessions to countries that violated commonly agreed upon standards.

---

[1]Martin Khor, "How the South Is Getting a Raw Deal at the WTO," in *Views from the South: The Effects of Globalization and the WTO on the Third World*, ed. Sarah Anderson, 1–49 (San Francisco: International Forum on Globalization, 1999).

John Miller develops this proregulation perspective. He claims that available evidence does not suggest that global labor standards will reduce the number of manufacturing jobs available in developing countries. Nor does he believe that sweatshops will disappear as a natural consequence of development. Sweatshops will disappear, he argues, only if governments use regulation—national and international—to eliminate them.

POINTS **TO PONDER**

1. What economic concept underlies Krugman's assertion that sweatshop jobs should be seen as good rather than bad jobs?

2. What argument does Miller advance to counter Krugman? How do you think Krugman would respond?

3. How does Miller define the concept "living wage"? Is this a good definition? What are the arguments for and against an internationally regulated minimum wage using the living wage standard?

4. Should developing countries be required to have the same labor standards as advanced industrialized countries? Why or why not?

Paul Krugman

In Praise of Cheap Labor: Bad Jobs at Bad Wages Are Better than No Jobs at All

For many years a huge Manila garbage dump known as Smokey Mountain was a favorite media symbol of Third World poverty. Several thousand men, women, and children lived on that dump—enduring the stench, the flies, and the toxic waste in order to make a living combing the garbage for scrap metal and other recyclables. And they lived there voluntarily, because the $10 or so a squatter family could clear in a day was better than the alternatives.

The squatters are gone now, forcibly removed by Philippine police last year as a cosmetic move in advance of a Pacific Rim summit. But I found myself thinking about Smokey Mountain recently, after reading my latest batch of hate mail.

The occasion was an op-ed piece I had written for the *New York Times,* in which I had pointed out that while wages and working conditions in the new export industries of the Third World are appalling, they are a big improvement over the "previous, less visible rural poverty." I guess I should have expected that this comment would generate letters along the lines of, "Well, if you lose your comfortable position as an American professor you can always find another job—as long as you are 12 years old and willing to work for 40 cents an hour."

Such moral outrage is common among the opponents of globalization— of the transfer of technology and capital from high-wage to low-wage countries and the resulting growth of labor-intensive Third World exports. These critics take it as a given that anyone with a good word for this process is naive or corrupt and, in either case, a de facto agent of global capital in its oppression of workers here and abroad.

But matters are not that simple, and the moral lines are not that clear. In fact, let me make a counter-accusation: The lofty moral tone of the opponents of globalization is possible only because they have chosen not to think their position through. While fat-cat capitalists might benefit from globalization, the biggest beneficiaries are, yes, Third World workers.

After all, global poverty is not something recently invented for the benefit of multinational corporations. Let's turn the clock back to the Third World as it was only two decades ago (and still is, in many countries). In those days, although the rapid economic growth of a handful of small Asian nations had started to attract attention, developing countries like Indonesia or Bangladesh were still mainly what they had always been: exporters of raw materials, importers of manufactures. Inefficient manufacturing sectors served their domestic markets, sheltered behind import quotas, but generated few jobs. Meanwhile, population pressure pushed desperate peasants into cultivating ever more marginal land or seeking a livelihood in any way possible—such as homesteading on a mountain of garbage.

Given this lack of other opportunities, you could hire workers in Jakarta or Manila for a pittance. But in the mid-1970s, cheap labor was not enough to allow a developing country to compete in world markets for manufactured goods. The entrenched advantages of advanced nations—their infrastructure and technical know-how, the vastly larger size of their markets and their proximity to suppliers of key components, their political stability and the subtle-but-crucial social adaptations that are necessary to operate an efficient economy—seemed to outweigh even a tenfold or twentyfold disparity in wage rates.

And then something changed. Some combination of factors that we still don't fully understand—lower tariff barriers, improved telecommunications, cheaper air transport—reduced the disadvantages of producing in developing countries. (Other things being the same, it is still better to produce in the First World—stories of companies that moved production to Mexico or East Asia, then moved back after experiencing the disadvantages of the Third World environment, are common.) In a substantial number of industries, low wages allowed developing countries to break into world markets. And so countries that had previously made a living selling jute or coffee started producing shirts and sneakers instead.

Workers in those shirt and sneaker factories are, inevitably, paid very little and expected to endure terrible working conditions. I say "inevitably" because their employers are not in business for their (or their workers') health; they pay as little as possible, and that minimum is determined by the other opportunities available to workers. And these are still extremely poor countries, where living on a garbage heap is attractive compared with the alternatives.

And yet, wherever the new export industries have grown, there has been measurable improvement in the lives of ordinary people. Partly this is because a growing industry must offer a somewhat higher wage than workers could get elsewhere in order to get them to move. More importantly, however, the growth of manufacturing—and of the penumbra of other jobs that the new export sector creates—has a ripple effect throughout the economy. The pressure on the land becomes less intense, so rural wages rise; the pool of unemployed urban dwellers always anxious for work shrinks, so factories start to compete with each other for workers, and urban wages also begin to rise. Where the process has gone on long enough—say, in South Korea or Taiwan—average wages start to approach what an American teenager can earn at McDonald's. And eventually people are no longer eager to live on garbage dumps. (Smokey Mountain persisted because the Philippines, until recently, did not share in the export-led growth of its neighbors. Jobs that pay better than scavenging are still few and far between.)

The benefits of export-led economic growth to the mass of people in the newly industrializing economies are not a matter of conjecture. A country like Indonesia is still so poor that progress can be measured in terms of how much the average person gets to eat; since 1970, per capita intake has risen from less than 2,100 to more than 2,800 calories a day. A shocking one-third of young children are still malnourished—but in 1975, the fraction was more than half. Similar improvements can be seen throughout the Pacific Rim, and even in places like Bangladesh. These improvements have not taken place because well-meaning people in the West have done anything to help—foreign aid, never large, has lately shrunk to virtually nothing. Nor is it the result of the benign policies of national governments, which are as callous and corrupt as ever. It is the indirect and unintended result of the actions of soulless multinationals and rapacious local entrepreneurs, whose only concern was to take advantage of the profit opportunities offered by cheap labor. It is not an edifying spectacle; but no matter how base the motives of those involved, the result has been to move hundreds of millions of people from abject poverty to something still awful but nonetheless significantly better.

Why, then, the outrage of my correspondents? Why does the image of an Indonesian sewing sneakers for 60 cents an hour evoke so much more feeling than the image of another Indonesian earning the equivalent of 30 cents an hour trying to feed his family on a tiny plot of land—or of a Filipino scavenging on a garbage heap?

The main answer, I think, is a sort of fastidiousness. Unlike the starving subsistence farmer, the women and children in the sneaker factory are working at slave wages *for our benefit*—and this makes us feel unclean. And so there are self-righteous demands for international labor standards: We should not, the opponents of globalization insist, be willing to buy those sneakers and shirts unless the people who make them receive decent wages and work under decent conditions.

This sounds only fair—but is it? Let's think through the consequences.

First of all, even if we could assure the workers in Third World export industries of higher wages and better working conditions, this would do nothing for the peasants, day laborers, scavengers, and so on who make up the bulk of these countries' populations. At best, forcing developing countries to adhere to our labor standards would create a privileged labor aristocracy, leaving the poor majority no better off.

And it might not even do that. The advantages of established First World industries are still formidable. The only reason developing countries have been able to compete with those industries is their ability to offer employers cheap labor. Deny them that ability, and you might well deny them the prospect of continuing industrial growth, even reverse the growth that has been achieved. And since export-oriented growth, for all its injustice, has been a huge boon for the workers in those nations, anything that curtails that growth is very much against their interests. A policy of good jobs in principle, but no jobs in practice, might assuage our consciences, but it is no favor to its alleged beneficiaries.

You may say that the wretched of the earth should not be forced to serve as hewers of wood, drawers of water, and sewers of sneakers for the affluent. But what is the alternative? Should they be helped with foreign aid? Maybe—although the historical record of regions like southern Italy suggests that such aid has a tendency to promote perpetual dependence. Anyway, there isn't the slightest prospect of significant aid materializing. Should their own governments provide more social justice? Of course—but they won't, or at least not because we tell them to. And as long as you have no realistic alternative to industrialization based on low wages, to oppose it means that you are willing to deny desperately poor people the best chance they have of progress for the sake of what amounts to an aesthetic standard—that is, the fact that you don't like the idea of workers being paid a pittance to supply rich Westerners with fashion items.

In short, my correspondents are not entitled to their self-righteousness. They have not thought the matter through. And when the hopes of hundreds of millions are at stake, thinking things through is not just good intellectual practice. It is a moral duty.

John Miller

Why Economists Are Wrong about Sweatshops and the Antisweatshop Movement

The student-led antisweatshop movement that took hold on many college campuses during the late 1990s should have pleased economists. Studying the working conditions faced by factory workers across the globe offered powerful lessons about the workings of the world economy, the dimensions of world poverty, and most students' privileged position in that economy.

On top of that, these students were dedicated not just to explaining sweatshop conditions, but also to changing them. They wanted desperately to do something to put a stop to the brutalization and assaults on human dignity suffered by the women and men who made their jeans, t-shirts, or sneakers.[1] On many campuses, student activism succeeded in pressuring college administrators by demanding that clothing bearing their college logo not be made under sweatshop conditions, and, at best, that it be made by workers earning a living wage (Featherstone and United Students Against Sweatshops 2002). But most mainstream economists were not at all pleased. No, they did not dispute these tales from the factory floor, many of which had been confirmed in the business press (Roberts and Bernstein 2000) and by international agencies (ILO 2000). Rather, mainstream economists rushed to defend the positive role of low-wage factory jobs, the very kind we usually call sweatshops, in economic development and in alleviating poverty.

What is more, these economists were generally dismissive of the student-led antisweatshop movement. In Summer 2000, the Academic Consortium on International Trade (ACIT), a group of advocates of globalization and free trade made up mostly of economists, took it upon themselves to write directly to the presidents of universities and colleges (see www.spp.umich.edu/rsie/acit/). The ACIT letter warned presidents that antisweatshop protesters on college campuses were often ill informed and that adopting codes of conduct requiring multinational corporations to pay higher wages recommended by the protesters may cost workers in poor countries their jobs.

The response of mainstream economists to the antisweatshop movement was hardly surprising. Economists have a penchant for playing the contrarian, and, for the most part, they oppose interventions into market outcomes, even interventions into the labor markets of the developing world.

No matter how predictable, their response was profoundly disappointing. Although it contains elements of truth, what economists have to say about sweatshops misses the mark. . . . First, the propositions that mainstream economists rely on to defend sweatshops are misleading, rooted in an exchange perspective that obscures sweatshop oppression. Sweatshop oppression is not defined by labor market exchanges but by the characteristics of a job. Second, policy positions based on these propositions are equally flawed. Economists' claim that market-led economic development, independent of labor and social movements and government regulation, will put an end to sweatshop conditions distorts the historical record. Finally, their assertion that demands for better working conditions in the world-export factories will harm third-world workers and frustrate poverty alleviation is also suspect.

With that said, the challenge issued by mainstream economists to the antisweatshop movement remains a formidable one. What economists have to say about the sweatshops has considerable power in the way of persuasion and influence, the protestations of Bhagwati and the ACIT notwithstanding. Often it is their writings that are being distilled in what journalists, government officials, and the general public have to say about sweatshops.

Supporters of the antisweatshop movement, and instructors of sweatshop seminars, need to be able to answer each count of the economists' indictments of their movement with arguments that are equally persuasive.

Today a group of economists is dedicated to doing just that. In the fall of 2001, Scholars Against Sweatshop Labor (SASL) issued a response to the ACIT indictment of the antisweatshop movement (SASL 2001). Its lead author, economist Robert Pollin, made the case that "the anti-sweatshop movement is taking constructive steps toward improving living and working conditions for millions of poor people throughout the world."

Teaching about sweatshops also convinced me that supporters of the antisweatshop movement need to respond to the criticisms of mainstream economists with actions as well as words. We need to link antisweatshop campaigns for the betterment of the women and men who toil in the world-export factories with efforts to improve the lot of their brothers and sisters, who often work under even more oppressive conditions in the informal and agricultural sectors of the developing world.

Just Enforce the Law

What to do about sweatshops? That is not a difficult question for most mainstream economists to answer. Just enforce the law, they say (Weidenbaum 1999, 26–28). And avoid other "institutional interventions" that might impair a market-led development that will enhance productivity and thereby raise wages and improve working conditions (Irwin 2002, 214; Sengenberger 1994, 10). By law, they mean local labor law, not some labor standard that ill-informed protesters (or even the International Labor Organization, for that matter) would impose on multinational corporations and their subcontractors in developing economies.

No one in the antisweatshop movement would quarrel with the insistence that the law be obeyed. In fact, several U.S. antisweatshop groups define a sweatshop in legal terms. According to Feminists Against Sweatshops (2002), for instance, sweatshop operators are employers who violate two or more labor laws, from the prohibition of child labor, to health, safety, fire, and building codes and to forced overtime and the minimum wage.[2]

Effective enforcement of local labor law in the developing world, where labor legislation in many countries—on paper, at least—is quite extensive, would surely help to combat sweatshop abuse as well (Portes 1994, 163). For instance, *Made in China,* a report of the National Labor Committee, the leading U.S.-based antisweatshop group, found that subcontractors producing goods for U.S. corporations, including Wal-Mart and Nike, "routinely violate" Chinese labor law. In some of these factories, young women work as long as seventy hours a week and are paid just pennies an hour after pay deductions for board and room, clear violations of China's labor law (Kernaghan 2000). A three-month *Business Week* investigation of the Chun Si Enterprise Handbag Factory in southern China, which makes Kathie Lee Gifford handbags sold by Wal-Mart stores, confirmed that workers there confronted labor practices that included illegally collected fines, confiscated identity papers, and beatings (Roberts and Bernstein 2000).

But the limitations of this legal prescription for curing sweatshop abuse become obvious when we go to apply it to countries where local labor law, even on paper, does not measure up to the most minimal, internationally agreed-upon labor standards. Take the case of the high-performance economies of Southeast Asia, Indonesia, Malaysia, and Thailand. In those countries, several core labor conventions of the International Labour Organization (ILO) have gone unratified—including the right to organize. Minimum wages are well below the level necessary to lift a family of three above the poverty line, the usual definition of a living wage. And in those countries (as well as China), independent trade union activity is systematically and sometimes brutally suppressed.[3]

When labor law protections are limited and international labor conventions are neither ratified nor respected, then insisting "the law should be fully obeyed" will do little to prevent sweatshop abuse. In those cases, enforcing the law would seem to be a shaky foundation on which to build a strategy of alleviating sweatshop labor through improved market outcomes.[4]

A Defense of Sweatshops?

The defense of sweatshops offered up by mainstream economists turns on two elegantly simple and ideologically powerful propositions. The first is that workers freely choose to enter these jobs, and the second is that these sweatshop jobs are better than the alternative employments available to them in developing economies. Both propositions have a certain truth in them.

An Exchange Perspective

From the perspective of mainstream economics, every exchange, including the exchange between worker and boss, is freely entered into and only takes place because both parties are made better off. Hiring workers to fill the jobs in the world-export factories is no exception.

Of course, in some cases, workers do not freely enter into sweatshop employment even by the usual standards of wage labor. Sometimes workers are held captive. For example, a 1995 police raid of a fenced-in compound of seven apartments in El Monte, California, found a clandestine garment sweatshop where some seventy-two illegal Thai immigrants were held in virtual captivity as they sewed clothes for brand-name labels (Su 1997, 143). Other times, workers find themselves locked into walled factory compounds surrounded by barbed wire, sometimes required to work fifteen hours a day, seven days a week, subject to physical abuse, and, after fines and charges are deducted from their paycheck, left without the money necessary to repay exorbitant hiring fees. That was the case for the more than 50,000 young female immigrants from China, the Philippines, Bangladesh, and Thailand who were recently discovered in Saipan (part of the Commonwealth of the Northern Mariana Islands, a territory of the United States) working under these near-slavelike conditions as they produced clothing for major American distributors bearing the label "Made in the United States" (ILO 2000).

But in most cases, workers do choose these jobs, if hardly freely or without the coercion of economic necessity. Seen from the exchange perspective of mainstream economics, that choice alone demonstrates that these factory jobs are neither sweatshops nor exploitative.

Listen to how mainstream economists and their followers make this argument. In response to the National Labor Committee's exposé of conditions in the Honduran factories manufacturing Kathie Lee clothing for Wal-Mart, El Salvadoran economist Lucy Martinez-Mont assured us that "People choose to work in maquila shops of their own free will, because those are the best jobs available to them" (Martinez-Mont 1996, sec. A, p. 14). For economic journalist Nicholas Kristof (1998), the story of Mrs. Tratiwoon, an Indonesian woman, makes the same point. She sustains herself and her son by picking through a garbage dump outside of Jakarta in search of metal scraps to sell. She tells Kristof of her dreams for her three-year-old son as she works. "She wants him to grow up to work in a sweatshop."

Stories such as this one are powerful. The fact that many in the developing world are worse off than workers in the world-export factories is a point that economists supportive of the antisweatshop movement do not deny. For instance, a few years back, economist Arthur MacEwan . . . made much the same point. He observed that in a poor country like Indonesia, where women working in agriculture are paid wages one-fifth those of women working in manufacturing, sweatshops do not seem to have a hard time finding workers (MacEwan 1998). And the Scholars Against Sweatshop Labor statement (2001) admits that "even after allowing for the frequent low wages and poor working conditions in these jobs, they are still generally superior to 'informal' employment in, for example, much of agriculture or urban street vending."

This is not meant to suggest that these exchanges between employers and poor workers with few alternatives are in reality voluntary or that world-export factory jobs are not sweatshops or places of exploitation. Rather, as political philosopher Michael Waltzer argues, these exchanges should be seen as "trades of last resort" or "desperate" exchanges that need to be protected by labor legislation regulating such things as limits on hours, a wage floor, and guaranteed health and safety requirements (Rodrik 1997, 35).[5]

Prevailing Wages and Working Conditions

What mainstream economists say in defense of sweatshops is limited in other ways as well. For instance, an ACIT letter (2000) misstates the argument. The ACIT writes that multinational corporations "commonly pay their workers more on average in comparison to the prevailing market wage for similar workers employed elsewhere in the economy." But, as the SASL authors correctly point out, "While this is true, it does not speak to the situation in which most garments are produced throughout the world— which is by firms subcontracted by multinational corporations, not the [multinational corporations] themselves." The ACIT authors implicitly acknowledge as much, for in the next sentence they write that "in cases where subcontracting is involved, workers are generally paid no less than the prevailing market wage."[6]

The SASL statement also warns that the ACIT claim that subcontractors pay the prevailing market wage does not by itself make a persuasive case that the world-export factories we commonly call sweatshops are anything but that. The SASL authors (2001) emphasize that "the prevailing market wage is frequently extremely low for garment workers in less developed countries. In addition, the recent university-sponsored studies as well as an October 2000 report by the International Labor Organization consistently find that serious workplace abuses and violations of workers' rights are occurring in the garment industry throughout the world."

The same can be said about other world-export factories. Consider for a minute the working conditions at the Indonesian factories that produce footwear for Reebok, the Stoughton, Massachusetts–based international corporation that "goes to great lengths to portray itself as a conscientious promoter of human rights in the Third World" (Zuckoff 1994). Despite its status as a model employer, working conditions at factories that make Reebok footwear became the focus of the *Boston Globe* 1994 series entitled "Foul Trade" (Zuckoff 1994). The *Globe* tells the story of Yati, a young Indonesian woman in Tangerang, Indonesia. She works sewing bits of leather and lace for tennis shoes sold as Reeboks.

Yati sits at a sewing machine, which is one of sixty in her row. There are forty-six rows on the factory floor. For working sixty-three hours a week, Yati earns not quite $80 a month—just about the price of a pair of Reeboks in the United States. Her hourly pay is less than 32 cents per hour, which exceeds the minimum wage for her region of Indonesia. Yati lives in a nearby ten-by-twelve-foot shack with no furniture. She and her two roommates sleep on the mud and tile floor.

A factory like the one Yati works in is typically owned by an East Asian company. For instance, PT Tong Yang Indonesia, a South Korean–owned factory, pumped out 400,000 pairs of Reeboks a month in 1993. In return, Reebok paid its owner, Tan Chuan Cheng, $10.20 for each pair of shoes and then sold them for $60 or more in the United States. Most of Tan's payment went to purchase materials. Tan told the *Globe* that wages accounted for as little as $1.40 of the cost of a pair of shoes (Zuckoff 1994).[7]

A More Effective Response

As I taught my seminar on sweatshops, I settled on a more effective response to the mainstream economic argument. It is simply this: Their argument is irrelevant for determining if a factory is a sweatshop or if workers are exploited. Sweatshop conditions are defined by the characteristics of a job. If workers are denied the right to organize, suffer unsafe and abusive working conditions, are forced to work overtime, or are paid less than a living wage, then they work in a sweatshop, regardless of how they came to take their jobs or if the alternatives they face are worse yet.

A careful reading of what the mainstream exchange perspective suggests about sweatshop jobs is not they are "good news" for the world's poor but "less bad news" than the usual conditions of work in the agricultural and informal sectors. The oppressive conditions of the work in the world-export factories are not denied by their argument. For instance, ACIT leader Jagdish Bhagwati says sweatshop jobs are a "ticket to slightly less impoverishment" (Goldberg 2001, 30).

Confronting Critics of the Antisweatshop Movement

Still, none of the above speaks directly to the contention of mainstream economists that imposing "enlightened standards" advocated by the antisweatshop activists onto conditions for employment in the export factories of the developing world will immiserate the very workers the movement intends to help (ACIT 2000).

Core Labor Standards

To begin with, as labor economist Richard Freeman (1994, 80) writes, "Everyone, almost everyone is for *some* standards" (emphasis in the original). Surely that includes economists who would combat sweatshops by insisting that local labor law be respected. Even their position recognizes that the "voluntary" exchange of labor for wages must be delimited by rules, collectively determined and obeyed by all.

The relevant question is, What are those rules, and are any rules so basic that they should be applied universally, transcending the normal bounds of sovereignty? For the most part, economists, trained after all as economists and not as political philosophers, have little to say on this matter other than to caution that outside of the condemnation of slavery, there is no universal agreement about the appropriateness of labor standards even when it comes to bonded labor and child labor (Bhagwati 1995, 754; Brown 2001, 94; Irwin 2002, 216).

Nonetheless, other economists, even some critical of the antisweatshop movement, are favorably disposed toward international labor standards about safety and health, forced labor, and the right to organize. For instance, Alice Amsden, an economist who opposes establishing wage standards on developing economies, favors the imposition of other labor standards. "The issue," she says, "is not health and safety conditions, the right of workers to be treated like human beings—not to be murdered for organizing unions, for example. These rights are inviolate" (Amsden 1995). At times, even Jagdish Bhagwati has taken a similar position (Bhagwati 2002, 60).

The ILO, in its 1998 Declaration on Fundamental Principles at Work, took a similar position. The ILO held that each of its 175 members (even if they have not ratified the conventions in question) was obligated "to respect, to promote, and to realize" the fundamental rights of "freedom of association and the effective recognition of the right to collective bargaining, the elimination of all forms of forced or compulsory labor, the effective abolition of child labor and the elimination of discrimination in respect of employment and occupation" (2002a).

The empirical evidence of the effect of these core labor standards on economic development is ambiguous. For instance, the Organization for Economic Cooperation and Development (OECD) found that countries that strengthen these core labor standards "can increase economic growth and efficiency" (OECD 2000, 14). International trade economist Jai Mah, on the other hand, found that ratification of the ILO Conventions on freedom of association and on the right to nondiscrimination negatively affected the export performance of developing countries (Mah 1997, 781). And a study conducted by Dani Rodrik, another international trade economist, suggested that low core labor standards enhanced a country's comparative advantage in the production of labor-intensive goods but deterred rather than attracted direct foreign investment (Rodrik 1996, 59).

The Living Wage

Nevertheless, almost all mainstream economists draw the line at labor codes designed to boost wages as opposed to leaving the determination of wages to labor market outcomes. That surely goes for labor codes that call for the payment of a living wage, usually defined as a wage adequate to lift a worker and two dependents out of poverty. The ACIT worries that if multinational corporations are persuaded to increase their wages (and those of their subcontractors) "in response to what the ongoing studies by the anti-sweatshop movement may conclude are appropriate wage levels, the net result would be shifts in employments that will worsen the collective welfare of the very workers who are supposed to be helped" (2001). And ACIT leader Bhagwati dismisses the call for multinationals and their subcontractors to pay a living wage as so much first-world protectionism cloaked in the language of "social responsibility" (Bhagwati 2000, 11). As he sees it, students' demand that a "living wage" be paid in developing countries would dull the one competitive advantage enjoyed by these countries—cheap labor.

But, in practice, would a labor standard demanding that multinational corporations and their subcontractors boost their wages beyond the local minimum wage and toward a living wage be a jobs killer? On that point the ACIT letter is silent. . . .

Still, we can ask just how responsive are the hiring decisions of multinational corporations and their subcontractors to higher wages. There is real reason to believe that the right answer is: not very responsive.

Economists Robert Pollin, James Heintz, and Justine Burns recently looked more closely at this question (Pollin et al. 2001). They examined the impact that a 100 percent increase in the pay for apparel workers in Mexico and in the United States would have on costs relative to the retail price those garments sell for in the United States. Their preliminary findings are that doubling the pay of nonsupervisory workers would add just 50 cents to the production costs of a men's casual shirt sold for $32 in the United States, or just 1.6 percent of the retail price. And even if the wage increase were passed on to consumers, which seems likely because retailers in the U.S. garment industry enjoy substantial market power, Pollin et al. argue that the increase in price is well within the amount that recent surveys suggest U.S. consumers are willing to pay to purchase goods produced under "good" working conditions as opposed to sweatshop conditions. (See Elliot and Freeman [2000] for a detailed discussion of survey results.) More generally, using a sample of forty-five countries over the period 1992–1997, Pollin et al. found no statistically significant relationship between real wages and employment growth in the apparel industry. Their results suggest that the mainstream economists' claim that improving the quality of jobs in the world-export factories (by boosting wages) will reduce the number of jobs is not evident in the data (Pollin et al. 2001).

Even if this counterexample is not convincing, it is important to recall that the demand curve that defines the responsiveness of multinational corporations and their subcontractors to wage increases for factory workers is a theoretical device drawn while holding other economic circumstances constant, including public policy. In reality, those circumstances are neither fixed nor unalterable. In fact, to counteract any negative effect that higher wages might have on employment, the SASL statement calls for the adoption of new policies, which include "measures to expand the overall number of relatively high quality jobs; relief from excessive foreign debt payments; raising worker job satisfaction and productivity and the quality of goods they produce; and improving the capacity to bring final products to retail markets" (SASL 2001).

"Shifting the demand curve for labor outward," says economic sociologist Peter Evans (2002), "is almost the definition of economic development—making people more valuable relative to the commodities they need to live." This "high road" approach to development, adds Evans, has the additional benefit of augmenting the demand for the commodities that workers produce.

Historical Change and Social Improvement

A labor code that requires multinational corporations and their subcontractors to pay a living wage, provide safe and healthy working conditions, and allow workers to organize would be likely to have yet more profound effects on these developing economies. On this point, the antisweatshop activists and their critics agree. What they disagree about is whether these broader effects will be a help or hindrance to economic development and an improved standard of living in the developing world (Freeman 1992).

Mainstream critics argue that labor codes are likely to have widespread debilitating effects. The institutionalization of these labor standards proposed by activists, they argue, would derail a market-led development process (Irwin 2002, 214; Sengenberger 1994, 10–11).

As they see it, labor-intensive sweatshops are good starter jobs—the very jobs that successful developing economies and developed countries used as "stepping-stones" to an improved standard of living for their citizens. And in each case, these countries outgrew their "sweatshop phase" through market-led development that enhanced productivity, not through the interventions of an antisweatshop movement (Krugman 1994, 116).

These economists often use the Asian economies as examples of national economies that abandoned "sweatshop practices" as they grew. Their list includes Japan, which moved from poverty to wealth early in the twentieth century, and the tiger economies—South Korea, Hong Kong, Singapore, and Taiwan—which grew rapidly in the second half of the century to become middle-income countries (Irwin 2002; Krugman 1994; Krugman 1997; Lim 1990; Weidenbaum 1999). Paul Krugman (1997) allows that some tigers relied on foreign plant owners (e.g., Singapore) while others shunned them (e.g., South Korea). Nonetheless, he maintains that their first stage of development had one constant: "It's always sweatshops" (Meyerson 1997).

• • •

But these arguments distort the historical record and misrepresent how social improvement is brought about with economic development. First, the claim that developed economies passed through a sweatshop stage does not establish that sweatshops caused or contributed to the enhanced productivity that they say improved working conditions. Second, in the developed world, the sweatshop phase was not extinguished by market-led forces alone but when economic growth combined with the very kind of social action, or enlightened collective choice, that defenders of sweatshops find objectionable.

Even Nobel Prize–winning economist Simon Kuznets, whose work did much to inspire economists' faith in the moderating effects of capitalist development on inequality, would find the mainstream economists' story of market-led social progress questionable. Kuznets based his famous hypothesis—that after initially increasing, inequality will diminish with capitalist economic development—not on the operation of market forces alone, but on the combined effect of economic growth and social legislation.[8] For instance, in his famous 1955 *American Economic Review* article, Kuznets writes, "In democratic societies the growing political power of the urban lower-income groups led to a variety of protective and supporting legislation, much of it aimed to counteract the worst effects of rapid industrialization and urbanization and to support the claims of the broad masses for more adequate shares of the growing income of the country" (1955, 17). The labor codes called for by the antisweatshop movement would seem to be an example of the "protective and supporting legislation" that Kuznets says is key to spreading the benefits of economic growth more widely.

To be sure, labor standards in the absence of economic growth will be hard put to make workers better off. Economist Ajit Singh and Ann Zammit of the South Centre, an intergovernmental organization dedicated to promoting cooperation among developing countries, make exactly this point in their article opposing compulsory labor standards (Singh and Zammit 2000, 37). As they note, over the last few decades, wages in rapidly growing South Korea increased much more quickly than those in slowly growing India, even though India had much better labor standards in the 1950s than South Korea did.[9] . . .

Fastidiousness or Commodity Fetishism?

Mainstream economists have one last probing question for antisweatshop activists: Why factory workers? Krugman (1997) asks the question in a most pointed way: "Why does the image of an Indonesian sewing sneakers for 60 cents an hour evoke so much more feeling than the image of another Indonesian earning the equivalent of 30 cents an hour trying to feed his family on a tiny plot of land, or of a Filipino scavenging on a garbage heap?"

It is a good question. There are plenty of poor people in the world. Some 1.2 billion people, about one-fifth of the world population, had to make do on less than U.S. $1 a day in 1998 (World Bank 2001). The world's poor are disproportionately located in rural areas. Most scratch out their livelihood from subsistence agriculture or by plying petty trades, while others on the edge of urban centers work in the informal sector as street-hawkers or the like (Todaro 2000, 151). In addition, if sweat is the issue, journalist Kristof (1998) assures us that "this kind of work, hoeing the field or working in paddies, often involves more perspiration than factory work."

So why has the plight of these rural workers, who are often poorer and sweat more than workers in the world-export factories, not inspired a first-world movement dedicated to their betterment?

"Fastidiousness" is Krugman's answer. "Unlike the starving subsistence farmer," says Krugman, "the women and children in the sneaker factory are working at slave wages *for our benefit*—and this makes us feel unclean. And so there are self-righteous demands for international labor standards" (1997; emphasis in the original).

Ironically, Krugman's answer is not so different from the one Marx would have given to the question. Marx's answer would be commodity fetishism or that commodities become the bearers of social relations in a capitalist economy (Marx 1967). Purchasing commodities brings us in contact with the lives of the factory workers who manufacture them. Buying jeans, t-shirts, or sneakers made in Los Angeles, Bangkok, or Jakarta, or the export zones of southern China and Latin America, connected students in my seminar to the women and men who work long hours in unhealthy and dangerous conditions for little pay in the apparel and athletic footwear industries. And it was the lives of those workers that my most political students sought to improve through their antisweatshop activism. Beyond that, as consumers and citizens they are empowered to change the employment practices of U.S. corporations and their subcontractors.

Krugman's complaint is no reason to dismiss the concerns of the antisweatshop movement. Historically, the organization of factory workers has been one of the most powerful forces for changing politics in the democratic direction that Kuznets outlines. Krugman's complaint does, however, suggest that the plight of sweatshop workers needs to be seen in the context of pervasive world poverty and the gaping inequalities of the global economy.

The global economy, to the extent that we live in a truly unified marketplace, connects us not just with sweatshop workers, but with oppressed workers outside the factory gates as well. By pointing out these connections to my students, I hoped to demonstrate the need to build a movement that would demand more for working people across the multiple dimensions of the world economy. Campaigns to improve conditions in the world-export factories should, of course, be part of that movement. But that movement must also tackle the often worse conditions of low-wage agricultural workers, poor farmers, street vendors, domestic servants, small-shop textile workers, and prostitutes. Only when conditions for both groups of workers improve might economists be able to say honestly, as something other than a Faustian bargain, that more world-factory jobs are good news for the world's poor.

ENDNOTES

1. While men and women suffer sweatshop abuse, young women overwhelmingly constitute the workforce of the "world market factories" in the developing world (Elson and Pearson 1997, 191). Women workers have also been the focus of the antisweatshop movement. Female employment is generally high in the clothing industry and in export-processing zones. In 1995, women made up 74 percent of the global workforce in the clothing industry (ILO 2000, 26).

2. There is no universal agreement about the definition of a sweatshop in the antisweatshop movement. For instance, sociologists Roger Waldinger and Michael Lapp argue that sweatshop labor is a form of what the Organisation for Economic Cooperation and Development (OECD) calls "concealed employment," which escapes state regulation (Waldinger and Lapp 1993, 8–9). Their definition would cover the return of sweatshops to the United States. It also covers subcontractors of first-world multinational corporations who employ workers in the formal sector of the third world under lax regulatory standards, as well as the minuscule firms in informal sectors of the developing world that are not subject to regulation. Other sweatshop critics, such as labor economist Michael Piore, insist that the term "sweatshop" should be reserved for "a specific organization of work" characterized by "very low fixed costs" (Piore 1997, 136). In sweatshops, workers are usually paid by the piece. Other fixed costs—rent, electricity, heat—are held to a minimum by operating substandard, congested, unhealthy factories, typically overseen by a "sweater" or subcontractor (Piore 1997, 135). Still others use the term *sweatshop* as a vivid metaphor to describe lousy jobs ranging from bicycle messengers who work in "Sweatshops of the Streets" (Lipsyte 1995) to cruise workers who endure "Sweatshops at Sea" (Reynolds and Weikel 2000) to adjunct professors at colleges "who might as well be sweatshop workers" (Scarff 2000).

3. In the case of China, the ILO writes that "the existence of a single trade union linked to the Communist Party [the All-China Federation of Trade Unions] in itself says much about freedom of association in the country" (ILO 2000, 66).

The Organisation for Economic Cooperation and Development reports that in China "the right to strike is not recognized" (OECD 2000, 101). In Indonesia, several core ILO conventions remained unratified until June 1999, when then President J. B. Habibie faced a national election. The Suharto regime never signed ILO labor convention 87, which recognizes the right of workers to organize; convention 138, establishing a minimum age of employment; convention 105, outlawing forced labor; and convention 111, banning discrimination in employment (ILO 1998; ILO 1999a; ILO 1999b). Thailand's and Malaysia's records are similarly dismal. Thailand has failed to ratify both ILO conventions recognizing the right of workers to organize (conventions 87 and 98) and the minimum age convention 138. The right to strike is not recognized in Thailand's state enterprises, and authorities can prohibit strikes in the Thai private sector (OECD 2000, 104). Malaysia has not ratified ILO convention 87 and not only has failed to sign convention 105 calling for the abolition of forced labor but has condemned it (ILO 1998). And the right to strike in Malaysia is "severely limited" (OECD 2000, 106). According to a study of wages at Indonesian factories producing Nike footwear, the minimum wage for Jakarta in 1997 provided a family of three less than $1 per day for each family member, the United Nations' definition of extreme poverty (Benjamin 1998). The same study found that to meet the minimum physical needs of a woman working for Nike in the Indonesian area required $35 a month and that the usual wage paid by Nike subcontractors fell well below even that amount (Benjamin 1998). In Thailand, Bangkok's minimum wage, which kept pace with inflation during the 1990s boom, never extended to most of the 800,000 Thai garment workers, the great bulk of whom were employed by subcontractors (Pasuk and Baker 1998, 139–40).

4. These arguments also apply to countries in the developed world. For instance, the United States has failed to ratify six of the ILO's eight Fundamental Human Rights Conventions, covering freedom of association and collective bargaining, elimination of forced and compulsory labor, elimination of discrimination in respect to employment and occupation, and the abolition of child labor (ILO 2002b). Bhagwati rightly complains that discussions of international labor standards have focused on conditions in the developing world while remaining silent about "the much-documented quasi-slavery conditions for migrant labor in American agriculture in Georgia and Mississippi" (Bhagwati 2002, 71–72). He adds that a recent Human Rights Watch report, *Unfair Advantage,* documents how U.S. legal doctrine violates internationally recognized workers' rights to organize by allowing employers to permanently replace workers on strike and by banning secondary boycotts (Bhagwati 2002, 77). Bhagwati's complaint makes it clear that merely enforcing local labor law, even in the United States, is insufficient for combating abusive working conditions.

5. This sort of "asymmetric bargaining power," actually any sort of bargaining power, goes unrecognized in standard economic models (Stiglitz 2000).

6. When correctly stated, the limitations of the claim that working for these manufacturing subcontractors is better than the other opportunities available

to the sons and daughters of recyclers and other poor workers are evident in the writings of defenders of sweatshops. For instance, the writings of economist Linda Lim, an ACIT signatory who is dismissive of the efforts of the antisweatshop movement (which she describes as "patronizing white-man's-burden stuff"), convinced several students in my sweatshop seminar that women who work in the world's export factories are exploited (Featherstone and Henwood 2001). In her earlier work, Lim reports that in East Asia, "the wages earned by women in export factories are usually higher than what they could earn as wage laborers in alternative low-skilled female occupations" (Lim 1990, 109). But at the same time, the wages of women in the export industries are lower than the wages of men who work in those industries and lower than those of first-world women who work in the same industries. That is true, even though third-world women's productivity "is acknowledged to be higher than that of either of these other groups" (Lim 1997, 223). Even for Lim, that makes these women "the most heavily exploited group of workers relative both to their output and other groups" (Lim 1997, 223). Whatever Lim's work suggests about the relative attractiveness of these factory jobs, it went a long way toward convincing my students that these workplaces are sites of exploitation and properly described as sweatshops.

7. How is Yati likely to be faring today? Thanks in part to aggressive consumer campaigns in the United States, spearheaded by such groups as Global Exchange, campus organizations, and unions, Reebok commissioned an independent Indonesian firm to study conditions in factories that do business with Reebok. Murray Weidenbaum acted as a consultant for that report. One of the factories investigated was PT Tong Yang. According to the *London Guardian* (October 19, 1999), the fourteen-month study "found evidence of health and safety abuses, sexual discrimination, and communication problems. Safety notices were often handed out in English, for example." Other safety problems include "lack of labels for dangerous chemicals . . . and inadequate ventilation." According to the report, women face special problems, such as access to few toilets despite the fact that they represent 80 percent of the workforce, and under-representation among higher-ranking workers. In response, Tong Yang Indonesia introduced new machinery that used safer water-based solvents, installed a new ventilation system, and bought new chairs with backs that provided more support than the older ones. Despite those efforts, more basic problems remain. Wages still hover just above the inadequate Jakarta-area minimum wage, and workers continue to go without effective collective bargaining, denied the right to form independent unions (Bernstein 2000).

8. For a thoroughgoing analysis of the progressive underpinnings of Kuznets's article and its subversive implications for the neoliberal policy agenda, see the third chapter of Arthur MacEwan's *Neo-Liberalism or Democracy? Economic Strategy, Markets, and Alternatives for the 21st Century* (1999).

9. For these reasons, Singh and Zammit favor measures intended to promote more equitable and stable economic growth in the developing world, such as managed world trade and controls on international capital movements, instead of compulsory labor standards (Singh and Zammit 2000, 67).

REFERENCES

Academic Consortium on International Trade (ACIT). 2000. Letter to Presidents of Universities and Colleges, July 29 (www.spp.umich.edu/rsie/acit/).

Amsden, Alice. 1995. "International Labor Standards: Hype or Help?" *Boston Review* 20, no. 6 (bostonreview.mit.edu/BR20.6/amsden.html). . . .

Benjamin, Medea. 1998. San Francisco: Global Exchange (www.globalexchange .org).

Bernstein, Aaron. 2000. "A World of Sweatshops: Progress Is Slow in the Drive for Better Conditions." *Business Week*, November 6: 84.

Bhagwati, Jagdish. 1995. "Trade Liberalization and 'Fair Trade' Demands: Addressing the Environmental and Labour Standards Issues." *World Economy* 18, no. 6: 745–59. . . .

_____. 2000. "Nike Wrongfoots the Student Critics." *Financial Times*, May 2: 11.

_____. 2002. *Free Trade Today.* Princeton: Princeton University Press.

Brown, Drusilla K. 2001. "Labor Standards: Where Do They Belong on the International Trade Agenda?" *Journal of Economic Perspectives* 15, no. 3 (summer): 89–112. . . .

Elliot, K.A., and R.B. Freeman. 2000. "White Hats or Don Quixotes? Human Rights Vigilantes in the Global Economy." National Bureau of Economic Research Conference on Emerging Labor Market Institutions (www.nber .org/~confer/2000/si2000/elliot.pdf).

Elson, Diane, and Ruth Pearson. 1997. "The Subordination of Women and the Internationalization of Factory Production." In *The Women, Gender, and Development Reader*, ed. Naline Visvanathan et al., pp. 191–202. London: Zed Books.

Evans, Peter B. 2002. Personal communication, April. . . .

Featherstone, Liza, and Doug Henwood. 2001. "Clothes Encounters: Activists and Economists Clash Over Sweatshops." *Lingua Franca* 11, no. 2 (March): 26–33 (www.linguafranca.com).

Featherstone, Liza, and United Students Against Sweatshops. 2002. *Students Against Sweatshops.* New York: Verso.

Feminists Against Sweatshops. 2002. www.feminist.org/other/sweatshops.html. . . .

Freeman, Richard B. 1992. "Labour Market Institutions and Policies: Help or Hindrance to Economic Development?" In *Proceedings of the World Bank Annual Conference on Development Economics*, pp. 117–56. Washington, DC: World Bank.

_____. 1994. "A Hard-Headed Look at Labour Standards." In *International Labour Standards and Economic Interdependence*, ed. Werner Sengenberger and Duncan Campbell, pp. 79–92. Geneva: International Labor Organization (International Institute for Labor Studies).

Goldberg, Jonah. 2001. "Sweatshop Chic: The Know-Nothings Find a Cause." *National Review*, April 4 . . . .

International Labour Organization (ILO). 1998. *The Social Impact of the Asian Financial Crisis.* Bangkok, Thailand.

_____. 1999a. *Toward Full Employment: Prospects and Problems in Asia and the Pacific.* Bangkok, Thailand.

_____. 1999b. "Indonesia Ratifies Core ILO Conventions." Press release, June 7.

_____. 2000. *Labour Practices in the Footwear, Leather, Textiles and Clothing Industries.* Geneva: International Labor Organization.

_____. 2002a. Declaration on Fundamental Principles at Work.ilo.org/public/ english/standards/deci/declaration/index.htm.

_____. 2002b. Ratifications. ilolex. ilo. ch:1567/english/docs/declworld. htm.

Irwin, Douglas A. 2002. *Free Trade Under Fire.* Princeton: Princeton University Press.

Kernaghan, Charles. 2000. *Made in China: The Role of U.S. Companies in Denying Human and Worker Rights.* New York: National Labor Committee . . . .

Kristof, Nicholas. 1998. "Asia's Crisis Upsets Rising Effort to Confront Blight of Sweatshops." *New York Times,* June 15: sec. A, p. 1.

Krugman, Paul. 1994. "Does Third World Growth Hurt First World Prosperity?" *Harvard Business Review* (July–August): 113–21.

_____. 1997. "In Praise of Cheap Labor: Bad Jobs at Bad Wages Are Better Than No Jobs at All." *Slate,* March 27.

Kuznets, Simon. 1955. "Economic Growth and Income Inequality." *American Economic Review* 45, no. 1 (March): 1–28.

Lim, Linda. 1990. "Women's Work in Export Factories." In *Persistent Inequalities,* ed. Irene Tinker, pp. 101–19. New York: Oxford University Press.

_____. 1997. "Capitalism, Imperialism, and Patriarchy." In Visvanathan et al., ed., *The Women, Gender, and Development Reader,* pp. 216–29.

Lipsyte, Robert. 1995. "Voices from the 'Sweatshop of the Streets.' " *New York Times,* May 14: sec. A, p. 18.

MacEwan, Arthur. 1998. "Ask Dr. Dollar." *Dollars & Sense,* no. 219 (September/ October): 51.

_____. 1999. *Neo-Liberalism or Democracy? Economic Strategy, Markets, and Alternatives for the 21st Century.* London: Zed Books.

Mah, Jai S. 1997. "Core Labor Standards and Export Performance in Developing Countries." *World Economy* 20, no. 6 (September): 773–85.

Martinez-Mont, Lucy. 1996. "Sweatshops Are Better Than No Shops." *Wall Street Journal,* June 25: sec. A, p. 14.

Marx, Karl. 1967. *Capital.* Vol. 1. New York: International.

Meyerson, Allen R. 1997. "In Principle, a Case for More 'Sweatshops,' " *New York Times,* June 22: sec. 4, p. 5 . . . .

Organization for Economic Cooperation and Development (OECD). 2000. *International Trade and Core Labour Standards.* Paris: OECD.

Pasuk, Phongpaichit, and Chris Baker. 1998. *Thailand's Boom and Bust.* Chiang Mai, Thailand: Silkworm Books.

Piore, Michael. 1997. "The Economics of the Sweatshop." In Ross, ed., *No Sweat,* pp. 135–42.

Pollin, Robert, Justine Burns, and James Heintz. 2001. "Global Apparel Production and Sweatshop Labor: Can Raising Retail Prices Finance Living Wages?" Political Economy Research Institute, Working Paper series, no. 19.

Portes, Alejandro. 1994. "By-Passing the Rules: The Dialectics of Labour Standards and Informalization in Less Developed Countries." In Sengenberger and Campbell, ed., *International Labour Standards and Economic Interdependence,* pp. 159–76.

Reynolds, Christopher, and Dan Weikel. 2000. "For Cruise Ship Workers, Voyages Are No Vacations." *Los Angeles Times,* May 30: pt. A, p. A-1.

Roberts, Dexter, and Aaron Bernstein. 2000. "A Life of Fines and Beatings." *Business Week,* October 2: 122.

Rodrik, Dani. 1996. "Labor Standards in International Trade: Do They Matter and What Do We Do About Them?" In *Emerging Agenda for Global Trade: High Stakes for Developing Countries,* ed. Robert Z. Lawrence, Dani Rodrik, and John Walley, pp. 35–79. Washington, DC: Johns Hopkins University Press for the Overseas Development Council.

———. 1997. *Has Globalization Gone Too Far?* Washington, DC: Institute for International Economics . . . .

Ross, Robert. 2002. "The New Sweatshops in the United States: How New, How Real, How Many, Why?" In *Free Trade and Uneven Development: The North American Apparel Industry,* ed. Gary Gereffi, David Spencer, and Jenniter Blair, pp. 100–122. Philadelphia: Temple University Press.

Scarff, Michelle. 2000. "The Full-Time Stress of Part-Time Professors: For the Pittance They're Paid, Adjunct Profs at Our Colleges Might as Well Be Sweatshop Workers." *Newsweek,* May 15: 10.

Scholars Against Sweatshop Labor (SASL). 2001. October (www.umass.edu/peri/sasl/).

Sengenberger, Werner. 1994. "International Labour Standards in a Globalized Economy: The Issues." In Sengenberger and Campbell, ed., *International Labour Standards and Economic Interdependence,* pp. 3–16.

Singh, A., and A. Zammit. 2000. "The Global Labour Standards Controversy: Critical Issues for Developing Countries." Geneva: South Centre (www.southcentre.org/publicatons/labour/toc.htm).

Stiglitz, Joseph. 2000. "Democratic Development as the Fruits of Labor." Keynote address of the annual meetings of the Industrial Relations Research Association, Boston (available at www.globalpolicy.org/socecon/bwi-wto/wbank/stieg2.htm).

Su, Julie. 1997. "El Monte Thai Garment Workers: Slave Sweatshops." In Ross, ed., *No Sweat,* pp. 143–50 . . . .

Todaro, Michael. 2000. *Economic Development.* 7th ed. New York: Addison Wesley. . . .

Waldinger, Roger, and Michael Lapp. 1993. "Back to the Sweatshop or Ahead to the Informal Sector?" *International Journal of Urban and Regional Research* 17, no. 1: 6–29.

Weidenbaum, Murray. 1999. "A Defense of Sweatshops." In *Child Labor and Sweatshops,* ed. Mary Williams, pp. 26–28. San Diego: Greenhaven.

World Bank. 2001. *World Development Report 2000/2001.* New York: Oxford University Press.

Zuckoff, Mitchell. 1994. "Taking a Profit, and Inflicting a Cost." First part of a series titled "Foul Trade." *Boston Globe,* July 10: sec. A, p. 1.

CHAPTER 8 THE MULTINATIONAL CORPORATION RACE TO THE BOTTOM *v.* THE MYTH OF THE MULTINATIONAL CORPORATION RACE TO THE BOTTOM

The Multinational Corporation Race to the Bottom
Advocate: Debora Spar and David Yoffie

Source: "Multinational Enterprises and the Prospects for Justice," *Journal of International Affairs* 52 (Spring 1999): 557–81

The Myth of the Multinational Corporation Race to the Bottom
Advocate: Daniel W. Drezner

Source: "Bottom Feeders," *Foreign Policy*, November/December 2000: 64–70

The growth of multinational corporations (MNCs) prompts concerns about a "race-to-the-bottom" dynamic in government regulation. Governments maintain different regulatory standards. At a broad level, labor and environmental regulations tend to be more strict in advanced industrialized countries than in developing countries. Governments in advanced industrialized countries enact and enforce stringent regulations that tightly constrain how firms must treat workers, how they must handle toxic waste and other environmental pollutants, and other business activities. Governments in developing societies adopt less stringent regulations and have less capacity to enforce even these laws. These different regulatory frameworks affect firms' production costs. It is more expensive, for example, for a firm to treat hazardous waste than simply to dump it in a landfill. Differences in regulatory standards can make it cheaper to produce in a developing country than in an advanced industrialized country.

Not only might firms shift their operations to countries with lax regulations, but also governments in advanced industrialized countries might alter their regulatory standards. To prevent existing factories from moving offshore and to attract new investments from domestic and foreign firms, governments in high-standard countries might find it necessary to relax their labor and environmental regulations. Governments in developing countries might then respond by further relaxing their regulations, prompting governments in advanced industrialized countries to relax theirs still further. Competition between governments to maintain and attract investment will thus drive regulator frameworks down toward the lowest common denominator.

THE MULTINATIONAL CORPORATION RACE TO THE BOTTOM

Those who first enunciated the race-to-the-bottom hypothesis argued that it is the dominant characteristic of the contemporary global economy. The "global economy has allowed multinational companies to escape developed countries' hard-won labor standards. Today these companies choose between workers in developing countries that compete against each other to attract foreign investment. . . . Multinational companies have turned back the clock, transferring production to countries with labor conditions [like those in nineteenth-century America]."[1] Confident that footloose companies were forcing governments to compete to attract investment by relaxing regulatory standards, these same analysts called for governments to develop common global standards to end such races.

Deborah Spar and David Yoffie advance a much more sophisticated and substantially nuanced version of this argument. They posit that races to the bottom are a possible but hardly inevitable consequence of globalization. Whether firms engage in such races depends on a range of incentives that the authors classify into necessary and sufficient conditions. In addition, the authors suggest that government-led efforts to stem such races by crafting global regulatory regimes may be helpful and even necessary in some cases. But they also highlight how firms can craft private agreements that limit races to the bottom. Such efforts, be they government or firm led, produce what they call a "race to the top."

THE MYTH OF THE MULTINATIONAL CORPORATION RACE TO THE BOTTOM

Perhaps the greatest challenge confronting those who voice concerns about races to the bottom is the absence of compelling evidence that firms in fact relocate production in response to regulatory differences. That is, there doesn't seem to be much racing going on. Indeed, the effort by Spar and Yoffie to develop a more sophisticated framework to think about races to the bottom reflects this lack of convincing evidence of such races. And if multinational companies

---

[1]Terry Collingsworth, J. William Goold, and Pharis J. Harvey, "Time for a Global New Deal," *Foreign Affairs* 73 (January/February 1994): 8.

are not moving production to countries with lax regulatory regimes, advanced industrialized countries need not worry that competition for investment will force them to dismantle the regulatory structures created over the last fifty years. Consequently, elaborate global efforts to harmonize regulations internationally are simply not necessary.

Daniel Drezner argues this position forcefully. He asserts that there is no evidence to support the claim that firms move production to countries with lax regulatory standards. He suggests that the race-to-the-bottom logic has become popular because it enables groups with competing interests to advance their political agendas. Opponents of globalization use the race-to-the-bottom myth to attempt to block further market-based integration. Deregulating politicians embrace the myth to avoid bearing political responsibility for their deregulatory orientation. The myth persists not because it is true, but because it is useful.

POINTS **TO PONDER**

1. According to Spar and Yoffie, under what conditions are we most and least likely to see races to the bottom? What industries are most and least likely to meet these conditions?

2. Why does Drezner believe that the race to the bottom is a myth? Why does the argument retain favor even though it is a myth?

3. Do you believe that the global economy is characterized by races to the bottom? What evidence would you need to collect to confidently answer this question?

4. If we assume that races to the bottom do occur, must governments take steps to prevent them? What would happen if governments did nothing?

Debora Spar and David Yoffie

Multinational Enterprises and the Prospects for Justice

One of the defining features of the modern era is the spread of business enterprises across international borders. Markets once considered peripheral or exotic are now often viewed as integral to a firm's success, and a global corps of businesses has replaced the once-scattered legion of expatriate firms. As corporations increasingly define their markets to encompass wide swathes of the globe, cross-border flows of capital, technology, trade, and currencies have skyrocketed. Indeed, cross-border activities of multinational firms are an integral piece—perhaps the integral piece—of globalization. They are also, in some quarters at least, highly controversial.

One of the controversies centers on the impact of global mobility. According to some scholars, the corporate scramble for ever-wider markets has a dark side. In addition to creating economies of scale and enhancing efficiency, globalization may create a deleterious "race to the bottom," a downward spiral of rivalry that works to lower standards among all affected parties. As described by proponents of this view, the dynamic behind such races is straightforward and compelling. As corporations spread throughout the international economy, their constant search for competitive advantage drives down all those factors that the global players seek to minimize. Tax and labor rates are pushed down, and health and environmental regulation are kept to a bare minimum. In the process, crucial functions of governance effectively slip from the grasp of national governments, and corporations and capital markets reap what societies and workers lose. Since justice is hardly a central concern of the modern corporate enterprise, it presumably gets lost in the shuffle.

Does corporate expansion necessarily lead to such race-to-the-bottom behavior? Or are there situations in which multinational enterprises might actually contribute to the pursuit of international justice? Common wisdom would probably suggest that because corporations are motivated solely by the desire to maximize profits, it would be unrealistic to expect them to play any positive role in the pursuit of international justice. This paper seeks to unbundle such arguments and looks in greater detail at races to the bottom and their impact on affected nations. In particular, it seeks to examine when such races really do occur and when they do not; when corporate expansion is liable to drive global standards to rock-bottom lows; and when it can, paradoxically perhaps, actually enhance prospects for global governance and international justice. . . .

. . . This article proposes a series of hypotheses about the impact of corporate mobility on international standards and international governance. Specifically, we suggest that races to the bottom only occur when border controls are minimal and regulation and factor costs differ across national markets. Once these preconditions are met, races will most likely occur when products are relatively homogeneous, cross-border differentials are significant, and both sunk costs and transaction costs are minimal. Likewise, we suggest that "governance from the top" will be facilitated by the strong presence of externalities within a particular issue area, by a cascading process that affects several states (racing that occurs in steps), by the presence of cross-cutting and powerful domestic coalitions, and occasionally, by incentives for self-governance among the racing firms.

Taken together, these hypotheses imply a more nuanced combination of races to the bottom and governance from the top. They describe globalization as a complex process with no determinate outcome and few clear winners. Sometimes, the integration of capital flows and corporate structures can indeed produce a deleterious spiral and an erosion of governance mechanisms. Yet sometimes it can also culminate in increased governance and more stringent international standards. The challenge for both scholars and policymakers is to separate these effects and probe their disparate causes.

Global Races

In an influential 1994 *Foreign Affairs* article, Terry Collingsworth, J. William Goold, and Pharis J. Harvey laid forth a bleak logic of globalization. According to the authors, the advent of the global economy has enabled multinational companies to escape from developed countries' labor standards and to depress working conditions and wages around the world. As corporations have ventured abroad, they have encouraged a fierce rivalry among the developing countries that seek to win their investment capital. In the process of wooing multinationals, countries "compete against each other to depress wages."[1] As a result, "First World components are assembled by Third World workers who often have no choice but to work under any conditions offered them. Multinational companies have turned back the clock, transferring production to countries with labor conditions that resemble those in the early period of America's own industrialization."[2]. . .

More specific arguments focus on the impact of globalization on labor, suggesting that, in a bid to attract multinational investment, countries may race to the regulatory bottom, lowering wages and abandoning any labor protection they might have offered in the past. In the process, international economic justice is almost certainly compromised, as labor demands give way to corporate rivalry.[3] In the environmental realm, numerous studies have likewise suggested that international competition for investment will compel governments to create "pollution havens," lowering their environmental regulations far below socially desirable levels.[4] These havens will, in turn, lure multinational firms, causing them to flee from more stringent environments. The result of this migration will be more lax standards around the world, increased environmental degradation and a massive migration of jobs and capital from the industrialized states.

Though "justice" is not an explicit theme in this work, the implications in its direction are clear: as corporations race around the world, they weaken the ability of governments to address social issues. Concerns about income distribution, for example, will be muted by a desire to retain multinational investment, and demands for unionization or free association will fall prey to corporate preferences for low wages and docile labor pools. As a result, society at large is bound to suffer and justice will take a back seat to profits. This is the basic logic that connects globalization with race-to-the-bottom effects.

Empirically, evidence of races is more difficult to discern.[5] Indeed, most of the research done tends to dispute the race-to-the-bottom hypothesis, arguing that firms do not actually trawl around the global economy looking for lower labor standards or weaker environmental regimes.[6] Admittedly, finding empirical evidence of race-to-the-bottom effects is bound to be a difficult endeavor since so many variables and motives are involved. Firms choose locations for a wide variety of reasons: to expand markets, to be close to customers, to follow competitors, and to reduce factor and regulatory costs. In most instances, it will be difficult to discern from aggregate data which motives predominate and how important cost or regulatory reduction has been in prompting firms' overseas movements. . . .

Yet even if the empirical evidence is somewhat dismissive, races to the bottom remain a troubling element of the global economy. Theoretically, they are also quite plausible. Firms undeniably seek to increase profits and create a competitive advantage, and if moving to less expensive or less onerous locations would serve these aims, then it is only logical to expect them to do so. It is also reasonable to expect these cross-border movements to increase as globalization tears down old barriers to international flows of capital, people, and technology. If these movements occur, and if they force governments to restrict their own policy options, then the outcomes will be distinctly troubling. In short, even the possibility of race-to-the-bottom effects is important enough to demand continued attention and rigorous inquiry.

At the same time, though, such inquiries must also not lose sight of a parallel possibility. Sometimes it appears that the very same forces that lead to downward spirals can simultaneously produce pressures for higher standards and increased levels of international governance.[7] In other words, some races to the bottom have let loose a countervailing force: supranational regulation, either by governments or by the firms themselves. Rather than directly competing for multinational investment, countries can sometimes agree to common standards for the treatment of multinationals and protocols for taxation. Rather than using wage differentials to compete in the trading arena, national governments can negotiate agreements that regulate their trade and promote more just outcomes. In at least a few cases, governance from the top has mitigated races to the bottom.

In the discussion below, we try to separate out these two effects and the relationship between them. What factors lead, theoretically, to a race to the bottom, and what factors can transform this dynamic into governance from the top?

Racing to the Bottom

. . . A race to the bottom is the progressive movement of capital and technology from countries with relatively high levels of wages, taxation, and regulation to countries with relatively lower levels. . . . Under what conditions, and in what areas, is a race to the bottom most likely to occur? Logically, the answers seem to fall into two distinct tiers: necessary conditions and facilitating factors.

Necessary Conditions

The necessary conditions for races to the bottom are fairly obvious. The first is simply mobility. As with any race, races to the bottom depend critically on the participants' ability to move. Corporations can only launch a race to the bottom once they are free to move across national borders.[8] This essential assumption is evident in many more formal treatments of races.[9] Practically, it also implies that races to the bottom can occur only where border controls are minimal. As countries remove barriers to trade and, particularly, investment, they fire the starting gun that allows corporations to race abroad. . . .

. . . By itself, however, the freedom to move is not sufficient to launch a full-scale race. For a race to occur, corporations must also have some incentives to search for lower cost or more attractive locations: there must be lower taxes and/or lower wage costs in an overseas location, less-expensive inputs, and/or less-onerous regulations. If these factors are the same across borders, then there is little incentive for firms to race across them.[10] Firms race only when regulation and factor costs are heterogeneous—and when this heterogeneity leaves gaps that can be turned to the firms' competitive advantage.

At a minimum, racing to the bottom demands that two necessary conditions be met. Firms must be mobile and markets must be heterogeneous; there must either be differential factor costs or regulatory differences that affect product costs. Without these conditions, firms either will not be able to move across international borders or will have no incentive to do so.

Yet does the mere existence of these conditions ensure that such races will occur? Empirically, it seems not. As mentioned above, numerous studies have demonstrated that even when the conditions for racing are met, races do not necessarily occur.[11] Less formally, we can observe that races simply do not happen everywhere and in every industry. . . . Clearly, there are other factors at work.

Facilitating Factors

We hypothesize that four variables raise the incentives for races to occur: homogeneity of products, regulatory differentials, transaction costs, and sunk costs. While all four capture different elements of the interaction between firms and states in a global economy, we believe that races are more likely when multiple combinations of these variables are present.

Homogeneity of Products

The first variable is what we label as homogeneity of products. In some industries, firms compete across a wide range of dimensions. They may have sharply different products, marketing operations, or research foci. For these firms, marginal cost differentials are unlikely to be all that important to their competitive performance. Intel, for example, does not compete with other semiconductor manufacturers by shaving a few pennies off the price of its Pentium chip. Merck does not undercut its rivals through cut-throat pricing on cancer drugs. These firms still compete, and they still worry about relative cost structures, but they are probably not predisposed to race across the world in order to seize either a cost or a regulatory advantage.

By contrast, firms that manufacture homogeneous products will be more inclined to leap for any advantages that location hopping might bring. If firms produce essentially the same product, and if their internal cost structures are similar, they will feel obligated to compete more at the margin, seizing whatever relative advantage they can find. Thus, firms such as Sony and Matsushita, which produce television sets, may well be tempted to search for lower labor costs in their assembly plants; bulk chemical producers may look for regulatory gaps that help to reduce their relative costs. The more homogeneous the products in any industry, the more we would expect to see competition lured by races toward the bottom.

An interesting twist here concerns the homogeneity of products within a firm's production chain. In developed economies, many firms produce high-profile brand goods: Nike shoes or Izod shirts, for example. At the product level, these goods are not homogeneous. A customer may refuse, for example, to purchase anything but Air Jordan shoes. Yet if we separate the marketing and distribution of these brand goods from their production, homogeneity becomes relevant once more. Only here homogeneity exists at the level of the supplier. Nike and Izod, after all, essentially still produce homogeneous goods—sneakers and T-shirts—that are sourced and assembled by a range of virtually interchangeable suppliers. Nike, for example, purchases nearly all its footwear from relatively small suppliers scattered across Asia. From Nike's perspective, these suppliers are basically homogeneous. Nike can pick and choose among them, chasing whatever cost advantages a particular subcontractor might provide. Nike can then act as an oligopolist in its own market, and can pocket the profit differential that lower-cost suppliers can offer. This combination of oligopolistic industry structure at home combined with homogeneity of international suppliers sharply increases the incentives for Nike (and indeed any firm from the apparel or footwear industries) to pursue lower-cost suppliers—that is, to race toward the bottom. Thus, races can occur not only when final products are homogeneous, but also when the producers of non-homogeneous products can disaggregate their own supply chain and wring advantages from the homogeneous components they employ.

Regulatory Differentials

A second factor concerns the relative cost of regulatory differentials. . . . If factor and regulatory costs vary widely across borders, and if these costs are important to the affected firms, then firms will have an incentive to follow these costs to their lowest possible point. If the differences are small and/or unimportant, firms will generally be more content to remain where they are or base any relocation decisions on a range of other factors. Consider, for example, the impact of regulatory variation on firms from two very different industries: toys and paper. For the paper firm, environmental regulation is a critical component of doing business. Under certain circumstances, therefore, it may be in the paper firm's interest to search the globe for more lax regulatory regimes and to invest wherever environmental regulation is least stringent. In this case, a race to the bottom is likely to occur. For a toy producer, however, environmental regulation is generally not that important. If being in a more lax regulatory regime does not affect a firm's way of doing business—or if this effect is minimal—a firm is unlikely to race toward a more lax country, in which case no race to the bottom will ensue. This dynamic may help to explain why evidence of industrial flight to "pollution havens" is limited, despite the obvious logic behind such proposed flights. In most industries, it appears that the costs of complying with pollution control measures are simply not that high.[12]

Transaction Costs and Sunk Costs

The third and fourth factors relate to the economists' well-worn notion of stickiness. In most cases, empirical evidence indicates that firms do not move with the ease suggested by economic models. Changes in production costs do not instantaneously manifest themselves in price changes, wage increases do not create instant layoffs, and firms do not change suppliers or supply patterns to accord perfectly with their relative prices. Such stickiness is particularly relevant for investment decisions, since investment involves a considerable outlay of firm resources. In the race-to-the-bottom literature, there is an underlying sense that firms move at the speed of relative cost change: they hop across borders as soon as they perceive a financial advantage. Yet the stickiness of investment is bound to slow the pace of relocation. Most firms cannot switch plant locations at will as most will incur substantial costs from any move across borders. The higher these costs, the stickier existing investments will prove to be—and stickier investments will decrease the momentum for any race to the bottom.

In particular, we can imagine two kinds of stickiness that would affect firms' propensity to engage in a race to the bottom. The first is that which arises from sunk costs: the more expensive and capital-intensive an operation is, the less likely its parent firm will be to relocate.[13] The second comes from transaction costs: the more difficult and time-consuming a move will be, the less likely it is to occur. Both of these points are largely intuitive, yet they explain considerable differences in industry structure and incentives.

Consider again the gap that separates apparel firms from paper mills. An apparel firm is a highly labor-intensive venture, with only a limited amount of in-the-ground capital investment. It may lease a building or a few floors and own some machinery, the total cost of which can be as low as $100,000. Neither relocating its operations nor opening additional facilities in a new location is particularly daunting. The sunk costs are low and the stickiness of the investment is thus minimal. Similar characteristics would adhere to firms in the footwear industry and many low-technology assembly operations. A paper mill, by contrast, has much lower levels of labor intensity and correspondingly higher levels of capital intensity. Instead of housing primarily laborers and easily duplicated machinery, a paper plant (or a chemical processing plant or semiconductor fabrication facility) typically contains highly specific machinery and complex interlocked processes. Such plants can be moved; they can also be closed in one location and supplanted by newer facilities elsewhere. Yet the propensity for such changes is significantly lower than in the apparel industry, since the sunk costs of any particular plant are much greater. We should expect, therefore, that paper mills are less likely to race abroad than apparel firms. . . .

A similar logic adheres to the stickiness created by transaction costs. As the literature on institutional economics makes clear, not all costs borne by firms are explicitly financial. There are also invisible costs such as the costs of hiring and training new employees, suffering productivity losses after introducing new technologies, and building contacts and reputation. All of these costs will be present, and frequently heightened, as firms move to new locations. The higher these costs, the more reluctant firms should be to engage in race-to-the-bottom behavior.[14] . . .

Taken together, these hypotheses sketch a two-tiered view of races and an argument that industry structure matters. In any industry, races can occur only when two key necessary conditions are met: corporations must be free to move their capital and technology across borders, and government regulation and factor costs must be heterogeneous across those borders. Once these conditions are in place, though, industry variation comes into play, meaning that not all firms will be equally predisposed to chase each other toward the lowest common denominator. Firms will be most inclined to race when they produce homogeneous, commodity-type products; when the costs that matter most to them are sharply divergent across national borders; and when their sunk costs of investment and transaction costs of relocation are both relatively low. When these conditions are not in place, races to the bottom are less likely to occur.

Racing toward Justice?

Thus far, we have described only how races to the bottom might be fore-stalled by the internal dynamics of various industries. Yet, as mentioned at the outset, there exists another realm of possibilities: races, once launched, might be curtailed by the imposition of external standards. A race to the bottom, in other words, can be transformed into governance from the top.[15] In the process, the prospects for justice are bound to increase.

To imagine how this transformation might occur, consider the dynamics of the race. Essentially, regulatory and/or factor arbitrage facilitates a downward spiral. In the absence of high sunk or transaction costs, firms chase competitive advantage to the lowest possible point; they will move investment to whatever location will support their operations at the lowest cost. Countries can reinforce the game by depressing the cost of factors under their control (taxes, regulation, minimum wages) and watering down standards in order to compete for scarce capital.

What would slow the race down, then, is any constraint that either prevents the firm from seizing the arbitrage opportunity or prevents the state from creating it. Theoretically, such possibilities are relatively easy to imagine. Consider the situation from the firm's perspective. What drives the race here is rivalry and relative costs. Firms need to chase lower costs primarily to keep (or get) a cost advantage relative to their competitors. If everyone were to stop chasing, then no one would be at a particular disadvantage. It is precisely the dynamic that describes cartels, the dynamic captured in Rousseau's classic parable of the stag hunt.[16] If firms were to cooperate and hold to a common standard, the race would stop. The problem, though, is that firms are rarely able to form this kind of collective endeavor. Indeed, as we know, the record of cartels is dismally poor: most succumb early on to the pressures of competition and defection.[17]

Where national governments are concerned, however, the prospects are considerably brighter. As the vast literature on international organizations and regimes makes clear, it is eminently possible for governments not only to govern effectively at home, but also to establish governance structures that stretch across borders. . . .

We know . . . that, in numerous cases, governments have . . . agreed on common, higher standards; and they have achieved (varying) degrees of compliance with the rules they set. The GATT [General Agreement on Tariffs and Trade], the World Trade Organization, the Nuclear Nonproliferation Treaty and the European Union all . . . enforce common standards that collectively enhance their members' well-being while simultaneously denying these members the advantages of certain unilateral actions. Conceptually, there is no reason to suspect that the global playing field could not be similarly leveled with regard to multinational investment and corporate mobility.

More challenging, though, is to imagine the precise conditions under which this "race to the top" might emerge to regulate races to the bottom. As a first cut, we might expect that a necessary condition for any kind of international governance is the strong presence of externalities within a particular issue area. Realistically, governance efforts are likely to cluster where state borders are most porous. The more that events in one country affect outcomes or welfare in another, the greater the need for cross-border governance to address any problems that might arise. . . . States, in short, will be more inclined to pursue international governance when the effect of races to the bottom is to damage their own domestic economy. The greater the damage, the greater their incentive to stop the race.

A final point along these lines, though, is that state identity matters. While all states may have similar interests in stopping races or forging governance structures, not all states will be similarly equipped to address these issues. . . . It seems reasonable to assume that some states will be better positioned to create and enforce arrangements of international governance. States that are more powerful in the international arena simply will carry more clout in the formation of cross-border rules. They will be better able to set higher standards, abide by them, and persuade others to do likewise. They will also generally be better prepared to perform the duty of enforcer, punishing those who wander too far from the rules established at the international level.[18] . . .

A second hypothesis concerns what might be labeled "cascading." When races occur, they rarely sweep downward in a single motion. Rather, firms move through a series of steps: from their home country to a less-expensive, less-onerous foreign location; from that spot to an even more lax alternative; then on to the next contender; and so forth. This is the process by which the spiral is widened and accelerated. Governments are most likely to get involved only after the process has already moved down several of the early steps. If firms move only from their home market to an overseas facility, pressure for governance will be muted by the inherent ambiguities described earlier. The firms may have moved for a whole range of reasons, and the state is unlikely to get involved. If these same firms move on from destination to destination, then the pressure for governance is likely to mount. There are more states that feel the negative consequences of [the firms'] movement, and more evidence that the movement is being driven by a race-to-the-bottom rivalry. Critically, in order for international governance to succeed, multiple states must share a common interest in arresting the race at any particular point and preventing any further downward movement. We should therefore expect to see more concerted efforts at international governance as the race cascades beyond its initial stages. . . .

A third hypothesis brings domestic politics back into the . . . picture. . . . Domestic groups typically put international governance issues on the state's agenda. The Multifiber Arrangement is the end result of extensive lobbying by U.S. textile firms and (particularly) their labor unions; pressure for environmental regulation has for decades been the work of concerted activist groups such as Greenpeace and the Environmental Defense Fund, and pressure for international labor standards comes from human rights groups, as well as labor organizations.[19] When these domestic groups have already forged their own alliances at the international level, the political pressure is likely to be even more effective and the governance swifter. The more that domestic groups care about a particular issue, and the more powerful these groups are, the higher levels of international governance we should expect to see.

A final hypothesis returns us to . . . firms. While it is easy to paint firms as the malevolent drivers of these downward spirals, . . . firms could play some role in redirecting their races back toward the top—that is, toward global regulation and higher international standards. Under some circumstances, firms might choose to self-regulate, settling upon common standards rather than competing for relative advantage along these lines. Admittedly, these circumstances are bound to be rare. Given the collective action dilemma . . . , firms generally will be wary of defection and thus not eager to bind themselves to a set of prescribed rules. Nevertheless, in some cases rules may triumph over races. If firms suspect that formal international governance is imminent, then they may choose to self-regulate in the hopes of pre-empting a more onerous set of restrictions. Likewise, if the race is becoming too costly for all of the players, or even for a solid and powerful majority of them, then they may choose again to self-regulate and set a common floor below which none of the players will compete.

Cases of this sort are actually quite common, more common by far than the race-to-the-bottom literature would suggest. As early as 1981, for example, when pressure for environmental regulation was just beginning to spread around the world, the International Chamber of Commerce (a private business group) passed its own set of environmental guidelines supporting the harmonization of global pollution regulations. After the 1984 disaster in Bhopal, India, the U.S.-based Chemical Manufacturers Association (CMA) enacted a set of environmental guidelines known as "Responsible Care" that applied to all of the association's 180 member firms. Consisting of ten "guiding principles" and six management codes, Responsible Care specifies requirements for many different aspects of the chemicals business, from community awareness and emergency response to pollution control and employee health and safety. While the initiative was largely a response to negative public opinion within the United States, its effects have ranged far beyond national borders. By mandating that Responsible Care be extended to cover the numerous foreign manufacturing facilities of member firms, the CMA has successfully exported United States environmental standards to developing nations.[20] Similar guidelines were adopted subsequently by the European Chemical Industries Council (CEFIC).[21] More recently, major producers of chemicals and pesticides adopted a voluntary and apparently highly effective system to ensure that exports of these substances follow certain well-defined rules and procedures.[22]

In the area of human rights and labor standards, private initiatives are also playing an increasingly important role. In 1997, for example, both the World Federation of the Sporting Goods Industry and the U.S.-based Sporting Goods Manufacturers Association pledged to eradicate child labor in the Pakistani soccer ball industry. Spurred by Reebok, a U.S. firm that had been hard hit by accusations that it had purchased balls made by 12-year-old workers, all members of the private industry associations eventually agreed to establish a system of independent monitors to ensure that no children were involved in the production of soccer balls. The firms also joined forces in establishing schools and other programs for the former child workers.[23] Similarly, public pressure in the United States has recently led to the formation of a private Apparel Industry Partnership, under which firms such as Liz Claiborne and L.L. Bean have agreed to ensure that all of their suppliers comply with specific workplace codes of conduct.[24] In the rug industry, importers in both the United States and Germany have agreed to monitor the source of the products they sell, affixing a "Rugmark" label to those carpets that are guaranteed to have been made without the use of child labor.[25] At the most general level, a number of major multinationals such as Toys 'R' Us and Avon announced in the spring of 1998 that their suppliers will henceforth need to comply with the provisions of SA8000, a certifiable set of labor and human rights standards. Modeled on the International Organization for Standardization system for ensuring compliance with technical and environmental standards, SA8000 is an ambitious attempt to create private standards for social accountability.[26] Under this system, corporations voluntarily agree to adhere to a list of social standards; for example, provisions regarding the use of child labor, the right to collective bargaining, nondiscrimination and so forth. Independent auditors then visit the firms and their suppliers to ensure compliance with the SA8000 code. . . .

Clearly, any scheme for private corporate governance must be regarded with some degree of caution. None of these arrangements have any formal structure around them, and all lack stringent enforcement mechanisms. They can all easily disintegrate into public relations efforts and will always bear the stigma of this possibility. Yet private corporate arrangements also have a number of advantages. They appear easier to forge than governmental structures, since the negotiation process involves fewer parties and does not have the same measure of public accountability as would a governmental initiative.[27] According to some evidence, they also actually have higher rates of compliance over a harder range of issues.[28]

Finally, from the firms' perspective, self-regulation can be an effective means of restoring or enhancing profitability. If racing becomes too costly, or if firms fear that governments are prepared to impose collective regulation upon them, then self-regulation can make sense. By leveling the playing field, firms can solve the collective action dilemma that binds them all. They can also use harmonized policies to shift the cost of compliance from producers to consumers: if all producers are held to the same standard, then the world price of their goods is likely to rise. Finally, if firms are already adhering to their own cross-national standards (a common practice for many firms from industrialized countries), then encouraging other firms to agree to these same standards can convey a significant advantage. As one American CEO recently commented in response to a U.S. proposal to include environmental standards in trade legislation: "We already have environmental standards . . . we want a level playing field."[29] Cooperation under these circumstances can prove a powerful competitive weapon.

Firms, States, and the Pursuit of Justice

Drawing a connection between multinational enterprises and international justice is no easy task. As stated at the outset, corporations are not designed as emissaries of justice. . . . Corporations can exploit host countries and peoples; they can capitalize on whatever advantages a location offers to them; and they can chase each other round the globe in a downward spiraling search for more lax regulations and lower costs. Yet they also can eschew all of these activities—not because they find them unsavory, but because it may be in their own best interest to do so. Under some circumstances, corporations may even act to raise global standards. Working either through national governments or private associations, corporations may cooperate to enact tougher environmental standards, bans on child labor, and tighter health and safety regulations. . . .

As a policy issue, of course, the key question is "how?" How can governments prod multinational firms into a race to the top rather than the bottom? How can they compel multinationals to work toward justice rather than against it? . . . The dilemma for government policy is that races to the bottom are largely driven by factors inherent in industry structure. Some industries—footwear, apparel, and toys, for example—are more likely to engage in this type of behavior than others. If countries explicitly woo these industries, then they should expect, eventually, that they will either be outbid by countries offering even more attractive terms, or that they will progressively have to lower their own standards in order to compete. Not surprisingly, it is also these industries that have witnessed some of the greatest allegations of labor abuse and unjust practices. If countries truly want to end corporate racing (and this, after all, remains an open question), they would be wise to promote investment in other spheres and to resist the temptation of using competitive deregulation as a sustainable policy tool.

Finally, if the arguments laid forth in this paper are correct, then multinationals may hold the most powerful key to their own regulation. To forestall racing to the bottom and enhance the prospects for corporate self-governance, states may want to facilitate a process in which multinationals forge their own common standards. They may wish, for example, to host or encourage intra-industry negotiations, perhaps even conducting these negotiations under governmental auspices. Such has been the case with the U.S. Apparel Industry Partnership, which was launched by (though not controlled by) the U.S. Department of Labor. Governments may also want to keep regulation as an ever-ready possibility, since a concern for impending formal regulation seems often to coalesce industry interest in informal self-regulation. . . .

Ultimately, it is unrealistic to expect that corporations will be leaders in the pursuit of international economic justice. Yet corporations are neither an impediment to justice nor an irrelevant instrument in its pursuit. Under certain conditions and with the prodding of concerned voices in both the public and private arenas, multinational enterprises may be surprisingly forceful means for pushing global standards to a higher, and more just, plateau.

ENDNOTES

1. . . . Terry Collingsworth, J. William Goold and Pharis J. Harvey, "Labor and Free Trade: Time for a Global New Deal," *Foreign Affairs*, 73, no. 1 (January/February 1994) p. 9.

2. Ibid. . . .

3. See Dani Rodrik, *Labour Standards and International Trade: Moving Beyond the Rhetoric* (Washington, DC: Institute for International Economics, 1995);

Ethan B. Kapstein, "Workers and the World Economy," *Foreign Affairs*, 75, no. 3 (May/June 1996) pp. 16–37; Adrian Wood, *North–South Trade, Employment and Inequality: Changing Fortunes in a Skill-Driven World* (New York: Oxford University Press, 1994); Richard B. Du Boff, "Globalization and Wages: The Down Escalator," *Dollars and Sense*, no. 213 (September/October 1997) pp. 36–40; and Werner Sengenberger, "Local Development and International Economic Competition," *International Labour Review*, 132, no. 3 (1993) pp. 313–329.

4. Eric Bond and Larry Samuelson, "Strategic Behavior and Rules for International Taxation of Capital," *Economic Journal*, 99, no. 398 (December 1989) pp. 1099–1111; Herman E. Daly, "The Perils of Free Trade," *Scientific American*, 269, no. 5 (November 1993) pp. 24–29. See also Arik Levinson, "Environmental Regulations and Industry Location: International and Domestic Evidence," in *Fair Trade and Harmonization: Prerequisites for Free Trade*, ed. Jagdish Bhagwati and Robert E. Hudec (Cambridge: The MIT Press, 1996) pp. 429–457; and H. Jeffrey Leonard, *Pollution and The Struggle for World Product* (Cambridge: Cambridge University Press, 1988).

5. See Eddy Lee, "Globalization and Labour Standards: A Review of Issues," *International Labour Review*, 136, no. 2 (Summer 1997) pp. 173–189; Maureen Cropper and Wallace Oates, "Environmental Economics: A Survey," *Journal of Economic Literature*, 30, no. 2 (June 1992) pp. 675–740; and Charles S. Pearson, "Environmental Standards, Industrial Relocation, and Pollution Havens," in *Multinational Corporations, Environment, and the Third World: Business Matters*, ed. Charles S. Pearson (Durham, NC: Duke University Press, 1987) pp. 113–128.

6. See Cletis Coughlin, Joseph V. Terza and Vachira Arromdee, "State Characteristics and the Location of Foreign Direct Investment Within the United States," *Review of Economics and Statistics*, 73, no. 4 (November 1991) pp. 675–683; Timothy J. Bartik, "Business Location Decisions in the United States: Estimates of the Effects of Unionization, Taxes, and Other Characteristics of States," *Journal of Business and Economic Statistics*, 3, no. I (January 1985) pp. 14–22; Richard B. Freeman, "Comments," in *Labor Markets and Integrating National Economies*, ed. Ronald G. Ehrenberg (Washington, DC: The Brookings Institution, 1994) pp. 107–110; G. Knogden, "Environment and Industrial Siting," *Zeitschrift fur Umweltpolitik* (December 1979); and Gene M. Grossman and Alan B. Krueger, "Environmental Impacts of a North American Free Trade Agreement," Woodrow Wilson School Discussion Papers in Economics, no. 158 (November 1991).

7. David Vogel, *Trading Up: Consumer and Environmental Regulation in a Global Economy* (Cambridge: Harvard University Press, 1995).

8. For a discussion of mobility and its dangers, see Daly, pp. 24–29.

9. William A. Fischel, "Fiscal and Environmental Considerations in the Location of Firms in Suburban Communities," in *Fiscal Zoning and Land Use Controls*, ed. Edwin S. Mills and Wallace Oates (Lexington, MA: DC Heath & Co., 1975) pp. 119–174; and Michelle J. White, "Firm Location in a Zoned Metropolitan Area," in Mills and Oates, eds., pp. 175–201. . . .

10. Except, perhaps, to service these markets with lower transportation costs.

11. Joseph Freidman, Daniel A. Gerlowski and Johnathan Silberman, "What Attracts Foreign Multinational Corporations? Evidence From Branch Plant Location in the United States," *Journal of Regional Science*, 32, no. 4 (November 1992) pp. 403–418.

12. H. David Robison, "Who Pays for Industrial Pollution Abatement?" *Review of Economics and Statistics*, 67, no. 4 (November 1985) pp. 702–706; Cropper and Oates, p. 698.

13. For a discussion of sunk costs in multinational investment, see David B. Yoffie, "From Comparative Advantage to Regulated Competition," in *Beyond Free Trade: Firms, Governments, and Global Competition*, ed. David B. Yoffie (Boston: Harvard Business School Press, 1993) pp. 1–25.

14. Robert Wade, "Globalization and Its Limits: Reports of the Death of the National Economy Are Greatly Exaggerated," in *National Diversity and Global Capitalism*, ed. Suzanne Berger and Ronald Dore (Ithaca, NY: Cornell University Press, 1996) pp. 80–81.

15. Or as Vogel puts it, the "Delaware effect" is replaced by the "California effect." Businesses relocate to Delaware due to its low corporate taxation rate, while California's stringent environmental regulations raise the standards of regulation across the country. Vogel, pp. 5–6.

16. For more on Rousseau's idea of the stag hunt, see R. Harrison Wagner, "The Theory of Games and the Problem of International Cooperation," *American Political Science Review*, 77, no. 2 (June 1993) pp. 330–346.

17. See Debora L. Spar, *The Cooperative Edge: The Internal Politics of International Cartels* (Ithaca, NY: Cornell University Press, 1994); and Jock A. Finlayson and Mark W. Zacher, *Managing International Markets: Developing Countries and the Commodity Trade Regime* (New York: Columbia University Press, 1988).

18. For more on this relationship, see James Alt, Randall Calvert and Brian D. Humes, "Reputation and Hegemonic Stability: A Game Theoretical Analysis," *American Political Science Review*, 82, no. 2 (June 1988) pp. 445–466; Spar (1994).

19. See Peter J. Spiro, "New Global Communities: Nongovernmental Organizations in International Decision-Making Institutions," *Washington Quarterly*, 18, no.1 (Winter 1995) pp. 45–56; and Lester M. Salamon, "The Rise of the Non-profit Sector," *Foreign Affairs*, 73, no. 4 (July/August 1994) pp. 109–122. For an argument that these concerns are linked solely to organized labor's disguised desire for protection, see International Labor Organization, *Extracts From Statements Made at the Ministerial Conference of the World Trade Organization*, Singapore: 9–13 December 1996 (Geneva: International Labor Organization, 1997).

20. Forest L. Reinhardt, "Business and the Environment," forthcoming manuscript (Boston: Harvard Business School Press, 1999) pp. 3–12.

21. M. Baram, "Multinational Corporations, Private Codes, and Technology Transfer for Sustainable Development," *Environmental Law*, 24 (1994) pp. 33–65.

22. David Victor, "The Operation and Effectiveness of the Montreal Protocol's Non-Compliance Procedure," in *The Implementation and Effectiveness of*

International Commitments: Theory and Practice, ed. David Victor, Kal Rustilia and Eugene B. Sholnikoff (Cambridge: MIT Press, 1998) pp. 137–176.

23. Steven Greenhouse, "Sporting Goods Concerns Agree to Combat Sale of Soccer Balls Made by Children," *New York Times*, 14 February 1997, p. A12.

24. Debora L. Spar, "The Spotlight and the Bottom Line," *Foreign Affairs*, 77, no. 2 (March/April 1998) pp. 7–12; and Michael Posner and Lynda Clarizio, "An Unprecedented Step in the Effort to End Sweatshops," *Human Rights*, 24, no. 4 (Fall 1997) p. 14.

25. Hugh Williamson, "Stamp of Approval," *Far Eastern Economic Review*, 158, no. 5 (2 February 1995) p. 26.

26. For more on the provisions of SA8000, see Pamela Sebastian, "A Special Background Report on Trends in Industry and Finance," *Wall Street Journal*, 16 July 1998, p. Al; and Aaron Bernstein, "Sweatshop Police," *Business Week* (20 October 1997) p. 39.

27. Richard Freeman also suggests that private standards are more market-friendly, since they essentially allow consumers to determine which standards they deem acceptable. See Richard Freeman, "A Hard-headed Look at Labor Standards," in *International Labour Standards and Economic Interdependence*, ed. Werner Sengenberger and Duncan Campbell (Geneva: International Institute for Labor Studies, 1994) pp. 79–92.

28. See Victor; for an opposing argument, see Baram, pp. 33–65.

29. W. Douglas Ellis Jr., CEO of Southern Mills, Inc., cited in Paul Magnusson, De'Ann Weimer and Nicole Harris, "Clinton's Trade Crusade," *Business Week* (8 June 1998) p. 35.

Daniel W. Drezner

Bottom Feeders

The "race to the bottom" in global labor and environmental standards has captivated journalists, politicians, and activists worldwide. Why does this myth persist? Because it is a useful scare tactic for multinational corporations and populist agitators peddling their policy wares.

The current debates over economic globalization have produced a seemingly simple and intuitive conclusion: Unfettered globalization triggers an unavoidable "race to the bottom" in labor and environmental standards around the world. The reduction of restrictions on trade and cross-border investment frees corporations to scour the globe for the country or region where they can earn the highest return. National policies such as strict labor laws or rigorous environmental protections lower profits by raising the costs of production. Multinational corporations will therefore engage in regulatory arbitrage, moving to countries with lax standards. Fearing a loss of their tax base, nation–states have little choice but to loosen their regulations to encourage foreign investment and avoid capital flight. The inevitable result: a Darwinian struggle for capital where all other values—including workers' rights and the environment—are sacrificed upon the altar of global commerce.

The fear of such a race to the bottom has helped forge an unlikely coalition of union leaders, environmentalists, and consumer groups; together, they have spearheaded significant public resistance to several recent international economic initiatives. These include the North American Free Trade Agreement (NAFTA), the abortive Multilateral Agreement on Investment (MAI), the 1999 World Trade Organization (WTO) talks in Seattle, China's admission into the WTO, and the African Growth and Opportunity Act that U.S. President Bill Clinton signed into law [in May 2000]. In each instance, protestors argued that unless globalization is reversed or at least slowed, a race to the bottom is inevitable.

At the opposite end of the political spectrum, the rhetoric and goals may differ, but the underlying imagery remains the same. Pro-market politicians and multinational corporations also cultivate the idea of an unstoppable global race—except they do so in order to advance environmental deregulation and "flexible" labor legislation that otherwise would become ensnared in fractious political debates. Multinational corporations argue that the pressures of the global marketplace force them to relocate or outsource their production to lower-cost facilities in poor nations.

The race-to-the-bottom hypothesis appears logical. But it is wrong. Indeed, the lack of supporting evidence is startling. Essayists usually mention an anecdote or two about firms moving from an advanced to a developing economy and then, depending on their political stripes, extrapolate visions of healthy international competition or impending environmental doom. However, there is no indication that the reduction of controls on trade and capital flows has forced a generalized downgrading in labor or environmental conditions. If anything, the opposite has occurred.

Given this dearth of evidence, why does the race to the bottom persist in policy debates? Because the image is politically useful for both pro- and anti-globalization forces. Unfortunately, by perpetuating the belief in a nonexistent threat, all sides contribute to a misunderstanding of both the effects of globalization and how governments in developing and advanced economies should—or should not—respond.

Running in Place

If economic globalization really does trigger a race to the bottom in regulatory standards, two trends should be evident. First, countries that are more open to trade and investment should have fewer and less demanding regulations affecting corporate production costs. Once barriers to trade and investment are lowered, the logic goes, nation–states must eliminate burdensome regulations or risk massive capital flight. Over time, therefore, more open economies should display lower labor and environmental standards. Second, multinational corporations should flock to countries with the lowest regulatory standards. The core of the race-to-the-bottom hypothesis is that profit-maximizing firms will locate to places where the production costs are relatively low. Since any regulatory standard presumably raises these costs, corporations will seek out countries with the weakest possible standards.

These predicted trends are, in fact, nonexistent. Consider labor standards. There is no real evidence that economic openness leads to the degradation of workers. In fact, some evidence suggests that openness actually improves worker standards. A comprehensive 1996 study by the Organisation for Economic Co-operation and Development (OECD) found that "successfully sustained trade reforms" were linked to improvements in core labor standards, defined as nondiscrimination in the workplace, the right to unionize, and the prohibition of forced labor and exploitative child labor. This linkage occurs because multinationals often pay higher-than-average wages in developing countries in order to recruit better workers. Moreover, since corporations have learned to work efficiently under rigorous regulatory standards in their home countries, they favor improving standards in their foreign production sites in order to gain a competitive advantage over local competitors, who are not accustomed to operating under such conditions. A recent World Bank survey of 3,800 workers in 12 Nike factories in Thailand

and Vietnam found that 72 percent of Thai workers were satisfied with their overall income levels, while a majority of Vietnamese workers preferred factory employment over lower-wage jobs in their country's agricultural sector.

The case of export processing zones (EPZs) in developing economies underscores the spuriousness of the race-to-the-bottom argument. EPZs are areas established in order to attract foreign investment. Typically, governments entice investors into EPZs with infrastructure investment and duty-free imports and exports. There are more than 850 [EPZs] worldwide, employing some 27 million workers; in some developing nations, like Mauritius, EPZs account for a majority of a country's exports. If there is a race to the bottom in labor standards, it should be particularly evident in EPZs.

There are a few countries, such as Bangladesh and Zimbabwe, that have attempted to preempt competitive pressures by exempting their EPZs from regulations covering labor standards. However, contrary to the race-to-the-bottom hypothesis, such policies have not compelled other countries to relax labor standards in their own EPZs. Indeed, several nations, including the Dominican Republic and the Philippines, actually reversed course in the mid-1990s and established labor standards in their EPZs when none previously existed. A 1998 International Labour Organization report found no evidence that countries with a strong trade-union presence suffered any loss of investment in their EPZs, while a 1997 World Bank study noted a strong positive correlation between higher occupational safety and health conditions and foreign investment in EPZs. Analysts also have found that wages in EPZs actually tend to exceed average wages elsewhere in the host country.

Similarly, openness to trade and investment does not lead to a race to the bottom in environmental conditions or regulations. Countries most open to outside investment—OECD nations—also have the most stringent environmental regulations. Even developing countries such as Malaysia, the Philippines, Thailand, Argentina, and Brazil have liberalized their foreign investment laws while simultaneously tightening environmental regulations. In Latin America, there is clear evidence that more protectionist countries, such as pre-NAFTA Mexico and Brazil under military rule, have been the biggest polluters. This finding is hardly surprising; the most protectionist economies in this century—the Warsaw Pact bloc—displayed the least concern for the environment. Privatization programs in these countries, which help attract foreign direct investment, have contributed to improved environmental performance as multinational corporations have transferred cleaner technologies from the developed world. In Brazil, for instance, the privatization of the petrochemicals sector in the early 1990s led to a greater acceptance of environmentally safe practices.

Race-to-the-bottom critics counter that stringent labor and environmental standards in developing economies are backed by purely nominal enforcement capabilities. Although it is difficult to quantify compliance and enforcement in developing economies, the emergence of watchdog groups—analogous to election observers and human rights organizations—that scrutinize the enforcement of national labor and environmental legislation is a positive development. The United States has recently pursued this strategy by bolstering the role of the International Labour Organization in monitoring core labor standards around the world. And even in the absence of uniform national enforcement, many multinational corporations have embraced self-monitoring programs for the environment—an effective complement to government regulations.

Perhaps most damaging to the race-to-the-bottom proponents, there is no evidence that corporations direct their investment to developing countries with lower labor or environmental standards. Indeed, the relationship between foreign direct investment (FDI) and labor standards is strongly positive. During the 1990s, an overwhelming majority of global FDI was directed toward advanced economies (which tend to have higher labor standards), not to poor nations. A similar story can be told with environmental standards. Comparing data on U.S. FDI in developed and developing countries reveals that pollution-intensive U.S. firms tend to invest in countries with stricter environmental standards.

Profit-maximizing corporations invest in countries with high labor and environmental standards not out of a sense of obligation, but for hard-nosed business reasons. Consumption has gone global along with production; many firms base their investment decisions not just on likely production costs but also on access to sizable markets. A 1994 survey by the U.S. Department of Commerce found that more than 60 percent of the production of U.S. corporate affiliates in developing countries was sold in the host country and less than 20 percent was exported back to the United States. In Mexico, which provides an ideal platform for reexporting to the United States, only 28 percent of production by U.S. affiliates made it back to the United States; more than two-thirds was marketed in Mexico. The great fear of the race-to-the-bottom crowd—that U.S. multinationals will locate production facilities in developing countries, exploit local resources, and reexport back to the United States—has not materialized. In fact, that type of activity characterizes less than 4 percent of total U.S. investment abroad. The oft-cited cases of garment facilities based in poor nations and geared to consumers in advanced economies are the exception, not the rule. This exception is largely due to the low capital investment and importance of labor costs in the textiles sector.

Since corporations invest overseas to tap into new, large markets, host countries actually wield considerable power. They can use that power to resist deregulatory pressures. Multinational corporations have invested large sums in China despite formidable regulatory hurdles, a blatant disregard for copyright laws, high levels of corruption, and strict requirements for technology transfers. The prospect of 1 billion consumers will cause that kind of behavior among chief executive officers. Mexico has enhanced its environmental protection efforts while trying to attract investment. The result? Foreign direct investment around Mexico City has exploded, while the air quality has actually improved.

Multinational firms are also well aware of the growing link between public opinion and profits. Increasingly, citizens care about the conditions under which their products are manufactured—an environmental or labor mishap can cripple a corporation's brand name. Thus, foreign investors in Costa Rican bananas or Asian lumber insist on higher standards than the local government in order to cater to environmentally savvy European consumers. And PepsiCo pulled out of Myanmar in 1997 because it did not want to be linked to that country's repressive regime. To be sure, some multinational corporations are hardly paragons of labor or environmental virtue, as the perilous labor conditions at Royal Dutch Shell and Chevron's operations in Nigeria make clear. But in general, corporations understand that it is smart business to stay in the good graces of their customers.

The lack of evidence for a race to the bottom is not surprising when put in historical perspective. In the late 19th century, there was an enormous increase in flows of capital, goods, and labor among countries in the Atlantic basin. On several dimensions, such as labor mobility and investment flows, the degree of market integration 100 years ago is much greater than today. Despite claims made at the time that these trends would lead to a world ruled by social Darwinism, the United States and Europe created national regulatory standards for consumer safety, labor, and the environment and developed regional institutions (including a predecessor to the European Central Bank) to cope with the vicissitudes of financial markets. Indeed, globalization does not eliminate the ability of sovereign states to make independent regulatory decisions. Nor does globalization render governments impervious to the preferences of their own citizens. Even authoritarian countries are not immune to public pressure; the beginning of the end of the Soviet bloc saw environmental protests against rising levels of pollution. Governments, particularly in democratic countries, must respond not only to domestic and foreign firms but also to the wishes of citizens·who prefer stricter regulatory standards.

The Scapegoat Factory

Of course, one can hardly dispute that developing countries often display deplorable environmental and labor standards and conditions, far below those in the world's advanced economies. But the evidence thus far indicates that globalization itself does not cause or aggravate this disparity. If anything, the opposite is true. So why do so many people seem to believe in a hypothesis that has yet to attract any evidence? Because the myth is politically convenient for all sides. Nongovernmental organizations (NGOs), corporations, politicians, and academics use the race to the bottom as an excuse to peddle their policy wares.

Opponents of globalization—including environmentalists, labor unions, and a multitude of NGOs—advance the myth of a race to the bottom to oppose further global market integration. The race to the bottom is a wonderful rallying tool for fundraising and coalition building and also serves as the perfect bogeyman, allowing these groups to use scare tactics derived from previous domestic policy campaigns against nuclear power and acid rain. Such strategies are consistent with a pattern of exaggerating dangers to capture the attention of the press and the public: Only by crying that the sky is falling can antiglobalization forces rouse complacent citizens. For example, Public Citizen, one of the most vocal NGOs on trade issues, has argued that steps toward economic liberalization will have devastating social effects. Its Web site notes that the Multilateral Agreement on Investment (MAI) would have "hasten[ed] the 'race to the bottom,' wherein countries are pressured to lower living standards and weaken regulatory regimes in an effort to attract needed investment capital." Whatever shortcomings the MAI may have displayed, it demanded discerning criticism, not knee-jerk attacks based on spurious reasoning.

The race to the bottom also provides a useful scapegoat for larger trends that adversely affect specific interest groups, such as labor unions. A recent statement by Philip Jennings, general secretary of the Geneva-based Union Network International, which represents more than 900 unions in 140 countries, provides an apt example. "Globalization is not working for working people," Jennings declared in July 2000. "It needs a human face." Similarly, union leaders in the United States have argued that globalization and the race to the bottom are responsible for the 30-year stagnation in the median real wages and the growing income inequality in the United States. Such simplistic views disregard other key factors—particularly advances in technology and the subsequent demand for high-skilled labor—affecting wage and employment levels. If, as race-to-the-bottom proponents suggest, U.S. workers are being replaced by their counterparts in developing economies, then the 2.6 million employees laid off by manufacturing multinationals in the United States over the past three decades were replaced with a mere 300,000 workers hired in developing nations over the same period. In other words, Third World laborers would have to be nearly nine times as productive as those in the United States—hardly a persuasive proposition. In fact, the U.S. labor force displays the highest productivity levels in the world.

The race-to-the-bottom myth also helps pro-globalization forces sell deregulatory policies that may result in short-term economic pain. But rather than take the responsibility of pushing for deregulation directly, advocates invoke globalization as an excuse. It does not matter whether one favors deregulation or not; globalization will punish those who fail to deregulate, so there is little choice in the matter. For example, Pacific Telesis (now part of SBC Communications) used globalization as an excuse for cutbacks and layoffs in its San Francisco offices and to lobby Washington for deregulation. Unocal has argued that because of the competitive pressures of globalization, it should not be forced by U.S. sanctions to pull out of Myanmar.

Politicians also exploit the need to compete in the global marketplace and the myth of a race to the bottom as excuses to support policies that would otherwise trigger fierce public debate. State governments in the United States have often claimed that widespread deregulation must occur in order to attract capital. Meanwhile, European politicians trotted out the specter of globalization to justify the Maastricht criteria, a series of stringent economic prerequisites for a European monetary union. It was a clever tactic; governments across the European Union were able to push through deregulation and painful spending cuts without an overwhelming electoral backlash.

Perhaps the most potent reason for deploying the race-to-the-bottom myth is the psychological effect it has on individuals. By depicting a world without choices, the race to the bottom taps into the primal fear of a loss of control. Governments and citizens appear powerless in a world dominated by faceless, passionless capital flows. This perceived lack of control prompts unease for the same reason that many people prefer driving a car to flying in an airplane even though the latter is safer: Even if driving is riskier, at least we are behind the steering wheel.

A Durable Myth

In his 1996 book *Jihad vs. McWorld*, Benjamin Barber warned that, by empowering owners of capital and disenfranchising voters, globalization would threaten democratic practices. Democracy may indeed be at risk, but not for the reasons Barber suggested. Globalization itself will not necessarily weaken democracy, but the rhetoric surrounding globalization may have that effect. If protestors persist in the indiscriminate trashing of multilateral institutions, they will only undermine the legitimacy of the mechanisms that democratic governments have established to deal with the very problems that concern them. And if enough leaders claim that globalization is an unstoppable trend demanding specific and formulaic policy responses, ordinary citizens will lose interest in a wide range of policy debates, believing their outcomes to be foregone conclusions determined by economic forces beyond their comprehension and control.

Can the race-to-the-bottom myth be debunked? In time, perhaps. As facts continue to contradict fiction, the claim will become untenable, much as the notion of Japan's global economic superiority died down by the mid-1990s. Ironically, some of the strongest voices speaking against the race-to-the-bottom myth emanate from the very developing countries that antiglobalization forces purport to defend. In a speech before the World Economic Forum in January 2000, Mexican President Ernesto Zedillo charged that antitrade activists wanted to save developing countries . . . from development. Even in Malaysia, where Prime Minister Mahathir Mohamad has become notorious for his diatribes against currency traders and global capitalism, the Federation of Malaysian Manufacturers recently stated that globalization and liberalization should be viewed "with an open mind and [in] an objective and rational manner." And economist Jagdish Bhagwati of Columbia University is spearheading the Academic Consortium on International Trade, a group of academic economists and lawyers arguing that the antisweatshop campaigns currently underway at several U.S. universities will only "worsen the collective welfare of the very workers in poor countries who are supposed to be helped."

Unfortunately, bad economics is often the cornerstone of good politics. The belief in a race to the bottom has helped cement an unwieldy coalition of interests and has enhanced the influence of antiglobalization activists both inside the corridors of power and in the mind of public opinion. Myths persist because they are useful; there is little incentive to abandon the race to the bottom now, even though there is no evidence to support it.

For those who wish to deepen the process of globalization, however, the implications are troubling. Historically, bouts of protectionism have occurred primarily during global economic downturns. But the rhetoric of a race to the bottom has gained adherents during a time of relative prosperity. If the current era has produced so many challenges for continued economic openness, what will happen when the economy hits the next speed bump? The image of a race to the bottom will likely endure in global policy debates well into the new century.

CHAPTER 9 SOVEREIGN WEALTH FUNDS THREATEN U.S. INTERESTS *v.* SOVEREIGN WEALTH FUNDS DO NOT THREATEN U.S. INTERESTS

Sovereign Wealth Funds Threaten U.S. Interests

Advocate: Gal Luft

Source: "Sovereign Wealth Funds, Oil, and the New World Economic Order," Testimony before the Committee on Foreign Affairs, U.S. House of Representatives, Washington, DC, May 21, 2008, http://foreignaffairs.house.gov/110/luf052108.htm

Sovereign Wealth Funds Do Not Threaten U.S. Interests

Advocate: Edwin M. Truman

Source: "The Rise of Sovereign Wealth Funds: Impacts on U.S. Foreign Policy and Economic Interests," Testimony before the Committee on Foreign Affairs, U.S. House of Representatives, Washington, DC, May 21, 2008, http://foreignaffairs.house. gov/110/tru052108.htm

Sovereign wealth funds (SWFs) have generated increasing public and political scrutiny in the United States and the European Union (EU). SWFs are government-owned funds that purchase private assets in foreign markets. More than twenty governments currently have SWFs, which together control approximately $3 trillion; projections suggest that they could grow to $10 trillion by 2012. The single largest fund, the United Arab Emirates' Abu Dhabi Investment Authority, controls approximately $875 billion. Norway's SWF, the second largest, controls just shy of $400 billion. Many SWFs are funded with revenues generated by state-owned oil companies. Others, such as the China Investment Corporation, are funded with foreign exchange reserves generated by persistent balance-of-payments surpluses.

The growth of SWFs has raised political concerns similar to those generated by multinational corporations (MNCs). First, through SWFs, concentrated foreign economic power gains some control over local productive assets. Thus, SWFs extend foreign control across national borders, just as MNCs do. Second, foreign control could be used to advance foreign interests rather than, and in some case at the expense of, local interests, again just as with MNCs. Thus, even though SWFs are distinct from MNCs, their activities raise concerns and generate policy debates quite similar to those sparked by MNCs. The issue of foreign control is heightened in the case of SWFs, however, because foreign governments rather than foreign firms control the investments.

SOVEREIGN WEALTH FUNDS THREATEN U.S. INTERESTS

Some analysts fear that SWFs pose novel risks to U.S. economic and security interests. The core fear is that governments will use their investments to pursue political rather than economic objectives. Government-controlled investment funds might select which firms to invest in with an eye toward their political rather than economic value. Governments might use their investments once acquired as leverage in pursuit of political objectives. The businesses that are affiliated with a foreign SWF might also exploit that connection to advance its economic interests. In short, once governments become involved, cross-border investments are much less likely to be undertaken for purely economic gain and much more likely to have political ramifications.

Gal Luft, the executive director of the Institute for the Analysis of Global Security, expresses these concerns in his testimony to the U.S. House of Representatives Committee on Foreign Affairs. Governments may use their SWFs to enhance their geopolitical influence and to advance anti-Western ideologies. Luft finds particularly worrying the fact that many of the largest SWFs are owned by Persian Gulf states. Although Luft recognizes that none of the threats he lists have yet materialized, he argues that they are likely to materialize in the future as SWFs continue to grow.

SOVEREIGN WEALTH FUNDS DO NOT THREATEN U.S. INTERESTS

Other observers believe that SWFs pose no threat to U.S. interests. But even these more sanguine observers do raise concerns about SWFs' impact on financial markets. Many of these concerns reflect the lack of transparency in SWF operations and the absence of a common regulatory framework. Few SWFs are open about the strategies that motivate their investment decisions or about the assets they own. As they grow in size, their investment decisions will increasingly affect markets. In the absence of better information about what they own and what motivates their purchases, other market participants will wind up guessing. Such dynamics could give rise to disruptive and potentially destabilizing trading activity.

Edwin Truman, a senior fellow at the Peterson Institute, advances this argument. He asserts that SWFs do not pose a substantial threat to American interests but do raise a set of issues that require governmental responses. The central area for concern is the lack of transparency in SWF activities in conjunction with their growing importance in the global economy. The appropriate government response, Truman argues, includes efforts to promote a code of conduct that increases transparency within SWF operations.

POINTS **TO PONDER**

1. In what ways are the issues raised by SWFs and MNCs similar and in what ways are they different?

2. Do you believe that SWFs are likely to emerge as significant security threats in the future? Would the remedies that Truman proposes help reduce the likelihood of this eventuality?

3. Luft distinguishes between the behavior of the Norwegian SWF and that of a Persian Gulf state SWF. Do you agree that Norway's SWF constitutes a lower threat than a Persian Gulf SWF? Why or why not?

4. Which of Truman's proposals do you think the U.S. government should enact?

Gal Luft

Sovereign Wealth Funds, Oil, and the New World Economic Order

Mr. Chairman, members of the Committee, less than a decade ago Washington was consumed by a debate on what would be the best policy to absorb the then multibillion dollar federal surplus. Reductions in outstanding debt, tax cuts, and spending increases were the most touted solutions. The least popular policy was for the government to invest the accumulated excess balances in private-sector financial markets. Former Office of Management and Budget (OMB) Director Alice Rivlin wrote in 1992, "No good would come of making the government a big shareholder in private companies or the principal owner of state and local bonds." [Federal Reserve] Chairman Alan Greenspan said in a 1999 testimony that federal investment in the private sector "would arguably put at risk the efficiency of our capital markets and thus our economy." Two years later, on January 25, 2001, he underscored this point at a Senate Budget Committee hearing: "The federal government should eschew private asset accumulation because it would be exceptionally difficult to insulate the government's investment decisions from political pressures. Thus, over time, having the federal government hold significant amounts of private assets would risk suboptimal performance by our capital markets, diminished economic efficiency, and lower overall standards of living than would be achieved otherwise." These words are worth remembering today as we are again facing a similar dilemma about what to do with government surpluses, just that this time it is not our own government's surplus that knocks on the door of our financial system but that of some of the world's least democratic, least transparent, and least friendly governments.

The rise of sovereign wealth funds (SWFs) as new power brokers in the world economy should not be looked at as a singular phenomenon but rather as part of what can be defined [as] a new economic world order. This new order has been enabled by several mega-trends [that] operate in a self-reinforcing manner, among them the meteoric rise of developing Asia, accelerated globalization, the rapid flow of information, and the sharp increase in the price of oil by a delta of over $100 per barrel in just six years which has enabled Russia and OPEC [Organization of Petroleum Exporting Countries] members to accumulate unprecedented wealth and elevate themselves to the position of supreme economic powers. Oil-rich countries of OPEC and Russia have more than quadrupled their revenues, raking in some $1.2 trillion in revenues last year alone. At $125-a-barrel oil they are expected to earn close to $2 trillion dollars in 2008.

The resulting transfer of wealth from consumers to exporters has already caused the following macroeconomic trends:

1. **Regressive tax on the world economy.** As a result [of] the rise in oil prices consuming countries face economic dislocations such as swollen trade deficits, loss of jobs, sluggish economic growth, inflation, and if prices continue to soar, inevitable recessions. The impact on developing countries, many of which still carry debts from the previous oil shocks of the 1970s, is the most severe. Three-digit oil will undoubtedly slow down their economic growth and exacerbate existing social illnesses; it would also make them economically and politically dependent on some of the world's most nasty petro-regimes.

2. **Change in the direction of the flow of capital.** Historically the flow of capital has always been from industrialized countries to the developing ones. The rise in oil prices coupled with growing dependence on oil and other commodities by the industrialized world [has] reversed this course, and today it is the developing world [that] feeds the industrialized world with capital.

3. **Change in ownership patterns.** During the post–Cold War era, there has been a decline in direct state ownership of business and a significant strengthening of the private sector. Throughout the world private businesses took ownership over what were once state-owned companies. In some cases, like Russia, such privatization happened too fast, leading to various socio-economic problems. The tide is now turning against the private sector as governments accumulate unprecedented wealth, which allows them to buy stakes in what were once purely private companies.

In this context, we should view SWFs as enablers of the new economic order. SWFs are pouring billions into hedge funds, private equity funds, real estate, natural resources, and other nodes of the West's economy. No one knows precisely how much money is held by SWFs, but it is estimated that they currently own $3.5 trillion in assets and [that] within one decade they could balloon to $10–$15 trillion, equivalent to America's gross domestic product. While much of the economic activity is generated by the Asian funds, particularly China's and Singapore's, I will focus my testimony on the activities of the SWFs from oil-producing countries, primarily the five Persian Gulf states that account for nearly half of the world SWF assets—Abu Dhabi, Dubai, Qatar, Kuwait, and Saudi Arabia—as well as SWFs owned by oil-producing countries like Nigeria, Oman, Kazakhstan, Angola, and Russia, which have been among the fastest growing over the last five years.

Before I delve into the specific issues related to SWFs, I would like to remind the Committee that those funds are not the only way states can exert influence in global financial markets. High net worth individuals, government controlled companies, and central banks are just as important in this context. Each one of the governments [that] are concentrating wealth has a different portfolio of investment instruments. Saudi Arabia, for example, accounts for roughly half of the GCC [Gulf Cooperation Council]'s private foreign wealth, yet unlike the UAE [United Arab Emirates], where SWFs control foreign assets, most Saudi foreign wealth is in the hands of private investors who are mostly members of the royal family. Only recently the Kingdom announced its intention to create a large SWF. While I applaud the Committee for holding this hearing on this important topic, we should realize that SWFs are only part of a much bigger problem.

The second thing to bear in mind is that to date there has been little evidence that SWFs attempt to assume control of firms they invest in or use their wealth to advance political ends. This is perhaps why so many experts dismiss the fear of foreign money acquiring portions of Western economies as a new form of jingoism, deriding the "fear mongers" as disciples of those who propelled the "Japanese-are-coming" hysteria of the 1980s. I do not share their dismissive view. The key issue to understand is that there is a fundamental difference between state versus private ownership, and that because governments operate differently from other private sector players, their investments should be governed by rules designed accordingly. Unlike ordinary shareholders and high-net-wealth private investors who are motivated solely by the desire to maximize the value of their shares, governments have a broader agenda—to maximize their geopolitical influence and sometime to promote ideologies that are in essence anti-Western. Nondemocratic and nontransparent governments can allow the use of their intelligence agencies and other covert as well as overt instruments of power to acquire valuable commercial information. Unlike pure commercial enterprises, state-owned investment funds can leverage the political and financial power of their governments to promote their business interests. Governments may enter certain transactions in order to extract a certain technology or alternatively in order to "kill" a competing one. The reason the Japan analogy is incorrect is that Mitsubishi Estate, the Japanese company that bought the Rockefeller Center in 1989 was not Tokyo's handmaid and Japan was—and still is—an American ally. This can hardly be said about Russia, Communist China, or OPEC members, some of whom use their revenues to fund the proliferation of an anti-Western agenda, develop nuclear capabilities, fan the flames of the Arab-Israeli conflict, and serially violate human rights. As it is now known to all, for decades the de facto leader of OPEC, Saudi Arabia, has been actively involved in the promotion of Wahhabism, the most puritan form of Islam, and its charities and other governmental and nongovernmental institutions have been bankrolling terrorist organizations and Islamic fundamentalism. To this day, the Kingdom's petrodollars pay for a hateful education system and fuel conflicts from the Balkans to Pakistan. With a little over 1% of the world's Muslim population, Saudi petrodollars support today 90% of the expenses of the entire faith. U.S. Undersecretary of the Treasury in charge of fighting terrorist financing Stuart Levey recently said in an interview: "If I could snap my fingers and cut off the funding from one country, it would be Saudi Arabia."

Mr. Chairman, from an international relations perspective most of the concerns raised about SWFs only really matter if in the years to come the relations between the United States and the investing countries were to deteriorate. If tension between the United States and the Muslim world subsided and if China maintained its peaceful rise without undermining U.S. strategic interests there would hardly be a reason for concern; if the opposite occurs, then indulging on Arab or Chinese wealth could be outright dangerous. The best example here is CITGO. PDV's successful acquisition of CITGO in the United States (50% in 1986, the remainder in 1990) triggered very few concerns at the time. But if such a takeover were attempted by Hugo Chavez today, when U.S.–Venezuela relations are acrimonious, the public outcry would be huge. Therefore, our discussion on foreign investment should not be dominated only by "what is happening today" but also in view of "where we are headed," considering the trajectories and patterns we can already begin to observe, the most important of which are the unabated rise in oil prices combined with questionable international behavior of some of the major oil-producing countries.

Despite the attention given to SWFs, they are still relatively small players in the global economic system. Their assets exceed the $1.4 trillion managed by hedge funds, but they are far below the $15 trillion managed by pension funds, the $16 trillion managed by insurance companies, or the $21 trillion managed by investment companies. Here again it is more important to look at the trend rather than the present situation. At their current growth rate of 24% a year SWFs are beginning to present tough competition to other institutional investors over access to investment opportunities. To understand the anatomy of the competition between government entities and commercial firms one needs only to observe the process in which international oil companies (IOCs) have gradually lost their competitive edge vis-à-vis national oil companies (NOCs). IOCs find themselves unable to compete against the deep-pocketed NOCs, which do not face the same regulatory limitations, do not have to provide the same measures of transparency, and do not have to abide by stringent environmental and humanitarian constraints. As SWFs gain strength and volume they could sideline other players vying for investments. Unlike pension funds and other institutional investors who are slow in their decision-making process, following strict timelines set by their investment committees, SWFs are agile. They have the in-house structure and the resources to make investment decisions quickly.

New Economic Balance of Power

No doubt perpetual high oil prices will shift the economic balance between OPEC and the West in the direction of those who own the precious commodity. As Robert Zubrin points out in his book *Energy Victory*, in 1972 the United States spent $4 billion on oil imports, an amount that equaled to 1.2% of our defense budget. In 2006, it paid $260 billion, which equals half of our defense budget. In 2008, it is likely to pay over $500 billion, which is equivalent to our full defense budget. Over the same period, Saudi oil revenues grew from $2.7 billion to roughly $400 billion and with it their ability to fund radical Islam. In the years to come this economic imbalance will grow by leaps and bounds. To understand the degree of the forces in play it is instructive to visualize the scale of OPEC's wealth in comparison to the consuming countries. The value of OPEC's proven oil and gas resources using today's prices is $137 trillion. This is roughly equivalent to the world's total financial assets—stocks, bonds, other equities, government and corporate debt securities, and bank deposits—or almost three times the market capitalization of all the companies traded in the world's top twenty-seven stock markets. Saudi Arabia's oil and gas alone is worth $36 trillion, ten times the total value of all the companies traded in the London Stock Exchange. If one adds the additional oil and gas reserves that have not yet been discovered, OPEC's wealth more than doubles. If oil prices climb to $200, as OPEC's president Chakib Khelil recently warned, the wealth nearly doubles again. In an economic system of $200-barrel oil we can expect the value of financial institutions to shrink while the transfer of wealth to the oil-producing countries increases in velocity. Such monumental wealth potential will enable buying power of the oil countries that far exceeds that of the West. For demonstration sake, at $200 oil OPEC could potentially buy Bank of America in one month worth of production, Apple Computers in a week, and General Motors in just three days. It would take less than two years of production for OPEC to own a 20% stake (which essentially ensures a voting block in most corporations) in every S&P 500 company. Of course, takeovers of such magnitude are unlikely, but $200 oil and additional trillions of dollars in search of a parking spot are very likely. What is clear about the new economic reality is that while the economic power of America and its allies is constantly eroding, OPEC's "share" price is on a solid upward trajectory and with it an ever-growing foreign ownership over our economy.

Vulnerable Sectors

SWFs have lost $25 billion on their recent investments in struggling banks and securities firms worldwide. In the near future, they are not likely to be as enthusiastic to bail out additional financial institutions. But with high oil prices here to stay and with the International Energy Agency projecting that "we are ending up with 95% of the world relying for its economic well-being on decisions made by five or six countries in the Middle East," it is hard to see how OPEC's massive buying power would not upset the West's economic and political sovereignty. This is particularly true in light of the prospects of potential future bailouts in sectors other than banking should the U.S. economy continue to decline. As populations in Western countries age and dwindle, it is only a matter of time before the underfunded health care and retirement systems begin to face similar liquidity problems. Foreign governments have already put their sight on auto manufacturers, buying stakes in companies like Ferrari and Daimler. In 2004, Abu Dhabi attempted to buy 25% of Volkswagen's shares after the German automaker's profits fell sharply. The danger here is that SWFs might be the first to step in to save the ailing U.S. auto industry from its pension obligations if the industry continues to underperform. What would this mean for the effort to make our cars less dependent on petroleum is a question policymakers should think about before such crisis occurs.

Media organizations are another sector worthy of attention. In September 2006, with mainstream news organizations in the United States reporting falling earnings and downbeat financial assessments, information ministers, tycoons, and other officials of the 57-nation Organization of the Islamic Conference (OIC) gathered in Saudi Arabia where OIC Secretary General Ekmeleddin Ihsanoglu urged them to buy stakes in Western media outlets to help correct what he views as misconceptions on Islam around the world. To date, though private investors from the Middle East have made substantial acquisitions of global media, SWFs have not bought holdings in this sector. A change in SWF behavior [that] leads to attempts to gain control over media organizations could lead to an erosion in freedom of speech and freedom of information. Pervasive influence of Saudi money in the publishing world, coupled with a growing litigation against scholars critical of Saudi Arabia, is shielding from public scrutiny the one country that is most responsible for the proliferation of radical Islam.

Opaque Investment Patterns and the Risk of Predatory Behavior

When it comes to governance, transparency, and accountability SWFs are not cut from the same cloth. There is a profound difference between SWFs of democratic countries like Norway and the United States and those of nondemocratic regimes. In some of the latter countries, like Kuwait, SWFs are barred by the country's laws from revealing their assets. The Linaburg–Maduell Transparency Index, which was developed at the Sovereign Wealth Funds Institute, shows significantly lower SWF transparency ranking among nondemocratic countries as opposed to democratic ones. Not surprisingly, nine out of the ten worst ranked funds are those of oil-producing nations. Lack of transparency and accountability among those SWFs makes them a disruptive factor in our overall highly transparent market economy. To avoid scrutiny, SWFs have fostered new alliances with private equity funds, which offer a culture of secrecy. SWFs already account for approximately 10% of private equity investments globally, and this number will grow further in the coming years. Last year, Chinese entities bought the largest external stake in Blackstone, [which], indirectly through its holdings, is one of the largest employers in the United States. Carlyle Group sold [a] 7.5% stake to a fund owned by Abu Dhabi, which also bought 9% of Apollo Management. The situation is similar in hedge funds. One of the dangers here is that through their investments SWFs can shape market conditions in sectors where their governments have economic and/or political interests or where they enjoy comparative advantage. In recent months, for example, commodity futures have increased dramatically, largely due to astronomical growth in speculation and bidding up of prices, while actual deliveries are far behind. Commodity markets are easily manipulated, and the impact of such manipulations could often reverberate throughout the world, as the current food crisis shows. While U.S. companies are not allowed to buy their own products and create shortage to increase revenues, foreign governments with economic interest in a particular commodity face no similar restrictions bidding on it, via their proxies, in the commodity market. Under the current system, oil countries can, via their SWFs as well as other investment vehicles that receive investment from SWFs structure long future contracts and commodity derivatives and hence affect oil futures in a way that benefits them. This would be tantamount to the U.S. government using its position as the world's largest exporter of corn to bid up corn futures.

Boardroom Presence

To date, the influx of petrodollars has not translated into overbearing presence of government agents in corporate boardrooms. In fact, many of the SWFs buy holdings under the 5% benchmark that triggers regulatory scrutiny and forego board seats. But at the current rate of investment and many more years of three-digit oil combined with deepening geopolitical tensions, foreign governments might be more willing to translate their wealth into power, dictating business practices, vetoing deals, appointing officers sympathetic to their governments, and dismissing those who are critical of them. Direct influence of a foreign governments could lead to inefficiencies, capital misallocations, and political interference in business decisions. This is why it is my view that SWF acquisitions should be restricted to nonvoting stakes.

The Rise of Sharia Finance

The gradual penetration of Shariah (Islamic Law) into [the] West's corporate world is another characteristic of the new geo-economic order. Islamic countries operating on the basis of compliance with Shariah have strict guidelines of economic conduct. Banks and investment houses gradually employ a new breed of executive—the Chief Shariah Officer (CSO)—whose sole job is to ensure compliance with Islamic law and hence attract more business from the Muslim investors. Over time, such compliance could put pressure on companies not consistent with Islamic principles to become more "Islamic." Imams sitting on Shariah boards could be pressured to withhold their approval of any business dealing directly or indirectly connected with countries or institutions that are offensive to Islam. One can only guess what this would mean for publishing houses, Hollywood movie studios, the alcohol and gambling industries. A sure casualty of the Islamization of the corporate world would be Israel, which has for years been subjected to the Arab boycott. According to the U.S. Department of Commerce, last year American companies reported no fewer than 486 requests from UAE companies alone to boycott Israel.

Building a Fireless Firewall

None of the potential risks to which I alluded entail lifting the drawbridge and becoming economic hermits. America's commitment to open markets has been a source of respect and admiration around the world, and reversing it through investment protectionism would only hurt U.S. prestige while undermining economic growth and job creation at home. To arrest the current economic trend and to hedge the risk of sovereignty loss the United States should apply a healthy dosage of vigilance and develop a system of indicators to determine and examine when SWFs pursue different approaches from other institutional investors. Willingness to pay above-market prices, use government assets to back up financial deals, or manipulate prices to increase returns should all be red flags that trigger response. The United States already has rigorous safeguard mechanisms against undesirable foreign investors. The Committee on Foreign Investment in the U.S. (CFIUS) protects national security assets in sectors such as telecommunications, broadcasting, transportation, energy, and minerals in which there is a clear potential danger to national security. I am delighted that many of the concerns about foreign investments have already been addressed in the CFIUS reform legislation entitled the Foreign Investment and National Security Act of 2007. The range of regulatory and supervisory tools available to the Federal Reserve Board as described in the Federal Reserve Act are quite satisfactory [in] case SWFs make an investment in a U.S. banking organization that triggers one of the Fed's thresholds. But in order to protect ourselves against sovereignty loss more safeguards are needed.

Reciprocity

While enjoying almost unlimited access to investment opportunities in the West, oil-rich governments do not feel the need to reciprocate by opening their economies to foreign investment. The opposite is true: They obstruct international companies from investing in their midst, limiting them to, at best, minority shares. This is the root cause of insufficient production of new oil. Oil countries, together owning 80% of the world's reserves, practice resource nationalism, stick to quotas, [and] refuse to provide transparency of oil activities including reserve studies and terms of contract with their own national oil companies, and they are riddled with corruption and cronyism.

The least we can do is demand that foreigners treat us as we treat them. Despite being the lead violator of free trade by dint of its leadership of the OPEC cartel, three years ago, with U.S. support, the Saudis were admitted to the World Trade Organization (WTO). This was a terrible mistake. Since the admission, the world's generosity toward the Saudis was rewarded with nothing but continuous manipulation of oil prices and behavior that can only be described as antithetical to free trade. Enjoying the benefits of free trade is an earned privilege, not an entitlement, and foreign governments wishing to acquire assets in the West should be obliged only if they show similar hospitality to Western companies. We should not be shy to use retaliatory measures against serial violators of free-trade principles. There are currently four OPEC members in waiting to accede to the WTO—Algeria, Iran, Iraq, and Libya. Oil-producing countries with growing SWFs like Russia, Kazakhstan, and Azerbaijan are also on the waiting list. These countries' admittance to the organization should be contingent on compliance with those principles and on an unequivocal commitment to refrain from noncompetitive behavior and anti-market activities. You cannot seek a seat at the WTO and at the same time promote a natural gas cartel.

Increase Transparency

The scope and growth rate of SWFs are so vast that their actions can have far-reaching influence on world financial markets, whether intentionally or mistakenly. This begs for the introduction of intermediary asset managers and the creation of disclosure standards for SWFs as well as other foreign institutional investors that are at least as stringent as those applied to other regulated investors. However, any go-it-alone effort to force SWFs to adopt higher transparency standards would be unworkable and easy to circumvent. The guidelines of working with SWFs should therefore be drawn in collaboration with the EU and other countries on the receiving end of sovereign money.

Break the Oil Cartel

In the long run, the only way to roll back the new economic order and restrain OPEC's control over the world economy is to reduce the inherent value of its commodity. This cannot be done as long as we continue to put on our roads cars that can run on nothing but petroleum. Every year 17 million new cars roll onto America's roads. Each of these cars will have a lifespan of nearly 17 years. In the next Congressional session 35 million new cars will be added. If the next president presides for two terms he or she will preside over the introduction of 150 million new cars. If we allow all those cars to be gasoline only we are locking our future to petroleum for decades to come. I cannot think of something more detrimental to America's security than Congress allowing this to happen. Congress can break OPEC's monopoly over the transportation sector by instituting fuel choice. The cheapest, easiest, and most immediate step should be a federal Open Fuel Standard, requiring that every new car put on the road be a flex fuel car, which looks and operates exactly like a gasoline car but has a $100 feature [that] enables it to run on any combination of gasoline and alcohol. Millions of flex fuel cars will begin to roll back oil's influence by igniting a boom of innovation and investment in alternative fuel technologies. The West is not rich in oil, but it is blessed with a wealth of other energy sources from which alcohol fuels—such as ethanol and methanol—capable of powering flexible fuel vehicles can be affordably and cleanly generated. Among them: vast rich farmland, hundreds of years' worth of coal reserves, and billions of tons a year of agricultural, industrial, and municipal waste. Even better: In an alcohol economy, scores of poor developing countries, which right now struggle under the heavy economic burden caused by high oil prices, would be able to become net energy exporters. With hot climate and long rainy seasons, countries in south Asia, Africa, and Latin America enjoy the perfect conditions for the production of sugarcane ethanol, which costs roughly half the price and is five times more efficient than corn ethanol. Hence, a shift to alcohol-enabled cars will enable developing countries to generate revenues and emerge as a powerful force that could break OPEC's dominance over the global transportation sector.

In addition to alcohols, coal, nuclear power, [and] solar and wind energy can make electricity to power pure electric and plug-in hybrid cars. The latter have an internal combustion engine and fuel tank, and thus are not limited in size, power, or range, but also have a battery that can be charged from an electric socket and can power 20–40 miles of driving, giving the consumer the choice of driving on electricity or liquid fuel. Only 2% of U.S. electricity is generated from oil today. While plug-in hybrids have unlimited range and a cost premium of several thousand dollars, pure electric cars are planned to be sold at competitive prices in several countries, including the

United States and Japan, as early as 2010. Because pure electric cars have a range limitation—at least two countries, Israel and Denmark, are now in the process of developing an infrastructure for battery replacement to address this problem—they may not satisfy the needs of many Americans. But electric cars can easily serve as a second or third family car. This "niche market" is roughly two thirds of America. Thirty-one percent of America's households own two cars, and an additional 35% own three or more vehicles. These are not the cars a family would use to visit Grandma out of town but cars that drive routinely well below the full battery range. There are over 75 million households in the United States that own more than one vehicle and that can potentially replace one or more gasoline-only cars with cars powered by made-in-America electricity.

Mr. Chairman, the new economic order is shaping up right before our eyes, increasingly invalidating much of the economic paradigm to which we have been accustomed. For America, a continuation of the petroleum standard guarantees economic decline and perpetual economic and political enslavement to the OPEC cartel and its whims. If we want to address the challenge of SWFs and increased foreign government control over our economy we must focus on policies that can empower countries that share our values rather than the petro-dictators of the world. We must bring down the price of oil before it hits a critical point beyond which sovereignty loss becomes inevitable.

Edwin M. Truman

The Rise of Sovereign Wealth Funds: Impacts on U.S. Foreign Policy and Economic Interests

The broadest definition of a sovereign wealth fund (SWF) is a collection of government-owned or government-controlled assets. Narrower definitions may exclude government financial or nonfinancial corporations, purely domestic assets, foreign exchange reserves, assets owned or controlled by subnational governmental units, or some or all government pension funds. I use "sovereign wealth fund" as a descriptive term for a separate pool of government-owned or government-controlled assets that includes some international assets. I include all government pension, as well as nonpension, funds to the extent that they manage marketable assets. The basic objectives of both types are essentially the same. They raise virtually identical issues of best practice—the focus of my research and analysis—in government control and accountability regardless of their specific objectives, mandates, or sources of funding.

SWFs are funded from foreign exchange reserves, earnings from commodity exports, receipts from privatizations, other fiscal revenues, or pension contributions. These funds have been around for more than half a century with a range of structures, mandates, and economic, financial, and political (domestic and international) objectives—normally a mixture. Consequently, it is perilous to generalize about SWFs and associated potential threats to U.S. foreign policy, national security, or economic interests.

Nevertheless, my summary conclusions are three:

First, SWFs do not pose a significant new threat to U.S. security or economic interests. We have adequate mechanisms to manage any potential threats they pose, which at this point are likely to be minimal.

Second, SWFs are one of the many challenges of global economic and financial change in the twenty-first century. Whether these particular challenges of globalization are appropriately addressed will have profound implications for the United States and for the world economy and financial system.

Third, the United States should continue to press countries with SWFs to design and embrace best practices for these funds to enhance their accountability to citizens of the countries with the funds as well as to the citizens and markets in which they invest. At the same time, the United States should continue to try to minimize economic and political barriers to foreign investment in all forms from all sources here and around the world. Financial protectionism is the wrong answer to the very real challenges of financial globalization and the associated potential for global financial turbulence. The United States cannot disengage from evolving changes in the global financial system. If we were merely to hint that we are tempted to do so, we would risk catastrophic damage to the U.S. and world economies.

It is useful to place the activities of SWFs in a broader perspective. At the end of 2006, the estimated size of global capital markets was $190 trillion. A conservative estimate of financial assets owned or controlled by governments is $15 trillion, or about 8% of global financial assets. Governments in the United States own or control more than $3 trillion (20%) of the total. Thus, the United States is in the business of sovereign wealth management. Consequently, we should be careful what we wish for.

International assets owned or controlled by governments are at least $10 trillion: $6 trillion in foreign exchange reserves, $2.7 trillion in assets of nonpension SWFs, and at least $1.3 trillion in government pension funds. Excluding our modest holdings of foreign exchange reserves, international assets of U.S. SWFs are about $800 billion mostly in the form of the pension funds of state and local governments. Thus, U.S. SWFs, as a group, are second to the United Arab Emirates in their holdings of international assets.

As an additional point of reference, at the end of 2006, U.S. total holdings of foreign assets were $13.8 trillion. About 92% was managed by the private sector. Foreign holdings of U.S. assets were $16.3 trillion. At least 17% was managed by the public sector. U.S. holdings of international financial assets are at least 20% of the global total. In other words, the U.S. economy is thoroughly intertwined with the global financial system on both the asset and liability side of our balance sheet through both the private and public sectors.

Over the past five years, the size of the global capital market has doubled, but asset holdings of SWFs have at least tripled. The explosive growth of SWFs reflects the sustained rise in commodity prices as well as global imbalances. However, the increased international diversification of financial portfolios—the weakening of so-called home bias—is at least as important as macroeconomic factors in explaining the growth of SWFs.

The increasing relative importance of SWFs has exposed two tensions as part of the ongoing globalization of the international financial system.

The first is the dramatic redistribution of international (or cross-border) wealth from the traditional industrial countries, like the United States, to countries that historically have not been major players in international finance. The newcomers have had little or no role in shaping the practices, nouns, and conventions governing the system.

The second is the fact that governments own or control a substantial share of the new international wealth. This redistribution from private to public hands implies a decision-making orientation that is at variance with the traditional private-sector, market-oriented framework with which most of us are comfortable even though [the] system does not fully conform to that ideal.

These twin tensions, in turn, are manifested in five broad concerns.

First, governments may mismanage their international investments to their own economic and financial detriment, including large-scale corruption in handling the huge amounts involved. It is a well known, though often ignored, regularity that governments are not good at picking economic winners; for example, government-owned banks tend to be less profitable than private banks. This concern about mismanagement is the principal reason why it is in the interests of every country with a SWF to favor the establishment of internationally agreed SWF best practices. Moreover, greater accountability of such funds is in the foreign policy interest of the United States because the mismanagement of SWF investments could lead to political as well as economic instability in countries with such funds.

Second, governments may manage SWF investments in pursuit of political objectives—raising national security concerns—or economic power objectives—for example, promoting state-owned or state-controlled national champions as global champions. Such behavior contributes not only to political conflicts between countries but also to economic distortions.

Third, financial protectionism may be encouraged in host countries in anticipation of the pursuit of political or economic objectives by the funds or in response to their actual actions. Development of and compliance with SWF best practices would help to diffuse this source of backlash against globalization. At the same time, countries receiving SWF investments should be as open as possible to such investments, subject to the constraints of national security considerations narrowly defined.

Fourth, in the management of their international assets, SWFs may contribute to market turmoil and uncertainty. They also may contribute to financial stability, but their net contribution is difficult to establish *a priori,* in particular if their operations are opaque, but also because judgments can only be reached on a case by case basis.

Fifth, foreign government owners of the international assets may come into conflict with the governments of the countries in which they are investing. For example, government ownership adds a further dimension in balancing open markets and appropriate macroprudential regulation.

At this point, these concerns, with the important exception of the first—potential adverse implications for the home countries—are largely in the realm of the hypothetical. The others are much more salient in the context of cross-border investments by government-owned or government-controlled financial or nonfinancial corporations. Nevertheless, a loud, often acrimonious public discourse about SWFs is underway in many countries, and not only in countries receiving SWF investments.

In my view, the challenge is to make the world safe for SWFs through the establishment of an internationally agreed voluntary set of best practices. The natural place to start is with the current practices of individual funds today. To this end, I have created with the assistance of Doug Dowson a scoreboard for the largest SWFs. The scoreboard rates funds on their current practices and includes thirty-three elements grouped in four categories: structure, governance, accountability and transparency, and behavior. We have scored the funds based on systematic, regularly available public information. At least one fund receives a positive score on each element. In fact, at least several do.

First, all SWFs are not the same. Nor is there one cluster of "good" funds and another cluster of "bad" funds. The overall scores range from 95 to 9 out [of] a possible 100. The rating of each of them can be improved. The funds fall in three broad groups: twenty-two funds with scores above 60, fourteen funds with scores below 30, and ten funds in a middle group. Moreover, the grouping of scores is essentially identical if one examines only the category of accountability and transparency.

Second, although each of the twelve representative pension SWFs is in the top group, that group of twenty-two funds also includes ten nonpension SWFs. Thus, it is not unreasonable to hold nonpension SWFs to the standard of accountability of pension funds. Chile's pension and nonpension SWFs both score in the top group. On the other hand, China's National Social Security Fund is in the top group, but the China Investment Corporation is in the bottom group.

Third, it is essentially impossible to correlate the ratings of the individual funds with the economic or political characteristics of their government owners. For example, the top group includes seven of the fourteen funds with estimated assets of more than $100 billion, but four are in the second group, and two are in the third group. The top group includes funds of a number of developing countries, including Azerbaijan, Chile, China, Kazakhstan, Thailand, and Timor-Leste. The middle group includes funds of nonindustrial countries as diverse as Russia, Mexico, Kuwait, and Singapore, whose two funds are in this group. Singapore's two funds have close-to-identical overall scores, but their scores differ on many individual elements. The bottom group includes three funds from Abu Dhabi, each of which has an excellent reputation in financial markets.

For some this diversity of current practice illustrates the challenge in developing a common set of best practices. In my view, it illustrates the opportunity to converge on a common high standard. A senior representative of the Abu Dhabi Investment Authority is co-chairing, with the director of the IMF [International Monetary Fund]'s monetary and capital markets department, the International Working Group of Sovereign Wealth Funds to develop "a set of SWF principles that properly reflects their investment practices and objectives." The decision by the authorities of the United Arab Emirates to provide a co-chairman for this group implies a commitment by them to enhance substantially the accountability and transparency of their SWFs.

In his letter of invitation to testify before this committee today, Chairman Berman raised three issues, other than the phenomenon of SWFs and their accountability and transparency, on which I have not yet commented explicitly.

First, he asked whether SWFs have the potential to disrupt financial markets. All investors with large portfolios have the potential to disrupt financial markets whatever their motivation. However, the very size of their portfolios helps to inhibit them from doing so—in other words, discourages them from shooting themselves in their feet.

At the same time, it is inappropriate in my opinion to view SWFs as cornucopias available to be tapped to rescue the U.S. or the global financial system. For every SWF investment in a U.S. financial institution, that fund has to disinvest, or not invest, in some other asset, normally in the United States or at least in U.S. dollars.

Some observers of private equity firms and hedge funds have concerns about their implications for the stability of our economy and financial system. I do not share most of those concerns, though I have long favored increased transparency for large private equity firms and hedge funds. However, the facts do not support those who argue that SWFs are not like hedge funds and private equity firms in their speculative activities. SWFs invest in hedge funds, in private equity firms, and in other highly leveraged financial institutions whose activities, including the use of leverage, are indistinguishable from hedge funds and private equity firms. In effect, SWFs are providing the capital that those firms subsequently leverage to generate high rates of return for the funds. They are no different from other investors except that their stakes may be measured in the billions rather than in the hundreds of millions of dollars.

Second, Chairman Berman asked more generally whether the foreign policy and national security interests of countries with SWFs pose a threat to the United States. It follows from what I have already said that my short answer is no.

I am not an expert on the foreign policy and national interests of each of the more than 30 countries with nonpension SWFs, to say nothing of the additional countries that only have pension SWFs. However, it is clear that the interests [of] the individual countries are diverse, and perceptions of those countries fluctuate over time, in part, reflecting differences in the development and evolution of their political and social systems.

Policymakers are primarily interested in issues of underlying investment control even if they do not agree on how to define that concept. In this context, government-owned or -controlled financial and nonfinancial corporations are much more relevant because, in general, their activities are more focused and more easily integrated with foreign policy and national security objectives.

Although some SWFs do take controlling interests via their investments, more than half of the forty-six funds we scored have explicit policies against doing so. A substantial proportion of the remaining twenty-two funds also do not seek controlling interests, but they do not have explicit, public policies in this area. Of course, it is possible to pursue foreign policy or national security interests without taking a controlling investment interest, but it is more difficult, and the investment interest is likely to be more narrowly focused and more easily identified. The essential point is that the activities of a few countries that have SWFs and may use them to pursue political and economic interests should not be conflated with the motivations of the vast majority of countries that have such funds.

Finally, Chairman Berman asked for thoughts on how the U.S. Congress and the Administration can best "manage" SWF investing in the United States. I interpret his question as asking how the Congress and Administration should best respond to the phenomenon of SWFs.

Notwithstanding my view that the greatest risks associated with SWFs are to the citizens of the countries whose governments have accumulated the large stocks of international assets, authorities in the United States and other countries where those assets are invested also have legitimate concerns about how they will be managed. Those concerns focus primarily on acquisition of large or controlling stakes by foreign governments in private institutions. As noted, at present this is the exception not the rule for SWFs. However, one area of concern and potential conflict is the apparent use by a few countries, such as China and potentially Brazil, [of] their SWFs to promote the expansion of their own economic enterprises.

Of course, the current, largely benign, pattern could change, and foreign government-owned or government-controlled financial and nonfinancial corporations do acquire stakes in companies in other countries, including controlling stakes. The 2007 Foreign Investment and National Security Act (FINSA) revised the framework and procedures of the Committee on Foreign Investment in the United States (CFIUS). With these changes and the existing powers of the Securities and Exchange Commission, as well as other U.S. financial regulators, we are well positioned to evaluate and, if necessary, to mitigate, to block, or to pursue any U.S. acquisitions or investment by an SWF or other foreign government entity to protect our national security or to enforce our laws and regulations governing financial markets and institutions.

With respect to economic security concerns, the greatest risk to the U.S. economy is that we will erect unnecessary barriers to the free flow of capital into our economy and, in the process, contribute to the erection of similar barriers in other countries to the detriment of the health and continued prosperity of the U.S. and global economies. We may not in all cases be comfortable with the consequences of the free flow of finance and investment either internally or across borders, but on balance it promotes competition and efficiency. We should exhaust all multilateral approaches before pursuing bilateral remedies, and any such bilateral remedies should be narrowly focused.

To this end, I endorse the Administration's support of the OECD [Organisation for Economic Co-operation and Development] process designed to strengthen the framework that the United States and other OECD member countries use to govern foreign investment, including by governmental entities. At present that framework does not, in principle, extend to nonmembers of the OECD, though often it does in practice. The United States should support its explicit extension to all countries.

My hope is that the OECD process will provide sufficient reassurance to countries with SWFs so that, with the facilitation of the IMF, they can reach agreement on and fully comply with a voluntary set of best practices for their funds.

One test is whether the resulting set of best practices covers substantively all the elements included in my scoreboard. Of course, it is not essential to cover them precisely in the form outlined. However, each element should be adequately addressed. A significant omission should be seen as falling short of expectations.

A second test of success is whether the best practices are embraced by substantially all countries with large SWFs. If each of the fourteen SWFs with more than $100 billion in total assets were to adhere to the prospective set of best practices, it is less critical that the others do so immediately. For each country, including those that choose not to adhere fully or at all, the minimum expectation should be that the country would comply, or it should explain why it does not do so in whole or in part.

A third test is the quality of compliance by the countries that embrace the best practices. If they are drawn up properly, the best practices should be self-enforcing. Politicians, the media, financial-market participants, and the general public in the home and host countries should be able to determine the degree of compliance.

On the other hand, if the voluntary best practices agreed to under the auspices of the IMF are less precise than they should be, it will be necessary to have some mechanism to report on compliance. That function might be lodged in the IMF or the World Bank, which have experience with respect to overseeing compliance with twelve of the many existing international standards and codes. As is the case with existing standards subject to IMF and World Bank surveillance and oversight, the resulting process of implicit naming and shaming, combined with peer pressure from other SWFs that want to avoid the application of draconian restrictions to their activities, should contribute to a high level of compliance within a short period.

Some may favor supervisory inspections of SWFs beyond those that would be covered by IMF and World Bank surveillance, plus published, independent audits as called for in my scoreboard. To my knowledge, no official has said so publicly. However, to advocate this type of supervision would sharply escalate the SWF debate from one about the content of and adherence to internationally agreed to voluntary best practices to one about explicit regulation. At this point, such an escalation is neither appropriate nor justified on the merits.

On the recipient side, many countries today have (very diverse) regimes covering foreign direct investment in their countries. Pending the establishment of a broad consensus on those regimes as they apply to government investments, such as is being pursued within the OECD, and perhaps even in that context, the United States and other similarly situated countries might reasonably decide to take account of a country's voluntary compliance with the international best practices for SWFs as one of a number of factors considered in making determinations about whether a particular SWF's investment should be blocked because of a threat to national security. For example, in a March 13 letter sent to U.S. Treasury Secretary Henry Paulson, Representatives Barney Frank, Carolyn Maloney, and Luis Gutierrez suggested that a country's compliance with aspects of SWF best practices could be used by the CFIUS as a factor in determining whether the committee should grant that country a waiver from a full investigation under FINSA of an investment, for example, by a government-owned pension fund.

More controversially, some observers have suggested that an SWF that takes even a noncontrolling stake in a company should be forbidden from voting its shares, presumably increasing the probability that the investment is "passive." My understanding is that there is no generally accepted legal definition of a passive investment. (I note that the proposed CFIUS regulations implementing the FINSA instead seek to define interests that are "solely for the purpose of investment," which is a more limited approach.) To limit the voting rights of government investors, if applied uniformly, would disenfranchise as much as several trillion dollars of investments by U.S. state and local government pension funds. If the United States did not apply this type of restriction to domestic pension SWFs, it would still risk disenfranchising U.S. government pension funds in their investment operations abroad. The reason is that it would be difficult to apply such a restriction to foreign non-pension SWFs and not to foreign pension SWFs. As a consequence, foreign governments almost certainly would retaliate in kind.

U.S. Treasury Assistant Secretary Clay Lowery has suggested a more sensible approach: Either an SWF should choose voluntarily not to vote its shares or it should disclose how it votes, as is now done voluntarily by some U.K. institutional investors and is required by the Securities and Exchange Commission for U.S. mutual funds. The objective of the SEC rule for mutual funds is to address concerns about conflicts of interest and, as noted earlier, similar concerns arise with respect to SWFs. Presumably, the SWF would not face a formal SEC reporting requirement in this area; that would raise a host of other process and jurisdictional issues and also serve to escalate the SWF debate.

In conclusion, the phenomenon of SWFs is a permanent feature of our global economy and financial system. Their potential impacts on U.S. foreign policy, national security, and economic interests may be disquieting, but they do not endanger the United States. U.S. authorities should exhaust all multilateral approaches to make the world safe for SWFs—in the form of SWF best practices and open financial environments—before turning to any additional, bilateral remedies for concerns that to date are between minimal and nonexistent.

PART IV
INTERNATIONAL MONETARY ISSUES

The international monetary system is supposed to facilitate international trade and promote adjustment of large trade imbalances. Our current international monetary system has been in place for thirty-five years. It facilitates trade by according the dollar a key role. Many internationally traded goods are priced in dollars—or at least relative to dollars— and most cross-border payments typically are made in dollars. The international monetary system is designed to promote adjustment of imbalances through exchange-rate movements. The currencies of countries with large surpluses should appreciate, while the currencies of countries with large deficits should depreciate. Contemporary debates about the international monetary system focus on whether the system will persist in its current form and whether it effectively promotes adjustment. This section examines two specific contemporary manifestations of these broader questions.

Chapter 10 explores the role of markets and states in the recent global financial crisis. The fundamental question here is whether the crisis was a consequence of too little government regulation of the financial system or instead was a result of too much government involvement in the economy. Many analysts argue that financial deregulation since the 1980s exposed societies to risks inherent in financial markets. Joseph Stiglitz, for example, argues that excessive faith in markets led to deregulation, excessive lending, and the resulting financial crisis. He suggests that preventing further crises requires new and much tighter regulation. Others argue that the crisis reflected too much government involvement in the economy. Lawrence White, for example, suggests that the crisis emerged from a loose monetary policy that made credit too cheap and congressional efforts that encouraged home ownership among traditionally disadvantaged groups. His solution to the problem involves getting government out of the business of influencing the availability and use of credit.

Chapter 11 delves into the role of exchange-rate movements in promoting adjustment of the U.S.–China bilateral trade imbalance. Some economists, and many members of Congress, argue that the Chinese government has intentionally undervalued its currency, the renminbi, against the dollar. China's exchange-rate policy sits next to a very large U.S.–China trade imbalance. Indeed, the U.S. trade deficit with China— about $290 billion in 2007—accounts for a large share of the U.S. overall trade deficit. The question at the center of this debate is whether Chinese exchange-rate policy is the cause of the trade imbalance.

C. Fred Bergsten argues that it is. The bilateral imbalance, he argues, is a direct consequence of China's exchange rate policy. Adjustment of this trade imbalance, therefore, requires the renminbi to appreciate against the dollar by a substantial amount. David Hale and Lyric Hughes Hale argue that the trade imbalance is not a consequence of China's exchange-rate policy. Instead, they say the trade imbalance is not a consequence of macroeconomic imbalances—especially in savings and investment rates—in the United States and China.

CHAPTER 10

TOO LITTLE MARKET REGULATION CAUSED THE FINANCIAL CRISIS *v.* **TOO MUCH GOVERNMENT INTERVENTION CAUSED THE FINANCIAL CRISIS**

Too Little Market Regulation Caused the Financial Crisis

Advocate: Joseph E. Stiglitz

Source: "The Anatomy of a Murder: Who Killed America's Economy," *Critical Review* 21: 2–3 (2009): 329–39

Too Much Government Intervention Caused the Financial Crisis

Advocate: Lawrence H. White

Source: *How Did We Get into This Financial Mess?* Briefing Paper 110 (Washington, DC: CATO Institute, November 18, 2008)

The collapse of the U.S. subprime mortgage market led to the worst global financial crisis and recession since the Great Depression. Almost immediately, debate began over who was responsible. Many blamed private market actors—Wall Street, mortgage lenders, people who bought homes they could not afford—while others blamed government officials for poor regulation, loose monetary policy, and bailouts. Governments around the world responded with a series of stabilization policies and reform proposals.

It did not take long before the question of proximate causes turned into a broader ideological clash between those who favor a heavy role for government in regulating the economy and those who do not. While this debate is not new, the financial crisis, fiscal bailouts, and financial and economic reform proposals brought it into sharp focus.

TOO LITTLE MARKET REGULATION CAUSED THE FINANCIAL CRISIS

Proponents of a strong role for government in regulating the economy focus on the instability of markets. They argue that free market ideology makes unreasonable assumptions about human rationality, the quality of information about risk,

235

and the efficiency of markets in utilizing that information. In reality, they claim, humans make mistakes, information is far from perfect, and markets regularly generate inefficient outcomes. It is the role of governments to tightly regulate markets in order to mitigate the effects of these flaws so as to prevent economic collapses.

Joseph Stiglitz, winner of the 2001 Nobel Memorial Prize in Economic Sciences, argues that the financial crisis was the result of the pervasiveness of market fundamentalism. This faith in markets led to lax regulation and the encouragement of Wall Street excesses, which in turn led to the financial crisis and economic collapse.

TOO MUCH GOVERNMENT INTERVENTION CAUSED THE FINANCIAL CRISIS

Opponents of government management of the economy argue that financial markets were not free of government interference before the crisis. Regulatory requirements, monetary policies, and government agencies altered the incentives of banks and mortgage lenders, which led to distorted markets. Criticizing free market ideology for the subprime crisis presupposes that markets were free when they were not and thus places blame in the wrong place. If we want to avoid future crises, they say, we should reduce the ability of government to distort markets for political gain.

Lawrence White highlights two policy areas where the government was heavily involved in the run-up to the crisis: first, the loose monetary policy of the Federal Reserve, which provided the funds necessary to make risky subprime loans; and second, a variety of housing policies that encouraged the issuance of those loans. The combination of the two created incentives for banks to take more risks than they otherwise would.

POINTS **TO PONDER**

1. What, according to Stiglitz, are the flaws in free market ideology that led to the crisis? Does White address those claims?

2. Do Stiglitz and White disagree about policy or about ideology? Both? Neither?

3. Given the arguments presented here, do you think governments should try to do more or less to influence markets?

Joseph E. Stiglitz

The Anatomy of a Murder: Who Killed America's Economy?

The search is on for whom to blame for the global economic crisis. It is not just a matter of vindictiveness; it is important to know who or what caused the crisis if one is to figure out how to prevent another, or perhaps even to fix this one.

The notion of causation is, however, complex. Presumably, it means something like, "If only the guilty party had taken another course of action, the crisis would not have occurred." But the consequences of one party changing its actions depend on the behavior of others; presumably the actions of other parties, too, may have changed.

Consider a murder. We can identify who pulled the trigger. But somebody had to sell that person the gun. Somebody may have paid the gunman. Somebody may have provided inside information about the whereabouts of the victim. All of these people are party to the crime. If the person who paid the gunman was determined to have his victim shot, then even if the particular gunman who ended up pulling the trigger had refused the job, the victim would have been shot; someone else would have been found to pull the trigger.

There are many parties to this crime—both people and institutions. Any discussion of "who is to blame" conjures up names like Robert Rubin, co-conspirator in deregulation and a senior official in one of the two financial institutions into which the American government has poured the most money. Then there was Alan Greenspan, who also pushed the deregulatory philosophy; who failed to use the regulatory authority that he had; who encouraged homeowners to take out highly risky adjustable mortgages; and who supported President Bush's tax cut for the rich,[1]—making lower interest rates, which fed the bubble, necessary to stimulate the economy. But if these people hadn't been there, others would have occupied their seats, arguably doing similar things. There were others equally willing and able to perpetrate the crimes. Moreover, the fact that similar problems arose in other countries—with different people playing the parts of the protagonists—suggests that there were more fundamental economic forces at play.

The list of institutions that must assume considerable responsibility for the crisis includes the investment banks and the investors; the credit rating agencies; the regulators, including the S.E.C. and the Federal Reserve; the mortgage brokers; and a string of administrations, from Bush to Reagan, that pushed financial-sector deregulation. Some of these institutions contributed to the crisis in multiple roles—most notably the Federal Reserve, which failed in its role as regulator, but which also may have contributed to the crisis by mishandling interest rates and credit availability. All of these—and some others discussed below—share some culpability.

The Main Protagonists

But I would argue that blame should be centrally placed on the banks (and the financial sector more broadly) and the investors.

The banks were supposed to be the experts in risk management. They not only didn't manage risk; they created it. They engaged in excessive leverage. At a 30-to-1 leverage ratio, a mere 3 percent change in asset values wipes out one's net worth. (To put matters in perspective, real-estate prices have fallen some 20 percent and, as of March 2009, are expected to fall another 10–15 percent, at least.) The banks adopted incentive structures that were designed to induce short-sighted and excessively risky behavior. The stock options that they used to pay some of their senior executives, moreover, provided incentives for bad accounting, including incentives to engage in extensive off-balance-sheet accounting.

The bankers seemingly didn't understand the risks that were being created by securitization—including those arising from information asymmetries: The originators of the mortgages did not end up holding onto them, so the originators didn't bear the consequences of any failure at due diligence. The bankers also misestimated the extent of correlation among default rates in different parts of the country—not realizing that a rise in the interest rate or an increase in unemployment might have adverse effects in many parts of the country—and they underestimated the risk of real-estate price declines. Nor did the banks assess with any degree of accuracy the risks associated with some of the new financial products, such as low- or no-documentation loans.

The only defense that the bankers have—and it's admittedly a weak defense—is that their investors made them do it. Their investors didn't understand risk. They confined high returns brought on by excessive leverage in an up market with "smart" investment. Banks that didn't engage in excessive leverage, and so had lower returns, were "punished" by having their stock values beaten down. The reality, however, is that the banks exploited this investor ignorance to push their stock prices up, getting higher short-term returns at the expense of higher risk.

Accessories to the Crime

If the banks were the main perpetrators of the crime, they had many accomplices.

Rating agencies played a central role. They believed in financial alchemy, and converted F-rated subprime mortgages into A-rated securities that were safe enough to be held by pension funds. This was important, because it allowed a steady flow of cash into the housing market, which in turn provided the fuel for the housing bubble. The rating agencies' behavior may have been affected by the perverse incentive of being paid by those that they rated, but I suspect that even without these incentive problems, their models would have been badly flawed. Competition, in this case, had a perverse effect: It caused a race to the bottom—a race to provide ratings that were most favorable to those being rated.

Mortgage brokers played a key role: They were less interested in originating good mortgages—after all, they didn't hold the mortgages for long—than in originating *many* mortgages. Some of the mortgage brokers were so enthusiastic that they invented new forms of mortgages: The low- or no-documentation loans to which I referred earlier were an invitation to deception, and came to be called liar loans. This was an "innovation," but there was a good reason that such innovations hadn't occurred before. . . .

The mortgage originators didn't focus on risk but rather focussed on transactions costs. But they weren't trying to minimize transactions costs; they were trying to maximize them—devising ways that they could increase them, and thereby their revenues. Short-term loans that had to be refinanced—and left open the risk of not being able to be refinanced—were particularly useful in this respect.

The transactions costs generated by writing mortgages provided a strong incentive to prey on innocent and inexperienced borrowers—for instance by encouraging more short-term lending and borrowing, entailing repeated loan restructurings, which helped generate high transactions costs.

The regulators, too, were accomplices in crime. They should have recognized the inherent risks in the new products; they should have done their own risk assessments rather than relying on self-regulation or on the credit-rating agencies. They should have realized the risks associated with high leverage, with over-the-counter derivatives, and especially the risks that were compounding as these were not netted out.

The regulators deceived themselves into thinking that if only they ensured that each bank managed its own risk (which they had every incentive, presumably, to do), then the system would work. Amazingly, they did not pay any attention to *systemic risk*, though concerns about systemic risk constitute one of the primary rationales for regulation in the first place. Even if every bank were, "on average," sound, they could act in a correlated way that generated risks to the economy as a whole.

In some cases, the regulators had a defense: They had no legal basis for acting, even had they discovered something was wrong. They had not been given the power to regulate derivatives. But that defense is somewhat disingenuous, because some of the regulators—most notably Greenspan—had worked hard to make sure that appropriate regulations were not adopted.

The repeal of the Glass–Steagall Act played an especial role, not just because of the conflicts of interest that it opened up . . . , but also because it transmitted the risk-taking culture of investment banking to commercial banks, which should have acted in a far more prudential manner.

It was not just *financial* regulation and regulators that were at fault. There should have been tougher enforcement of antitrust laws. Banks were allowed to grow to be too big to fail—or too big to be managed. And such banks have perverse incentives. When it's heads I win, tails you lose, too-big-to-fail banks have incentives to engage in excessive risk taking.

Corporate governance laws, too, are partly to blame. Regulators and investors should have been aware of the risks that the peculiar incentive structures engendered. These did not even serve shareholder interests well. In the aftermath of the Enron and WorldCom scandals, there was much discussion of the need for reform, and the Sarbanes–Oxley Act represented a beginning. But it didn't attack perhaps the most fundamental problem: stock options.

Bush's and Clinton's capital-gains tax cuts, in conjunction with the deductibility of interest, provided enhanced incentives for leverage—for homeowners to take out, for instance, as large a mortgage as they could.

Credentialed Accomplices

There is one other set of accomplices—the economists who provided the arguments that those in the financial markets found so convenient and self-serving. These economists provided models—based on unrealistic assumptions of perfect information, perfect competition, and perfect markets—in which regulation was unnecessary.

Modern economic theories, particularly those focusing on imperfect and asymmetric information and on systematic irrationalities, especially with respect to risk judgments, had explained how flawed those earlier "neoclassical" models were. They had shown that those models were not robust—even slight deviations from the extreme assumptions destroyed the conclusions. But these insights were simply ignored.

Some important strands in recent economic theory, moreover, encouraged central bankers to focus solely on fighting inflation. They seemed to argue that low inflation was necessary, and almost sufficient, for stable and robust growth. The result was that central bankers (including the Fed) [paid] little attention to the financial structure.

In short, many of the most popular micro-economic and macro-economic theories aided and abetted regulators, investors, bankers, and policymakers—they provided the "rationale" for their policies and actions.

They made the bankers believe that in pursuing their self-interest, they were, in fact, advancing the well-being of society; they made the regulators believe that in pursuing their policies of benign neglect, they were allowing the private sector to flourish, from which all would benefit.

Rebutting the Defense

Alan Greenspan (2009) has tried to shift the blame for low interest rates to China because of its high savings rate. Clearly, Greenspan's defense is unpersuasive: The Fed had enough control, at least in the short run, to have raised interest rates in spite of China's willingness to lend to America at a relatively low interest rate. Indeed, the Fed did just that in the middle of the decade, which contributed—predictably—to the popping of the housing bubble.

Low interest rates did feed the bubble. But that is not the necessary consequence of low interest rates. Many countries yearn for low interest rates to help finance needed investment. The funds could have been channeled into more productive uses. Our financial markets failed to do that. Our regulatory authorities allowed the financial markets (including the banks) to use the abundance of funds in ways that were not socially productive. They allowed the low interest rates to feed a housing bubble. They had the tools to stop this. They didn't use the tools that they had.

If we are to blame low interest rates for "feeding" the frenzy, then we have to ask what induced the Fed to pursue low interest rates. It did so, in part, to maintain the strength of the economy, which was suffering from inadequate aggregate demand as a result of the collapse of the tech bubble.

In that regard, Bush's tax cut for the rich was perhaps pivotal. It was not designed to stimulate the economy and did so only to a limited extent. His war in Iraq, too, played an important role. In its aftermath, oil prices rose from $20 a barrel to $140 a barrel. (We don't have to parse out here what fraction of this increase is due to the war; but there is little doubt that it played a role. See Stiglitz and Bilmes 2008.) Americans were now spending hundreds of billions of dollars a year more to import oil. This was money not available to be spent at home. . . .

Given the war and the consequent soaring oil prices and given Bush's poorly designed tax cuts, the burden of maintaining economic strength fell to the Fed. The Fed could have exercised its authority as a regulator to do what it could do to direct the resources into more productive uses. Here, the Fed and its chairman have a double culpability. Not only did they fail in their regulatory role, they became cheerleaders for the bubble that eventually consumed America. When asked about a possible bubble, Greenspan suggested there was none—only a little froth. That was clearly wrong. The Fed argued that you could not tell a bubble until after it broke. That, too, was not fully correct. You can't be *sure* there is a bubble until after it breaks, but one can make strong probabilistic statements.

All policies are made in the context of uncertainty. House prices, especially at the lower end, soared, yet the real incomes of most Americans stagnated: There was a clear problem. And it was clear that the problem would get worse once interest rates rose. Greenspan had encouraged people to take out variable-rate mortgages when interest rates were at historically low levels. And he allowed them to borrow up to the hilt—assuming interest rates would remain at the same low level. But because interest rates were so low—real interest rates were negative—it was unreasonable to expect them to remain at that level for long. When they rose, it was clear that many Americans would be in trouble—and so would the lenders who had lent to them.

Apologists for the Fed sometimes try to defend this irresponsible and short-sighted policy by saying they had no choice: Raising interest rates would have killed the bubble, but also would have killed the economy. But the Fed has more tools than just the interest rate. There were, for instance, a number of regulatory actions that would have dampened the bubble. It chose not to employ these tools. It could have reduced maximum loan-to-value ratios as the likelihood of a bubble increased; it could have lowered the maximum house payment-to-income ratios allowed. If it believed it did not have the requisite tools, it could have gone to Congress and requested them.

This doesn't provide a *fully* satisfactory counterfactual. True, perhaps the money could have been deployed by financial markets more productively, to support, for instance, more innovation, or important projects in developing countries. But perhaps the financial markets would have found another scam to support irresponsible borrowing—for instance, a new credit-card boom.

Defending the Innocent

Just as all of the accomplices are not equally culpable, some suspects should be acquitted.

In the long list of possible culprits, there are two that many Republicans often name. They find it difficult to accept that markets fail, that market participants could act in such an irresponsible manner, that the wizards of finance didn't understand risk, that capitalism has serious flaws. It is government, they are sure, which is to blame.

I have suggested government is indeed to blame, but for doing too little. The conservative critics believe that government is to blame for doing too much. They criticize the Community Reinvestment Act (CRA) requirements imposed on banks, which required them to lend a certain fraction of their portfolio to underserved minority communities. They also blame Fannie Mae and Freddie Mac, the peculiar government-sponsored enterprises, which, though privatized in 1968, play a very large role in mortgage markets. Fannie and Freddie were, according to conservatives, "under pressure" from Congress and the president to expand home ownership (President Bush often talked about the "ownership society").

This is clearly just an attempt to shift blame. A recent Fed study showed that the default rate among CRA mortgagors is actually *below* average (Kroszner 2008). The problems in America's mortgage markets began with the subprime market, while Fannie Mae and Freddie Mac primarily financed "conforming" (prime) mortgages. . . .

. . . To be sure, Fannie Mae and Freddie Mac did get into the high-risk high leverage "games" that were the fad in the private sector, though rather late, and rather ineptly. Here, too, there was regulatory failure; the government-sponsored enterprises have a special regulator which should have constrained them, but evidently, amidst the deregulatory philosophy of the Bush Administration, did not. Once they entered the game, they had an advantage, because they could borrow somewhat more cheaply because of their (ambiguous at the time) government guarantee. They could arbitrage that guarantee to generate bonuses comparable to those that they saw were being "earned" by their counterparts in the fully private sector.

Politics and Economics

There is one more important culprit, which, in fact, has played a key behind-the-scenes role in many various parts of this story: America's political system, and especially its dependence on campaign contributions. This allowed Wall Street to exercise the enormous influence that it has had, to push for the stripping of regulations and . . . the appointment of regulators who didn't believe in regulations—with the predictable and predicted consequences (Stiglitz 2003) that we have seen. Even today, that influence is playing a role in the design of effective means of addressing the financial crisis.

Any economy needs rules and referees. Our rules and referees were shaped by special interests; ironically, it is not even clear whether those rules and referees served those special interests well. It is clear that they did not serve the national interests well.

In the end, this is a crisis of our economic and political system. Each of the players was, to a large extent, doing what they thought they should do. The bankers were maximizing their incomes, given the rules of the game. The rules of the game said that they should use their political influence to get regulations and regulators that allowed them, and the corporations they headed, to walk away with as much money as they could. The politicians responded to the rules of the game: They had to raise money to get elected, and to do that, they had to please powerful and wealthy constituents. There were economists who provided the politicians, the bankers, and the regulators with a convenient ideology: According to this ideology, the policies and practices that they were pursuing would supposedly benefit all.

There are those who now would like to reconstruct the system as it was prior to 2008. They will push for regulatory reform, but it will be more cosmetic than real. Banks that are too big to fail will be allowed to continue little changed. There will be "oversight," whatever that means. But the banks will continue to be able to gamble, and they will continue to be too big to fail. Accounting standards will be relaxed, to give them greater leeway. Little will be done about incentive structures or even risky practices. If so, then, another crisis is sure to follow.

ENDNOTE

1. Greenspan supported the 2001 tax cut even though he should have known that it would have led to the deficits which previously he had treated as such an anathema. His argument that, unless we acted now, the surpluses that were accumulating as a result of Clinton's prudent fiscal policies would drain the economy of all of its T-bills, which would make the conduct of monetary policy difficult, was one of the worst arguments from a respected government official I have ever heard; presumably, if the contingency he imagined—the wiping out of the national debt—was imminent, Congress had the tools and incentives with which to correct the situation in short order.

Joseph E. Stiglitz, University Professor and Professor of Economics at Columbia University, 814 Uris Hall, MC 3308, 420 West 118th Street, New York, NY 10027, a 2001 Nobel Laureate in economics, is the author, inter alia, *of* The Roaring Nineties *(Norton, 2003).*

Critical Review *21(2–3); 329–339   ISSN 0891-3811 print, 1933-8007 online*

© 2009 Critical Review Foundation DOI: 10.1080/08913810902934133

REFERENCES

Greenspan, Alan. 2009. "The Fed Didn't Cause the Housing Bubble." *Wall Street Journal,* 11 March.
Kroszner, Randall S. 2008. "The Community Reinvestment Act and the Recent Mortgage Crisis." Speech to the Confronting Concentrated Poverty Policy Forum, Board of Governors of Federal Reserve System, Washington, D.C., 3 December.
Stiglitz, Joseph E. 2003. *The Roaring Nineties.* New York: W.W. Norton.
Stiglitz, Joseph E., and Linda Bilmes. 2008. *The Three Trillion Dollar War: The True Costs of the Iraq Conflict.* New York: W.W. Norton.

Lawrence H. White

How Did We Get into This Financial Mess?

Introduction

Mortgage foreclosure rates in the United States have risen to the highest level since the Great Depression. The nation's two largest financial institutions, the government—sponsored mortgage purchasers and repackagers Fannie Mae and Freddie Mac, have gone into bankruptcy-like "conservatorship." Several major investment banks, insurance companies, and commercial banks heavily tied to real estate lending have gone bankrupt outright or have been sold for cents on the dollar. Prices and trading volumes in mortgage-backed securities have shrunk dramatically. Reluctance to lend has spread to other markets. To prepare the ground for a return to normalcy in American credit markets we must understand the character of the problems we currently face and how those problems arose.

What *Didn't* Happen

Some commentators (and both presidential candidates) have blamed the current financial mess on greed. But if an unusually high number of airplanes were to crash this year, would it make sense to blame gravity? No. Greed, like gravity, is a constant. It can't explain why the number of financial crashes is higher than usual. There has been no unusual epidemic of blackheartedness.

Others have blamed deregulation or (in the words of one representative) "unregulated free market lending run amok." Such an indictment is necessarily skimpy on the particulars, because there has actually been no recent dismantling of banking and financial regulations. Regulations were in fact intensified in the 1990s in ways that fed the development of the housing finance crisis, as discussed below. The last move in the direction of financial deregulation was the bipartisan Financial Services Modernization Act of 1999, also known as the Gramm–Leach–Bliley Act, signed by President Clinton. That act opened the door for financial firms to diversify: a holding company that owns a commercial bank subsidiary may now also own insurance, mutual fund, and investment bank subsidiaries. Far from contributing to the recent turmoil, the greater freedom allowed by the act has clearly been a blessing in containing it. Without it. JPMorgan Chase could not have acquired Bear Stearns, nor could Bank of America have acquired Merrill Lynch—acquisitions that avoided losses to Bear's and Merrill's bondholders. Without it, Goldman Sachs and Morgan Stanley could not have switched specialties to become bank holding companies when it became clear that they could no longer survive as investment banks.

What *Did* Happen—and Why?

The actual causes of our financial troubles were unusual monetary policy moves and novel federal regulatory interventions. These poorly chosen public policies distorted interest rates and asset prices, diverted loanable funds into the wrong investments, and twisted normally robust financial institutions into unsustainable positions.

Let's review how the crisis has unfolded. Problems first surfaced in "exotic" or "flexible" home mortgage lending. Creative lenders and originators had expanded the volume of unconventional mortgages with high default risks (reflected in nonprime ratings), which are the housing market's equivalent of junk bonds. Unconventional mortgages helped to feed a run-up in condo and house prices. House prices peaked and turned downward. Borrowers with inadequate income relative to their debts, many of whom had either counted on being able to borrow against a higher house value in the future in order to help them meet their monthly mortgage payments, or on being able to "flip" the property at a price that would more than re-pay their mortgage, began to default. Default rates on nonprime mortgages rose to unexpected highs. The high risk on the mortgages came back to bite mortgage holders, the financial institutions to whom the monthly payments were owed. Firms directly holding mortgages saw reduced cash flows. Firms holding securitized mortgage bundles (often called "mortgage-backed securities") additionally saw the expectation of continuing reductions in cash flows reflected in declining market values for their securities. Uncertainty about future cash flows impaired the liquidity (resalability) of their securities.

Doubts about the value of mortgage-backed securities led naturally to doubts about the solvency of institutions heavily invested in those securities. Financial institutions that had stocked up on junk mortgages and junk-mortgage-backed securities found their stock prices dropping. The worst cases, like Countrywide Financial, the investment banks Lehman Brothers and Merrill Lynch, and the government-sponsored mortgage purchasers Fannie Mae and Freddie Mac, went broke or had to find a last-minute purchaser to avoid bankruptcy. Firms heavily involved in guaranteeing mortgage-backed securities, like the insurance giant AIG, likewise ran aground. Suspect Financial institutions began finding it difficult to borrow, because potential lenders could not confidently assess the chance that an institution might go bankrupt and be unable to pay them back. Credit flows among financial institutions became increasingly impeded by such solvency worries.

Given this sequence of events, the explanation of our credit troubles requires an explanation for the unusual growth of mortgage lending—particularly nonprime lending, which fed the housing bubble that burst—leading in turn to the unusual number of mortgage defaults, financial institution crashes, and attendant credit-market inhibitions.

There is no doubt that private miscalculation and imprudence have made matters worse for more than a few institutions. Such mistakes help to explain which particular firms have run into the most trouble. But to explain *industrywide* errors, we need to identify policy distortions capable of having industrywide effects.

We can group most of the unfortunate policies under two main headings: (1) Federal Reserve credit expansion that provided the means for unsustainable mortgage financing, and (2) mandates and subsidies to write riskier mortgages. The enumeration of regrettable policies below is by no means exhaustive.

Providing the Funds: Federal Reserve Credit Expansion

In the recession of 2001, the Federal Reserve System, under Chairman Alan Greenspan, began aggressively expanding the U.S. money supply. Year-over-year growth in the M2 monetary aggregate rose briefly above 10 percent, and remained above 8 percent entering the second half of 2003. The expansion was accompanied by the Fed repeatedly lowering its target for the federal funds (interbank short-term) interest rate. . . . The *real* Fed funds rate was negative—meaning that nominal rates were lower than the contemporary rare of inflation—for two and a half years. In purchasing-power terms, during that period a borrower was not paying but rather gaining in proportion to what he borrowed. Economist Steve Hanke has summarized the result: "This set off the mother of all liquidity cycles and yet another massive demand bubble." . . .

The demand bubble thus created went heavily into real estate. From mid-2003 to mid-2007, while the dollar volume of final sales of goods and services was growing at 5 percent to 7 percent, real estate loans at commercial banks were growing at 10–17 percent.[1] Credit-fueled demand pushed up the sale prices of existing houses and encouraged the construction of new housing on undeveloped land, in both cases absorbing the increased dollar volume of mortgages. Because real estate is an especially long-lived asset, its market value is especially boosted by low interest rates. . . .

The Fed's policy of lowering short-term interest rates not only fueled growth in the dollar volume of mortgage lending but had unintended consequences for the *type* of mortgages written. By pushing very-short-term interest rates down so dramatically between 2001 and 2004, the Fed lowered short-term rates relative to 30-year rates. Adjustable-rate mortgages (ARMs), typically based on a one-year interest rate, became increasingly cheap relative to 30-year fixed-rate mortgages. Back in 2001, nonteaser

ARM rates on average were 1.13 percent cheaper than 30-year fixed mortgages (5.84 percent vs. 6.97 percent). By 2004, as a result of the ultra-low federal funds rate, the gap had grown to 1.94 percent (3.90 percent *vs.* 5.84 percent).[2] Not surprisingly, increasing numbers of new mortgage borrowers were drawn away from mortgages with 30-year rates into ARMs. The share of new mortgages with adjustable rates, only one-fifth in 2001, had more than doubled by 2004. An adjustable-rate mortgage shifts the risk of refinancing at higher rates from the lender to the borrower. Many borrowers who took out ARMs implicitly (and imprudently) counted on the Fed to keep short-term rates low indefinitely. They have faced problems as their monthly payments have adjusted upward. The shift toward ARMs thus compounded the mortgage-quality problems arising from regulatory mandates and subsidies. . . .

The excess investment in new housing has resulted in an overbuild of housing stock. Assuming that the federal government does not follow proposals (tongue-in-cheek or otherwise) that it should buy up and then raze excess houses and condos, or proposals to admit a large number of new immigrants, house prices and activity in the U.S. housing construction industry are going to remain depressed for a while. The process of adjustment, already well under way but not yet completed, requires house prices to fall and workers and capital to be released from the construction industry to find more appropriate employment elsewhere. Correspondingly, an adjustment requires the book value of existing financial assets based on housing to be written down and workers and capital to be released from writing and trading mortgages to find more appropriate employment elsewhere. No matter how painful the adjustment process, delaying it only delays the economy's recovery.

Mandates and Subsidies to Write Risky Mortgages

In 2001, the share of existing mortgages classified as nonprime (subprime or the intermediate category "Alt-A") was below 10 percent. That share began rising rapidly. The non-prime share of all *new* mortgage originations rose close to 34 percent by 2006, bringing the nonprime share of existing mortgages to 23 percent. Meanwhile the quality of loans within the nonprime category declined, because a smaller share of nonprime borrowers made 20 percent down payments on their purchases.[3]

The expansion in risky mortgages to under-qualified borrowers was an imprudence fostered by the federal government. As elaborated in the paragraphs to follow, there were several ways that Congress and the executive branch encouraged the expansion. The first way was loosening down-payment standards on mortgages guaranteed by the Federal Housing Administration. The second was strengthening the Community Reinvestment Act [CRA]. The third was pressure on lenders by the Department of

Housing and Urban Development. The fourth and most important way was subsidizing, through implicit taxpayer guarantees, the dramatic expansion of the government-sponsored mortgage buyers Fannie Mae and Freddie Mac; pointedly refusing to moderate the moral hazard problem of implicit guarantees or otherwise rein in the hyper-expansion of Fannie and Freddie; and increasingly pushing Fannie and Freddie to promote "affordable housing" through expanded purchases of nonprime loans to low-income applicants.

The Federal Housing Administration was founded in 1934 to insure mortgage loans made by private firms to qualifying borrowers. For a borrower to qualify, the FHA originally required—among other things—that the borrower provide a nonborrowed 20 percent down payment on the house being purchased. Private mortgage lenders like savings banks considered that to be a low down payment at the time. But private down payment requirements began falling toward the FHA level. The FHA reduced its requirements below 20 percent. Private mortgage insurance arose for non-FHA borrowers with down payments below 20 percent. Apparently concerned for bureaucratic reasons with preventing its "market share" from shrinking too far, the FHA began lowering its standards to stay below those of private lenders. By 2004, the required down payment on the FHA's most popular program had fallen to only 3 percent, and proposals were afoot in Congress to lower it to zero.[4] Mortgages with very low down payments have had very high default rates.

The Community Reinvestment Act, first enacted in 1977, was relatively innocuous for its first 12 years or so, merely imposing reporting requirements on commercial banks regarding the extent to which they lent funds back into the neighborhoods where they gathered deposits. Congress amended the CRA in 1989 to make banks' CRA ratings public information. Further amendments in 1995 gave the CRA serious teeth: regulators could now deny a bank with a low CRA rating approval to merge with another bank—at a time when the arrival of interstate banking made such approvals especially valuable—or even to open new branches. . . .

In response to the new CRA rules, some banks joined into partnerships with community groups to distribute millions in mortgage money to low-income borrowers previously considered noncreditworthy. Other banks took advantage of the newly authorized option to boost their CRA rating by purchasing special "CRA mortgage-backed securities," that is, packages of disproportionately nonprime loans certified as meeting CRA criteria and securitized by Freddie Mac. No doubt a small share of the total current crop of bad mortgages has come from CRA loans. But for the share of the increase in defaults that *has* come from the CRA-qualifying borrowers (who would otherwise have been turned down for lack of creditworthiness) rather than from, say, would-be condo-flippers on the outskirts of Las Vegas—the CRA bears responsibility.

Defaults and foreclosures are, of course, a drag on real estate values in poor neighborhoods just as in others. Federal Reserve Chairman Ben Bernanke aptly commented in a 2007 speech that "recent problems in mortgage markets illustrate that an underlying assumption of the CRA—that *more* lending equals *better* outcomes for local communities may not always hold."[5] . . .

Congress and HUD also pressured Fannie Mae and Freddie Mac. A 1992 law, as described by Bernanke, "required the government-sponsored enterprises, Fannie Mae and Freddie Mac, to devote a large percentage of their activities to meeting affordable housing goals."[6] Russell Roberts has cited some relevant numbers in the *Wall Street Journal:*

> Beginning in 1992, Congress pushed Fannie Mae and Freddie Mac to increase their purchases of mortgages going to low- and moderate-income borrowers. For 1996, the Department of Housing and Urban Development (HUD) gave Fannie and Freddie an explicit target—42 percent of their mortgage Financing had to go to borrowers with income below the median in their area. The target increased to 50 percent in 2000 and 52 percent in 2005.
>
> For 1996, HUD required that 12 percent of all mortgage purchases by Fannie and Freddie be "special affordable" loans, typically to borrowers with income less than 60% of their area's median income. That number was increased to 20% in 2000 and 22% in 2005. The 2008 goal was to be 28%. Between 2000 and 2005, Fannie and Freddie met those goals every year, funding hundreds of billions of dollars worth of loans, many of them subprime and adjustable-rate loans, and made to borrowers who bought houses with less than 10% down.[7]

Wayne Barrett of *The Village Voice* has likewise drawn attention to how Andrew Cuomo, as Secretary of HUD between 1997 and 2001, actively pushed Fannie Mae and Freddie Mac into backing the enormous expansion of the nonprime mortgage market. In the short run, Fannie Mae and Freddie Mac found that their new flexible lending lines were profitable, and they continued to expand their purchases of nonprime mortgages under the rising goals set by subsequent HUD Secretaries.[8]

The hyperexpansion of Fannie Mae and Freddie Mac was made possible by their implicit backing from the U.S. Treasury. To fund their enormous growth, Fannie Mae and Freddie Mac had to borrow huge sums in wholesale financial markets. Institutional investors were willing to lend to the government-sponsored mortgage companies cheaply—at rates only slightly above those on the Treasury's risk-free securities and well below those paid by other financial intermediaries—despite the risk of default that would normally attach to private firms holding such highly leveraged and poorly diversified portfolios. The investors were so willing only because they thought that the Treasury would repay them should Fannie or Freddie be unable to. As it turns out, they were right. The Treasury did explicitly guarantee Fannie's and Freddie's debts when the two giants collapsed and were placed into conservatorship.

Congress was repeatedly warned by credible observers about the growing dangers posed by Fannie Mae's and Freddie Mac's implicit federal backing. A leading critic was William Poole, then president of the Federal Reserve Bank of St. Louis, who as far back as 2003 pointedly warned that the companies had insufficient capital to survive adverse conditions, and that the problem would continue to fester unless Congress explicitly removed the federal backing from the two companies so that they would face market discipline.[9]

Congress did nothing. Efforts to rein in Fannie and Freddie came to naught because the two giants had cultivated powerful friends on Capitol Hill. . . .

Conclusion

The housing bubble and its aftermath arose from market distortions created by the Federal Reserve, government backing of Fannie Mae and Freddie Mac, the Department of Housing and Urban Development, and the Federal Housing Authority. We are experiencing the unfortunate results of perverse government policies.

The traditional remedy for the severely mistaken investment policies of private firms—shut and dismantle those firms to stop the bleeding, free their assets and personnel to go where they can add value, and make room for firms with better entrepreneurial ideas—is as relevant as ever. A financial market in which failed enterprises like Freddie Mac or AIG are never shut down is like an *American Idol* contest in which the poorest singers never go home. The closure of Lehman Brothers (and the near-closure of Merrill Lynch), by raising the interest rate that the market charges to highly leveraged investment banks, forced Goldman Sachs and Morgan Stanley to change their business models drastically. The most effective and appropriate form of business regulation is regulation by profit and loss.

The long-term remedy for the severely mistaken government monetary and regulatory policies that have produced the current financial train wreck is similar. We need to identify and undo policies that distort housing and financial markets and dismantle failed agencies whose missions require them to distort markets. We should be guided by recognizing the two chief errors that have been made. Cheap-money policies by the Federal Reserve System do not produce a sustainable prosperity. Hiding the cost of mortgage subsidies off-budget, as by imposing affordable housing regulatory mandates on banks and by providing implicit taxpayer guarantees on Fannie Mae and Freddie Mac bonds, does not give us more housing at nobody's expense.

Lawrence H. White is the F. A. Hayek Professor of Economic History at the University of Missouri St. Louis and an adjunct scholar at the Cato Institute. He is the author of Competition and Currency, Free Banking in Britain, *and* The Theory of Monetary Institutions.

ENDNOTES

1. Federal Reserve Bank of St. Louis FRED database, series FINSAL and REALLN, year-over-year percentage changes, http://research.stlouisfed.org/fred2/series/FINSAL?cid=106 and http://research.stlouisfed.org/fred2/series/REALLN?cid=100. My thanks to George Selgin for drawing my attention to these numbers.
2. As reported by Freddie Mac, http://www.freddiemac.com/pmms/pmms30.htm.
3. William R. Emmons, "The Mortgage Crisis: Let Markets Work, But Compensate the Truly Needy," *Regional Economist* (July 2008), http://www.stlouisfed.org/publications/re/2008/c/pages/mortgage.html.
4. John Berlau, "The Subprime FHA," *Wall Street Journal* (October 15, 2007), http://cei.org/gencon/019,06195.cfm.
5. Ben S. Bernanke, "The Community Reinvestment Act: Its Evolution and New Challenges." (March 30, 2007), http://www.federalreserve.gov/newsevents/speech/Bemanke20070330a.htm.
6. Bernanke, "The Community Reinvestment Act."
7. Russell Roberts, "How Government Stoked the Mania," *Wall Street Journal* (October 3, 2008), http://online.wsj.com/article/SB122298982558700341.html?mod=special_page_campaign2008_most-pop.
8. Wayne Barrett, "Andrew Cuomo and Fannie and Freddie: How the Youngest Housing and Urban Development Secretary in History Gave Birth to the Mortgage Crisis," *Village Voice* (August 5, 2008), http://www.villagevoice.com/2008-08-05/news/how-andrew-cuomo-gave-birth-to-the-crisis-at-fannie-mae-and-freddie-mac/1.
9. "Official Cites Risks of Fannie, Freddie," *Los Angeles Times* (March 11, 2003), http://articles.latimes.com/2003/mar/11/business/fi-freddie11.

CHAPTER 11

CHINA MUST REVALUE TO CORRECT GLOBAL IMBALANCES *v.* CHINESE REVALUATION WILL NOT CORRECT GLOBAL IMBALANCES

China Must Revalue to Correct Global Imbalances

Advocate: C. Fred Bergsten

Source: "The Dollar and the Renminbi," Statement at the Hearing on U.S. Economic Relations with China: Strategies and Options on Exchange Rates and Market Access, Subcommittee on Security and International Trade and Finance, Committee on Banking, Housing, and Urban Affairs, U.S. Senate, Washington, DC, May 23, 2007

Chinese Revaluation Will Not Correct Global Imbalances

Advocate: David D. Hale and Lyric Hughes Hale

Source: "Reconsidering Revaluation: The Wrong Approach to the U.S.–Chinese Trade Imbalance," *Foreign Affairs* 87 (January/February 2008): 57–66

Should China revalue its currency, the renminbi (whose principal unit is the yuan), against the dollar? Officially, the Chinese government pegs the renminbi to a basket of currencies in a crawling peg regime. Unofficially, China continues to maintain the renminbi at a fairly stable exchange rate against the dollar. Many economists have argued that the renminbi is undervalued against the dollar and that China's exchange-rate policy intentionally maintains this undervaluation to promote exports. Such concerns prompted Congress to pressure first the Bush administration and now the Obama administration to urge the Chinese government to revalue the renminbi and to threaten to impose tariffs on imports from China if it doesn't.

Efforts to pressure China to revalue its currency come in the broader context of global current account imbalances. The United States has run current account deficits of unprecedented magnitude since 2000; in 2007, this deficit reached $731 billion, about 5 percent of U.S. income. For its part, China has run very large current account surpluses—about $231 billion or 10 percent of its gross domestic product (GDP) in 2007. Moreover, the United States runs its largest bilateral deficit with China: $289 billion in 2007. Many observers conclude from these facts that the U.S. current account deficit is largely a consequence of the bilateral deficit with China and that the bilateral deficit in turn is a consequence of the exchange rate between the dollar and the renminbi.

CHINA MUST REVALUE TO CORRECT GLOBAL IMBALANCES

Advocates of renminbi revaluation assert that the imbalance in U.S.–China trade is a direct consequence of China's exchange-rate policy. Because China pegs its currency to the dollar at an undervalued rate, it reduces the price of Chinese-made products in the U.S. market and raises the price of American products in the Chinese market. Consequently, demand for Chinese goods rises, while demand for American goods falls. Renminbi revaluation would reverse these relative prices, leading to greater demand for American goods, falling demand for Chinese goods, and an adjustment of the trade imbalance.

C. Fred Bergsten develops this argument in detail here. Bergsten argues that the global current account imbalances that are the consequence of Chinese exchange-rate policies pose a serious threat to global economic stability. Adjustment of these imbalances requires exchange-rate realignments wherein the renminbi is revalued by as much as 40 percent against the dollar. And although Bergsten calls for other changes in Chinese practices, he claims that "China's currency policy . . . is thus by far the single most important issue in U.S.–China economic relations."

CHINESE REVALUATION WILL NOT CORRECT GLOBAL IMBALANCES

Others are more skeptical about the need for a change in China's exchange-rate policy and the impact that any such change would have on the U.S. current account deficit. These observers analyze contemporary global imbalances through an economic model that emphasizes cross-national differences in savings and investment rates rather than exchange rates. Within this framework, the U.S. current account deficit is a consequence of a very low national savings rate relative to investment. For the past few years, the U.S. savings rate has been close to zero. In contrast, China's current account surplus is a consequence of a very high national savings rate relative to its investment. Indeed, China saved almost 50 percent of its national income in 2008. Adjustment of the imbalance will thus require changes in these national savings rates. Americans must consume less and save more, and the Chinese must consume more and save less.

Such logic underpins the analysis of David Hale and Lyric Hughes Hale. They suggest that Congress has placed far too much emphasis on the bilateral relationship with China. What matters is the multilateral position. Moreover, focusing on the exchange rate is unwise because a revaluation will not only do little to correct the imbalance but also create a backlash in China. Instead, they advocate a broader range of reforms designed to integrate China more firmly into the global economy. In addition, China must reform its tax system, restructure its corporate and banking sectors, and encourage consumption.

POINTS **TO PONDER**

1. What industries in China have an interest in an undervalued exchange rate? Does this valuation hurt any group in China?

2. What are the arguments for and against Bergsten's proposition that a revaluation of the renminbi will correct the bilateral trade imbalance?

3. What, if anything, could the U.S. Congress do to reduce the U.S. multilateral current account deficit?

4. How should the burden of adjustment be distributed between surplus and deficit countries?

C. Fred Bergsten

The Dollar and the Renminbi

The Central Role of China in the Global Imbalances

The U.S. global merchandise trade and current account deficits rose to $857 billion in 2006. This amounted to about 6.5 percent of our GDP [gross domestic product], twice the previous record of the middle 1980s and by far the largest deficit ever recorded by a single country.[1] The deficits have risen by an annual average of $100 billion over the past four years.

China's global current account surplus soared to about $250 billion in 2006, more than 9 percent of its GDP. Its trade surplus has doubled again in the first quarter of 2007, suggesting that its current account deficit will exceed $300 billion in 2007—the largest ever recorded by any country. China has become by far the largest surplus country in the world, recently passing Japan and far ahead of all others. Its foreign exchange reserves have also passed Japan's to become the largest in the world and now exceed $1 trillion, an enormous waste of resources for a country where most of the huge population remains very poor.

China's role in the global imbalances is even greater than these numbers might suggest. A substantial increase in the value of the Chinese currency is an essential component of reducing the imbalances, but China has blocked any significant rise in the RMB [renminbi] by intervening massively in the foreign exchange markets. It has been buying $15–$20 billion per month for several years to hold its currency down, and its level of intervention jumped to a monthly average of $45 billion in the first quarter of this year.

By keeping its own currency undervalued, China has also deterred a number of other Asian countries from letting their currencies rise very much (if at all) against the dollar for fear of losing competitive position against China. Hence, China's currency policy has taken much of Asia out of the international adjustment process. This is critical because Asia accounts for about half the global surpluses that are the counterparts of the U.S. current account deficit, has accumulated the great bulk of the increase in global reserves in recent years, and is essential to the needed correction of the exchange rate of the dollar because it makes up about 40 percent of the dollar's trade-weighted index. The most obvious Asian candidates for sizable currency appreciation in addition to China are Japan, whose currency is also substantially undervalued despite the absence of intervention for over three years, Taiwan, Hong Kong, Singapore, and Malaysia.

China has recently let the RMB rise marginally against the dollar. Since China continues to link its exchange rate to the dollar and the dollar has fallen against virtually all other currencies, however, the average exchange rate of the RMB is weaker now than in 2001 when China's current account surplus accounted for a modest 1 percent of its GDP. The world's most competitive economy has become even more competitive through a deliberate policy of currency undervaluation.

About one quarter of all of China's economic growth in the past two years has stemmed from the continued sharp rise in its trade surplus. China is thus overtly exporting unemployment to other countries and apparently sees its currency undervaluation as an off-budget export and job subsidy that, at least to date, has avoided effective international sanction.

The Risks for the U.S. and World Economies

These global imbalances are unsustainable for both international financial and U.S. domestic political reasons. On the international side, the United States must now attract about $8 billion of capital from the rest of the world every working day to finance our current account deficit and our own foreign investment outflows. Even a modest reduction of this inflow, let alone its cessation or a sell-off from the $14 trillion of dollar claims on the United States now held around the world, could initiate a precipitous decline in the dollar. Especially under the present circumstances of nearly full employment and full capacity utilization in the United States, this could in turn sharply increase U.S. inflation and interest rates, severely affecting the equity and housing markets and potentially triggering a recession. The global imbalances represent the single largest threat to the continued growth and stability of the U.S. and world economies.

The domestic political unsustainability derives from the historical reality that sizable dollar overvaluation, and the huge and rising trade deficits that it produces, are the most accurate leading indicators of resistance to open trade policies in the United States. Such overvaluation and deficits alter the domestic politics of U.S. trade policy, adding to the number of industries seeking relief from imports and dampening the ability of exporters to mount effective countervailing pressures. Acute trade policy pressures of this type, threatening the basic thrust of U.S. trade policy and thus the openness of the global trading system, prompted drastic policy reversals by the Reagan Administration to drive the dollar down by more than 30 percent via the Plaza Agreement in the middle 1980s, and by the Nixon Administration to impose an import surcharge and take the dollar off gold to achieve a cumulative devaluation of more than 20 percent in the early 1970s.

The escalation of trade pressures against China at present, despite the strength of the U.S. economy and the low level of unemployment, is the latest evidence of this relationship between currency values and trade policies.

With deep-seated anxieties over globalization already prevalent in our body politic, and the failure of the Doha Round to maintain the momentum of trade liberalization around the world, continued failure to correct the currency misalignments could have a devastating impact on the global trading system.

The Policy Implications

It is thus essential to reduce the U.S. and China imbalances by substantial amounts in as orderly a manner as possible. The goal of the global adjustment should be to cut the U.S. global current account deficit to 3–3½ percent of GDP, about half its present level, at which point the ratio of U.S. foreign debt to GDP would eventually stabilize and should be sustainable. China's goal, already accepted in principle by its political leadership but without any significant policy follow-up, should be to totally eliminate its global current account surplus and stop the buildup of foreign exchange reserves.

The United States should take the lead in addressing the imbalances by developing a credible program to convert its present, and especially foreseeable, budget deficits into modest surpluses like those that were achieved in 1998–2001. Such a shift, of perhaps 3–4 percent of our GDP, would have two crucial payoffs vis-à-vis our external economic position: It would reduce the excess of our domestic spending relative to domestic output, which can only be met by additional net imports, and it would reduce the shortfall of our domestic savings relative to domestic investment, thereby cutting our reliance on the foreign capital inflows that drive up the value of the dollar and undermine our trade competitiveness. Fiscal tightening is the only available policy instrument that will produce such adjustments. Hence I strongly recommend that the new Congress take effective and immediate steps in that direction.[2]

China needs to adopt policies to promote an opposite adjustment, reducing its uniquely high national saving rate by increasing domestic consumption. China can increase domestic spending directly through higher government expenditures on health care, pensions, and education. Such new government programs are needed for purely internal reasons because of the unrest in China that has resulted from the demise of state-owned enterprises that provided these benefits in previous times. They would also reduce the precautionary motive for household saving in China; this would boost private as well as government demand, contributing importantly to the needed international adjustment.[3] A number of important Chinese policy goals, such as increasing employment and curbing energy consumption, would also be served by such shifts in the composition of China's growth strategy.[4]

Large changes in exchange rates will also have to be a major component of the adjustment process. The dollar will need to fall, hopefully in a gradual and orderly manner over the next several years, by a trade-weighted average of about 20 percent. A change in China's currency policy, in both the short and longer runs, is thus by far the single most important issue in U.S.–China economic relations.[5]

An increase of at least 20 percent in the average value of the RMB against all other currencies, which would imply an appreciation of about 40 percent against the dollar,[6] and sizable appreciations against the dollar of other key Asian currencies will be required to achieve an orderly correction of the global imbalances.[7] Such a change could be phased in over several years to ease the transitional impact on China.[8] It could be accomplished either by a series of step-level revaluations, like the 2.1-percent change of July 2005 against the dollar, but of much larger magnitudes and with a substantial initial "down payment" of at least 10–15 percent, or by a much more rapid upward managed float of the RMB than is underway at present. An increase of 40 percent in the RMB and other Asian currencies against the dollar would reduce the U.S. global current account deficit by about $150 billion per year, more than one third of the total adjustment that is required.

Over the longer run, China should adopt a more flexible exchange rate that will respond primarily to market forces. These forces would clearly have pushed the RMB to much higher levels by now in the absence of China's official intervention. There is some justification, however, for China's fears that an abrupt move to a freely floating exchange rate now, particularly if accompanied by abolition of its controls on financial outflows, could trigger capital flight and jeopardize its economy in view of the fragility of its banking system. Full-scale reform of China's exchange rate system will have to await completion of the reform of its banking system, which will take at least several more years. Hence the adoption of a flexible exchange rate regime in China, which is essential to avoid re-creation of the present imbalances in the future, can be only a second stage in the resolution of the currency problem, and the immediate need is for a substantial increase in the price of the RMB (especially against the dollar) through whatever technique is most feasible for the Chinese authorities.[9]

A U.S. Strategy for the Renminbi

It is obvious that China is extremely reluctant to make the needed changes in its currency policy. It is equally obvious that U.S. efforts on the issue over the past three years, whether the "quiet diplomacy" of the Administration or the threats of Congressional action, have borne little fruit to date. A new U.S. policy is clearly needed.

One cardinal requirement is for the Administration and Congress to adopt a unified, or at least consistent, position. To date, there has been something of "good cop" (Administration)–"bad cop" (Congress, e.g., the threat of the Schumer–Graham legislation) bifurcation between the two branches. China has exploited these differences, essentially counting on the Administration to protect it from the Congress—a bet that, to date, has paid off.

I would therefore suggest a new five-part strategy for U.S. policy on the currency issue.

First, it is clear that China has aggressively blocked appreciation of the RMB through its massive intervention in the currency markets and that the Treasury Department has severely jeopardized its credibility on the issue by failing to carry out the requirements of current law to label China a "currency manipulator."[10] The Treasury report of May 2005 indicated that "if current trends continue *without substantial alteration* (italics added), China's policies will likely meet the statute's technical requirements for designation." The report of May 2006 sharply criticized China for its currency policies, clearly suggesting that there has been no "substantial alteration" in those practices, but inexplicably failed to draw the obvious conclusion of its own analysis.[11] The latest report, submitted last December, was much milder. Treasury has thus been reducing its criticism of China's currency practices even as the RMB has become increasingly undervalued and China's external surpluses have soared.

The Treasury policy needs to be changed sharply and quickly. The Administration should notify the Chinese that, if China fails to make a significant "down payment" appreciation of at least 10 percent prior to the release of Treasury's next semiannual report, it will be labeled a "manipulator." This would trigger an explicit U.S. negotiation with China on the currency issue.

Second, the Administration should notify its G-7 [Group of Seven] partners and the IMF [International Monetary Fund] that it plans to make such a designation in the absence of major preventive action by China. These other countries would prefer to avoid a U.S.–China confrontation on the issue and could be brought into a multilateral effort on the issue, reducing its confrontational bilateral character, if they were convinced that the United States was serious about pursuing it. The objective of that international effort, hopefully spearheaded by the IMF,[12] should be a "Plaza II" or "Asian Plaza" agreement that would work out the needed appreciation of all the major Asian currencies through which the impact on the individual countries involved (including China) would be tempered because they would not be moving very much vis-à-vis each other.[13] The Europeans have an especially large incentive to join the United States in such an initiative because their own currencies will rise much more sharply when the dollar experiences its next large decline if China and the other Asians continue to block their own adjustment (and perhaps to head off the incipient United States–China "G-2" implied by the Strategic Economic Dialogue).

Third, the Administration (with as many other countries as it can mobilize) should also take a new multilateral initiative on the trade side by filing a WTO [World Trade Organization] case against China's currency intervention as an export subsidy and/or as a violation of the provision in Article XV (4) that member countries "shall not, by exchange action, frustrate the intent of the provisions of the Agreement." As Chairman Ben Bernanke indicated in his highly publicized speech in Beijing in December 2006, in connection with the first Strategic Economic Dialogue, China's exchange rate intervention clearly represents an effective subsidy (to exports, as well as an import barrier) in economic terms. It should be addressed as such.[14]

Fourth, if the multilateral efforts fail, the United States will have to address the China currency issue unilaterally. Treasury can pursue the most effective unilateral approach by entering the currency markets itself. It is impossible to buy RMB directly, because of its inconvertibility on capital account, so Treasury would have to select the best available proxies in the financial markets. The message of U.S. policy intent would be crystal clear, however, and at a minimum there would be a further sharp increase in inflows into the RMB that would make it even more difficult for the Chinese authorities to resist their inflationary consequences and thus the resultant pressures to let the exchange rate appreciate. (All other undervalued Asian currencies, including the Japanese yen, could be purchased directly, with immediate impact on their exchange rates against the dollar.)[15]

The United States has of course conducted such currency intervention on many occasions in the past, most dramatically via the Plaza Agreement in 1985 and most recently when it bought yen to counter the excessive weakness of that currency in 1998 (when it approached 150:1, about the same level in real terms as its current rate of about 120:1). All those actions have been taken with the agreement of the counterpart currency country, however, and usually in cooperation with that country. This would be the essence of the proposed "Plaza II" or "Asian Plaza" agreement, as suggested above, and the multilateral approach would be preferable and should be pursued vigorously by the Administration. Failing such agreement, however, the unilateral option is available and might have to be adopted.

Fifth, the Administration should quietly notify the Chinese that it will be unable to oppose responsible Congressional initiatives to address the issue. Congress should then proceed, hopefully in cooperation with the Administration, to craft legislation that would effectively sanction the Chinese (and perhaps some other Asians) for their failure to observe their international currency obligations.

Such unilateral steps by the United States, although decidedly inferior to the multilateral alternatives proposed above and as long as they are compatible with the rules of the WTO, could hardly be labeled "protectionist" since they are designed to counter a massive distortion in the market (China's intervention) and indeed promote a market-oriented outcome. Nor could they be viewed as excessively intrusive in China's internal affairs, since they would be no more aggressive than current U.S. efforts on intellectual property rights and other trade policy issues (including the filing of subsidy and other cases on such issues with the WTO). Such steps should therefore be considered seriously if China continues to refuse to contribute constructively to the needed global adjustments and if the Treasury Department continues to whitewash the Chinese policies by failing to carry out the clear intent of the law fashioned by this Committee [U.S. Senate Subcommittee on Security and International Trade and Finance, Committee on Banking, Housing and Urban Affairs] almost two decades ago.

ENDNOTES

1. I note with pride that, based on the work of my colleague Catherine L. Mann, I predicted precisely such an outcome for 2006 in the third paragraph of my testimony before the full Committee on May 1, 2002.

2. See my testimonies on that topic to the House Budget Committee on January 23 and the Senate Budget Committee on February 1. I suggest there that the external imbalances are in fact the most likely source of a crisis that could force the United States into precipitous and thus unpalatable budget adjustments if preemptive action is not taken.

3. See Chapter 2 of *China: The Balance Sheet* and Nicholas Lardy, "China: Toward a Consumption-Driven Growth Path," Washington: Institute for International Economics, October 2006.

4. See Daniel H. Rosen and Trevor Houser, "What Drives China's Demand for Energy (and What It Means for the Rest of Us)," in C. Fred Bergsten, Nicholas Lardy, Bates Gill and Derek Mitchell, eds. *The China Balance Sheet in 2007 and Beyond*, Washington: Peter G. Peterson Institute for International Economics and Center for Strategic and International Studies, April 2007.

5. The short-term success of the new Strategic Economic Dialogue [SED] will be judged largely by whether it achieves effective resolution of this problem. The SED also has the long-term potential to foster a more constructive relationship between the two countries that will inevitably lead the world economy over the coming years and perhaps decades. It thus begins to implement the "G-2" concept proposed in my "A New Foreign Economic Policy for the United States" in C. Fred Bergsten and the Institute for International Economics, *The United States and the World Economy: Foreign Economic Policy for the Next Decade*, Washington: Institute for International Economics, 2005, pp. 53–4.

6. See William R. Cline, *The United States as a Debtor Nation*, Washington: Institute for International Economics, 2005, especially Table 6.2 on page 242.

7. I have studiously refrained from mentioning the very large Chinese bilateral trade surplus with the United States, which should not be a primary focus of policy because of the multilateral nature of international trade and payments. At present, however, the bilateral imbalance is a fairly accurate reflection of the global imbalances and is thus more relevant than usual.

8. See Morris Goldstein and Nicholas Lardy, "A New Way to Deal with the Renminbi," *Financial Times*, January 20, 2006.

9. This two-step approach was initially proposed by my colleagues Morris Goldstein and Nicholas Lardy, "Two-Stage Currency Reform for China," *Financial Times*, September 12, 2003.

10. See Morris Goldstein, "Paulson's First Challenge," *The International Economy*, Summer 2006.

11. Treasury (and the IMF) has justified their inaction on the grounds that there is insufficient evidence that China is manipulating its exchange rate with the "intent" of frustrating effective current account adjustment. This is of course ludicrous because it is highly unlikely that China (or any country) would admit such a motive and it is impossible to discern any other purpose for the policy. It might be desirable to amend U.S. law, however, by replacing the controversial (and pejorative) term "manipulation" with the unambiguous (and emotionally neutral) term "intervention."

12. Congress could direct Treasury to use the "voice and vote" of the United States to seek effective implementation by the IMF of its existing rules against competitive currency undervaluation.

13. See William R. Cline's "The Case for a New Plaza Agreement," Washington: Institute for International Economics, December 2005.

14. These ideas are analyzed in Gary Clyde Hufbauer, Yee Wong, and Ketki Sheth, *US–China Trade Disputes: Rising Tide, Rising Stakes*, Washington: Institute for International Economics, August 2006, pp. 16–24. Congress could require the Administration to bring such a case or cases, once a country was found to be violating its currency obligations, in any legislation that it passed on these issues.

15. Congress could write a requirement for such action, once a country was found to be violating its currency obligations, into legislation on these issues.

David D. Hale and Lyric Hughes Hale

Reconsidering Revaluation: The Wrong Approach to the U.S.–Chinese Trade Imbalance

China's economy has grown dramatically in the last decade: it is more than twice as large as it was ten years ago. This spectacular rise means that Beijing can influence the global economy today in ways that would have been unimaginable in the 1990s—a development that has led to widespread concerns in the United States. Many officials in Washington and small U.S. manufacturing companies allege that Beijing has deliberately undervalued its currency and manipulated markets in order to promote the growth of its exports.

Consequently, many U.S. politicians are clamoring for action to redress China's growing annual trade surplus with the United States, which currently stands at $250 billion. They assume that increasing the value of the yuan against the dollar will simultaneously decrease Chinese exports to the United States by making them more expensive and boost U.S. imports to China by making them cheaper. As the 2008 presidential election [approached], the U.S. Congress [was] actively discussing protectionist legislation and new tariffs that would punish China if its currency does not appreciate faster than the current rate of five percent.

But revaluation—no matter how vehemently it is advocated—is unlikely to achieve the desired result of reducing the U.S. trade imbalance with China. Taxation reform, the restructuring of the corporate and banking sectors, the gradual opening of capital accounts, and the encouragement of domestic consumer spending would each have a more measurable and lasting effect on China's current account surplus. There is also scant reason to believe that Beijing will accept the large-scale revaluation of 20 percent or more sought by certain members of the U.S. Congress. Such a policy could result in fewer exports, lost jobs, and capital flight to other emerging markets with cheaper labor costs, not to mention increased currency speculation and exchange-rate losses on hundreds of billions of dollars worth of U.S. Treasury debt now held by the Chinese government.

In addition, the trade imbalance that a revaluation of the yuan is supposed to fix is not the dire threat that many in Congress have made it out to be. The growing Chinese trade surplus has actually produced numerous benefits for the world economy and for U.S. corporations and consumers. It has handsomely rewarded U.S. companies, such as

Wal-Mart, which have enjoyed record profitability as a result of low labor and production costs in China. Critics forget that China's central bank, the People's Bank of China, uses the surplus to buy U.S. debt, which benefits the U.S. economy, Furthermore, some 27 percent of China's exports are actually generated by U.S.-owned corporations, which pass on their savings to consumers back home.

Simply strengthening the yuan will not correct the U.S.–Chinese trade imbalance, much less bring China's dynamic economy into lasting equilibrium; at best, it is a flawed solution to an ancillary problem. The greater and far more critical challenge is to properly complete China's integration into the global economy. China is but one cog, and revaluation just one lever, in the complex machinery of international trade. Unfortunately, many U.S. politicians with little knowledge of economic theory, trade flows, or investment patterns have not grasped the intricacies of the Chinese economy and its place in the global marketplace. And so they seek a jingoistic, politically popular solution to a complex and multifaceted problem.

The Perils of Revaluation

This is not the first time Washington has sought to intervene in Beijing's monetary affairs. In the early 1930s, President Franklin Roosevelt's administration supported legislation to raise the price of silver in order to both garner support for the New Deal from western senators in silver-producing states and increase U.S. exports to China. But this proved to be a disaster for China, which was then on the silver standard rather than the gold standard. Unlike the rest of the world, China had experienced economic growth during the early years of the Great Depression due to low silver prices and rapid industrialization. The Silver Purchase Act of 1934 compelled China to revalue its currency, decreased its exports by almost 60 percent, and plunged the Chinese economy into chaos—while failing to increase U.S. exports to China. In the twenty-first-century world of highly mobile capital, information, talent, and technology, similar policies of economic containment, such as those currently circulating in Congress, are even more likely to fail.

Nevertheless, Washington remains obsessed with China's exchange-rate policy. Labor unions and second-tier U.S. manufacturing firms insist that China has kept its currency artificially undervalued in order to boost its international competitive position. They point out that China has a trade surplus with the United States equal to nearly two percent of its GDP [gross domestic product], compared with a peak of 1.2 percent for Japan in the 1980s, when the U.S. government last panicked about trade imbalances with Asia.

Washington has already taken punitive action. The U.S. Commerce Department shocked the financial markets on March 30, 2006, by announcing new trade measures against China's paper industry, potentially opening the door to many more attempts by U.S. companies to block Chinese imports. It introduced duties on Chinese paper imports because of allegations that the paper industry in China benefits from unfair subsidies, such as low tax rates and low-cost loans. This announcement broke with the 23-year-old U.S. policy of treating China as a nonmarket economy not subject to countervailing duties. Before this change, U.S. companies could only file antidumping cases against Chinese firms. The Bush administration's decision to pursue these sanctions reflects the new political mood inside the Beltway.

Washington may have forgotten how its silver policy affected China in the 1930s, but Chinese policymakers remember, and they do not want to undertake another massive revaluation that could produce domestic deflation and cripple exports, leading to massive job losses. Such caution is especially understandable given the experience of other Asian countries that heeded international advice. When China's neighbors followed the International Monetary Fund's prescription to liberalize their financial systems during the 1990s, they experienced a major crisis because of their large current account deficits and huge dollar debts. China was actually on the road to a freely floating exchange rate and full convertibility just prior to the East Asian financial crisis of 1998. But after the meltdown throughout the region, Beijing was convinced that in a world of hedge funds and rampant speculation, it was safer to protect one's currency.

In the aftermath of the Asian crash, there was a risk that China would devalue the yuan, leading to a cascade of other devaluations throughout Asia, which would have deepened the crisis. Instead, China took a long-term view. It exhibited regional leadership and left the yuan alone. After all, it did not really need to take the risk. In fact, due to forced devaluations elsewhere in the region, China's real exchange rate actually appreciated by 30 percent during the crisis. Nevertheless, its exports remained resilient due to high productivity growth. As late as 2002, Beijing continued to resist the temptation to devalue, even though doing so would have been to the country's immediate export advantage. China was unafraid to stand alone; its steadfastness proved to be its first act of global citizenship in the postwar period.

Traditionally, it has been China's banks that have opposed currency revaluation, out of fear that it might damage the financial sector. But today, resistance to a more flexible exchange rate is also coming from interest groups in China, such as industrialists and farmers, who fear losing their competitive edge in the export market. China depends on manufacturing employment for 109 million jobs—compared with the United States' 14 million manufacturing jobs—and the government is naturally concerned that a significant exchange-rate appreciation could reduce manufacturing employment in China: export prices would rise, and markets for cheap

Chinese products abroad could dry up. Some textile companies in the manufacturing hub of Guangdong Province are moving factories to Cambodia and Vietnam because of rapidly rising wages and uncertainty over Beijing's exchange-rate policy. Chinese farmers are also worried in the longer term about international competition now that World Trade Organization agreements have made the Chinese market more porous to imports. These farmers are a potentially powerful constituency given that two thirds of China's population resides in the countryside and increased imports would have a major impact on the developing rural economy.

China's Global Trade Deficit

Unlike many of their counterparts in Washington, officials in Beijing understand that U.S.–Chinese trade imbalances are a function of something much greater than exchange rates or even bilateral trade. Production has become so globally integrated today that very few manufactured goods are actually made in a single country from start to finish. Unlike Japan, for example, China does not have a vertically integrated domestic economy that can produce an entire product line from raw materials to finished goods. Instead, China is the last stop on the global assembly line. It imports components from other Asian countries, completes the manufacturing process, and then exports finished products to the United States. In 2003, intermediate goods produced by companies in Japan, Singapore, South Korea, and Taiwan accounted for 34 percent of all Chinese imports, compared with 18 percent in 1992—and the percentage is probably several points higher today. Also, because China serves essentially as a finishing shop, barely 20 percent of the value of the products it exports is actually captured by the Chinese economy. As a result, although China has a trade surplus with the United States, it has a trade deficit with the rest of Asia. In fact, China's trade deficit with East Asia grew more than threefold, from $39 billion to $130 billion, between 2000 and 2007, just as China's trade surplus with the United States increased nearly threefold, from $90 billion to over $250 billion, during the same period.

As these figures make clear, far too much emphasis has been placed on bilateral issues between the United States and China—rather than on trade imbalances as a global issue. For one thing, they suggest that being on the short end of a trade imbalance is not necessarily an economic liability. China supporters in the United States, including the Club for Growth and a number of academic and Wall Street economists, have warned against anti-China protectionism precisely on the grounds that the Chinese trade surplus is not necessarily such a bad thing for the United States. Ballooning corporate profits have given China a savings surplus, which it recycles into U.S. Treasury securities as part of its foreign exchange reserves. U.S. firms have also shared in this boom: their profits from business in China rose to over $4 billion this year—50 percent more than a year ago.

Furthermore, as a recent study by the Hong Kong Institute for Monetary Research ([HKIMR,] the think tank of Hong Kong's de facto central bank, the Hong Kong Monetary Authority) shows, the yuan's value is a function of China's overall trade balance, not simply of its surplus vis-à-vis the United States. In fact, the HKIMR researchers argue, currency appreciation would not have the expected effect of decreasing China's exports. It could actually have the opposite effect by decreasing the cost of the imports China needs in order to create finished goods for export to the United States and Europe.

Beyond Revaluation

The real challenge, as Beijing well understands, is helping China integrate its booming economy into the international system. As China's growth rate continues to rise, many in China, including Zhou Xiaochuan, the head of the People's Bank of China, have begun to worry about inflation, which is now at its highest level in 11 years. China's foreign exchange reserves now exceed $1.4 trillion—equal to approximately 50 percent of GDP. During the past two years, the Shanghai stock-market index has risen from 1,000 to 6,000. Last May, the trading volume on the stock markets in Shanghai and Shenzhen exceeded that on all the stock markets of the rest of Asia and Australia combined. Today, China accounts for five percent of all global stock-market activity.

So far, China's monetary policy alone has failed to curtail its very high growth rate, now over 11 percent. The People's Bank of China cannot use one common tool to restrain the stock market, regulating margin debt, which allows investors to use borrowed funds in order to buy stocks: such debt does not exist in China. It has instead responded by steadily increasing bank reserve requirements and nudging up interest rates. But if it raises interest rates sharply, it could attract capital inflows from foreign investors, which would bolster the currency. Higher interest rates could also keep even more Chinese money at home. Neither outcome would slow down the economy. Chinese policymakers will therefore need to look beyond monetary policy and focus instead on reforming tax laws, increasing consumer spending, encouraging capital outflows, and changing the regulations governing Chinese corporations.

China traditionally refunded to producers the 17 percent value-added tax (VAT) on production inputs that was paid on exports. But last June, it announced that it would phase out the VAT rebates on 25 percent of the products it exports. It has eliminated rebates on energy-intensive goods such as coal, refined copper, primary aluminum, crude steel, and activated carbon, all of which are produced in industries suffering from overinvestment. China will maintain the VAT rebates on higher-value-added products, such as machinery, because it regards them as the locomotive for growth in the future.

Due to its growing domestic market and the sheer scale of its manufacturing activities, China has managed to accrue corporate and government savings at an unprecedented rate. But the transition to capitalism has been rocky and imperfect. China's failure to pay corporate dividends has swollen corporate treasuries, leading to a cycle of overinvestment in capital equipment and to a form of corporate speculation on the stock market that is similar to the Japanese practice of using surplus capital for short-term, high-risk investing, known as Zaitekku. A change in the regulations governing Chinese corporations that would force them to pay dividends to all shareholders would cure a major distortion.

Ultimately, China will also have to shift to a new policy that boosts domestic consumption and reduces the country's dependence on exports. Consumer spending has not kept pace with overall GDP growth: its share of GDP has slumped from 50 percent in the 1980s to 36 percent today. Consumption has been eclipsed by huge gains in capital spending and exports. The government has made some moves to increase consumer spending, such as introducing measures abolishing the taxation of farmers and increasing government spending on health care and education. Nevertheless, Chinese households still have the world's highest savings rate—between 23 and 25 percent. This is because the country's social safety net remains so inadequate that many people save more in order to pay for education, health care, and retirement. Ironically, to decrease the household savings rate and boost consumer spending, the government will have to reinstate some socialist policies that disappeared in the 1990s.

Beijing is also trying to slow the growth of its foreign exchange reserves by encouraging more capital outflows. Last May, Beijing changed the rules in this area, permitting Chinese special investment funds to invest in foreign equities and foreign firms to invest in Chinese equities. The change produced an immediate rally on the Hong Kong exchange, where Chinese institutions routinely buy "H" shares, shares of Chinese companies approved for listing in Hong Kong. (These sell at a significant discount compared with similar shares on the Shanghai exchange due to lower retail demand and a smaller market.) The Chinese government magnified the rally by announcing that it would give Chinese citizens more freedom to purchase Hong Kong equities and allow mutual funds to invest in a wider range of foreign markets. China hopes that this strategy of encouraging capital outflows will succeed in the same way that it did in Japan a few years ago—by reducing bloated foreign exchange reserves and bringing the economy into lasting equilibrium.

A Global Player

Despite Beijing's understandable reluctance to cave in to U.S. demands, the odds are good that China will eventually change tack and allow its exchange rate to appreciate more rapidly due to political pressure from Washington. But exchange-rate appreciation will have a far less significant impact on China's trade surplus than the economic policy changes China is already pursuing. For the past 30 years, China has been engaged in a complex process of integration into the world economy. No matter how many sensible economic reforms are implemented in Beijing, much of the burden for integrating China into the global economy will fall on the international community. And this process will require more than unilateral efforts by the United States to protect its own interests; it should instead be approached as a multilateral issue that will affect almost every nation on earth.

The time has come for a broad international effort to integrate China into the global economy. The United States should reform the traditional G-8 [Group of Eight] summits to include China as its ninth member. The G-7 ([Group of Seven,] the group of highly industrialized states) admitted Russia during the late 1990s, and China is a far more important economic player now than Russia was then. Indeed, there cannot be a serious discussion of global economic issues without the active participation of Beijing. The admission of China to the G-8 process would create a major global forum in which the leading industrialized countries could discuss the impact of China's export boom on other nations' economies and address the environmental impact of Beijing's growing demand for commodity imports and energy resources. In the end, only a skillful combination of structural reforms in China and coordinated multilateral efforts will create a more balanced economic relationship between Washington and Beijing.

PART V

DEVELOPMENT IN THE GLOBAL ECONOMY

Do developing societies benefit from participating in the global economy? Do they experience more rapid growth if they actively manage their participation in the global economy or if they simply open their borders and allow the global market to work? This basic question—Is development best promoted by markets or by the state?—has been at the center of the debate over development since at least 1950. The last twenty-five years have brought a dramatic shift in government orientations. The state played the central role and international markets a much smaller role in development strategies until the early 1980s. Today, the state's role is greatly reduced, and the role of markets is greatly enhanced. Has this change in the relative importance of the state and the markets been good for development, or would developing societies realize more rapid progress with a more active state role? Each chapter in this part looks at this question in a different context.

Chapter 12 takes a close look at the relationship between participation in the international trade system and participation in the economic growth. Since the mid-1980s, governments in developing societies have opted to integrate their economies into the global trade system. This strategy is quite distinct from the policy of the post–World War II period, when governments sought to develop by insulating themselves from the global trade system. The shift toward development strategies based on trade openness has generated a debate about the relationship among trade, economic development, and poverty reduction. David Dollar and Aart Kraay argue that trade boosts development and provides income gains that are distributed widely across society. In short, trade reduces poverty. Dani Rodrik argues that trade is not a "magic bullet" for development. There is little evidence, he argues, to support the claim that trade openness, by itself, is a recipe for sustained growth.

Chapter 13 considers the debate over the impact of foreign aid on the least developed societies. Policy makers have long believed that development requires investment and that developing economies lack the savings required to finance the needed investment. Governments devised foreign-aid programs to provide the necessary financing. Yet governments have been disappointed with the postwar foreign-aid record. The billions of dollars provided do not appear to have had much positive impact. David Dollar argues that foreign aid can be made to work more effectively by focusing on different objectives. Rather than focusing on investment in physical capital, aid should target institutional development. William Easterly doubts that foreign aid can become more effective. He believes that aid fails because aid providers care more about keeping Western governments happy than about achieving success in developing societies. Consequently, improvements in aid effectiveness will require fundamental reform of how governments supply aid.

Chapter 14 concludes this section by examining the contribution that microcredit can make to development. Disappointing results with traditional foreign aid has led policymakers to a search for alternative mechanisms. One contender is microcredit, whereby entrepreneurs in poor countries are given very small loans to create or expand small businesses. Although enthusiasm about the potential of microcredit, as well as the actual growth of microcredit services have both dramatically increased in recent years, debate continues about the effect of microcredit on development. Nobel Laureate Muhammad Yunus, founder of the one of the first microcredit institutions, argues that microcredit transforms societies and can eradicate poverty. Karol Boudreaux and Tyler Cowen argue that microcredit is unlikely to eradicate poverty but may alleviate some of poverty's harsher consequences.

CHAPTER 12 TRADE PROMOTES GROWTH v. TRADE DOES NOT PROMOTE GROWTH

Trade Promotes Growth

Advocate: David Dollar and Aart Kraay

Source: "Spreading the Wealth," *Foreign Affairs* 81 (January/February 2002): 120–33

Trade Does Not Promote Growth

Advocate: Dani Rodrik

Source: "Trading in Illusions," *Foreign Policy*, March/April 2001: 55–62

Active participation in the global economy, as well as pursuit of market-oriented economic policies, is a recent innovation for most developing countries. Until the mid-1980s, most developing countries pursued inward-looking development strategies called import substitution industrialization (ISI). ISI was a "statist" approach to development in which the state played the lead role in promoting industrialization. By using trade barriers to protect favored domestic producers, by subsidizing credit, and by sometimes creating and owning enterprises, policy makers used state power to transform largely agricultural societies into industrialized countries. Because this inward-looking strategy placed little emphasis on exports and depended on barriers to imports, developing countries participated little in the General Agreement on Tariffs and Trade process.

This policy orientation changed dramatically in the mid-1980s. Facing internal problems with ISI, accumulating large foreign debts that they could not easily service, and confronting a deteriorating international climate, many governments were forced to turn to the International Monetary Fund and the World Bank for financial assistance. Structural adjustment was the price of this assistance. Structural adjustment programs encouraged governments to scale back the state's role in the economy and increase the role of the markets. Structural adjustment encouraged governments to shift from an inward-looking to an export-oriented development strategy. To that end, governments liberalized trade, deregulated the economy, and privatized state-owned industries. Most became active participants in the World Trade Organization.

TRADE PROMOTES GROWTH

By the late 1990s, scholars and policy makers were beginning to evaluate the consequences of these reforms. Were the countries that had moved the farthest on the reform trajectory and opened the most to global trade performing better than the countries that had reformed less and opened less to the global economy? Research conducted by economists working with and independent from the World Bank suggested that economic reform had delivered improved economic performance.

David Dollar and Aart Kraay, World Bank economists, summarize the results of perhaps the most comprehensive of these studies. They argue that the preponderance of evidence illustrates a positive relationship between trade openness and economic growth. Developing countries that liberalized trade and foreign investment have experienced more rapid growth than have countries that remained relatively insulated from the global economy. For Dollar and Kraay, therefore, developing countries intent on reducing poverty should take further steps to integrate into the global economy.

TRADE DOES NOT PROMOTE GROWTH

Others argue that participation in the global economy is not causally related to better economic performance. Some of these critics accept the apparent correlation between trade openness and economic performance but deny any causal relationship. Other critics are even skeptical about the existence of a relationship between trade openness and economic performance. Some suggest that causality runs in the other direction—growth spurts are followed by, rather than caused by, a growth of trade. The broader point such critics develop is that trade openness, although certainly not harmful, will not produce economic development. An important role remains for the state.

Dani Rodrik, a political economist at Harvard University, is perhaps the most prominent advocate of this alternative view. Rodrik is deeply skeptical about the claim that trade openness and economic performance are positively correlated. He argues that countries that opened most to the global economy during the 1980s and 1990s in fact grew more slowly than they grew during the 1960s and 1970s when they were more closed. He also claims that countries that have recently experienced long periods of rapid growth, such as China and India, liberalized trade gradually and only after growth had taken off. Hence, for Rodrik, trade openness is not the magic bullet of economic development.

POINTS **TO PONDER**

1. How would Dollar and Kraay respond to Rodrik's argument, and how would they evaluate the policies Rodrik recommends?

2. What countries do Dollar and Kraay point to as illustrations of the positive relationship between trade and growth? Does Rodrik agree with their interpretation of the reasons for rapid growth in these countries?

3. What complicates any attempt to evaluate the relationship among trade openness, broader market-friendly policy reform, and subsequent economic performance?

4. What is at stake in the debate about the relationship between trade and development? Do you think that there exists a single proper development strategy appropriate for all countries?

David Dollar and Aart Kraay
Spreading the Wealth

A Rising Tide

One of the main claims of the antiglobalization movement is that globalization is widening the gap between the haves and the have-nots. It benefits the rich and does little for the poor, perhaps even making their lot harder. As union leader Jay Mazur put it . . . , "globalization has dramatically increased inequality between and within nations" ("Labor's New Internationalism," [*Foreign Affairs*,] January/February 2000). The problem with this new conventional wisdom is that the best evidence available shows the exact opposite to be true. So far, the current wave of globalization, which started around 1980, has actually promoted economic equality and reduced poverty.

Global economic integration has complex effects on income, culture, society, and the environment. But in the debate over globalization's merits, its impact on poverty is particularly important. If international trade and investment primarily benefit the rich, many people will feel that restricting trade to protect jobs, culture, or the environment is worth the costs. But if restricting trade imposes further hardship on poor people in the developing world, many of the same people will think otherwise.

Three facts bear on this question. First, a long-term global trend toward greater inequality prevailed for at least 200 years; it peaked around 1975. But since then, it has stabilized and possibly even reversed. The chief reason for the change has been the accelerated growth of two large and initially poor countries: China and India.

Second, a strong correlation links increased participation in international trade and investment on the one hand and faster growth on the other. The developing world can be divided into a "globalizing" group of countries that have seen rapid increases in trade and foreign investment over the last two decades—well above the rates for rich countries—and a "nonglobalizing" group that trades even less of its income today than it did 20 years ago. The aggregate annual per capita growth rate of the globalizing group accelerated steadily from one percent in the 1960s to five percent in the 1990s. During that latter decade, in contrast, rich countries grew at two percent and nonglobalizers at only one percent. Economists are cautious about drawing conclusions concerning causality, but they largely agree that openness to foreign trade and investment (along with complementary reforms) explains the faster growth of the globalizers.

Third, and contrary to popular perception, globalization has not resulted in higher inequality within economies. Inequality has indeed gone up in some countries (such as China) and down in others (such as the Philippines). But those changes are not systematically linked to globalization measures such as trade and investment flows, tariff rates, and the presence of capital controls. Instead, shifts in inequality stem more from domestic education, taxes, and social policies. In general, higher growth rates in globalizing developing countries have translated into higher incomes for the poor. Even with its increased inequality, for example, China has seen the most spectacular reduction of poverty in world history—which was supported by opening its economy to foreign trade and investment.

Although globalization can be a powerful force for poverty reduction, its beneficial results are not inevitable. If policymakers hope to tap the full potential of economic integration and sustain its benefits, they must address three critical challenges. A growing protectionist movement in rich countries that aims to limit integration with poor ones must be stopped in its tracks. Developing countries need to acquire the kinds of institutions and policies that will allow them to prosper under globalization, both of which may be different from place to place. And more migration, both domestic and international, must be permitted when geography limits the potential for development.

The Great Divide

Over the past 200 years, different local economies around the world have become more integrated while the growth rate of the global economy has accelerated dramatically. Although it is impossible to prove causal linkage between the two developments—since there are no other world economies to be tested against—evidence suggests the arrows run in both directions. As Adam Smith argued, a larger market permits a finer division of labor, which in turn facilitates innovation and learning by doing. Some of that innovation involves transportation and communications technologies that lower costs and increase integration. So it is easy to see how integration and innovation can be mutually supportive.

Different locations have become more integrated because of increased flows of goods, capital, and knowledge. From 1820 to 1914, international trade increased faster than the global economy. Trade rose from about 2 percent of world income in 1820 to 18 percent in 1914. The globalization of trade took a step backward during the protectionist period of the Great Depression and World War II, and by 1950 trade (in relation to income) was lower than it had been in 1914. But thanks to a series of multilateral trade liberalizations under the General Agreement on Tariffs and Trade (GATT), trade dramatically expanded among industrialized countries between 1960 and 1980. Most developing countries remained largely isolated from this trade because of their own inward-focused policies, but the success of such notable exceptions as Taiwan and South Korea eventually helped encourage other developing economies to open themselves up to foreign trade and investment.

International capital flows, measured as foreign ownership of assets relative to world income, also grew during the first wave of globalization and declined during the Great Depression and World War II; they did not return to 1914 levels until 1980. But since then, such flows have increased markedly and changed their nature as well. One hundred years ago, foreign capital typically financed public infrastructure projects (such as canals and railroads) or direct investment related to natural resources. Today, in contrast, the bulk of capital flows to developing countries is direct investments tied to manufacturing and services.

The change in the nature of capital flows is clearly related to concurrent advances in economic integration, such as cheaper and faster transportation and revolutionary changes in telecommunications. Since 1920, seagoing freight charges have declined by about two-thirds and air travel costs by 84 percent; the cost of a three-minute call from New York City to London has dropped by 99 percent. Today, production in widely differing locations can be integrated in ways that simply were not possible before.

Another aspect of integration has been the movement of people. Yet here the trend is reversed: there is much more international travel than in the past but much less permanent migration. Between 1870 and 1910, about ten percent of the world's population relocated permanently from one country to another; over the past 25 years, only one to two percent have done so.

As economic integration has progressed, the annual growth rate of the world economy has accelerated, from 1 percent in the mid–nineteenth century to 3.5 percent in 1960–2000. Sustained over many years, such a jump in growth makes a huge difference in real living standards. It now takes only two to three years, for example, for the world economy to produce the same amount of goods and services that it did during the entire nineteenth century. Such a comparison is arguably a serious understatement of the true difference, since most of what is consumed today—airline travel, cars, televisions, synthetic fibers, life-extending drugs—did not exist 200 years ago. For any of these goods or services, therefore, the growth rate of output since 1820 is infinite. Human productivity has increased almost unimaginably.

All this tremendous growth in wealth was distributed very unequally up to about 1975, but since then growing equality has taken hold. One good measure of inequality among individuals worldwide is the mean log deviation—a measure of the gap between the income of any randomly selected person and a general average. It takes into account the fact that income distributions everywhere are skewed in favor of the rich, so that the typical person is poorer than the group average; the more skewed the distribution, the larger the gap. Per capita income in the world today, for example, is around $5,000, whereas a randomly selected person would most likely be living on close to $1,000—80 percent less. That gap translates into a mean log deviation of 0.8.

Taking this approach, an estimate of the world distribution of income among individuals shows rising inequality between 1820 and 1975. In that period, the gap between the typical person and world per capita income increased from about 40 percent to about 80 percent. Since changes in income inequality within countries were small, the increase in inequality was driven mostly by differences in growth rates across countries. Areas that were already relatively rich in 1820 (notably, Europe and the United States) grew faster than poor areas (notably, China and India). Global inequality peaked sometime in the 1970s, but it then stabilized and even began to decline, largely because growth in China and India began to accelerate.

Another way of looking at global inequality is to examine what is happening to the extreme poor—those people living on less than $1 per day. Although the percentage of the world's population living in poverty has declined over time, the absolute number rose fairly steadily until 1980. During the Great Depression and World War II, the number of poor increased particularly sharply, and it declined somewhat immediately thereafter. The world economy grew strongly between 1960 and 1980, but the number of poor rose because growth did not occur in the places where the worst-off live. But since then, the most rapid growth has occurred in poor locations. Consequently the number of poor has declined by 200 million since 1980. Again, this trend is explained primarily by the rapid income growth in China and India, which together in 1980 accounted for about one-third of the world's population and more than 60 percent of the world's extreme poor.

Upward Bound

The shift in the trend in global inequality coincides with the shift in the economic strategies of several large developing countries. Following World War II, most developing regions chose strategies that focused inward and discouraged integration with the global economy. But these approaches were not particularly successful, and throughout the 1960s and 1970s developing countries on the whole grew less rapidly than industrialized ones. The oil shocks and U.S. inflation of the 1970s created severe problems for them, contributing to negative growth, high inflation, and debt crises over the next several years. Faced with these disappointing results, several developing countries began to alter their strategies starting in the 1980s.

For example, China had an extremely closed economy until the mid-1970s. Although Beijing's initial economic reform focused on agriculture, a key part of its approach since the 1980s has involved opening up foreign trade and investment, including a drop in its tariff rates by two-thirds and its nontariff barriers by even more. These reforms have led to unprecedented economic growth in the country's coastal provinces and more moderate growth in the interior. From 1978 to 1994 the Chinese economy grew annually by 9 percent, while exports grew by 14 percent and imports by 13 percent. Of course, China and other globalizing developing countries have pursued a wide range of reforms, not just economic openness. Beijing has strengthened property rights through land reform and moved from a planned economy toward a market-oriented one, and these measures have contributed to its integration as well as to its growth.

Other developing countries have also opened up as a part of broader reform programs. During the 1990s, India liberalized foreign trade and investment with good results; its annual per capita income growth now tops four percent. It too has pursued a broad agenda of reform and has moved away from a highly regulated, planned system. Meanwhile, Uganda and Vietnam are the best examples of very low-income countries that have increased their participation in trade and investment and prospered as a result. And in the western hemisphere, Mexico is noteworthy both for signing its free-trade agreement with the United States and Canada in 1993 and for its rapid growth since then, especially in the northern regions near the U.S. border.

These cases illustrate how openness to foreign trade and investment, coupled with complementary reforms, typically leads to faster growth. India, China, Vietnam, Uganda, and Mexico are not isolated examples; in general, countries that have become more open have grown faster. The best way to illustrate this trend is to rank developing countries in order of their increases in trade relative to national income over the past 20 years. The top third of this list can be thought of as the "globalizing" camp, and the bottom two-thirds as the "nonglobalizing" camp. The globalizers have increased their trade relative to income by 104 percent over the past two decades, compared to 71 percent for rich countries. The nonglobalizers, meanwhile, actually trade less today than they did 20 years ago. The globalizers have also cut their import tariffs by 22 percentage points on average, compared to only 11 percentage points for the nonglobalizers.

How have the globalizers fared in terms of growth? Their average annual growth rates accelerated from 1 percent in the 1960s to 3 percent in the 1970s, 4 percent in the 1980s, and 5 percent in the 1990s. Rich countries' annual growth rates, by comparison, slowed to about 2 percent in the 1990s, and the nonglobalizers saw their growth rates decline from 3 percent in the 1970s to 1 percent in the 1980s and 1990s.

The same pattern can be observed on a local level. Within both China and India, the locations that are integrating with the global economy are growing much more rapidly than the disconnected regions. Indian states, for example, vary significantly in the quality of their investment climates as measured by government efficiency, corruption, and infrastructure. Those states with better investment climates have integrated themselves more closely with outside markets and have experienced more investment (domestic and foreign) than their less-integrated counterparts. Moreover, states that were initially poor and then created good investment climates had stronger poverty reduction in the 1990s than those not integrating with the global economy. Such internal comparisons are important because, by holding national trade and macroeconomic policies constant, they reveal how important it is to complement trade liberalization with institutional reform so that integration can actually occur.

The accelerated growth rates of globalizing countries such as China, India, and Vietnam are consistent with cross-country comparisons that find openness going hand in hand with faster growth. The most that these studies can establish is that more trade and investment is highly correlated with higher growth, so one needs to be careful about drawing conclusions about causality. Still, the overall evidence from individual cases and cross-country correlation is persuasive. As economists Peter Lindert and Jeffrey Williamson have written, "even though no one study can establish that openness to trade has unambiguously helped the representative Third World economy, the preponderance of evidence supports this conclusion." They go on to note that "there are no anti-global victories to report for the postwar Third World."

Contrary to the claims of the antiglobalization movement, therefore, greater openness to international trade and investment has in fact helped narrow the gap between rich and poor countries rather than widen it. During the 1990s, the economies of the globalizers, with a combined population of about 3 billion, grew more than twice as fast as the rich countries. The nonglobalizers, in contrast, grew only half as fast and nowadays lag further and further behind. Much of the discussion of global inequality assumes that there is growing divergence between the developing world and the rich world, but this is simply not true. The most important development in global inequality in recent decades is the growing divergence within the developing world, and it is directly related to whether countries take advantage of the economic benefits that globalization can offer.

The Path Out of Poverty

The antiglobalization movement also claims that economic integration is worsening inequality within countries as well as between them. Until the mid-1980s, there was insufficient evidence to support strong conclusions on this important topic. But now more and more developing countries have begun to conduct household income and consumption surveys of reasonable quality. (In low-income countries, these surveys typically track what households actually consume because so much of their real income is self-produced and not part of the money economy.) Good surveys now exist for 137 countries, and many go back far enough to measure changes in inequality over time.

One way of looking at inequality within countries is to focus on what happens to the bottom 20 percent of households as globalization and growth proceed apace. Across all countries, incomes of the poor grow at around the same rate as GDP. Of course, there is a great deal of variation around that average relationship. In some countries, income distribution has shifted in favor of the poor; in others, against them. But these shifts cannot be explained by any globalization-related variable. So it simply cannot be said that inequality necessarily rises with more trade, more foreign investment, and lower tariffs. For many globalizers, the overall change in distribution was small, and in some cases (such as the Philippines and Malaysia) it was even in favor of the poor. What changes in inequality do reflect are country-specific policies on education, taxes, and social protection. It is important not to misunderstand this finding. China is an important example of a country that has had a large increase in inequality in the past decade, when the income of the bottom 20 percent has risen much less rapidly than per capita income. This trend may be related to greater openness, although domestic liberalization is a more likely cause. China started out in the 1970s with a highly equal distribution of income, and part of its reform has deliberately aimed at increasing the returns on education, which financially reward the better schooled. But the Chinese case is not typical; inequality has not increased in most of the developing countries that have opened up to foreign trade and investment. Furthermore, income distribution in China may have become more unequal, but the income of the poor in China has still risen rapidly. In fact, the country's progress in reducing poverty has been one of the most dramatic successes in history.

Because increased trade usually accompanies more rapid growth and does not systematically change household-income distribution, it generally is associated with improved well-being of the poor. Vietnam nicely illustrates this finding. As the nation has opened up, it has experienced a large increase in per capita income and no significant change in inequality. Thus the income of the poor has risen dramatically, and the number of Vietnamese living in absolute poverty dropped sharply from 75 percent of the population in 1988 to 37 percent in 1998. Of the poorest 5 percent of households in 1992, 98 percent were better off six years later. And the improved well-being is not just a matter of income. Child labor has declined, and school enrollment has increased. It should be no surprise that the vast majority of poor households in Vietnam benefited immediately from a more liberalized trading system, since the country's opening has resulted in exports of rice (produced by most of the poor farmers) and labor-intensive products such as footwear. But the experience of China and Vietnam is not unique. India and Uganda also enjoyed rapid poverty reduction as they grew along with their integration into the global economy.

The Open Societies

These findings have important implications for developing countries, for rich countries such as the United States, and for those who care about global poverty. All parties should recognize that the most recent wave of globalization has been a powerful force for equality and poverty reduction, and they should commit themselves to seeing that it continues despite the obstacles lying ahead.

It is not inevitable that globalization will proceed. In 1910, many believed globalization was unstoppable; they soon received a rude shock. History is not likely to repeat itself in the same way, but it is worth noting that antiglobalization sentiments are on the rise. A growing number of political leaders in the developing world realize that an open trading system is very much in their countries' interest. They would do well to heed Mexican President Vicente Fox, who said recently,

> We are convinced that globalization is good and it's good when you do your homework, . . . keep your fundamentals in line on the economy, build up high levels of education, respect the rule of law. . . . When you do your part, we are convinced that you get the benefit.

But today the narrow interests opposed to further integration—especially those in the rich countries—appear to be much more energetic than their opponents. In Quebec City last spring and in Genoa last summer, a group of democratically elected leaders gathered to discuss how to pursue economic integration and improve the lives of their peoples. Antiglobalization demonstrators were quite effective in disrupting the meetings and drawing media attention to themselves. Leaders in developed and developing countries alike must make the proglobalization case more directly and effectively or risk having their opponents dominate the discussion and stall the process.

In addition, industrialized countries still raise protectionist measures against agricultural and labor-intensive products. Reducing those barriers would help developing countries significantly. The poorer areas of the world would benefit from further openings of their own markets as well, since 70 percent of the tariff barriers that developing countries face are from other developing countries.

If globalization proceeds, its potential to be an equalizing force will depend on whether poor countries manage to integrate themselves into the global economic system. True integration requires not just trade liberalization but wide-ranging institutional reform. Many of the nonglobalizing developing countries, such as Myanmar, Nigeria, Ukraine, and Pakistan, offer an unattractive investment climate. Even if they decide to open themselves up to trade, not much is likely to happen unless other reforms are also pursued. It is not easy to predict the reform paths of these countries; some of the relative successes in recent years, such as China, India, Uganda, and Vietnam, have come as quite a surprise. But as long as a location has weak institutions and policies, people living there are going to fall further behind the rest of the world.

Through their trade policies, rich countries can make it easier for those developing countries that do choose to open up and join the global trading club. But in recent years, the rich countries have been doing just the opposite. GATT was originally built around agreements concerning trade practices. Now, institutional harmonization, such as agreement on policies toward intellectual property rights, is a requirement for joining the WTO [World Trade Organization]. Any sort of regulation of labor and environmental standards made under the threat of WTO sanctions would take this requirement for harmonization much further. Such measures would be neoprotectionist in effect, because they would thwart the integration of developing countries into the world economy and discourage trade between poor countries and rich ones.

The WTO meeting in Doha was an important step forward on trade integration. More forcefully than in Seattle, leaders of industrial countries were willing to make the case for further integration and put on the table issues of central concern to developing nations: access to pharmaceutical patents, use of antidumping measures against developing countries, and agricultural subsidies. The new round of trade negotiations launched at Doha has the potential to reverse the current trend, which makes it more difficult for poor countries to integrate with the world economy.

A final potential obstacle to successful and equitable globalization relates to geography. There is no inherent reason why coastal China should be poor; the same goes for southern India, northern Mexico, and Vietnam. All of these locations are near important markets or trade routes but were long held back by misguided policies. Now, with appropriate reforms, they are starting to grow rapidly and take their natural place in the world. But the same cannot be said for Mali, Chad, or other countries or regions cursed with "poor geography"—i.e., distance from markets, inherently high transport costs, and challenging health and agricultural problems. It would be naive to think that trade and investment alone can alleviate poverty in all locations. In fact, for those locations with poor geography, trade liberalization is less important than developing proper health care systems or providing basic infrastructure—or letting people move elsewhere.

Migration from poor locations is the missing factor in the current wave of globalization that could make a large contribution to reducing poverty. Each year, 83 million people are added to the world's population, 82 million of them in the developing world. In Europe and Japan, moreover, the population is aging and the labor force is set to shrink. Migration of relatively unskilled workers from South to North would thus offer clear economic benefits to both. Most migration from South to North is economically motivated, and it raises the living standard of the migrant while benefiting the sending country in three ways. First, it reduces the South's labor force and thus raises wages for those who remain behind. Second, migrants send remittances of hard currency back home. Finally, migration bolsters transnational trade and investment networks. In the case of Mexico, for example, ten percent of its citizens live and work in the United States, taking pressure off its own labor market and raising wages there. India gets six times as much in remittances from its workers overseas as it gets in foreign aid.

Unlike trade, however, migration remains highly restricted and controversial. Some critics perceive a disruptive impact on society and culture and fear downward pressure on wages and rising unemployment in the richer countries. Yet anti-immigration lobbies ignore the fact that geographical economic disparities are so strong that illegal immigration is growing rapidly anyway, despite restrictive policies. In a perverse irony, some of the worst abuses of globalization occur because there is not enough of it in key economic areas such as labor flows. Human traffic, for example, has become a highly lucrative, unregulated business in which illegal migrants are easy prey for exploitation.

Realistically, none of the industrialized countries is going to adopt open migration. But they should reconsider their migration policies. Some, for example, have a strong bias in their immigration rules toward highly skilled workers, which in fact spurs a "brain drain" from the developing world. Such policies do little to stop the flow of unskilled workers and instead push many of these people into the illegal category. If rich countries would legally accept more unskilled workers, they could address their own looming labor shortages, improve living standards in developing countries, and reduce illegal human traffic and its abuses. In sum, the integration of poor economies with richer ones over the past two decades has provided many opportunities for poor people to improve their lives. Examples of the beneficiaries of globalization can be found among Mexican migrants, Chinese factory workers, Vietnamese peasants, and Ugandan farmers. Many of the better-off in developing and rich countries alike also benefit. After all the rhetoric about globalization is stripped away, many of the policy questions come down to whether the rich world will make integrating with the world economy easy for those poor communities that want to do so. The world's poor have a large stake in how the rich countries answer.

Dani Rodrik

Trading in Illusions

Advocates of global economic integration hold out utopian visions of the prosperity that developing countries will reap if they open their borders to commerce and capital. This hollow promise diverts poor nations' attention and resources from the key domestic innovations needed to spur economic growth.

A senior U.S. Treasury official recently urged Mexico's government to work harder to reduce violent crime because "such high levels of crime and violence may drive away foreign investors." This admonition nicely illustrates how foreign trade and investment have become the ultimate yardstick for evaluating the social and economic policies of governments in developing countries. Forget the slum dwellers or *campesinos* who live amidst crime and poverty throughout the developing world. Just mention "investor sentiment" or "competitiveness in world markets" and policymakers will come to attention in a hurry.

Underlying this perversion of priorities is a remarkable consensus on the imperative of global economic integration. Openness to trade and investment flows is no longer viewed simply as a component of a country's development strategy; it has mutated into the most potent catalyst for economic growth known to humanity. Predictably, senior officials of the World Trade Organization (WTO), International Monetary Fund (IMF), and other international financial agencies incessantly repeat the openness mantra. In recent years, however, faith in integration has spread quickly to political leaders and policymakers around the world.

Joining the world economy is no longer a matter simply of dismantling barriers to trade and investment. Countries now must also comply with a long list of admission requirements, from new patent rules to more rigorous banking standards. The apostles of economic integration prescribe comprehensive institutional reforms that took today's advanced countries generations to accomplish, so that developing countries can, as the cliché goes, maximize the gains and minimize the risks of participation in the world economy. Global integration has become, for all practical purposes, a substitute for a development strategy.

This trend is bad news for the world's poor. The new agenda of global integration rests on shaky empirical ground and seriously distorts policymakers' priorities. By focusing on international integration, governments in poor nations divert human resources, administrative capabilities, and political capital away from more urgent development priorities such as education, public health, industrial capacity, and social cohesion. This emphasis also undermines nascent democratic institutions by removing the choice of development strategy from public debate.

World markets are a source of technology and capital; it would be silly for the developing world not to exploit these opportunities. But globalization is not a shortcut to development. Successful economic growth strategies have always required a judicious blend of imported practices with domestic institutional innovations. Policymakers need to forge a domestic growth strategy by relying on domestic investors and domestic institutions. The costliest downside of the integrationist faith is that it crowds out serious thinking and efforts along such lines.

Excuses, Excuses

Countries that have bought wholeheartedly into the integration orthodoxy are discovering that openness does not deliver on its promise. Despite sharply lowering their barriers to trade and investment since the 1980s, scores of countries in Latin America and Africa are stagnating or growing less rapidly than in the heyday of import substitution during the 1960s and 1970s. By contrast, the fastest growing countries are China, India, and others in East and Southeast Asia. Policymakers in these countries have also espoused trade and investment liberalization, but they have done so in an unorthodox manner—gradually, sequentially, and only after an initial period of high growth—and as part of a broader policy package with many unconventional features.

The disappointing outcomes with deep liberalization have been absorbed into the faith with remarkable aplomb. Those who view global integration as the prerequisite for economic development now simply add the caveat that opening borders is insufficient. Reaping the gains from openness, they argue, also requires a full complement of institutional reforms.

Consider trade liberalization. Asking any World Bank economist what a successful trade-liberalization program requires will likely elicit a laundry list of measures beyond the simple reduction of tariff and nontariff barriers: tax reform to make up for lost tariff revenues; social safety nets to compensate displaced workers; administrative reform to bring trade practices into compliance with WTO rules; labor market reform to enhance worker mobility across industries; technological assistance to upgrade firms hurt by import competition; and training programs to ensure that export-oriented firms and investors have access to skilled workers. As the promise of trade liberalization fails to materialize, the prerequisites keep expanding. For example, Clare Short, Great Britain's secretary of state for international development, recently added universal provision of health and education to the list.

In the financial arena, integrationists have pushed complementary reforms with even greater fanfare and urgency. The prevailing view in Washington and other Group of Seven (G-7) capitals is that weaknesses in banking systems, prudential regulation, and corporate governance were at the heart of the Asian financial crisis of the late 1990s. Hence the ambitious efforts by the G-7 to establish international codes and standards covering fiscal transparency, monetary and financial policy, banking supervision, data dissemination, corporate governance, and accounting standards. The Financial Stability Forum (FSF)—a G-7 organization with minimal representation from developing nations—has designated 12 of these standards as essential for creating sound financial systems in developing countries. The full FSF compendium includes an additional 59 standards the agency considers "relevant for sound financial systems," bringing the total number of codes to 71. To fend off speculative capital movements, the IMF and the G-7 also typically urge developing countries to accumulate foreign reserves and avoid exchange-rate regimes that differ from a "hard peg" (tying the value of one's currency to that of a more stable currency, such as the U.S. dollar) or a "pure float" (letting the market determine the appropriate exchange rate).

A cynic might wonder whether the point of all these prerequisites is merely to provide easy cover for eventual failure. Integrationists can conveniently blame disappointing growth performance or a financial crisis on "slippage" in the implementation of complementary reforms rather than on a poorly designed liberalization. So if Bangladesh's freer trade policy does not produce a large enough spurt in growth, the World Bank concludes that the problem must involve lagging reforms in public administration or continued "political uncertainty" (always a favorite). And if Argentina gets caught up in a confidence crisis despite significant trade and financial liberalization, the IMF reasons that structural reforms have been inadequate and must be deepened.

Free Trade-Offs

Most (but certainly not all) of the institutional reforms on the integrationist agenda are perfectly sensible, and in a world without financial, administrative, or political constraints, there would be little argument about the need to adopt them. But in the real world, governments face difficult choices over how to deploy their fiscal resources, administrative capabilities, and political capital. Setting institutional priorities to maximize integration into the global economy has real opportunity costs.

Consider some illustrative trade-offs. World Bank trade economist Michael Finger has estimated that a typical developing country must spend $150 million to implement requirements under just three WTO agreements (those on customs valuation, sanitary and phytosanitary measures, and trade-related intellectual property rights). As Finger notes, this sum equals a year's development budget for many least-developed countries. And while the budgetary burden of implementing financial codes and standards has never been fully estimated, it undoubtedly entails a substantial diversion of fiscal and human resources as well. Should governments in developing countries train more bank auditors and accountants, even if those investments mean fewer secondary-school teachers or reduced spending on primary education for girls?

In the area of legal reform, should governments focus their energies on "importing" legal codes and standards or on improving existing domestic legal institutions? In Turkey, a weak coalition government spent several months during 1999 gathering political support for a bill providing foreign investors the protection of international arbitration. But wouldn't a better long-run strategy have involved reforming the existing legal regime for the benefit of foreign and domestic investors alike?

In public health, should governments promote the reverse engineering of patented basic medicines and the importation of low-cost generic drugs from "unauthorized" suppliers, even if doing so means violating WTO rules against such practices? When South Africa passed legislation in 1997 allowing imports of patented AIDS drugs from cheaper sources, the country came under severe pressure from Western governments, which argued that the South African policy conflicted with WTO rules on intellectual property.

How much should politicians spend on social protection policies in view of the fiscal constraints imposed by market "discipline"? Peru's central bank holds foreign reserves equal to 15 months of imports as an insurance policy against the sudden capital outflows that financially open economies often experience. The opportunity cost of this policy amounts to almost 1 percent of gross domestic product annually—more than enough to fund a generous antipoverty program.

How should governments choose their exchange-rate regimes? During the last four decades, virtually every growth boom in the developing world has been accompanied by a controlled depreciation of the domestic currency. Yet financial openness makes it all but impossible to manage the exchange rate.

How should policymakers focus their anticorruption strategies? Should they target the high-level corruption that foreign investors often decry or the petty corruption that affects the poor the most? Perhaps, as the proponents of permanent normal trade relations with China argued in the recent U.S. debate, a government that is forced to protect the rights of foreign investors will become more inclined to protect the rights of its own citizens as well. But this is, at best, a trickledown strategy of institutional reform. Shouldn't reforms target the desired ends directly—whether those ends are the rule of law, improved observance of human rights, or reduced corruption?

The rules for admission into the world economy not only reflect little awareness of development priorities, they are often completely unrelated to sensible economic principles. For instance, WTO agreements on anti-dumping, subsidies and countervailing measures, agriculture, textiles, and trade-related intellectual property rights lack any economic rationale beyond the mercantilist interests of a narrow set of powerful groups in advanced industrial countries. Bilateral and regional trade agreements are typically far worse, as they impose even tighter prerequisites on developing countries in return for crumbs of enhanced "market access." For example, the African Growth and Opportunity Act signed by U.S. President Clinton in May 2000 provides increased access to the U.S. market only if African apparel manufac-turers use U.S.-produced fabric and yarns. This restriction severely limits the potential economic spillovers in African countries.

There are similar questions about the appropriateness of financial codes and standards. These codes rely heavily on an Anglo-American style of corporate governance and an arm's-length model of financial development. They close off alternative paths to financial development of the sort that have been followed by many of today's rich countries (for example, Germany, Japan, or South Korea).

In each of these areas, a strategy of "globalization above all" crowds out alternatives that are potentially more development-friendly. Many of the institutional reforms needed for insertion into the world economy can be independently desirable or produce broader economic benefits. But these priorities do not necessarily coincide with the priorities of a comprehensive development agenda.

Asian Myths

Even if the institutional reforms needed to join the international economic community are expensive and preclude investments in other crucial areas, pro-globalization advocates argue that the vast increases in economic growth that invariably result from insertion into the global marketplace will more than compensate for those costs. Take the East Asian tigers or China, the advocates say. Where would they be without international trade and foreign capital flows?

That these countries reaped enormous benefits from their progressive integration into the world economy is undeniable. But look closely at what policies produced those results, and you will find little that resembles today's rule book.

Countries like South Korea and Taiwan had to abide by few international constraints and pay few of the modern costs of integration during their formative growth experience in the 1960s and 1970s. At that time, global trade rules were sparse and economies faced almost none of today's common pressures to open their borders to capital flows. So these countries combined their outward orientation with unorthodox policies: high levels of tariff and nontariff barriers, public ownership of large segments of banking and industry, export subsidies, domestic-content requirements, patent and copyright infringements, and restrictions on capital flows (including on foreign direct investment). Such policies are either precluded by today's trade rules or . . . highly frowned upon by organizations like the IMF and the World Bank.

China also followed a highly unorthodox two-track strategy, violating practically every rule in the guidebook (including, most notably, the requirement of private property rights). India, which significantly raised its economic growth rate in the early 1980s, remains one of the world's most highly protected economies.

All of these countries liberalized trade gradually, over a period of decades, not years. Significant import liberalization did not occur until after a transition to high economic growth had taken place. And far from wiping the institutional slate clean, all of these nations managed to eke growth out of their existing institutions, imperfect as they may have been. Indeed, when some of the more successful Asian economies gave in to Western pressure to liberalize capital flows rapidly, they were rewarded with the Asian financial crisis.

That is why these countries can hardly be considered poster children for today's global rules. South Korea, China, India, and the other Asian success cases had the freedom to do their own thing, and they used that freedom abundantly. Today's globalizers would be unable to replicate these experiences without running afoul of the IMF or the WTO. The Asian experience highlights a deeper point: A sound overall development strategy that produces high economic growth is far more effective in achieving integration with the world economy than a purely integrationist strategy that relies on openness to work its magic. In other words, the globalizers have it exactly backwards. Integration is the result, not the cause, of economic and social development. A relatively protected economy like Vietnam is integrating with the world economy much more rapidly than an open economy like Haiti because Vietnam, unlike Haiti, has a reasonably functional economy and polity.

Integration into the global economy, unlike tariff rates or capital-account regulations, is not something that policymakers control directly. Telling finance ministers in developing nations that they should increase their "participation in world trade" is as meaningful as telling them that they need to improve technological capabilities—and just as helpful. Policymakers need to know which strategies will produce these results, and whether the specific prescriptions that the current orthodoxy offers are up to the task.

Too Good to Be True

Do lower trade barriers spur greater economic progress? The available studies reveal no systematic relationship between a country's average level of tariff and nontariff barriers and its subsequent economic growth rate. If anything, the evidence for the 1990s indicates a positive relationship between import tariffs and economic growth. The only clear pattern is that countries dismantle their trade restrictions as they grow richer. This finding explains why today's rich countries, with few exceptions, embarked on modern economic growth behind protective barriers but now display low trade barriers.

The absence of a strong negative relationship between trade restrictions and economic growth may seem surprising in view of the ubiquitous claim that trade liberalization promotes higher growth. Indeed, the economics literature is replete with cross-national studies concluding that growth and economic dynamism are strongly linked to more open trade policies. A particularly influential study finds that economies that are "open," by the study's own definition, grew 2.45 percentage points faster annually than closed ones—an enormous difference.

Upon closer look, however, such studies turn out to be unreliable. In a detailed review of the empirical literature, University of Maryland economist Francisco Rodriguez and I have found a major gap between the results that economists have actually obtained and the policy conclusions they have typically drawn. For example, in many cases economists blame poor growth on the government's failure to liberalize trade policies, when the true culprits are ineffective institutions, geographic determinants (such as location in a tropical region), or inappropriate macroeconomic policies (such as an overvalued exchange rate). Once these misdiagnoses are corrected, any meaningful relationship across countries between the level of trade barriers and economic growth evaporates.

The evidence on the benefits of liberalizing capital flows is even weaker. In theory, the appeal of capital mobility seems obvious: If capital is free to enter (and leave) markets based on the potential return on investment, the result will be an efficient allocation of global resources. But in reality, financial markets are inherently unstable, subject to bubbles (rational or otherwise), panics, shortsightedness, and self-fulfilling prophecies. There is plenty of evidence that financial liberalization is often followed by financial crash—just ask Mexico, Thailand, or Turkey—while there is little convincing evidence to suggest that higher rates of economic growth follow capital-account liberalization.

Perhaps the most disingenuous argument in favor of liberalizing international financial flows is that the threat of massive and sudden capital movements serves to discipline policymakers in developing nations who might otherwise manage their economies irresponsibly. In other words, governments might be less inclined to squander their societies' resources if such actions would spook foreign lenders. In practice, however, the discipline argument falls apart. Behavior in international capital markets is dominated by mood swings unrelated to fundamentals. In good times, a government with a chronic fiscal deficit has an easier time financing its spending when it can borrow funds from investors abroad; witness Russia prior to 1998 or Argentina in the 1990s. And in bad times, governments may be forced to adopt inappropriate policies in order to conform to the biases of foreign investors; witness the excessively restrictive monetary and fiscal policies in much of East Asia in the immediate aftermath of the Asian financial crisis. A key reason why Malaysia was able to recover so quickly after the imposition of capital controls in September 1998 was that Prime Minister Mahathir Mohamad resisted the high interest rates and tight fiscal policies that South Korea, Thailand, and Indonesia adopted at the behest of the International Monetary Fund.

Growth Begins at Home

Well-trained economists are justifiably proud of the textbook case in favor of free trade. For all the theory's simplicity, it is one of our profession's most significant achievements. However, in their zeal to promote the virtues of trade, the most ardent proponents are peddling a cartoon version of the argument, vastly overstating the effectiveness of economic openness as a tool for fostering development. Such claims only endanger broad public acceptance of the real article because they unleash unrealistic expectations about the benefits of free trade. Neither economic theory nor empirical evidence guarantees that deep trade liberalization will deliver higher economic growth. Economic openness and all its accouterments do not deserve the priority they typically receive in the development strategies pushed by leading multilateral organizations.

Countries that have achieved long-term economic growth have usually combined the opportunities offered by world markets with a growth strategy that mobilizes the capabilities of domestic institutions and investors. Designing such a growth strategy is both harder and easier than implementing typical integration policies. It is harder because the binding constraints on growth are usually country specific and do not respond well to standardized recipes. But it is easier because once those constraints are targeted, relatively simple policy changes can yield enormous economic payoffs and start a virtuous cycle of growth and additional reform.

Unorthodox innovations that depart from the integration rule book are typically part and parcel of such strategies. Public enterprises during the Meiji restoration in Japan; township and village enterprises in China;

an export processing zone in Mauritius; generous tax incentives for priority investments in Taiwan; extensive credit subsidies in South Korea; infant-industry protection in Brazil during the 1960s and 1970s—these are some of the innovations that have been instrumental in kick-starting investment and growth in the past. None came out of a Washington economist's tool kit.

Few of these experiments have worked as well when transplanted to other settings, only underscoring the decisive importance of local conditions. To be effective, development strategies need to be tailored to prevailing domestic institutional strengths. There is simply no alternative to a homegrown business plan. Policymakers who look to Washington and financial markets for the answers are condemning themselves to mimicking the conventional wisdom du jour, and to eventual disillusionment.

CHAPTER 13 FOREIGN AID PROMOTES DEVELOPMENT *v.* FOREIGN AID IS INEFFECTIVE

Foreign Aid Promotes Development

Advocate: David Dollar

Source: "Eyes Wide Open: On the Targeted Use of Foreign Aid," *Harvard International Review* 25 (Spring 2003): 48–52

Foreign Aid Is Ineffective

Advocate: William Easterly

Source: "The Cartel of Good Intentions," *Foreign Policy*, July/August 2002: 40–44

In the last ten years, governments and multilateral lending agencies have made important changes in their thinking about foreign aid. For most of the post–World War II period, agencies based the rationale for foreign aid on an economic model called the "finance gap." According to this approach, poverty was a result of insufficient physical and human capital. Creating such capital by investing in manufacturing industries would thus generate growth and rising per capita incomes. Lending agencies encouraged governments to develop investment plans and then calculate the amount of local savings they had available. The difference between planned investment and available savings was the finance gap, which multilateral agencies filled with foreign aid.

Lenders became disenchanted with this aid model in the 1990s. Almost four decades of experience failed to produce compelling results. World Bank studies found little relationship between the amount of foreign aid a country received and its subsequent economic performance. Although foreign aid contributed to growth in some countries, there was little evidence that the postwar regime was successful overall. Growing disenchantment, in conjunction with the end of the Cold War, led governments to reduce their aid expenditures and rethink the underlying rationale for aid. As governments began to increase aid in the wake of the 9/11 terrorist attacks, multilateral agencies searched for a framework that would ensure that aid expenditures had a positive impact.

FOREIGN AID PROMOTES DEVELOPMENT

Most advocates of aid suggest that aid can work if it targets the right things. A key conclusion of the recent reevaluation was that aid had been directed toward the wrong goal. Rather than focusing on the creation of physical and human capital, governments should use aid to build high-quality institutions. Rather than thinking of foreign aid as an input into manufacturing, as the finance gap model did, this new approach conceives of aid as an input into governance. By helping to build effective institutions, aid helps create the infrastructure within which individuals can make the investments that will drive economic development. Moreover, by providing aid to societies where governance is already strong, the chances that the aid will be misdirected or consumed by corrupt officials are reduced substantially.

David Dollar, a World Bank official, develops this argument here. He argues that foreign aid must promote high-quality institutions. Institutions that enable the state to act effectively within society are of particular importance. Dollar argues that property rights need protection and that state bureaucracies must be able to provide essential public services.

FOREIGN AID IS INEFFECTIVE

Other participants argue that the problem lies not in what aid targets but in the structure of the foreign-aid regime itself. William Easterly, a professor of economics at New York University, is the most prominent advocate of this position. Easterly argues that a central limitation of aid's effectiveness lies in the multilateral organizations that manage aid provision. Focusing on what he calls the "foreign aid cartel," Easterly argues that the bureaucratic agencies responsible for delivering and administering aid are accountable solely to politicians in wealthy donor countries. They, therefore, concentrate on projects that please their constituents rather than on projects that would generate a higher return in developing societies. Making foreign aid more effective, Easterly argues, requires fundamental reform of the international organizations that manage it. These organizations must be made accountable to their clients in developing countries. He suggests that bringing market competition into the distribution of foreign aid could create such accountability.

POINTS TO PONDER

1. Dollar stresses the importance of high-quality institutions. What specific institutions does he have in mind? Why does aid have a greater impact on countries with high-quality institutions?

2. Does Dollar believe that traditional forms of aid conditionality can be used to promote high-quality institutions? What are the consequences of this for the distribution of aid across countries?

3. What does Easterly mean by the "foreign aid cartel," and why does he call it that? What impact does this cartel have on the projects that aid agencies fund?

4. What solutions does Easterly propose for the problems created by the aid cartel?

5. Which author do you believe offers the best strategy for making aid more effective?

David Dollar

Eyes Wide Open: On the Targeted Use of Foreign Aid

Conventional wisdom on international development holds that "the rich get richer while the poor get poorer." This saying does not capture exactly what has happened between the rich and poor regions of the world over the past century, but it comes pretty close. In general, poor areas of the world have not become poorer, but their per capita income has grown quite slowly. On the other hand, income in the club of rich countries (Western Europe, the United States, Canada, Japan, Australia, and New Zealand) has increased at a much more rapid pace. As a result, by 1980 an unprecedented level of worldwide inequality had developed. The richest fifth of the world's population—which essentially corresponds to the population of the rich countries—produced and consumed 70 percent of the world's goods and services, while the poorest fifth of the global population, in contrast, held only two percent.

There has been a modest decline in global inequality since 1980 because two large poor countries—China and India—have outperformed the rich countries economically. This shift represents an interesting change that has important lessons for development. However, if one ignores the performance of China and India, much of the rest of the developing world still languishes, and there continues to be an appalling gap between rich countries and poor countries.

Inequality within countries is an important issue as well, but it pales in comparison with inequality between countries across the world. A homeless person pan-handling for two U.S. dollars a day on the streets of Boston would sit in the top half of the world income distribution. Without traveling through rural parts of the developing world, it is difficult to comprehend the magnitude of this gap, which is not just one of income. Life expectancy in the United States has risen to 77 years whereas in Zambia it has fallen to 38 years. Infant mortality is down to seven deaths per 1,000 live births in the United States, compared to 115 in Zambia. How can these gaps in living standards be understood? And, more importantly, what can be done about it?

Traditionally, one part of the answer to the latter question has been foreign aid. Since the end of the Cold War, aid has been in decline, both in terms of volume (down to about 0.2 percent of the gross national product of the rich countries) and popularity as an effective policy. However, since before September 11, 2001, aid has made something of a comeback, with a number of European countries, notably the United Kingdom, arguing for the importance of addressing global poverty by implementing reforms to make aid more effective. Since September 11, the U.S. government has shown renewed interest as well.

What can come from this renewed interest in foreign aid? Foreign aid bureaucracies have a long history of mistaking symptoms for causes. If this trend continues uncorrected, then it is unlikely that greater volumes of aid will make much of a dent in global poverty and inequality. On the other hand there is much more evidence about what leads to successful development and how aid can assist in that process. Thus, the potential exists to make aid a much more important tool in the fight against poverty. My argument on this matter is comprised of four points.

First, countries are poor primarily because of weak underlying institutions and policies. Features such as lack of capital, poor education, or absence of modern industry are symptoms rather than causes of underdevelopment. Aid focused on these symptoms has not had much lasting impact.

Second, local institutions in developing countries are persistent, and foreign aid donors have little influence over them. Efforts to reform countries through conditionality of aid from the Bretton Woods organizations have generally failed to bring about lasting reform within developing country institutions. It is difficult to predict when serious movements will emerge, but the positive developments in global poverty in the past 20 years have been the result of home-grown reform movements in countries such as China, India, Uganda, and Vietnam.

Third, foreign aid has had a positive effect in these and other cases, and arguably its most useful role has been to support learning at the state and community level. Countries and communities can learn from each other, but there are no simple blueprints of institutional reform that can be transferred from one location to the next. Thus, helping countries analyze, implement, and evaluate options is useful, whereas promoting a "best-practice" approach to each issue through conditionality is not.

Fourth, the financial aspect of foreign aid is also important. In poor countries that have made significant steps toward improving their institutions and policies, financial aid accelerates growth and poverty reduction and helps cement popular support for reform. Hence, large-scale financial assistance needs to be "selective," targeting countries that can put aid to effective use building schools, roads, and other aspects of social infrastructure.

Institutions and Policies

Economists have long underestimated the importance of state institutions in explaining the differences in economic performance between countries. Recent work in economic history and development is beginning to rectify this oversight. In their 2001 study, "Colonial Origins of Comparative Development: An Empirical Investigation," Daron Acemoglu, Simon Johnson, and James Robinson find that much of the variation in per capita income across countries can be explained by differences in institutional quality. They look at a number of different institutional measures, which generally capture the extent to which the state effectively provides a framework in which property is secure and markets can operate. Thus, indicators of institutional quality try to measure people's confidence in their property rights and the government bureaucracy's ability to provide public services relatively free of interest group appropriation and corruption. All countries have some problems with appropriation and corruption, so the practical issue is the extent of these problems. While these differences are inherently hard to measure, some contrasts are obvious; there is, for example, no doubt that Singapore or Finland has a better environment of property rights and clean government than Mobutu's Zaire or many similar locations in the developing world.

Differences in institutional quality explain much of the variation in per capita income across countries, an empirical result that is very intuitive. In a poor institutional environment, households must focus on day-to-day subsistence. The state fails to provide the complementary infrastructure—such as roads and schools—necessary to encourage long-term investment, while the lack of confidence in property rights further discourages entrepreneurial activity. In this type of setting, any surplus accumulated by individuals is more likely to fund capital flight, investment abroad, or emigration than to be reinvested in the local economy.

In addition, there is evidence that access to markets is also important as well for economic growth. If a region is cut off from larger markets either because of its natural geography or because of man-made trade barriers, then the incentives for entrepreneurial activity and investment are again reduced. In 1999, Jeffrey Frankel and David Romer cautiously concluded that the converse holds as well: better trading opportunities do lead to faster growth. There is still some debate among economists about the relative importance of institutions and trade, but it seems likely that both are important and that in fact they complement each other. Several years ago, Kenneth Sokoloff found that rates of invention were extremely responsive to the expansion of markets during the early industrialization of the United States by examining how patenting activity varied over time and with the extension of navigable waterways. For example, as the construction of the Erie Canal progressed westward across the state of New York, patenting per capita rose sharply county-by-county. The United States had a good system of protecting these intellectual properties, and the development of transport links to broader markets stimulated individuals and firms to invest more in developing new technologies.

Indeed, looking back over the past century, locations with access to markets and good property rights have generally prospered, while locations disconnected from markets and with poor property rights have remained poor. Many of the features that we associate with underdevelopment are therefore results of these underlying weaknesses in institutions and policies. In such environments, there is little incentive to invest in equipment or education and develop modern industry.

But these symptoms have often been mistaken by aid donors as causes of underdevelopment. If low levels of investment are a problem, then give poor countries foreign aid to invest in capital. If a lack of education is a problem, finance broad expansion of schools. If modern industry is absent, erect infant-industry protection to allow firms to develop behind a protected wall. All of these approaches have been pushed by aid donors. In poor countries with weak underlying institutions, however, the results have not been impressive.

Over several decades, Zambia received an amount of foreign aid that would have made every Zambian rich had it achieved the kind of return that is normal in developed economies. If lack of capital was the key problem in Zambia, then that was certainly addressed by massive amounts of aid; but the result was virtually no increase in the country's per capita income. Similarly, large amounts of aid targeted at expanding education in Africa yielded little measurable improvement in achievement or skills. Donors financed power plants, steel mills, and even shoe factories behind high levels of protection, but again there was virtually no return on these investments.

The recent thinking in economic history and development suggests that these efforts failed because they were aimed at symptoms rather than at underlying causes. If a government is very corrupt or dominated by powerful special interests, then giving it money, or schools, or shoe factories will not promote lasting growth and development. These findings suggest that much of the frustration about foreign aid comes from the many failed efforts to develop social infrastructure in weak institutional environments where governments and communities cannot make effective use of these resources—not from the intrinsic inability of aid itself to generate positive results.

There are a number of important caveats about these findings on aid effectiveness. First, humanitarian or food aid is a different story. When there is a famine or humanitarian crisis, international donors have shown that they can bring in short-term relief effectively. Second, there are some health interventions that can be delivered in a weak institutional environment. In much of Africa, donors have collaborated to eradicate river blindness, a disease that can be controlled by taking a single pill each year. That intervention—and certain types of vaccinations—can be carried out in almost any environment. But many other social services require an effective institutional delivery system; other health projects in countries with weak institutions have tended to fail without producing any benefits.

Persistent Institutions

A second important finding from recent work in economic history is that institutions are persistent. Last year, Stanley Engerman and Sokoloff showed how differences in the natural endowments of South and North American colonies centuries ago led to the development of different institutions in the two environments. Furthermore, many of these institutional differences have persisted to this day. If institutions are important and if they typically change slowly over time, then it is easy to understand the pattern of rising global inequality over the past century. Locations with better institutions have consistently grown faster than ones with poor institutions, widening inequalities. Because it is relatively rare for a country to switch from poor institutions and policies to good ones, countries that began at a disadvantage only fell further behind in the years that followed.

The importance of good institutions and policies for development in general and for aid effectiveness in particular is something that donors have gradually realized through experience and research. International donors' first instincts were to make improved institutions and policies a condition of their assistance. In the 1980s in particular, donors loaded assistance packages with large numbers of conditions concerning specific institutional and policy reforms. Some World Bank loans, for example, had more than 100 specific reform conditions. However, the persistence of institutions and policies hints at the difficulty of changing them. There are always powerful interests who benefit from bad policies, and donor conditionality has proved largely ineffective at overcoming these interest groups. A 2000 study that I coauthored with Jakob Svensson examined a large sample of World Bank structural adjustment programs to find that the success or failure of reform can largely be predicted by underlying institutional features of the country, including whether or not the government is democratically elected and how long the executive has been in power. Governments are often willing to sign aid agreements with large amounts of conditionality, but in many low-income countries the government is either uninterested in implementing reform or politically blocked from doing so. "Aid and Reform in Africa," a set of case studies written by African scholars on 10 African states, reaches similar conclusions: institutional and policy reform is driven primarily by domestic movements and not by outside agents.

Prospects for Reform

The good news is that a number of important developing countries have accomplished considerable reforms in the past two decades. In 1980, about 60 percent of the world's extreme poor—those living on less than one U.S. dollar per day—lived in just two countries: China and India. At that time, neither country seemed a particularly likely candidate for reform. Both had rather poor property rights and government efficiency according to the measures used in cross-country studies, and both were extremely closed to the world market. Over the past two decades, however, China has introduced truly revolutionary reforms, restoring property rights over land, opening the economy to foreign trade and investment, and gradually making the legal and regulatory changes that have permitted the domestic private sector to become the main engine of growth. Reforms in India have not been quite as dramatic, but have still been very successful at reducing the government's heavy-handed management of the economy and dismantling the protectionist trade regime. Among low-income countries, there have been a number of other notable reformers as well; Uganda is a good example in Africa, and Vietnam in Southeast Asia.

The general point about all of these low-income reformers is that outside donors were not particularly important at the start of these reform efforts. These movements are home-grown and each has an interesting and distinct political-economy story behind it. Once these reforms began, however, foreign assistance played an important supporting role in each case. Institutional reform involves much social and political experimentation. The way that China has gradually strengthened private property rights is an excellent example, as is the way India reformed its energy sector. Foreign assistance can help governments and communities examine options, implement innovations, and evaluate them. To do this effectively, donor agencies need to have good technical staff, worldwide experience, and an open mind about what might work in different circumstances.

The World Bank is often criticized for giving the same advice everywhere, but this simply is not true. World Bank reports on different countries show that the World Bank typically makes quite different recommendations in different countries. The criticism that comes from government officials in the developing world is a different and more telling one: that the World Bank tends to make a single strong recommendation on each issue, instead of helping clients analyze the pros and cons of different options so that communities can make up their own minds about what to do. We do not know much about institutional change, so it is more useful to promote community learning than to push particular institutional models.

For example, the Education, Health, and Nutrition Program—known by its Spanish acronym, PROGRESA—is a successful program of cash transfers that encourages poor families to keep their children in school that was developed and evaluated in Mexico without any donor support. A number of donors now have helped communities in Central American countries to implement similar programs. In each case, communities need to tailor the program to their particular situation. Systematic re-evaluation is important because the same idea will not necessarily work everywhere. But this is a good example of how donors can promote learning across countries and support institutional change by presenting a variety of reform options for developing countries to follow.

Money Matters

While supporting country and community learning is probably the most useful role for aid, and the one that will have the largest impact, there is still a role for large-scale financial aid. Studies have shown that there is little relationship between aid amounts and growth rates in developing countries, but there is a rather strong relationship between growth and the interaction of aid and economic policies. This finding, as well as microeconomic evidence about in-dividual projects, suggests that the growth effect of aid is greater in countries with reasonably good institutions and policies. The success of the Marshall Plan is a classic historical example. More recently, states such as Uganda show that the combination of substantial reform and large-scale aid goes together with rapid growth and poverty reduction. In a poor institutional environ-ment, however, large-scale aid seems to have little lasting economic impact and may even make things worse by sustaining a bad government.

What follows from this is that aid is going to have more impact on poverty reduction if it is targeted to countries that are poor and have favorable institutions and policies. This philosophy underlies a number of new initiatives in foreign aid—European countries, including the United Kingdom and the Netherlands, have reformed and expanded their aid program along these lines. The new U.S. Millennium Challenge Account is based on these principles as well.

Using aid to support learning and being selective in the allocation of large-scale financial resources are linked. When donors tried to push large amounts of money into weak institutional environments, they naturally wanted to have large numbers of conditions dictating how institutions and policies would change. But this neither promoted effective learning nor led to good use of money. The new model argues for much less conditionality—encouraging countries and communities to figure out what works for them—but retaining some form of selectivity in the allocation of financial resources.

Keeping in mind the persistence of institutions and the difficulty of changing them, one should have modest hopes for what foreign aid can ac-complish. But as long as there are countries and communities around the world struggling to change, the international community must support them. Afghanistan today is a good example. The country is trying to develop new institutions at the national and local levels, and the world has a big stake in helping it succeed. The international community does not know for sure what will work, but outsiders dictating a new set of institutions will almost certainly fail. On the other hand, donor agencies can help both national and local governments learn about options, implement policies, evaluate results, and re-design if necessary. As a sound institutional framework develops, there will be increasing scope for large-scale funding of roads, schools, and other social infrastructure. The effort may fail. No doubt the lack of good institutions in Afghanistan reflects extensive historical and political factors that will be hard to overcome. It is important to go in with eyes wide open; trying to reform aid based on what we know is preferable to giving up on aid and closing our eyes to the massive poverty that remains throughout the developing world.

William Easterly

The Cartel of Good Intentions

The world's richest governments have pledged to boost financial aid to the developing world. So why won't poor nations reap the benefits? Because in the way stands a bloated, unaccountable foreign aid bureaucracy out of touch with sound economics. The solution: Subject the foreign assistance business to the forces of market competition.

The mere mention of a "cartel" usually strikes fear in the hearts and wallets of consumers and regulators around the globe. Though the term normally evokes images of greedy oil producers or murderous drug lords, a new, more well-intentioned cartel has emerged on the global scene. Its members are the world's leading foreign aid organizations, which constitute a near monopoly relative to the powerless poor.

This state of affairs helps explain why the global foreign aid bureaucracy has run amok in recent years. Consider the steps that beleaguered government officials in low-income countries must take to receive foreign aid. Among other things, they must prepare a participatory Poverty Reduction Strategy Paper (PRSP)—a detailed plan for uplifting the destitute that the World Bank and International Monetary Fund (IMF) require before granting debt forgiveness and new loans. This document in turn must adhere to the World Bank's Comprehensive Development Framework, a 14-point checklist covering everything from lumber policy to labor practices. And the list goes on: Policymakers seeking aid dollars must also prepare a Financial Information Management System report, a Report on Observance of Standards and Codes, a Medium Term Expenditure Framework, and a Debt Sustainability Analysis for the Enhanced Heavily Indebted Poor Countries Initiative. Each document can run to hundreds of pages and consume months of preparation time. For example, Niger's recently completed PRSP is 187 pages long, took 15 months to prepare, and sets out spending for a 2002–05 poverty reduction plan with such detailed line items as $17,600 a year on "sensitizing population to traffic circulation."

Meanwhile, the U.N. International Conference on Financing for Development held in Monterrey, Mexico, in March 2002 produced a document—"the Monterrey Consensus"—that has a welcome emphasis on partnership between rich donor and poor recipient nations. But it's somewhat challenging for poor countries to carry out the 73 actions that the document recommends, including such ambitions as establishing democracy, equality between boys and girls, and peace on Earth.

Visitors to the World Bank Web site will find 31 major development topics listed there, each with multiple subtopics. For example, browsers can explore 13 subcategories under "Social Development," including indigenous peoples, resettlement, and culture in sustainable development. This last item in turn includes the music industry in Africa, the preservation of cultural artifacts, a seven-point framework for action, and—well, you get the idea.

It's not that aid bureaucrats are bad; in fact, many smart, hardworking, dedicated professionals toil away in the world's top aid agencies. But the perverse incentives they face explain the organizations' obtuse behavior. The international aid bureaucracy will never work properly under the conditions that make it operate like a cartel—the cartel of good intentions.

All Together Now

Cartels thrive when customers have little opportunity to complain or to find alternative suppliers. In its heyday during the 1970s, for example, the Organization of the Petroleum Exporting Countries (OPEC) could dictate severe terms to customers; it was only when more non-OPEC oil exporters emerged that the cartel's power weakened. In the foreign aid business, customers (i.e., poor citizens in developing countries) have few chances to express their needs, yet they cannot exit the system. Meanwhile, rich nations paying the aid bills are clueless about what those customers want. Nongovernmental organizations (NGOs) can hold aid institutions to task on only a few high-visibility issues, such as conspicuous environmental destruction. Under these circumstances, even while foreign aid agencies make good-faith efforts to consult their clients, these agencies remain accountable mainly to themselves.

The typical aid agency forces governments seeking its money to work exclusively with that agency's own bureaucracy—its project appraisal and selection apparatus, its economic and social analysts, its procurement procedures, and its own interests and objectives. Each aid agency constitutes a mini-monopoly, and the collection of all such monopolies forms a cartel. The foreign aid community also resembles a cartel in that the IMF, World Bank, regional development banks, European Union, United Nations, and bilateral aid agencies all agree to "coordinate" their efforts. The customers therefore have even less opportunity to find alternative aid suppliers. And the entry of new suppliers into the foreign assistance business is difficult because large aid agencies must be sponsored either by an individual government (as in the case of national agencies, such as the U.S. Agency for International Development) or by an international agreement (as in the case of multilateral agencies, such as the World Bank). Most NGOs are too small to make much of a difference.

Of course, cartels always display fierce jostling for advantage and even mutual enmity among members. That explains why the aid community concludes that "to realize our increasingly reciprocal ambitions, a lot of hard work, compromises and true goodwill must come into play." Oops, wait, that's a quote from a recent OPEC meeting. The foreign aid community simply maintains that "better coordination among international financial institutions is needed." However, the difficulties of organizing parties with diverse objectives and interests and the inherent tensions in a cartel render such coordination forever elusive. Doomed attempts at coordination create the worst of all worlds—no central planner exists to tell each agency what to do, nor is there any market pressure from customers to reward successful agencies and discipline unsuccessful ones.

As a result, aid organizations mindlessly duplicate services for the world's poor. Some analysts see this duplication as a sign of competition to satisfy the customer—not so. True market competition should eliminate duplication: When you choose where to eat lunch, the restaurant next door usually doesn't force you to sit down for an extra meal. But things are different in the world of foreign aid, where a team from the U.S. Agency for International Development produced a report on corruption in Uganda in 2001, unaware that British analysts had produced a report on the same topic six months earlier. The Tanzanian government churns out more than 2,400 reports annually for its various donors, who send the poor country some 1,000 missions each year. (Borrowing terminology from missionaries who show the locals the one true path to heaven, "missions" are visits of aid agency staff to developing countries to discuss desirable government policy.) No wonder, then, that in the early 1990s, Tanzania was implementing 15 separate stand-alone health-sector projects funded by 15 different donors. Even small bilateral aid agencies plant their flags everywhere. Were the endless meetings and staff hours worth the effort for the Senegalese government to receive $38,957 from the Finnish Ministry for Foreign Affairs Development Cooperation in 2001?

By forming a united front and duplicating efforts, the aid cartel is also able to diffuse blame among its various members when economic conditions in recipient countries don't improve according to plan. Should observers blame the IMF for fiscal austerity that restricts funding for worthy programs, or should they fault the World Bank for failing to preserve high-return areas from public expenditure cuts? Are the IMF and World Bank too tough or too lax in enforcing conditions? Or are the regional development banks too inflexible (or too lenient) in their conditions for aid? Should bilateral aid agencies be criticized for succumbing to national and commercial interests, or should multilateral agencies be condemned for applying a "one size fits all" reform program to all countries? Like squabbling children, aid organizations find safety in numbers. Take Argentina. From 1980 to 2001, the Argentine government received 33 structural adjustment loans from the IMF and World Bank, all under the watchful eye of the U.S. Treasury. Ultimately, then, is Argentina's ongoing implosion the fault of the World

Bank, the IMF, or the Treasury Department? The buck stops nowhere in the world of development assistance. Each party can point fingers at the others, and bewildered observers don't know whom to blame—making each agency less accountable.

The $3,521 Quandary

Like any good monopoly, the cartel of good intentions seeks to maximize net revenues. Indeed, if any single objective has characterized the aid community since its inception, it is an obsession with increasing the total aid money mobilized. Traditionally, aid agencies justify this goal by identifying the aid "requirements" needed to achieve a target rate of economic growth, calculating the difference between existing aid and the requirements, and then advocating a commensurate aid increase. In 1951, the U.N. Group of Experts calculated exactly how much aid poor countries needed to achieve an annual growth rate of 2 percent per capita, coming up with an amount that would equal $20 billion in today's dollars. Similarly, the economist Walt Rostow calculated in 1960 the aid increase (roughly double the aid levels at the time) that would lift Asia, Africa, and Latin America into self-sustaining growth. ("Self-sustaining" meant that aid would no longer be necessary 10 to 15 years after the increase.) Despite the looming expiration of the 15-year aid window, then World Bank President Robert McNamara called for a doubling of aid in 1973. The call for doubling was repeated at the World Bank in its 1990 "World Development Report." Not to be outdone, current World Bank President James Wolfensohn is now advocating a doubling of aid.

The cartel's efforts have succeeded: Total assistance flows to developing countries have doubled several times since the early days of large-scale foreign aid. (Meanwhile, the World Bank's staff increased from 657 people in 1959–60 to some 10,000 today.) In fact, if all foreign aid given since 1950 had been invested in U.S. Treasury bills, the cumulative assets of poor countries by 2001 from foreign aid alone would have amounted to $2.3 trillion. This aid may have helped achieve such important accomplishments as lower infant mortality and rising literacy throughout the developing world. And high growth in aid-intensive countries like Botswana and Uganda is something to which aid agencies can (and do) point. The growth outcome in most aid recipients, however, has been extremely disappointing. For example, on average, aid-intensive African nations saw growth decline despite constant increases in aid as a percentage of their income.

Aid agencies always claim that their main goal is to reduce the number of poor people in the world, with poverty defined as an annual income below $365. To this end, the World Bank's 2002 aid accounting estimates that an extra $1 billion in overseas development assistance would lift more than

284,000 people out of poverty. (This claim has appeared prominently in the press and has been repeated in other government reports on aid effectiveness.) If these figures are correct, however, then the additional annual aid spending per person lifted out of poverty (whose annual income is less than $365) comes to $3,521. Of course, aid agencies don't follow their own logic to this absurd conclusion—common sense says that aid should help everyone and not just target those who can stagger across the minimum poverty threshold. Regrettably, this claim for aid's effect on poverty has more to do with the aid bureaucracy's desperate need for good publicity than with sound economics.

A Framework for Failure

To the extent that anyone monitors the performance of global aid agencies, it is the politicians and the public in rich nations. Aid agencies therefore strive to produce outputs (projects, loans, etc.) that these audiences can easily observe, even if such outputs provide low economic returns for recipient nations. Conversely, aid bureaucrats don't try as hard to produce less visible, high-return outputs. This emphasis on visibility results in shiny showcase projects, countless international meetings and summits, glossy reports for public consumption, and the proliferation of "frameworks" and strategy papers. Few are concerned about whether the showcase projects endure beyond the ribbon-cutting ceremony or if all those meetings, frameworks, and strategies produce anything of value.

This quest for visibility explains why donors like to finance new, high-profile capital investment projects yet seem reluctant to fund operating expenses and maintenance after high-profile projects are completed. The resulting problem is a recurrent theme in the World Bank's periodic reports on Africa. In 1981, the bank's Africa study concluded that "vehicles and equipment frequently lie idle for lack of spare parts, repairs, gasoline, or other necessities. Schools lack operating funds for salaries and teaching materials, and agricultural research stations have difficulty keeping up field trials. Roads, public buildings, and processing facilities suffer from lack of maintenance." Five years later, another study of Africa found that "road maintenance crews lack fuel and bitumen . . . teachers lack books . . . [and] health workers have no medicines to distribute." In 1986, the World Bank declared that in Africa, "schools are now short of books, clinics lack medicines, and infrastructure maintenance is avoided." Meanwhile, a recent study for a number of different poor countries estimated that the return on spending on educational instructional materials was up to 14 times higher than the return on spending on physical facilities.

And then there are the frameworks. In 1999, World Bank President James Wolfensohn unveiled his Comprehensive Development Framework, a checklist of 14 items, each with multiple subitems. The framework covers clean government, property rights, finance, social safety nets, education, health, water, the environment, the spoken word and the arts, roads, cities, the countryside, microcredit, tax policy, and motherhood. (Somehow, macroeconomic policy was omitted.) Perhaps this framework explains why the World Bank says management has simultaneously "refocused and broadened the development agenda." Yet even Wolfensohn seems relatively restrained compared with the framework being readied for the forthcoming U.N. World Summit on Sustainable Development in Johannesburg in late August 2002, where 185 "action recommendations"—covering everything from efficient use of cow dung to harmonized labeling of chemicals—await unsuspecting delegates.

Of course, the Millennium Development Goals (MDGs) are the real 800-pound gorilla of foreign aid frameworks. The representatives of planet Earth agreed on these goals at yet another U.N. conference in September 2000. The MDGs call for the simultaneous achievement of multiple targets by 2015, involving poverty, hunger, infant and maternal mortality, primary education, clean water, contraceptive use, HIV/AIDS, gender equality, the environment, and an ill-defined "partnership for development." These are all worthy causes, of course, yet would the real development customers necessarily choose to spend their scarce resources to attain these particular objectives under this particular timetable? Economic principles dictate that greater effort should be devoted to goals with low costs and high benefits, and less effort to goals where the costs are prohibitive relative to the benefits. But the "do everything" approach of the MDGs suggests that the aid bureaucracy feels above such trade-offs. As a result, government officials in recipient countries and the foreign aid agency's own frontline workers gradually go insane trying to keep up with proliferating objectives—each of which is deemed Priority Number One.

All Payin', No Gain

A 2002 World Bank technical study found that a doubling of aid flows is required for the world to meet the U.N. goals. The logic is somewhat circular, however, since a World Bank guidebook also stipulates that increasing aid is undoubtedly "a primary function of targets set by the international donor community such as the [Millennium] Development Goals." Thus increased aid becomes self-perpetuating—both cause and effect.

Foreign Aid and Abet

Pity the poor aid bureaucracy that must maintain support for foreign assistance while bad news is breaking out everywhere. Aid agencies have thus perfected the art of smoothing over unpleasant realities with diplomatic language. A war is deemed a "conflict-related reallocation of resources." Countries run by homicidal warlords like those in Liberia or Somalia are "low-income countries under stress." Nations where presidents loot the treasury experience "governance issues." The meaning of other aid community jargon, like "investment climate," remains elusive. The investment climate will be stormy in the morning, gradually clearing in the afternoon with scattered expropriations.

Another typical spin-control technique is to answer any criticism by acknowledging that, "Indeed, we aid agencies used to make that mistake, but now we have corrected it." This defense is hard to refute, since it is much more difficult to evaluate the present than the past. (One only doubts that the sinner has now found true religion from the knowledge of many previous conversions.) Recent conversions supposedly include improved coordination among donors, a special focus on poverty alleviation, and renewed economic reform efforts in African countries. And among the most popular concepts the aid community has recently discovered is "selectivity"—the principle that aid will only work in countries with good economic policies and efficient, squeaky-clean institutions. The moment of aid donors' conversion on this point supposedly came with the end of the Cold War, but in truth, selectivity (and other "new" ideas) has been a recurrent aid theme over the last 40 years.

Unfortunately, evidence of a true conversion on selectivity remains mixed. Take Kenya, where President Daniel arap Moi has mismanaged the economy since 1978. Moi has consistently failed to keep conditions on the 19 economic reform loans his government obtained from the World Bank and IMF (described by one NGO as "financing corruption and repression") since he took office. How might international aid organizations explain the selectivity guidelines that awarded President Moi yet another reform loan from the World Bank and another from the IMF in 2000, the same year prominent members of Moi's government appeared on a corruption "list of shame" issued by Kenya's parliament? Since then, Moi has again failed to deliver on his economic reform promises, and international rating agencies still rank the Kenyan government among the world's most corrupt and lawless. Ever delicate, a 2002 IMF report conceded that "efforts to bring the program back on track have been only partially successful" in Kenya. More systematically, however, a recent cross-country survey revealed no difference in government ratings on democracy, public service delivery, rule of law, and corruption between those countries that received IMF and World Bank reform loans in 2001 and those that did not. Perhaps the foreign aid community applies the selectivity principle a bit selectively.

Dismantling the Cartel

How can the cartel of good intentions be reformed so that foreign aid might actually reach and benefit the world's poor? Clearly, a good dose of humility is in order, considering all the bright ideas that have failed in the past. Moreover, those of us in the aid industry should not be so arrogant to think we are the main determinants of whether low-income countries develop—poor nations must accomplish that mainly on their own.

Still, if aid is to have some positive effect, the aid community cannot remain stuck in the same old bureaucratic rut. Perhaps using market mechanisms for foreign aid is a better approach. While bureaucratic cartels supply too many goods for which there is little demand and too few goods for which there is much demand, markets are about matching supply and demand. Cartels are all about "coordination," whereas markets are about the decentralized matching of customers and suppliers.

One option is to break the link between aid money and the obligatory use of a particular agency's bureaucracy. Foreign assistance agencies could put part of their resources into a common pool devoted to helping countries with acceptably pro-development governments. Governments would compete for the "pro-development" seal of approval, but donors should compete, too. Recipient nations could take the funds and work with any agency they choose. This scenario would minimize duplication and foster competition among aid agencies.

Another market-oriented step would be for the common pool to issue vouchers to poor individuals or communities, who could exchange them for development services at any aid agency, NGO, or domestic government agency. These service providers would in turn redeem the vouchers for cash out of the common pool. Aid agencies would be forced to compete to attract aid vouchers (and thus money) for their budgets. The vouchers could also trade in a secondary market; how far their price is below par would reflect the inefficiency of this aid scheme and would require remedial action. Most important, vouchers would provide real market power to the impoverished customers to express their true needs and desires.

Intermediaries such as a new Washington-based company called Development Space could help assemble the vouchers into blocks and identify aid suppliers; the intermediaries could even compete with each other to attract funding and find projects that satisfy the customers, much as venture capital firms do. (Development Space is a private Web-based company established last year by former World Bank staff members—kind of an eBay for foreign aid.) Aid agencies could establish their own intermediation units to add to the competition. An information bank could facilitate transparency and communication, posting news on projects searching for funding, donors searching for projects, and the reputation of various intermediaries.

Bureaucratic cartels probably last longer than private cartels, but they need not last forever. President George W. Bush's proposed Millennium Challenge Account (under which, to use Bush's words, "countries that live by these three broad standards—ruling justly, investing in their people, and encouraging economic freedom—will receive more aid from America") and the accompanying increase in U.S. aid dollars will challenge the IMF and World Bank's near monopoly over reform-related lending. Development Space may be the first of many market-oriented endeavors to compete with aid agencies, but private philanthropists such as Bill Gates and George Soros have entered the industry as well. NGOs and independent academic economists are also more aggressively entering the market for advice on aid to poor countries. Globalization protesters are not well informed in all areas, but they seem largely on target when it comes to the failure of international financial institutions to foment "adjustment with growth" in many poor countries. Even within the World Bank itself, a recent board of directors paper suggested experimenting with "output-based aid" in which assistance would compensate service providers only when services are actually delivered to the poor—sadly, a novel concept. Here again, private firms, NGOs, and government agencies could compete to serve as providers.

Now that rich countries again seem interested in foreign aid, pressure is growing to reform a global aid bureaucracy that is increasingly out of touch with good economics. The high-income countries that finance aid and that genuinely want aid to reach the poor should subject the cartel of good intentions to the bracing wind of competition, markets, and accountability to the customers. Donors and recipients alike should not put up with $3,521 in aid to reduce the poverty head count by one, 185-point development frameworks, or an alphabet soup of bureaucratic fads. The poor deserve better.

CHAPTER 14

MICROCREDIT FACILITATES DEVELOPMENT *v.* MICROCREDIT DOES NOT FACILITATE DEVELOPMENT

Microcredit Facilitates Development

Advocate: Muhammad Yunus

Source: "Poverty Is a Threat to Peace," Nobel Lecture, December 10, 2006, http://nobelprize.org/nobel_prizes/peace/laureates/2006/yunus-lecture-en.html

Microcredit Does Not Facilitate Development

Advocate: Karol Boudreaux and Tyler Cowen

Source: "The Micromagic of Microcredit," *The Wilson Quarterly,* Winter 2008: 27–31

The failure of traditional foreign aid to foster economic development in poor countries has led governments and aid organizations to look for new solutions. One contender is microcredit, whereby entrepreneurs in poor countries are given very small loans to create or expand small businesses. These microcredit loans are designed to extend financing to those who have no other access to credit or to replace usurious interest rates on loans from local lenders.

The use of microcredit has grown exponentially over the past twenty-five years. The United Nations declared 2005 to be "The International Year of Microcredit," and that year private microcredit lending doubled. Between 2004 and 2008, the average rate of growth of microcredit institutions was 43 percent, and well over 100 million people are now estimated to be microcredit clients.[1] While it is clear that the availability of microcredit services has dramatically increased in recent years, it is less clear what effect microcredit has had on poverty and development.

MICROCREDIT FACILITATES DEVELOPMENT

Proponents of microcredit claim that lending small amounts to poor people can have a profound effect on their standard of living by allowing them to pursue economic opportunities previously unavailable to them. They also note that

---

[1]http://microfinance.cgap.org/2010/05/17/microfinance-in-2010/

repayment rates for microloans are very high, so microlending can be considered a business opportunity rather than charity. Microloans provide opportunities for growth potential that do not otherwise exist for poor societies.

In 2006, the Nobel Peace Prize was given to Muhammad Yunus, founder of the Grameen Bank, one of the first microcredit institutions. Yunus, in his Nobel acceptance lecture, argues that microcredit transforms the societies that have access to it, while allowing lending institutions to profit. He claims that an expansion of microcredit to more of the world's poor can eradicate poverty.

MICROCREDIT DOES NOT FACILITATE DEVELOPMENT

Others are more skeptical that microcredit can play a leading role in reducing global poverty. They point out that, while interest rates on microloans are much less than those on loans from other sources, they are still 50 to 100 percent per year. Many microcredit lenders will lend only to those with previously existing businesses. And Bangladesh, where Grameen Bank was founded more than thirty-five years ago and where microcredit has most penetrated society, remains extremely poor.

Karol Boudreaux and Tyler Cowen are among those skeptical of micro-credit as a development tool. They point out that acquiring microcredit often requires one to have an existing business rather than a plan to start a new one. In addition, they argue that microloans frequently finance consumption rather than investment. These loans often provide funding for emergencies, such as taking a sick child to the hospital or enrolling a child in a school. Microcredit may not be able to eradicate poverty, then claim, but it may be able to help alleviate some of poverty's effects.

POINTS **TO PONDER**

1. To what extent is Yunus is disagreement with Boudreaux and Cowen? Could you craft a statement about microcredit with which all would agree?

2. If one of the benefits of microcredit is that it is self-financing (i.e., repayment of previous loans plus interest finances future loans), then should governments get involved with microlending or rely on the market?

3. Can you think of policy measures that might enhance the utility of microcredit in reducing poverty?

Muhammad Yunus

Poverty Is a Threat to Peace

Ladies and Gentlemen:

By giving us this prize, the Norwegian Nobel Committee has given important support to the proposition that peace is inextricably linked to poverty. Poverty is a threat to peace.

World's income distribution gives a very telling story. Ninety four percent of the world income goes to 40 percent of the population while sixty percent of people live on only 6 percent of world income. Half of the world population lives on two dollars a day. Over one billion people live on less than a dollar a day. This is no formula for peace.

The new millennium began with a great global dream. World leaders gathered at the United Nations in 2000 and adopted, among others, a historic goal to reduce poverty by half by 2015. Never in human history had such a bold goal been adopted by the entire world in one voice, one that specified time and size. But then came September 11 and the Iraq war, and suddenly the world became derailed from the pursuit of this dream, with the attention of world leaders shifting from the war on poverty to the war on terrorism. Till now over $530 billion has been spent on the war in Iraq by the USA alone.

I believe terrorism cannot be won over by military action. Terrorism must be condemned in the strongest language. We must stand solidly against it, and find all the means to end it. We must address the root causes of terrorism to end it for all time to come. I believe that putting resources into improving the lives of the poor people is a better strategy than spending it on guns.

Poverty is Denial of All Human Rights

Peace should be understood in a human way—in a broad social, political and economic way. Peace is threatened by unjust economic, social and political order, absence of democracy, environmental degradation and absence of human rights.

Poverty is the absence of all human rights. The frustrations, hostility and anger generated by abject poverty cannot sustain peace in any society. For building stable peace we must find ways to provide opportunities for people to live decent lives.

The creation of opportunities for the majority of people—the poor—is at the heart of the work that we have dedicated ourselves to during the past 30 years.

Grameen Bank

I became involved in the poverty issue not as a policymaker or a researcher. I became involved because poverty was all around me, and I could not turn away from it. In 1974, I found it difficult to teach elegant theories of economies in the university classroom, in the backdrop of a terrible famine in Bangladesh. Suddenly, I felt the emptiness of those theories in the face of crushing hunger and poverty. I wanted to do something immediate to help people around me, even if it was just one human being, to get through another day with a little more ease. That brought me face to face with poor people's struggle to find the tiniest amounts of money to support their efforts to eke out a living. I was shocked to discover a woman in the village, borrowing less than a dollar from the money-lender, on the condition that he would have the exclusive right to buy all she produces at the price he decides. This, to me, was a way of recruiting slave labor.

I decided to make a list of the victims of this money-lending "business" in the village next door to our campus.

When my list was done, it had the names of 42 victims who borrowed a total amount of US $27. I offered US $27 from my own pocket to get these victims out of the clutches of those money-lenders. The excitement that was created among the people by this small action got me further involved in it. If I could make so many people so happy with such a tiny amount of money, why not do more of it?

That is what I have been trying to do ever since. The first thing I did was to try to persuade the bank located in the campus to lend money to the poor. But that did not work. The bank said that the poor were not credit-worthy. After all my efforts, over several months, failed I offered to become a guarantor for the loans to the poor. I was stunned by the result. The poor paid back their loans, on time, every time! But still I kept confronting difficulties in expanding the program through the existing banks. That was when I decided to create a separate bank for the poor, and in 1983, I finally succeeded in doing that. I named it Grameen Bank or Village Bank.

Today, Grameen Bank gives loans to nearly 7.0 million poor people, 97 percent of whom are women, in 73,000 villages in Bangladesh. Grameen Bank gives collateral-free income generating, housing, student and micro-enterprise loans to the poor families and offers a host of attractive savings, pension funds and insurance products for its members. Since it introduced them in 1984, housing loans have been used to construct 640,000 houses. The legal ownership of these houses belongs to the women themselves. We focused on women because we found giving loans to women always brought more benefits to the family.

In a cumulative way the bank has given out loans totaling about US $6.0 billion. The repayment rate is 99%. Grameen Bank routinely makes profit. Financially, it is self-reliant and has not taken donor money since 1995.

Deposits and own resources of Grameen Bank today amount to 143 percent of all outstanding loans. According to Grameen Bank's internal survey, 58 percent of our borrowers have crossed the poverty line.

Grameen Bank was born as a tiny homegrown project run with the help of several of my students, all local girls and boys. Three of these students are still with me in Grameen Bank, after all these years, as its topmost executives. They are here today to receive this honour you give us.

This idea, which began in Jobra, a small village in Bangladesh, has spread around the world and there are now Grameen type programs in almost every country.

Second Generation

It is 30 years now since we began. We keep looking at the children of our borrowers to see what has been the impact of our work on their lives. The women who are our borrowers always gave topmost priority to the children. One of the Sixteen Decisions developed and followed by them was to send children to school. Grameen Bank encouraged them, and before long all the children were going to school. Many of these children made it to the top of their class. We wanted to celebrate that, so we introduced scholarships for talented students. Grameen Bank now gives 30,000 scholarships every year.

Many of the children went on to higher education to become doctors, engineers, college teachers and other professionals. We introduced student loans to make it easy for Grameen students to complete higher education. Now some of them have PhD's. There are 13,000 students on student loans. Over 7,000 students are now added to this number annually.

We are creating a completely new generation that will be well equipped to take their families way out of the reach of poverty. We want to make a break in the historical continuation of poverty.

Beggars Can Turn to Business

In Bangladesh 80 percent of the poor families have already been reached with microcredit. We are hoping that by 2010, 100 percent of the poor families will be reached.

Three years ago we started an exclusive programme focusing on the beggars. None of Grameen Bank's rules apply to them. Loans are interest-free; they can pay whatever amount they wish, whenever they wish. We gave them the idea to carry small merchandise such as snacks, toys or household items, when they went from house to house for begging. The idea worked. There are now 85,000 beggars in the program. About 5,000 of them have already stopped begging completely. Typical loan to a beggar is $12.

We encourage and support every conceivable intervention to help the poor fight out of poverty. We always advocate microcredit in addition to all other interventions, arguing that microcredit makes those interventions work better.

Information Technology for the Poor

Information and communication technology (ICT) is quickly changing the world, creating distanceless, borderless world of instantaneous communications. Increasingly, it is becoming less and less costly. I saw an opportunity for the poor people to change their lives if this technology could be brought to them to meet their needs.

As a first step to bring ICT to the poor we created a mobile phone company, Grameen Phone. We gave loans from Grameen Bank to the poor women to buy mobile phones to sell phone services in the villages. We saw the synergy between microcredit and ICT.

The phone business was a success and became a coveted enterprise for Grameen borrowers. Telephone-ladies quickly learned and innovated the ropes of the telephone business, and it has become the quickest way to get out of poverty and to earn social respectability. Today there are nearly 300,000 telephone ladies providing telephone service in all the villages of Bangladesh. Grameen Phone has more than 10 million subscribers, and is the largest mobile phone company in the country. Although the number of telephone-ladies is only a small fraction of the total number of subscribers, they generate 19 percent of the revenue of the company. Out of the nine board members who are attending this grand ceremony today 4 are telephone-ladies.

Grameen Phone is a joint-venture company owned by Telenor of Norway and Grameen Telecom of Bangladesh. Telenor owns 62 percent share of the company, Grameen Telecom owns 38 percent. Our vision was to ultimately convert this company into a social business by giving majority ownership to the poor women of Grameen Bank. We are working towards that goal. Someday Grameen Phone will become another example of a big enterprise owned by the poor.

Free Market Economy

Capitalism centers on the free market. It is claimed that the freer the market, the better is the result of capitalism in solving the questions of what, how, and for whom. It is also claimed that the individual search for personal gains brings a collective optimal result.

I am in favor of strengthening the freedom of the market. At the same time, I am very unhappy about the conceptual restrictions imposed on the players in the market. This originates from the assumption that entrepreneurs are one-dimensional human beings, who are dedicated to one mission in their business lives—to maximize profit. This interpretation of capitalism insulates the entrepreneurs from all political, emotional, social, spiritual, environmental dimensions of their lives. This was done perhaps as a reasonable simplification, but it stripped away the very essentials of human life.

Human beings are a wonderful creation embodied with limitless human qualities and capabilities. Our theoretical constructs should make room for the blossoming of those qualities, not assume them away.

Many of the world's problems exist because of this restriction on the players of the free market. The world has not resolved the problem of crushing poverty that half of its population suffers. Healthcare remains out of the reach of the majority of the world population. The country with the richest and freest market fails to provide healthcare for one-fifth of its population.

We have remained so impressed by the success of the free market that we never dared to express any doubt about our basic assumption. To make it worse, we worked extra hard to transform ourselves, as closely as possible, into the one-dimensional human beings as conceptualized in the theory, to allow smooth functioning of free market mechanism.

By defining "entrepreneur" in a broader way we can change the character of capitalism radically, and solve many of the unresolved social and economic problems within the scope of the free market. Let us suppose an entrepreneur, instead of having a single source of motivation (such as maximizing profit), now has two sources of motivation, which are mutually exclusive, but equally compelling—a) maximization of profit and b) doing good to people and the world.

Each type of motivation will lead to a separate kind of business. Let us call the first type of business a profit-maximizing business, and the second type of business a social business.

Social business will be a new kind of business introduced in the market place with the objective of making a difference in the world. Investors in the social business could get back their investment, but will not take any dividend from the company. Profit would be ploughed back into the company to expand its outreach and improve the quality of its product or service. A social business will be a non-loss, non-dividend company.

Once social business is recognized in law, many existing companies will come forward to create social businesses in addition to their foundation activities. Many activists from the non-profit sector will also find this an attractive option. Unlike the non-profit sector where one needs to collect donations to keep activities going, a social business will be self-sustaining and create surplus for expansion since it is a non-loss enterprise. Social business will go into a new type of capital market of its own, to raise capital.

Young people all around the world, particularly in rich countries, will find the concept of social business very appealing since it will give them a challenge to make a difference by using their creative talent. Many young people today feel frustrated because they cannot see any worthy challenge, which excites them, within the present capitalist world. Socialism gave them a dream to fight for. Young people dream about creating a perfect world of their own.

Almost all social and economic problems of the world will be addressed through social businesses. The challenge is to innovate business models and apply them to produce desired social results cost-effectively and efficiently. Healthcare for the poor, financial services for the poor, information technology for the poor, education and training for the poor, marketing for the poor, renewable energy—these are all exciting areas for social businesses.

Social business is important because it addresses very vital concerns of mankind. It can change the lives of the bottom 60 percent of world population and help them to get out of poverty.

Grameen's Social Business

Even profit maximizing companies can be designed as social businesses by giving full or majority ownership to the poor. This constitutes a second type of social business. Grameen Bank falls under this category of social business.

The poor could get the shares of these companies as gifts by donors, or they could buy the shares with their own money. The borrowers with their own money buy Grameen Bank shares, which cannot be transferred to non-borrowers. A committed professional team does the day-to-day running of the bank.

Bilateral and multi-lateral donors could easily create this type of social business. When a donor gives a loan or a grant to build a bridge in the recipient country, it could create a "bridge company" owned by the local poor. A committed management company could be given the responsibility of running the company. Profit of the company will go to the local poor as dividend, and towards building more bridges. Many infrastructure projects like roads, highways, airports, seaports, and utility companies could all be built in this manner.

Grameen has created two social businesses of the first type. One is a yogurt factory, to produce fortified yogurt to bring nutrition to malnourished children, in a joint venture with Danone. It will continue to expand until all malnourished children of Bangladesh are reached with this yogurt. Another is a chain of eye-care hospitals. Each hospital will undertake 10,000 cataract surgeries per year at differentiated prices to the rich and the poor.

Social Stock Market

To connect investors with social businesses, we need to create a social stock market where only the shares of social businesses will be traded. An investor will come to this stock-exchange with a clear intention of finding a social business, which has a mission of his liking. Anyone who wants to make money will go to the existing stock market.

To enable a social stock-exchange to perform properly, we will need to create rating agencies, standardization of terminology, definitions, impact measurement tools, reporting formats, and new financial publications, such as *The Social Wall Street Journal*. Business schools will offer courses and business management degrees on social businesses to train young managers how to manage social business enterprises in the most efficient manner, and, most of all, to inspire them to become social business entrepreneurs themselves.

Role of Social Businesses in Globalization

I support globalization and believe it can bring more benefits to the poor than its alternative. But it must be the right kind of globalization. To me, globalization is like a hundred-lane highway criss-crossing the world. If it is a free-for-all highway, its lanes will be taken over by the giant trucks from powerful economies. Bangladeshi rickshaw will be thrown off the highway. In order to have a win–win globalization we must have traffic rules, traffic police, and traffic authority for this global highway. Rule of "strongest takes it all" must be replaced by rules that ensure that the poorest have a place and piece of the action, without being elbowed out by the strong. Globalization must not become financial imperialism.

Powerful multi-national social businesses can be created to retain the benefit of globalization for the poor people and poor countries. Social businesses will either bring ownership to the poor people, or keep the profit within the poor countries, since taking dividends will not be their objective. Direct foreign investment by foreign social businesses will be exciting news for recipient countries. Building strong economies in the poor countries by protecting their national interest from plundering companies will be a major area of interest for the social businesses.

We Create What We Want

We get what we want, or what we don't refuse. We accept the fact that we will always have poor people around us, and that poverty is part of human destiny. This is precisely why we continue to have poor people around us. If we firmly believe that poverty is unacceptable to us, and that it should not belong to a civilized society, we would have built appropriate institutions and policies to create a poverty-free world.

We wanted to go to the moon, so we went there. We achieve what we want to achieve. If we are not achieving something, it is because we have not put our minds to it. We create what we want.

What we want and how we get to it depends on our mindsets. It is extremely difficult to change mindsets once they are formed. We create the world in accordance with our mindset. We need to invent ways to change our perspective continually and reconfigure our mindset quickly as new knowledge emerges. We can reconfigure our world if we can reconfigure our mindset.

We Can Put Poverty in the Museums

I believe that we can create a poverty-free world because poverty is not created by poor people. It has been created and sustained by the economic and social system that we have designed for ourselves; the institutions and concepts that make up that system; the policies that we pursue.

Poverty is created because we built our theoretical framework on assumptions which under-estimate human capacity, by designing concepts which are too narrow (such as concept of business, credit-worthiness, entrepreneurship, employment) or developing institutions which remain half-done (such as financial institutions, where poor are left out). Poverty is caused by the failure at the conceptual level, rather than any lack of capability on the part of people.

I firmly believe that we can create a poverty-free world if we collectively believe in it. In a poverty-free world, the only place you would be able to see poverty is in the poverty museums. When school children take a tour of the poverty museums, they would be horrified to see the misery and indignity that some human beings had to go through. They would blame their forefathers for tolerating this inhuman condition, which existed for so long, for so many people.

A human being is born into this world fully equipped not only to take care of him or herself, but also to contribute to enlarging the well being of the world as a whole. Some get the chance to explore their potential to some degree, but many others never get any opportunity, during their lifetime, to unwrap the wonderful gift they were born with. They die unexplored and the world remains deprived of their creativity, and their contribution.

Grameen has given me an unshakeable faith in the creativity of human beings. This has led me to believe that human beings are not born to suffer the misery of hunger and poverty.

To me poor people are like bonsai trees. When you plant the best seed of the tallest tree in a flower-pot, you get a replica of the tallest tree, only inches tall. There is nothing wrong with the seed you planted, only the soil-base that is too inadequate. Poor people are bonsai people. There is nothing wrong in their seeds. Simply, society never gave them the base to grow on. All it needs to get the poor people out of poverty for us to create an enabling environment for them. Once the poor can unleash their energy and creativity, poverty will disappear very quickly.

Let us join hands to give every human being a fair chance to unleash their energy and creativity.

Ladies and Gentlemen, let me conclude by expressing my deep gratitude to the Norwegian Nobel Committee for recognizing that poor people, and especially poor women, have both the potential and the right to live a decent life, and that microcredit helps to unleash that potential.

I believe this honor that you give us will inspire many more bold initiatives around the world to make a historical breakthrough in ending global poverty.

Thank you very much.

Karol Boudreaux and Tyler Cowen

The Micromagic of Microcredit

Microcredit has star power. In 2006, the Nobel Committee called it "an important liberating force" and awarded the Nobel Peace Prize to Muhammad Yunus, the "godfather of microcredit." The actress Natalie Portman is a believer too; she advocates support for the Village Banking Campaign on its MySpace page. The end of poverty is "just a mouse click away," she promises. A button on the site swiftly redirects you to paypal.com, where you can make a contribution to microcredit initiatives.

After decades of failure, the world's aid organizations seem to think they have at last found a winning idea. The United Nations declared 2005 the "international Year of Microcredit." Secretary-General Kofi Annan declared that providing microloans to help poor people launch small businesses recognizes that they "are the solution, not the problem. It is a way to build on their ideas, energy, and vision. It is a way to grow productive enterprises, and so allow communities to prosper."

Many investors agree. Hundreds of millions of dollars are flowing into microfinance from international financial institutions, foundations, governments, and, most important, private investors—who increasingly see microfinance as a potentially profitable business venture. Private investment through special "microfinance investment vehicles" alone nearly doubled in 2005, from $513 million to $981 million.

On the charitable side, part of microcredit's appeal lies in the fact that the lending institutions can fund themselves once they are launched. Pierre Omidyar, the founder of eBay, explains that you can begin by investing $60 billion in the world's poorest people, "and then you're done!"

But can microcredit achieve the massive changes its proponents claim? Is it the solution to poverty in the developing world, or something more modest—a way to empower the poor, particularly poor women, with some control over their lives and their assets?

On trips to Africa and India we have talked to lenders, borrowers, and other poor people to try to understand the role microcredit plays in their lives. We met people like Stadile Menthe in Botswana. Menthe is, in many ways, the classic borrower. A single mother with little formal education, she borrowed money to expand the small grocery store she runs on a dusty road on the outskirts of Botswana's capital city, Gaborone. Menthe's store has done well, and she has expanded into the lucrative business of selling phone cards. In fact she's been successful enough that she has built two rental homes next to her store. She has diversified her income and made a better life for herself and her daughter. But how many borrowers are like Menthe? In our judgment, she is the exception, not the norm. Yes, microcredit is mostly a good thing. Very often it helps keep borrowers from even greater catastrophes, but only rarely does it enable them to climb out of poverty.

The modern story of microcredit began 30 years ago, when Yunus—then an economics professor at Chittagong University in southeastern Bangladesh—set out to apply his theories to improving the lives of the poor in the nearby village of Jobra. He began in 1976 by lending $27 to a group of 42 villagers, who used the money to develop informal businesses, such as making soap or weaving baskets to sell at the local market. After the success of the first experiment, Yunus founded Grameen Bank. Today, the bank claims more than five million "members" and a loan repayment rate of 98 percent. It has lent out some $6.5 billion.

At the outset, Yunus set a goal that half of the borrowers would be women. He explained, "The banking system not only rejects poor people, it rejects women. . . . Not even one percent of their borrowers are women." He soon discovered that women were good credit risks, and good at managing family finances. Today, more than 95 percent of Grameen Bank's borrowers are women. The UN estimates that women make up 76 percent of microcredit customers around the world, varying from nearly 90 percent in Asia to less than a third in the Middle East.

While 70 percent of microcredit borrowers are in Asia, the institution has spread around the world; Latin America and sub-Saharan Africa account for 14 and 10 percent of the number of borrowers, respectively. Some of the biggest microfinance institutions include Grameen Bank, ACCION International, and Pro Mujer of Bolivia.

The average loan size varies, usually in proportion to the income level of the home country. In Rwanda, a typical loan might be $50 to $200; in Romania, it is more likely to be $2,500 to $5,000. Often there is no explicit collateral. Instead, the banks lend to small groups of about five people, relying on peer pressure for repayment. At mandatory weekly meetings, if one borrower cannot make her payment, the rest of the group must come up with the cash.

The achievements of microcredit, however, are not quite what they seem. There is, for example, a puzzling fact at the heart of the enterprise. Most microcredit banks charge interest rates of 50 to 100 percent on an annualized basis (loans, typically, must be paid off within weeks or months). That's not as scandalous as it sounds—local moneylenders demand much higher rates. The puzzle is a matter of basic economics: How can people in new businesses growing at perhaps 20 percent annually afford to pay interest at rates as high as 100 percent?

The answer is that, for the most part, they can't. By and large, the loans serve more modest ends—laudable, but not world changing.

Microcredit does not always lead to the creation of small businesses. Many microlenders refuse to lend money for start-ups; they insist that a business already be in place. This suggests that the business was sustainable to begin with, without a microloan. Sometimes lenders help businesses to grow, but often what they really finance is spending and consumption.

That is not to say that the poor are out shopping for jewelry and fancy clothes. In Hyderabad, India, as in many other places, we saw that loans are often used to pay for a child's doctor visit. In the Tanzanian capital of Dares Salaam, Joel Mwakitalu, who runs the Small Enterprise Foundation, a local microlender, told us that 60 percent of his loans are used to send kids to school; 40 percent are for investments. A study of microcredit in Indonesia found that 30 percent of the borrowed money was spent on some form of consumption.

Sometimes consumption and investment are one and the same, such as when parents send their children to school. Indian borrowers often buy mopeds and motorbikes—they are fun to ride but also a way of getting to work. Cell phones are used to call friends but also to run businesses.

For better or worse, microborrowing often entails a kind of bait and switch. The borrower claims that the money is for a business, but uses it for other purposes. In effect, the cash allows a poor entrepreneur to maintain her business without having to sacrifice the life or education of her child. In that sense, the money is for the business, but most of all it is for the child. Such life-saving uses for the funds are obviously desirable, but it is also a sad reality that many microcredit loans help borrowers to survive or tread water more than they help them get ahead. This sounds unglamorous and even disappointing, but the alternative—such as no doctor's visit for a child or no school for a year—is much worse.

Commentators often seem to assume that the experience of borrowing and lending is completely new for the poor. But moneylenders have offered money to the world's poor for millennia, albeit at extortionate rates of interest. A typical moneylender is a single individual, well-known in his neighborhood or village, who borrows money from his wealthier connections and in turn lends those funds to individuals in need, typically people he knows personally. But that personal connection is rarely good for a break; a money-lender may charge 200 to 400 percent interest on an annualized basis. He will insist on collateral (a television, for instance), and resort to intimidation and sometimes violence if he is not repaid on time. The moneylender operates informally, off the books, and usually outside the law.

So compared to the alternative, microcredit is often a very good deal indeed. Microcredit critics often miss this point. For instance, Aneel Karnani, who teaches at the University of Michigan's business school, argues that microfinance "misses its mark." Karnani says that in some cases microcredit can make life for the planet's bottom billion even worse by reducing their cash flow. Karnani cites the high interest rates that microlenders charge and points out that "if poor clients cannot earn a greater return on their investment than the interest they must pay, they will become poorer as a result of microcredit, not wealthier." But the real question has never been credit vs. no credit; rather, it is moneylender vs. modern microcredit. Credit can bring some problems, but microcredit is easing debt burdens more than it is increasing them.

At microlender SERO Lease and Finance in Tanzania, borrower Margaret Makingi Marwa told us that she prefers working with a microfinance institution to working with a moneylender. Moneylenders demand quick repayment at high interest rates. At SERO, Marwa can take six months or a year to pay off her lease contract. Given that her income can vary and that she may not have money at hand every month, she prefers to have a longer-term loan.

Moneylenders do offer some advantages, especially in rural areas. Most important, they come up with cash on the spot. If your child needs to go to the doctor right now, the moneylender is usually only a short walk away. Even under the best of circumstances, a microcredit loan can lake several days to process, and the recipient will be required to deal with marry documents, not to mention weekly meetings.

There is, however, an upside to this "bureaucracy." In reality, it is the moneylender who is the "micro" operator. Microcredit is a more formal, institutionalized business relationship. It represents a move up toward a larger scale of trade and business organization. Microcredit borrowers gain valuable experience in working within a formal institution. They learn what to expect from lenders and fellow borrowers, and they learn what is expected of themselves. This experience will be a help should they ever graduate to commercial credit or have other dealings with the formal financial world.

The comparison to moneylending brings up another important feature of microcredit. Though its users avoid the kind of intimidation employed by moneylenders, microcredit could not work without similar incentives. The lender does not demand collateral, but if you can't pay your share of the group loan, your fellow borrowers will come and take your TV. That enforcement process can lead to abuses, but it is a gentler form of intimidation than is exercised by the moneylender. If nothing else, the group members know that at the next meeting any one of them might be the one unable to repay her share of the loan.

If borrowers are using microcredit for consumption and not only to improve a small business, how do they repay? Most borrowers are self-employed and work in the informal sector of the economy. Their incomes are often erratic; small, unexpected expenses can make repayment impossible in any given week or month. In the countryside, farmers have seasonal incomes and little cash for long periods of time.

Borrowers manage, at least in part, by relying on family members and friends to help out. In some cases, the help comes in the form of remittances from abroad. Remittances that cross national borders now total more than $300 billion yearly. A recent study in Tanzania found that microcredit borrowers get 34 percent of their income from friends and family, some of whom live abroad, but others of whom live in the city and have jobs in the formal sector. That's the most effective kind of foreign aid, targeted directly at the poor and provided by those who understand their needs.

Here again, microcredit does something that traditional banks do not. A commercial bank typically will not lend to people who work in the informal sector, precisely because their erratic incomes make them risky bets. The loan officer at a commercial bank does not care that your brother in Doha is sending money each month to help you out. But a microcredit institution cares only that you come to your weekly meeting with a small sum in hand for repayment. Because of microcredit, families can leverage one person's ability to find work elsewhere to benefit the entire group.

Sometimes microcredit leads to more savings rather than more debt. That sounds paradoxical, but borrowing in one asset can be a path toward (more efficient) saving in other assets.

To better understand this puzzle, we must set aside some of our preconceptions about how saving operates in poor countries, most of all in rural areas. Westerners typically save in the form of money or money-denominated assets such as stocks and bonds. But in poor communities, money is often an ineffective medium for savings: if you want to know how much net saving is going on, don't look at money. Banks may be a daylong bus ride away or may be plagued, as in Ghana, by fraud. A cash hoard kept at home can be lost, stolen, taken by the taxman, damaged by floods, or even eaten by rats. It creates other kinds of problems as well. Needy friends and relatives knock on the door and ask for aid. In small communities it is often very hard, even impossible, to say no, especially if you have the cash on hand. . . .

Under these kinds of conditions, a cow (or a goat or pig) is a much better medium for saving. It is sturdier than paper money. Friends and relatives can't ask for small pieces of it. If you own a cow, it yields milk, it can plow the fields, it produces dung that can be used as fuel or fertilizer, and in a pinch it can be slaughtered and turned into saleable meat or simply eaten. With a small loan, people in rural areas can buy that cow and use cash that might otherwise be diverted to less useful purposes to pay back the microcredit institution. So even when microcredit looks like indebtedness, savings are going up rather than down.

Microcredit *is* making people's lives better around the world. But for the most part, it is not pulling them out of poverty. It is hard to find entrepreneurs who start with these tiny loans and graduate to run commercial empires. Bangladesh, where Grameen Bank was born, is still a desperately poor country. The more modest truth is that microcredit may help some people, perhaps earning $2 a day, to earn something like $2.50 a day. That may not sound dramatic, but when you are earning $2 a day it is a big step forward. . . .

With microcredit, life becomes more bearable and easier to manage. The improvements may not show up as an explicit return on investment, but the benefits are very real. If a poor family is able to keep a child in school, send someone to a clinic, or build up more secure savings, its well-being improves, if only marginally. This is a big part of the reason why poor people are demanding greater access to microcredit loans. And microcredit, unlike many charitable services, is capable of paying for itself—which explains why the private sector is increasingly involved. . . .

If this portrait sounds a little underwhelming, don't blame microcredit. The real issue is that we so often underestimate the severity and inertia of global poverty. Natalie Portman may not be right when she says that an end to poverty is "just a mouse click away," but she's right to be supportive of a tool that helps soften some of poverty's worst blows for many millions of desperate people.

KAROL BOUDREAUX is a senior research fellow at the Mercatus Center at George Mason University. TYLER COWEN is a professor of economics at George Mason University and author of Discover Your Inner Economist: Use Incentives to Fall in Love. Survive Your Next Meeting, and Motivate Your Dentist *(2007).*

PART VI
THE FUTURE
OF GLOBALIZATION

We conclude our exploration of the global economy by returning to the questions with which we began: Will we see fundamental change in the structure of the global economy in the near future? Will the emergence of China and other large market countries, in combination with the recent financial crisis, accelerate a shift in global power? Will a shift in global power push the world economy away from the Anglo-American model upon which it has rested since World War II? If these developments do spark change, what form will the global economic structure assume? Are we moving toward a world shaped by an Asian or, more narrowly, a Chinese model of capitalism? Are we moving toward a world of less global integration—and thus greater economic nationalism? Or will the near future look much like the recent past? Such questions are at the center of current discussions about where the global economy is headed.

Chapter 15 explores whether China's development strategy, often referred to as the "Beijing Consensus," provides an alternative to the Washington Consensus. The question central to this debate is whether China has pursued a distinctive strategy that other emerging market countries can emulate. Xin Li and his co-authors set out ten principles that structure China's development strategy. They suggest that these principles offer a viable alternative to the Washington Consensus. Scott Kennedy questions the distinctiveness of China's strategy. He argues that China's development strategy has embraced core elements of the Washington Consensus and the developmental state model. Moreover, the ways in which China is distinctive—its population and market size, for example—cannot be emulated by other societies.

Chapter 16 explores whether the recent crisis has accelerated the world's transition to some alternative system. The question at the center of this debate is whether the crisis will catalyze fundamental change in the structure of the global economy. Roger Altman, a former Deputy Treasury Secretary in the Clinton administration, claims that the financial crisis was a "seismic global event" that will precipitate major alterations in the global economy. The crisis substantially reduced the ability of the United

States to lead and undermined global faith in markets. China has gained in relative terms. Niall Ferguson argues that the future will look much like the recent past. The crisis is unlikely to alter the global power distribution, and the U.S.–China relationship already dominates the global economy. Moreover, although the United States does face new constraints, it has always been able to resolve economic challenges.

CHAPTER 15 THE BEIJING CONSENSUS WILL REPLACE THE WASHINGTON CONSENSUS v. THE MYTH OF THE BEIJING CONSENSUS

The Myth of the Beijing Consensus

Advocate: Scott Kennedy

Source: "The Myth of the Beijing Consensus," *Journal of Contemporary China* 19 (June 2010): 461–77

The Beijing Consensus will Replace the Washington Consensus

Advocate: Xin Li, Kjeld Erik Brodsgaard, and Michael Jacobsen

Source: "Redefining Beijing Consensus: Ten Economic Principles," *China Economic Journal* 2 (November 2009): 297–311

China's unprecedented economic growth during the last thirty years has reinvigorated debate about development strategy. The Washington Consensus has held sway as the primary development strategy since the mid-1980s. The Washington Consensus holds that governments can best promote development by relying heavily on markets at home and abroad. Some have argued that China's growth has been based on a development strategy that departs sharply from this advice. In a 2004 essay, Joshua Cooper Ramo* named this distinctive Chinese strategy "the Beijing Consensus." Ramo argued that the Beijing Consensus rests on three theorems: a focus on continual innovation, a commitment to sustainable and equitable development, and the assertion of an independent or autonomous development path.

Ramo's essay sparked considerable debate, one that has intensified in the wake of the recent financial crisis. Many of the advocates for a Beijing Consensus point to disappointing economic performance generated by the Washington Consensus. For this group, China's success offers the promise of a new development model that governments in other countries can emulate with better results than delivered by the Washington Consensus. Others question whether

---

*Joshua Cooper Ramo. 2004. *The Beijing Consensus.* London: The Foreign Policy Centre.

the notion of a Beijing Consensus is useful. This group argues that China's development strategy has not been particularly distinctive. China has adhered to many of the tenets of the Washington Consensus and exhibits many of the characteristics of the developmental state model. Moreover, if China is distinctive, it is distinctive in ways that other developing societies cannot emulate—its population and market size, for example.

THE BEIJING CONSENSUS WILL REPLACE THE WASHINGTON CONSENSUS

Xin Li and his co-authors accept that Ramo's original formulation of the Beijing Consensus is deeply flawed. Rather than rejecting the idea of a distinctive Chinese approach altogether, however, they strive to reconstruct the Beijing Consensus on a broader—and they claim, more accurate—foundation. They elaborate ten general principles of China's development strategy that, they argue, attract a reasonable consensus in Beijing. They suggest that not only have these principles shaped Chinese strategy but also they offer a basis upon which other developing societies can construct an alternative to Washington Consensus policies.

THE MYTH OF THE BEIJING CONSENSUS

Scott Kennedy argues that there is no such thing as the Beijing Consensus as John Cooper Ramo formulated it. He asserts that Ramo's formulation fails to accurately characterize China's development experience. Moreover, Kennedy finds little to support the belief that even a slightly modified version of the Beijing Consensus tells us much about the Chinese state's role in China's economic development. Kennedy also claims that the distinctive aspects of China's strategy are unlikely to translate easily to other settings. Hence, even if China's strategy is distinctive, the strategy could not be copied by other governments.

POINTS **TO PONDER**

1. What are the key characteristics of the Beijing Consensus, and how does it differ from the Washington Consensus?

2. Do you believe that China has pursued a strategy distinctive from the strategies employed by governments in other East Asian countries? If so, in what way has the strategy been distinctive? If not, to what do you attribute China's remarkable economic performance?

3. To what extent are lessons drawn from China's experience usefully applied in other societies? That is, can policy developed in one context be applied to others?

Xin Li, Kjeld Erik Brødsgaard, and Michael Jacobsen

Redefining Beijing Consensus: Ten Economic Principles

The Fall of the Washington Consensus

In the 1960s and 1970s, in order to finance their ambitious industrialization, many Latin American countries, notably Brazil, Argentina, and Mexico, borrowed hugely from international creditors, largely by way of short-term loans. When the accumulation of their foreign debts reached a dangerous level at the end of the 1970s, the world economy went into a serious recession during 1979–82, in which record high interest rates in the U.S. and Europe made Latin America's debt payments unbearable. In August 1982, Mexico declared a moratorium on debt service, which within weeks plunged the whole region into what we henceforward call the debt crisis. Since then, Latin America has had a 'lost decade': although diverse efforts were made, they had not succeeded in either reducing foreign debt or growing their way out of debt (Vásquez 1996).

In 1989, when George H.W. Bush became the U.S. president, his Treasury Secretary Nicholas Brady announced a new plan to resolve the debt crisis, which urged Latin American debtor countries to implement market liberalizations in exchange for a 'voluntary' reduction of the commercial bank debts (Vásquez 1996). In order to understand to what extent Latin American policy reforms were being implemented, a conference under the title 'Latin American adjustment: How much has happened?' was convened by the Institute for International Economics in November 1989 (Kuczynski 2003). As the organizer of this conference, John Williamson wrote a background paper 'What Washington means by policy reform' to guide the commissioned country studies of individual Latin American debtor countries. In this paper, Williamson laid out 10 major policy reforms he believed to have reached 'a reasonable degree of consensuses in Washington as needed to restore Latin American economic growth' (Williamson 1990, 7).

The list of 10 policy recommendations that was termed by Williamson the 'Washington Consensus' included fiscal discipline, reordering public expenditure priorities, tax reform, liberalizing interest rates, a competitive exchange rate, trade liberalization, liberalization of inward foreign direct investment, privatization, deregulation, and property rights (Williamson 2004). However, Williamson later lamented that the concept of the Washington Consensus had become 'public property' (Williamson 2000, 252) and 'has been used to mean very different things by different people' (Williamson 2004, 6). He identified two versions that are very different from his original

Washington Consensus. One version refers to the policies the Bretton Woods institutions applied towards their client countries, or perhaps the attitude of the U.S. government plus the Bretton Woods institutions (i.e. the International Monetary Fund (IMF) and the World Bank). Another version uses the Washington Consensus as a synonym for neoliberalism or market fundamentalism (Williamson 2004).

Williamson pointed out that in the early days after 1989 there was not much difference between Bretton Woods institutions' policy packages applied to their client countries and his original concept of the Washington Consensus. But over time their policy package deviated substantively; for instance, their adoption of a bipolar doctrine of exchange rate, according to which countries should either float their exchange rate cleanly or else fix it firmly, is directly counter to Williamson's original call for a competitive exchange rate implying an intermediate regime. Another serious deviation Williamson singled out is that Bretton Woods institutions, or at least the IMF, came in the mid-1990s to urge client countries to liberalize their capital accounts, which, Williamson believes, bears the major responsibility for causing the Asian financial crisis of 1997. With the disastrous performance of the 'Shock Therapy' reforms in Eastern European and former Soviet Union countries (EEFSU) in the 1990s, strongly advocated by the U.S. Treasury and IMF, Bretton Woods institutions' version of the Washington Consensus was widely discredited.

Williamson regards the association of the Washington Consensus with neoliberalism or market fundamentalism as 'a thoroughly objectionable perversion' of his original version (Williamson 2004, 7) because he did not include most of the neoliberal innovations of the Reagan administration in the U.S. and Thatcher government in the UK, except privatization, nor does he believe that any of those distinctively neoliberal policies, such as supply-side economics, monetarism, and minimal government, commanded much of a consensus (Williamson 2004). However, the association of the Washington Consensus with neoliberalism or free market economics eventually has become the most widespread usage of the term. The current global financial crisis rooted in the U.S. is widely seen to have announced the fall of the free market or neoliberal economics. Following the 2009 G20 London summit, British Prime Minister Gordon Brown declared 'the Washington Consensus is over'. Williamson believes Brown's critique on the Washington Consensus actually refers to this neoliberal reinterpretation, rather than his original version (Williamson 2009).

Although John Williamson (2002) has repeatedly defended his original version of the Washington Consensus as 'motherhood and apple pie,' he recognizes 'the disappointing performance of many countries that made a conscientious attempt to implement the sort of reform agenda' of his original

Washington Consensus, and he has identified three defects in his formula: first, his original Washington Consensus did not emphasize crisis avoidance; second, there is incompleteness in his original reform agenda, and a second generation of reforms is needed; third, the objective that underlay the original Washington Consensus was excessively narrow (Williamson 2002, 973). No matter which version of the Washington Consensus people use, Harvard professor Dani Rodrik (2006) has argued that 'the debate now is not over whether the Washington Consensus is dead or alive, but over what will replace it.'

The Debate Over the Beijing Consensus . . .

China's phenomenal economic growth since its reform makes . . . China's development model distinctive and attractive. . . . Joshua Cooper Ramo, a former editor of *Time* magazine, argues that China's rise is remaking the international order and what is happening in China is not only a model for China, but a path for other nations around the world. At the heart of his conceptualization of the Beijing Consensus, which Ramo claimed replaces the widely discredited Washington Consensus, are three theorems: first, innovation-based development; second, giving sustainability and equality priority; third, self-determination in international relations.

Given China's success and increasing influence, the notion of the Beijing Consensus, once created, has generated widespread attention in China and beyond. Many people see the Chinese model as distinctive and successful and therefore representing an alternative way of development. China's economic miracle is now something that many countries in Africa, Latin America and other parts of Asia would like to emulate (Colley 2009). Leaders of Vietnam, Laos, India, Russia, Iran, Brazil, [and] Zimbabwe, among others, have shown interest in the 'Beijing Consensus' (Huang and Ding 2006, 29). Professor David Schweickart of Loyola University Chicago even argues that 'of all the countries in the world today, China is one of the best situated to make the transition to' what he terms 'Economic Democracy,' a viable, equitable market socialist society beyond capitalism featuring workplace democracy and social control of investment (Schweickart 2005, 5). . . .

. . . Ramo's conceptualization of the Beijing Consensus has some problems. On the one hand, his three 'theorems' are not accurate. Clearly, China is not yet an innovative country, and China's economic success has not been innovation-driven so far, although Chinese leaders have long realized innovation is very important and have made efforts to build China's national innovation system (OECD 2007). On the other hand, its three 'theorems' do not parallel those 10 policy reforms of the original Washington Consensus (Kennedy 2008, 10). Williamson's Washington Consensus is only about economic reform while the third theorem of Ramo's Beijing Consensus, using asymmetric power projection to achieve [a] global balance of power, is according to himself 'a new security doctrine' (p. 12). The fact that the term 'consensus' has a hegemonic connotation (Dirlik 2006) is because the Washington Consensus was put forward deliberately and systematically (Wu 2005). As China has repeatedly promised to rise peacefully and not to pursue hegemony, and the Chinese government does not say much on exporting China's developmental model (Colley 2009), we think Ramo's third theorem can hardly achieve a consensus in Beijing and should not be promoted as something the developing country can learn.

We believe the flaws of the original conceptualization of the Beijing Consensus should not be used to justify the rejection of the notion altogether. What we need to do is instead to come up with a sound new configuration. We intend to contribute to . . . redefining the concept in this paper. In the following section, we lay out 10 general principles that we believe command a moderate degree of consensus in Beijing. We acknowledge there might be more factors than these 10 principles that have contributed to Chinese success, but we believe these 10 principles are more widely accepted and represent more general policies rather than China-specific or technical factors. We are also aware that these 10 principles should be viewed as flexible guidance rather than a rigid recipe for any other country to copy. At the end of the day, what really makes a difference is how a country creatively adapts the best practice learned from other places to its own national situation.

Ten Principles as the Beijing Consensus
Principle One: Localization of Best Practices Borrowed

Chinese leaders firmly believe that, because of the different stages of development, developing nations face very different conditions and many constraints in economic construction, compared with developed countries (and differences also exist within the developing world), and therefore, any textbook economic theories and other countries' experiences should be adapted to their local situations, rather than copied without caution. Blindly imitating the so-called best-practice theories and policies without taking local conditions into consideration may result in unexpected outcomes.

During Mao Zedong's era, Chinese leaders were aware of this localization or adaptation principle. Mao himself wrote an important policy paper 'On Ten Great Relationships' in 1956 to warn his Party not to blindly imitate but to adapt [the] Stalinist model to Chinese domestic conditions. Some scholars argue that owing to this cautious approach China adopted an M-Form[1] (Qian and Xu 1993; Yusuf 1994, 75) instead of the Soviet U-Form economic administration structure, and therefore Chinese local governments had much autonomy and encouragement in building their local economies. This facilitated a fairly rapid growth in GDP [gross domestic product] even with the political disorder and disruption during the 10-year Cultural Revolution. . . .

This very first principle of localization clearly indicates that the Beijing Consensus is fundamentally different from the Washington Consensus in that China does not promote universal application of its development model; therefore China does not pursue hegemonic power by way of the Beijing Consensus vis-à-vis the Washington Consensus.

Principle Two: Combination of Market and Plan

No nation should be fettered by extreme ideology, i.e., free-market capitalism or fully-planned communism, in its economic construction. Any economy inevitably is or should be a mixed one in which both the market and planning have a role to play. Either the market or planning in isolation will ultimately fail due to information asymmetry[2] and economic calculation problems.[3] Greenwald and Stiglitz (1986) argue that it is only under exceptional circumstances that markets are efficient. Stiglitz (2003) also recognizes that the government is not always able to correct the limitations of markets. Therefore, the remedy to avoid failure is to find the right balance between the market and government. . . .

The essence of using the market is to induce competition for an efficient allocation of resources and effective mechanism of survival of the fittest. It is for this purpose that Deng Xiaoping made the decision of opening China up to the world and returning to the GATT [general agreement on Tariffs and Trade] and later joining the WTO [World Trade Organization]. One key success factor of China's market reform and opening up is the sequence and emphasis of liberalization and competition. It is obviously important to import investment and technology while giving a proper degree of protection to some strategically important industries, such as the financial industry and agriculture.

Mao and especially the Gang of Four tried to completely abolish the market mechanism as they saw it as an attachment of capitalism. An extreme example of this purely Communist thinking was to put all people into People's Communes where the central administration of the Commune had the power to decide everything concerning the life and work of commune members. With its huge failure, Deng Xiaoping realized that it was meaningless and misleading to debate whether a policy is capitalist or socialist; the final judgment should be 'the Three Helpful', i.e., whether such a policy is helpful for developing socialist productivity, for enhancing socialist comprehensive national power, for improving people's living standards.[4]

On the other hand, free-market economy evidently failed in the 1930s' Great Depression. In helping to understand and overcome the crisis the Keynesian

Revolution of economics helped the world to appreciate that macroeconomic intervention is necessary at some point in time and in some economic contexts. The most recent lesson we had of blindly believing 'free-market will maximize public welfare' (Adam Smith's (1776) 'invisible hand' theory) is the U.S. and global financial crisis caused by the credit crisis. The US $700bn bailout plan and a called-for global coordinated rescue plan once again prove government planning and market mechanisms are both viable and necessary. . . .

Principle Three: Flexible Means to a Common End

Western economic theories and policies have their merits, but they are based on the better conditions of developed markets. Hence, even though the general direction for developing countries' economic transition is to converge to those theories and policies, the route and pace . . . will be much more complex than . . . Western economic theorists have . . . expected. Therefore the process should be flexible in design and execution.

Chinese leaders themselves did not expect the complexity of economic reform at the outset. Their initial plan was to complete the reform within 5 to 10 years or at the latest by 1995[5] (Zhang 2008). Also, during the last 30 years of reform (still not yet completed), China has had three rounds of hot debates on how and whether to reform.[6] In the 1980s, China's reform was seen as 'liberalization in odd years and anti-liberalization in even years' (Zhu 2007). The most recent reform debate started in 2004 even triggered the anti-reform voices (Zhu 2007). All of these show the complex nature of the reform process.

Deng Xiaoping was a flexible pragmatist. The very idea of economic reform was a break away from the Maoist economic model. Although many Party leaders wanted to reform, it was taboo in the early years of reform to spell out the failure of Mao's policies. Deng's flexibility was to uphold the banner of 'Mao Zedong Thought'—the CCP's [Chinese Communist Party's] official theory under Mao's leadership—on the one hand and to reinterpret Maoism as 'freeing your mind and finding the truth from the fact' on the other hand (http://news.xinhuanet.com/ziliao/2002-03/04/content_2550275.htm). Therefore Deng's reform strategy was legitimated as an extension and development of Maoism, essentially guaranteeing the long-term continuation of the reform process.

Additional evidence of the power of the flexibility principle is the great idea and policy of 'one country, two systems', which Deng Xiaoping created for handling the issue of the return of Hong Kong and Macau in 1980s. To many people inside and outside China during that time, capitalism and socialism were as incompatible as water and fire. The British Prime Minister Thatcher even used this as an excuse to argue for keeping Hong Kong in British hands. Facing this knotty problem, Deng devised the 'one country, two systems' theory to unite seemingly conflicting systems.

Principle Four: Policy Rights

Chinese leaders consistently argue that every nation should have the freedom to choose its own strategy and policies for building its economy. Therefore China does not allow other countries to dictate China's domestic policies and in the meantime China promises not to intervene in the policies of other countries.

. . . [T]he first time a Chinese leader announced this view on an international occasion was in Premier Zhao Ziyang's speech at the International Meeting on Cooperation and Development[7] at Cancun city in Mexico on 22 October 1981. Zhao stated China's Five Principles on International Cooperation,[8] the fourth of which was 'developing countries have the rights to choose development strategies according to their domestic conditions; and developed nations should not make the domestic reform of developing countries as the precondition of establishing the new world order'.

. . . China's no-strings-attached approach is in sharp contrast to that of the Western powers which includes strict aid conditionality. In the 1990s, most of the Washington Consensus–based reforms worldwide failed to deliver the expected outcomes (cf. World Bank 2005), which helped make the Chinese development model attractive to the Global South. To many developing countries, China offers not only an effective model of economic development but also 'a new model for South–South cooperation' (Wen 2006) which is based on 'peaceful coexistence, equality, and respect for the social systems, sovereignty, and independence of [other nations]' and China's willingness 'to provide assistance without any political strings attached' (Wesley-Smith 2007, 23).

This argument concerning the freedom to choose one's own domestic policies is also supported by many development economists and is referred to as 'policy rights' (Alice Amsten, forthcoming; Crook 2003; Perales 2004, 416). Stiglitz (1998, 14) argues 'if policies are to be sustainable, developing countries must claim ownership of them'. The Chinese government has been consistently following this 'no interference' approach when dealing with international affairs and 'no-strings-attached' approach when granting international aid.

A strong argument is that policy rights and freedom were fully enjoyed in the history of industrialization of today's developed countries, e.g. the UK, France, the U.S. Germany, Japan, and the Newly Industrialized Countries and Economies (South Korea, Singapore, Hong Kong and Taiwan) (Wade 2004). Therefore, it is not right for the developed nations to 'kick away the ladder' (Chang 2002) for the developing countries and force them to accept some international rules designed to protect the interests of the advanced nations (Stiglitz 2000, 2003; Wade 1996, 2001, 2002).

Principle Five: Stable Political Environment

Chinese leaders have been well aware that a stable political environment domestically and internationally is a precondition for economic development.[9] So while economic reform has taken big steps forward, political reform has proceeded much more cautiously.[10] According to 'Jiang Zemin's thought of three representations',[11] one-party ruling is not the problem as long as the Chinese Communist Party represents the development needs of advanced production forces, the direction of advanced culture, and the basic interests of the majority of Chinese people. In China, the official slogan is 'stability overwhelms anything else'. Many scholars now agree that one important reason behind China's fast economic growth in recent years has been its relatively stable domestic political environment (Naughton and Yang 2004; Brødsgaard and Zheng 2004; Nathan 2003). The increased stability and predictability of Chinese politics was evidenced in China's rule-based and orderly transition from the third to fourth generation of political leaders (Brødsgaard 2004).

Some Washington-Consensus-minded scholars prescribed that political reform must precede economic reform because political institutions will directly impact on every economic transaction (North 1990); therefore getting the institutions right first can ensure minimized transaction costs (cf. Coase 1937; Williamson 1975). However, what they did not understand about the dynamics of the relationship between political environment and economic development is that these two are essentially mutually dependent and mutually constraining and reshaping one another. . . .

Principle Six: Self-Reliance

Chinese leaders always emphasize and encourage diligence and self-reliance. Mao enthusiastically praised the great potential of Chinese people's wisdom and creativity. In Mao's thinking, only people are the main source of generation of material wealth, scientific technology, and social progress. Chinese leadership after Mao inherited this self-reliance principle. On 17 November 2006, Chinese President Hu Jintao stated at the APEC CEO Summit 2006 that 'China's development is mainly based on self-reliance and Chinese people's hard work. In the meantime, China unshakably implements the opening-up policy, and executes reciprocal and win–win opening-up strategy'.[12]

As a result of the Cold War international order after the Second World War, Socialist China at its birth faced immense difficulties in its economic development and nation building. During the isolation and blockade by the West led by the U.S. in 1950s, China relied on the Soviet Union for economic help and assistance. However with deterioration of the China–Soviet relations from the early 1960s, China was forced to fully rely on her own efforts. But this forced self-reliance helped unite the whole Chinese people and created a sense of common destiny. In 1978, Deng Xiaoping announced that China would open the door to the outside world in order to import foreign capital, technology and management knowhow. After the 1989 Tiananmen student movement, Western countries led by the U.S. started to block China, and China had to once again rely on herself. One negative case is the policy of 'market exchanges for technology' started in 1992 (Lan 2005). After more than 10 years' practice, Chinese leaders have realized this policy has almost failed and China has to rely on herself to develop advanced manufacturing industries (Mei 2009). . . .

Principle Seven: Constantly Upgrading Industry

Chinese leadership knows well the importance of upgrading its industrial portfolio. This is exactly the idea of Lee Kuan Yew, as put straightforwardly in an interview with Joshua Ramo: 'we tried import substitution for a short while, we were making toothbrushes, mosquito coils, some shirts and garments, but it wasn't going to make us a living' (cited in Ramo 2004, 71). A former Japanese Ministry of Finance official Masaki Shiratori (1993) echoes this wisdom by arguing 'a latecomer to industrialization cannot afford to leave everything to the market mechanism. The trial and error inherent in market-driven industrialization is too risky and expensive considering the scarcity of resources' (cited in Wade 1996, 29).[13]

It is beyond the scope of this paper to make a detailed argument why some industries are more important than some others. Briefly put, certain strategic industries, say, capital-intensive, knowledge-intensive and high-tech industries, are more important than others for several reasons. First, these industries offer more space for technological learning, such as electronics, biochemical, and new material industries, etc. Secondly, these industries add more realizable value into their products hence generate more profit,[14] such as software, financial services, designing and marketing industries, etc. Thirdly, high-tech industries will have much more potential for export growth (Fagerberg, Srholec, and Knell 2007) with rising terms of trade. Fourthly, technology-sophisticated industries may have positive externality or spillover effect to other domestic industries. During the 1950s China adopted a development strategy which focused on heavy-industrial growth and massive investments. During the reform period attempts were made to channel more resources into agriculture and light industry (Brødsgaard 1991).

It is worth noting that it is necessary to foster competition (Stiglitz 1998, 7) among firms as well as among industries if an industrial upgrading strategy is to succeed. During the reform period, even though China opened its door to let foreign companies invest and operate in China, there was a reluctance to open up strategically important sectors such as finance, telecommunications, steel, and power generation. However, the current leadership realizes that Chinese industry needs to start competing on the global level playing field and has defined a group of 120 major companies ('national champions') that should be developed into major international players (Nolan 2001).

Principle Eight: Indigenous Innovation

A corollary of the need for constantly upgrading industry is the demand for indigenous innovation. This point is the first theorem in Ramo's original analysis of the Beijing Consensus (Ramo 2004, 11). . . .

China has invested heavily in education and technology. China used to rely more on technology import and transfer, but has realized it is crucial to develop the country's own innovation capabilities in order to compete in today's fast-changing world (Fagerberg, Srholec, and Knell 2007). China has now been geared to develop her national innovation system where her intention and strategy are to gradually transit from a government-centered to an enterprise-centered innovation web (OECD 2007). Some policy instruments for stimulating indigenous innovation are protecting intellectual property rights (IPR), fiscal decentralization and tax reform which fuelled up the incentives needed to each level of local governments.

It is worth noting that innovation is not just about technological innovation, but also about institutional innovation. Since the reform in 1978 China has shown considerable abilities in institutional innovation and reform. The decentralized social structure and reform leaders support the experimentation. Chinese society has rehabilitated the ability to innovate from below. Significantly, Chinese peasants have made several institutional innovations, such as the household contract responsibility system (HCRS), township and village enterprises (TVE), self-governance in village, rural special cooperatives, collective forest rights reform, etc.[15] With respect to the urban reform, Chinese leaders invented the 'dual-track system' which ensured a much more smooth transition from centrally planned to a market economy compared with the big bang reform in EEFSU. Some scholars highly praised this institutional innovation as a Pareto-improving method (Lau, Qian, and Roland 2000).

Principle Nine: Prudent Financial Liberalization

China has been very prudent and cautious when it comes to liberalization of financial markets, so China still has not opened her capital account. This might be partly because China has lacked the experience of managing stock and other financial markets, and partly because the Chinese leadership is worried about losing control of China's strategic national assets. But the most important reason is that Chinese leaders understand the enormous risk of rapid financial liberalization.

Chinese leaders' cautions and worries have been warranted by the chilly reality that those countries that have liberalized too quickly or relaxed regulations on financial markets have had to bear painful loses due to unexpected financial crises. One may point to the Latin American debt crisis in the 1980s and 1990s, the Asian financial crisis in 1997, the Russian financial crisis in 1998, and most recently the global financial crisis in 2008 caused by the U.S. subprime crisis.

What puzzles Chinese leaders is how come the rest of the world (LA, EA, EU, and U.S.) has not learnt a lesson from the string of financial crises in the last two decades of the twentieth century? To Chinese leaders, the main culprit of the global financial crisis was a blind belief in the market. Ironically, in his speech at the Manhattan Institute on 13 November 2008 'on the eve of' the G20 summit, the former U.S. president George W. Bush 'fervently defended U.S.-style free enterprise' as 'not the cause' but rather 'the cure' for the world's financial chaos (Feller 2008).

Principle Ten: Economic Growth for Social Harmony

Chinese leaders are enthusiastic about building a harmonious society and they believe they can achieve this by effectively growing the economy first. This belief can be traced back to the birth of the New China in 1949. Mao spent his whole life seeking a road toward a prosperous and strong China in which the Chinese people could enjoy a happy and equal life. Harmony in Mao's mind might mean no oppression and no exploitation. Based on this belief, he tried to make the oppressed stand up, the proletariat control the means of production, and the bourgeoisie be deprived of everything. The means of realizing his harmonious society proved to be wrong and had disastrous consequences, but it could be argued that his vision was clear; for instance, he even believed that by cultural revolution he could find a way from total chaos to total harmony (*cong tian xia da luan dao tian xia da zhi*).

Deng Xiaoping inherited Mao's vision but took another direction. Deng allowed some people to get rich first and reminded his Party never to forget his vision: let the people and regions that became rich first help the less wealthy people/regions to prosper and develop together. Deng Xiaoping and Jiang Zemin have done well in encouraging some Chinese people to get rich first, which in fact prepared the material basis for the new generation of Chinese leadership led by President Hu Jintao and Premier Wen Jiabao to take on the task of 'making all Chinese prosper together'. Hu and Wen have so far had a good start—they brought forth a new development plan called 'constructing a harmonious socialist society', which we argue will have far-reaching impact on China's peaceful rise in the twenty-first century. Part of this would be to correct the big income disparities that have emerged as a consequence of letting some people and regions prosper first.

Although we list this principle as the last one, it is actually very important because it indicates the ultimate purpose of reform and development. Chinese leaders since Mao have never lost their grand vision: to build a prosperous, democratic and civilized socialist country. Many Westerners criticize China's lack of democracy, human rights and freedom. However, we believe, it takes time for a huge country like China to realize its transformation from an underdeveloped, semi-colonized and semi-feudal country to an advanced modernized nation. What we have learned from the Chinese story is that China has prioritized economic development at the earlier stage and has gradually moved toward coordinated economic and social development when they feel they have accumulated sufficient material resources in the earlier stage. The best evidence is China's strategic switch to a strategy of building a harmonious society domestically and a harmonious world internationally.

Acknowledgements

Xin Li wishes to thank EAC Foundation in Denmark for sponsoring his PhD study at Copenhagen Business School.

Endnotes

1. M-form and U-form are concepts of organization theory. In M-form organizations, there are multiple autonomous divisions and the headquarters does not interfere much in the decision-making of individual divisions. In a U-form organization, the general manager exerts tight control through different functions, like finance, sales, operations, etc.
2. In 2001, the Nobel Prize in Economics was awarded to George Akerlof, Michael Spence, and Joseph E. Stiglitz 'for their analyses of markets with asymmetric information'. Source: http://en.wikipedia.org/wiki/Information_asymmetty (accessed 2 October 2009).
3. Hayek (1935, 1988) argues that central planners will never have enough information to carry out resource allocation reliably.
4. Source: http://www1.peopledaily.com.cn/GB/shizheng/252/5303/5304/20010626/497655.html (accessed November 29, 2008).
5. Source: http://www.tianjindaily.com.cn/epaper/mrxb/mrxb/2008-06/24/content_5748912.htm (accessed November 30, 2008).
6. Source: http://news.xinhuanet.com/fortune/2006-02/13/content_4173007.htm (accessed November 30, 2008).
7. This was the first international conference on cooperation and development where 14 developing countries including PR China and eight developed nations attended.
8. Source: http://cpc.people.com.cn/GB/64162/64165/70486/70508/4943078.html (accessed December 1, 2008).

9. Even the anti-socialist and anti-collectivist economist and political philosopher Friedrich Hayek once admitted 'Well, I would say that, as long-term institutions, I am totally against dictatorships. But a dictatorship may be a necessary system for a transitional period. At times it is necessary for a country to have, for a time, some form or other of dictatorial power'. Source: http://www.fahayek .org/index.php?option=com_content&task=view&id=121 (accessed November 29, 2008).

10. Deng Xiaoping called for political reform in 1980 and in 1986 he wanted to have a substantial start of political reform; however, the conservative forces within the Party succeeded in putting off such a bold move.

11. Source: http://news.xinhuanet.com/ziliao/2003-01/21/content_699933 .htm (accessed December 1, 2008).

12. Source: News of the Communist Party of China. http://cpc.people.com.cn/ GB/64093/64094/5057874.html (accessed November 27, 2008).

13. Stiglitz (1998, 11) points out two major market failures in developing countries: 'left to itself, the market will tend to underprovide human capital' and 'technology', which are crucial factors for economic development.

14. The Chinese ex-Minister for Commerce emotionally commented that 'Chinese people need to produce 800 million shirts in order to exchange an A380 plane'. His calculation was based on the harsh reality that the profit margin for a Chinese-made shirt was only US $0.35. Source: http://www.scol.com.cn/ comment/bbsnr/20060208/200628153736.htm (accessed November 25, 2008).

15. Source: China's official Xinhua news agency website http://news.xinhuanet. com/politics/2008-10/08/content_10165611.htm (accessed November 25, 2008).

References

Amsten, A. Forthcoming. Preface: Role models, policy 'rights', and peace. In *A farewell to theory: How developing countries learn from each other*. Department of Urban Studies in MIT (eds).

Brødsgaard, K.E. 1991. China's political economy in the nineties. *China Report 27*, no. 3: 177–96.

Brødsgaard. K.E. 2004. Jiang finally steps down: A note on military personnel changes and the CCP's governing capacity. *Copenhagen Journal of Asian Studies* 19: 82–8.

Brødsgaard, K.E., and Y. Zheng, eds. 2004. *Bringing the party back in: The role of the CCP in governing China*. London: Routledge.

Chang, H.J. 2002. *Kicking away the ladder: Development strategies in historical perspective*. London: Anthem.

Coase, R. 1937. The nature of the firm. *Economica, New Series*, 4, no. 16: 386–405.

Colley, C. 2009. China's reforms at 30 and the 'Beijing Consensus'. *Pambazuka News*, China–Africa Watch section, 2009-01-31, no. 417. http://pambazuka .org/en/category/africa_china/53757 (accessed May 6, 2009).

Crook, C. 2003. A cruel sea of capital: A survey of global finance. *The Economist*, 3, no. 5: 12–14.

Dirlik, A. 2006. Beijing Consensus: Beijing 'Gongshi'. Who recognizes whom and to what end? Position Paper, Globalization and Autonomy Online Compendium, January 17. http://www.globalau-tonomy.ca/globall/position.jsp?index=PP_Dirlik_BeijingConsensus.xml (accessed May 6, 2009).

Fagerberg, J., M. Srholec, and M. Knell. 2007. The competitiveness of nations: Why some countries prosper while others fall behind? *World Development* 35, no. 10: 1595–1620.

Feller, B. 2008. Bush defends capitalism on eve of economic summit. *Associated Press*, November 13. Accessed 3 February 2010 from http://usatoday.com/news/topstories/2008-11-13-1986009405_x.htm.

Gosset, D. 2006. The Dragon's metamorphosis. *The Asian Times*, December 9.

Greenwald, B.C., and J.E. Stiglitz. 1986. Externalities in economies with imperfect information and incomplete markets. *Quarterly Journal of Economics* 101, no. 2: 229–64.

Hayek, F. von, ed. 1935. *Collectivist Economic Planning*. London: Routledge.

Hayek, F. von, 1988. The fatal conceit: the errors of socialism. (The collected works of F. A. Hayek), ed. W. Bartley. London: Routledge.

Huang, P. 2005. Beijing gongshi haishi Zhongguo jingyan [Beijing Consensus or Chinese experience?]. *Tian Ya*, no. 6. http://theory.people.com.cn/GB/40557/54488/54489/3802568.html (accessed May 6, 2009).

Huang, Y., and S. Ding. 2006. Dragon's underbelly: An analysis of China's soft power. *East Asia* 23, no. 4: 22–44.

Kennedy, S. 2008. The myth of the Beijing Consensus. 1st draft. Paper presented at the 6th International Symposium of the Centre for China–U.S. Cooperation, May 30–31, Denver, Colorado, USA. http://www.indiana.edu/~rccpb/Myth%20Paper%20May%2008.pdf (accessed November 26, 2008).

Kuczynski, P. 2003. Setting the stage. In *After the Washington Consensus: Restarting growth and reform in Latin America*, ed. P. Kuczynski and J. Williamson, pp. 21–32. Washington, DC: Peterson Institute.

Lan, H. 2005. The past and present of 'market exchanges for technology'. *Global Financial Watch*, 24 April [in Chinese]. http://finance.sina.com.cn/review/observe/20050322/19011451207.shtml (accessed May 7, 2009).

Lau, L.J., Y. Qian, and G. Roland. 2000. Reform without losers: An interpretation of China's dual-track approach to transition. *Journal of Political Economy* 108, no. 1: 120–43.

Mei, X. 2009. China's strategy under the global trade protectionism. *China News Week*, May 5 [in Chinese], http://blog.ifeng.com/article/2321611.html (accessed May 7, 2009).

Nathan, A. 2003. Authoritarian resilience. *Journal of Democracy* 14, no. 1: 6–17.

Naughton, B., and D. Yang, eds. 2004. *Holding China together: Diversity and national integration in the post-Deng era*. Cambridge: Cambridge University Press.

Nolan, P. 2001. *China and the global economy*. London: Palgrave.

North, D.C. 1990. *Institutions, institutional change and economic performance*. Cambridge: Cambridge University Press.

Nye, J.S. 2005. The rise of China's soft power. *Wall Street Journal Asia*, December 29.

OECD (Organization for Economic Co-operation and Development). 2007. *OECD reviews of innovation policy: China–synthesis report*. Paris: OECD.

Perales, J.A.S. 2004. Consensus, dissensus, confusion: The 'Stiglitz debate' in perspective–a review essay. *Development in Practice* 14, no. 3: 412–23.

Qian, Y., and C.-G. Xu. 1993. Why China's economic reforms differ: the m-form hierarchy and entry/expansion of the non-state sector. Discussion Paper No. 154, Centre for Economic Performance, London School of Economics and Political Science, London. http://eprints.lse.ac.uk/3755/(accessed November 30, 2008).

Ramo, J.C. 2004. *The Beijing Consensus.* London: The Foreign Policy Centre.

Rodrik, D. 2006. Goodbye Washington Consensus, hello Washington confusion? A review of the World Bank's economic growth in the 1990s: Learning from a decade of reform. *Journal of Economic Literature* 44, no. 4: 973–87.

Schweickart, D. 2005. You can't get there from here: Reflections on the 'Beijing Consensus'. Paper presented at the International Symposium on the 'China Model or Beijing Consensus for Development', August 8, Tianjing Normal University, Tianjing, China. http://www.luc.edu/faculty/dschwei/beijingcon sensus.pdf (accessed November 30, 2008).

Shiratori, M. 1993. The role of government in economic development: Comments on the 'East Asian Miracle' study. Paper presented at the OECF seminar on the East Asian Miracle, December, 3, Tokyo.

Smith, A. 1776/1965. *The Wealth of nations.* New York: Modern Library.

Stiglitz, J. 1998 More instruments and broader goals: Moving toward the post-Washington Consensus. The 1998 WIDER Annual Lecture, January 7, Helsinki, Finland. http://www.adelinotorres.com/desenvolvimento/ STIGLITZ-Consenso%20de%20Washington.pdf (accessed November 30, 2008).

Stiglitz, J. 2000. The insider: What I learned at the world economic crisis. *The New Republic,* 17 April.

Stiglitz, J. 2003. Challenging the Washington Consensus. *The Brown Journal of World Affairs* 9, no. 2: 33–40.

Vásquez, 1. 1996. The Brady Plan and market-based solutions to debt crises. *The Cato Journal* 16, no. 2: 1–9.

Wade, R. 1996. Japan, the World Bank, and the art of paradigm maintenance: The East Asian Miracle in political perspective. *New Left Review* I/217: 3–36.

Wade, R. 2001. Showdown at the World Bank. *New Left Review* 7, January–February: 124–37.

Wade, R. 2002. U.S. hegemony and the World Bank: The fight over people and ideas. *Review of International Political Economy* 9, no. 2: 215–43.

Wade, R. 2004. Introduction to *Governing the market: Economic theory and the role of government in East Asian industrialization,* Princeton. NJ: Princeton University Press.

Wen, J. 2006. Win–win cooperation for common development. Keynote speech, China-Pacific Island Countries Economic Development and Cooperation Forum, April 5, Nadi, Fiji. http://news.xinhuanet.com/english/2006-04/05/ content_4385969.htm (accessed November 30, 2008).

Wesley-Smith, T. 2007. *China in Oceania: New forces in Pacific politics.* Honolulu, Hawaii: East–West Center.

Williamson. J. 1990. What Washington means by policy reform. In *Latin American adjustment: How much has happened.* Washington, DC: Institute for International Economics.

Williamson, J. 2000. What should the World Bank think about the Washington Consensus? *The World Bank Research Observer* 15, no. 2: 251–64.

Williamson, J. 2002. Did the Washington Consensus fail? Outline of remarks at the Center for Strategic & International Studies, November 6. Available from http://www.petersoninstitute.org/publications/papers/paper.cfm?ResearchID=488 (accessed 3 February 2010).

Williamson, J. 2004. A short history of the Washington Consensus. Paper presented at the conference 'From the Washington Consensus to a new Global Governance', September 24–25. Barcelona, Spain.

Williamson, J. 2009. The 'Washington Consensus': Another near-death experience? http://www.iie.com/realtime/?p=604 (accessed November 30, 2008).

Williamson, O.E. 1975. *Markets and hierarchies*. New York: Free Press.

World Bank. 2005. *Economic growth in the 1990s: Learning from a decade of reform*. Washington, DC: The World Bank.

Wu, S. 2005. The 'Washington Consensus' and 'Beijing Consensus'. *People's Daily Online*, June 18. http://english.peopledaily.com.cn/200506/18/eng20050618_190947.html (accessed November 30, 2008).

Yusuf, S. 1994. China's macroeconomic performance and management during transition. *Journal of Economic Perspectives* 8, no. 2: 71–92.

Zagha, R., and G.T. Nankani, eds. 2005. *Economic growth in the 1990s: Learning from a decade of reform*. Washington, DC: World Bank Publications.

Zedong, M. 1956/1977. On ten major relationships. *Selected works of Mao Tse-tung*. Peking: Foreign Language Press.

Zhang, W., ed. 2008. *Zhong Guo Gai Ge 30 Nian* [30 years of China's reform]. Shanghai: Shanghai People Press.

Zhao, X. 2004. Cong huashengdun gongshi dao Beijing gongsi [From Washington Consensus to Beijing Consensus].

Zhong guo Jingji Zhoukan. *China Economic Weekly*, no. 33. Accessed 3 February 2010 from http://people.com.cu/GB/paper1631/12870/1157164.html.

Zhu. X. 2007. Jidang 30 Nian: Gaige kaifang de jingyan zongjie [Exciting 30 years: Experiences and lessons from reform and opening up]. Lingnan Forum Lecture, December 15, Guangzhou, Guangdong. http://www.nddaily.com/special/lingnanforum/speech/200712/t20071217_603531.shtml (accessed November 30, 2008).

Scott Kennedy
The Myth of the Beijing Consensus

China's phenomenal economic success has given rise to a debate about the reasons for its achievements and the implications for broader debates about what constitutes the most appropriate development strategy for developing countries generally. Some believe that the broad liberalization of the last 30 years deserves the credit, which would be consistent with conventional explanations for economic development. Others suggest that just as significant as liberalization has been the measured pace and distinctive sequencing of reforms developed and carried out by a state with strong governing capabilities. They believe China's success challenges conventional theories about the most appropriate development strategies and the role of the state. One observer, Joshua Cooper Ramo, labels what he sees as China's unique approach as the 'Beijing Consensus, (BC, *beijing gongshi)*, thereby distinguishing it from the 'Washington Consensus, (WC, *huashengdun gongshi)*, which connotes a more conventional development approach.[1]

Ramo's argument, which he detailed in an extended essay in 2004, has touched off a wide debate among scholars and policymakers in China as well as scholars elsewhere.[2] In subsequent years, the power of this alternative vision has seemed to grow, particularly in the wake of the global financial crisis, which apparently laid bare the weaknesses of market fundamentalism and highlighted the importance of government regulation. Despite this turn of events, the original conception of the BC is not up to the task of being a worthwhile competitor to the alternative model from which its name was coined, not because of the WC's apparent worthiness, but rather because Ramo's Beijing Consensus is a misguided and inaccurate summary of China's actual reform experience. It not only gets the empirical facts wrong about China, it also disregards the similarities and differences China's experience shares with other countries, and it distorts China's place in international politics.

Yet in spite of these weaknesses, the Beijing Consensus is nevertheless a useful touchstone to consider the evolution of developmental paradigms, compare China's experience with that of others, identify the most distinctive features of China's experience, and evaluate its significance for the development prospects of other countries and for international relations. The BC is at once an unpleasant distraction and a useful tool to consider the true import of China's development experience.

The article begins with a discussion of the Beijing Consensus, both in its original form and how it has been interpreted and critiqued in China.

The BC is based on a misguided analysis of China's political economy. Although one might expect Chinese commentators to welcome such a laudatory label, ironically, opinion in China has been largely critical of the BC. Given the problems with the BC, we then consider another potentially more useful framework for distinguishing China's record, the China Model. In the conclusion, we discuss the implications of the BC and the China Model for the debate about economic development strategies of individual countries and policies of international institutions. The lessons taken from China may be less revolutionary than the advocates of the BC or China Model imagined. . . .

The Beijing Consensus

. . . [T]he Beijing Consensus (BC) originated with a single individual, in this case, Joshua Cooper Ramo, who in 2004 published the ambitiously sounding extended essay, 'The Beijing Consensus: notes on the new physics of Chinese power'. A former editor at *Time* magazine, he was a managing partner in the office of Goldman Sachs chairman John Thornton and a professor at Tsinghua University at the time the essay was published.[3] Virtually unknown among China specialists at the time, Ramo's tract took the field by storm and drew immediate attention from Chinese scholars and officialdom. For a time, the BC created a buzz similar to that of the term 'BRICs,' also invented by Goldman Sachs.[4]

If one reads 'The Beijing Consensus' as a manifesto meant to trumpet China's success and challenge the normative authority of the WC, then one can admire the boldness of Ramo's effort and the rhetorical flourishes of his prose. The ambition is commendable, particularly from the perspective of a professor whose students usually sit on the fence and are wont to challenge conventional wisdom. Moreover, to the extent the label gains cocket and resonates beyond China, it could serve as a challenge to the WC and as a symbol of China's growing soft power.[5] . . .

Ramo obviously chose the term 'Beijing Consensus' as a provocative response to the Washington Consensus.[6] . . . Ramo is explicitly concerned with explaining both China's impressive economic development and her growing international influence. The first tenet is that China's modernization has been rooted in innovation and technological leaps, which accounts for rapid increases in total factor productivity. As he puts it, 'The conventional wisdom is that Chinese growth is an example of what happens when you let loose lots of cheap labor. In fact, innovation-led productivity growth has sustained the Chinese economy and helped to offset disastrous internal imbalances'.[7] The second component is that China is intent on not only expanding the economic pie, but on achieving equitable distribution of wealth in which the benefits are widely shared. He notes that recently China's leaders and even local officials have made sustainable and balanced growth a 'central concern'. There is a widening commitment to reducing the environmental damage from growth; hence, the popularity of adopting 'green' as a more accurate measure of the economy's performance.[8]

The third element of Ramo's BC is the notion that China has been able to maintain control over its development policies and path and that China's success is leading it to challenge the United States by dint of China's attractiveness as a model to others and its own growing power. According to Ramo, China has not felt compelled to strictly follow the WC and instead has pursued policies suited to local circumstances: 'For China the main point of reference is and has been China itself'.[9] As a consequence, 'When measured in terms of comprehensive national power, China is already a rival of the United States in many important areas'.[10] Equally important, the developing world is flocking to China as an economic partner, political ally, and development model, all of which is eroding the U.S.'s global dominance.

Despite flamboyant flourishes and strategic references to China's wise political leadership, Ramo's Beijing Consensus deals in several myths. Granted, in some ways China has not strictly followed the tenets of the WC, and the country has become more influential globally. Yet making these points does not justify Ramo's grand vision. The following critique focuses primarily on those elements directly related to economic development and does not engage the debate about China's growing international influence and its potential challenge to American hegemony. Elements of the latter issues are taken up in the conclusion.

First, technological innovation has not been the centerpiece of China's growth. Ramo sounds like futurologist Alvin Toffler in suggesting China could jump several generations of technology and do so based on its own innovations.[11] It would be inaccurate to assert that innovation has been irrelevant in China's growth story. There doubtless have been a large number of incremental innovations in different sectors of the economy and, in particular, in manufacturing processes. Moreover, there is a rapidly growing pool of scientists, engineers, and entrepreneurs. The amount of funding dedicated to research and development has expanded in the past decade, particularly among companies. These investments are reflected in a rapid rise in the number of filed patents, copyrights, and trademarks.

Nevertheless, the Chinese have not been innovation leaders. For the most part, Chinese enterprises make products and provide services that have been designed or invented outside China. In high technology sectors, the most successful Chinese companies have integrated themselves into global production networks as assemblers and manufacturers of others' designs.[12] The great majority of the value added in China's information technology exports originates from outside China, and over 85% of these exports are produced in either joint ventures or wholly owned foreign subsidies of multinationals based in advanced capitalist countries.[13] Over the last few years China's leaders have trumpeted an effort to promote 'indigenous innovation' *(zizhu chuangxin)*. A centerpiece of this goal is to develop distinctive technical standards in information technology and then leverage China's huge market size to force other countries to produce to these standards. The record so far, though, has been poor. The great majority of these efforts have failed; only those that are compatible with other foreign technologies show much promise of commercial success.[14]

Second, the evidence that China is pursuing sustainable and equitable development is highly limited. At best, these can be seen as future goals which have not been the mainstream of Chinese policy during the Reform era. China has taken significant steps to create a regulatory infrastructure for environmental protection, but just about whenever there appears to be a tradeoff between the environment and growth, the latter wins.[15] Ramo notes the great interest in Hu Angang's green GDP [gross domestic product] calculations. However, although the Chinese government did allow a report based on 2004 data to be issued, it has not allowed similar reports to be issued in subsequent years because of the steep deductions in the growth data that emerge from such calculations.[16] Similarly, inequality, not equality, has been a chief hallmark of China's growth experience. Several hundred million people have been lifted out of poverty, but regardless of how it was measured—personal, sectoral, or regional—inequality has expanded. Ramo himself acknowledges this point.[17] Recently, Beijing has eliminated some preferential policies for coastal regions and increased investment in Western China, but the gap between coast and interior is still massive. Poorly constructed schools, homes, and office buildings which were decimated by the May 2008 earthquake in Sichuan are unfortunate evidence that these regional differences persist.

The third myth that Ramo offers is that China's economic development strategy is unique. In one sense, that is true. No other country has adopted the same mix of policies and achieved the same results, and certainly China's own development path has been to some extent conditioned in a way by the country's size and political institutions that set it apart from others. Yet extrapolating from having some distinctive elements to hail a new consensus does not say much. The same could be said of the world's every other 191 countries. It would certainly be meaningless to ascribe the label 'X-country Consensus' to every nation that has achieved successful development.

At the same time, one should note that if one were to measure China's policies against the original WC, one would find that China essentially followed eight of the ten elements.[18] China closely abided by the WC in terms of fiscal discipline, maintaining a competitive exchange rate (some would say too competitive), liberalizing trade, and liberalizing foreign direct investment. It has made gradual progress on four others: reordering spending away from non-merit subsidies toward public goods, expanding the tax base, easing barriers to market entry, and strengthening property rights. It has moved the least on liberalizing interest rates and privatization, but even on the latter, a substantial portion of SOEs have been privatized since the late 1990s.

Despite these areas of overlap, it is entirely reasonable to see that China's behavior has not approached the WC ideal. If we applied a more-nuanced comparative lens, we would discover that China's policies and trajectory share similarities and differences with a wide range of countries, including those with more liberal capitalist governance regimes and those with developmental states. This is in part because the intellectual source for most of China's economic reforms has been the experiences of other countries, and China's experts and officials have closely examined and borrowed from elsewhere.[19] Ramo would have been closer to the mark if he said China was following in the footsteps of other developmental states.[20] China's government has consistently intervened in the economy, using both macro and micro economic policy tools, and the Chinese have explicitly adopted some of the policies of their neighbors. Ramo says China's special economic zones (SEZs) were the inspiration for those in India, but China borrowed the idea from elsewhere.

At the same time, China diverges from its East Asian neighbors in several respects.[21] The fastest growing segments of China's economy, the coastal private sector, have achieved their success without central government encouragement and have had to survive in highly competitive markets. Efforts to 'rationalize' sectors by forming cartels or banning firms regularly fail. For the last decade, the central government has tried to raise the concentration of the steel sector, but China has over 6,000 steel companies, 2,000 more than when the initiative began. Whereas Japan and South Korea maintained extreme barriers to foreign direct investment [FDI] and imports, in relative terms, China has been far more open to the international economy. China has been the largest destination in the developing world of FDI for more than a decade, in part because of foreign political pressure and in part because of China's own economic weaknesses that necessitated attracting foreign managerial talent and technology.[22] Whereas Japan. South Korea, and Taiwan had highly organized systems for government–business consultation, industry associations are poorly developed in China. Chinese and foreign industries do influence China's economic policies, but most business contact with government occurs through informal, individualized channels, sharing more similarities with government–business relations in Russia and India. And China's social welfare system is far less developed than its neighbors and shares much more in common with other 'uneven developers' such as South Africa and Egypt.

The ultimate point of all of these examples is that a sweeping generalization of distinctiveness blurs more than it clarifies. Engaging in fine-tuned comparisons across the constituent elements of China's economy is more valuable.

The fourth problematic aspect of Ramo's thesis is that he assumes that the different elements of the Chinese state have acted in concert with each other, that together they have pursued a well-defined goal, and that China's economic performance is a reflection of those plans. Such a view ascribes the central role in the story to Deng Xiaoping and subsequent Chinese leaders. While no doubt immensely influential, the record indicates that they have not been all-powerful rulers able to force their vision on the rest of society. To a large extent, China's leadership has had to react to economic and political pressures not of their choosing. During the first 15 years of the Reform era, many policies reflected a compromise between liberal and conservative wings of the Communist Party.[23] Although ideological disagreements have diminished as a result of purges and death, bureaucratic conflicts have continued to shape the adoption and implementation of policies. More recently, lobbying by business interests and other components of society has become central to policy debates at the national and local levels.[24] Many of China's most successful policies were first adopted locally, not as centrally-approved experiments, but as violations of central policy, and then were only subsequently endorsed nationally.[25] The bottom line is that compromise between different groups, not consensus, has been the source for most of China's economic policies. . . .

From the Beijing Consensus to the China Model

Given the problems of the BC in terms of both substance and nomenclature, a more productive conversation about China's development experience needs to move in other directions. One of the most popular alternatives of late has been the 'China Model' *(zhongguo moshi)*. Although the term does not explicitly assume common agreement amongst China's elite and it has attracted more interest by Chinese analysts than the BC, interpretations of the China Model vary far and wide, and none stand up well as a rigorous summary of a distinctive Chinese developmental experience.

Unlike the BC, the China Model has no clear provenance, but it appears that the phrase originally was used to distinguish China's gradualist reform strategy from the 'shock therapy' approach adopted by post-Communist states of central Europe. In that regard, the China Model is a synonym for the more ideologically inspired, 'socialism with Chinese characteristics'.[26] Its purpose is to justify the Reform era's break from Maoist policies while at the same time suggesting it is entirely appropriate for China to follow a path different from its fellow former Socialist comrades. To some analysts, this coda only hides the reality that China is no longer genuinely socialist, and hence the emergence of the term 'capitalism with Chinese characteristics'.[27]

A second way the China Model has been deployed is as a synonym for the Beijing Consensus. Though not sharing the exact meaning, commentators emphasize that China has not followed the WC and permitted extensive state intervention in the economy yet not foisting its own development experience on to other countries.[28] Some who see the overlap between the BC and the China Model argue in favor of using the latter because the BC is more likely to arouse fears overseas of the Chinese threat to the international system.[29]

Another way the China Model has been used is to highlight the strategy of rapid economic reform while simultaneously maintaining China's original political institutions. Yao Yang, a professor at the influential China Center for Economic Research at Peking University, stresses that since officials do not have to be responsive to special interests, China's 'neutral government' *(zhongxing zhengfu)* has been able to consistently pursue policies that serve the general interest.[30] Although this claim may not hold up to detailed scrutiny, a key implication of the analysis is to distinguish China from India and other democratic developing countries and, in doing so, help to justify the continuation of the CCP's one-party rule.[31] Critics, on the other hand, use this label to criticize China for pursuing 'authoritarian capitalism'.[32] Whether meant as praise or criticism, if this is the only basis of the model, then surely it does not deserve the adjective China, since many countries have successfully pursued economic development in the context of a strong authoritarian state. The most obvious examples are several of China's neighbors in the decades after World War II, but one can find additional cases at other points in time (Meiji-era Japan) or in other regions (late nineteenth-century Mexico).

Most recently, in the wake of the global financial crisis, the China Model has been re-deployed to refer to China's export-oriented growth strategy. Some analysts believe China has overly embraced globalization and has been too dependent on foreign markets and instead needs to promote domestic consumption and higher productivity as the foundation for future economic growth.[33] In this usage, the model has been reduced to describe only one aspect of China's economy—its orientation toward the global economy. Observers such as Wang Yong note that China's heavy reliance on exports distinguishes it from large industrialized economies such as the United States, but China in many ways is following the strategy of many of its neighbors. The ironic implication of this last usage is that this strategy emphasizes extensive trade and investment liberalization, which is consistent with the Washington Consensus.

In addition to the difficulties noted above, no matter how deployed, the China Model faces two other analytical problems. The word 'model' implies a coherence and guiding plan that likely does not square with the reality of China's path. As noted earlier, despite the strong leadership of

Deng Xiaoping and subsequent CCP chiefs, many policies have been the product of compromises amongst elites, bureaucrats, and interest groups, and have been in response to short-term problems as much as long-term plans. Finally, the China Model implies a single, consistent strategy, when economic reform has actually proceeded through several stages, each different from the proceeding one. If the China Model is reduced to mean modifying China's policies as circumstances change over time or choosing policies through experimentation, then it is robbed of much analytical rigor.[34]

Conclusions

The proponents of the BC and China Model would have observers believe that China's experience directly violates the dogma of the WC and neoliberalism. Although China did not strictly adhere to Williamson's ten tenets or the various elaborations, in particular with regard to governing institutions, fundamentalists on either side may be overstating how far China diverges from standard economic theory. Rodrik argues that the goals of neoliberal analyses do not imply only one type of policy prescription. Hence, he writes that 'broad objectives of economic reform—namely market-oriented incentives, macroeconomic stability, and outward orientation—do not translate into a unique set of policy actions'.[35] For example, property rights can be secured in individuals, but China through the mid-1990s endowed local governments with such protections, which helps explain the phenomenal success of township and village enterprises (TVE). Rodrik's broader purpose is to show that extensive government intervention can be consistent with traditional economic logic. One of the greatest ironies is that traditional economics is flexible enough to make sense of and make peace with China, undercutting the very rationale for a BC or China Model as a challenger to orthodoxy.

Despite their problematic construction, the *perception* that a Beijing Consensus or China Model exists may still have consequences for China, other countries, and international institutions. These ideas are most likely to have an impact on the place that draws their inspiration. Because it is viewed as a foreign creation, China's leadership has not embraced the BC, and hence, it will never find a place as ideological supplements alongside 'socialism with Chinese characteristics' or 'reform and opening up'. But the government has at least implicitly endorsed the discussion of a China model. That there is no agreement on its contents or utility may be less relevant than that the discussion occurs, which gives legitimacy to any way in which China diverges from the free-market democratic ideal promoted by others.

China's experience also has implications for debates about the appropriate role of the state in the economy. Although the Bretton Woods institutions offer policy advice to clients, which is often still old-school or new-school WC, their analysts are coming to terms with the success of China and other countries where government has played a large role.[36] No longer is a limited non-interventionist state accepted as always appropriate. Japan and others in East Asia helped initiate this discussion, but perhaps China's success has made it seem appropriate for an even broader swath of countries. China's experience appears to give additional impetus to the breakdown of any universal dogma, a trend only reinforced by the responses of developed countries to the global financial crisis.[37]

Whereas the BC and China Model may have some lasting resonance on matters political, given the problems of these terms and the flexibility of standard economic theory, it should be clear that the economic significance of these ideas should not be overstated. There are individual elements of China's experience that deserve study and perhaps adoption by others, but they do not add up to a distinctive model. Even Yao Yang, the proponent of a 'neutral government' autonomous from social pressures, still stresses the need for China to center reforms around improving and supporting the market, not circumventing it.[38] The BC and China Model do not neatly crystallize features of China's experience that are unique to her or that can be packaged as simple prescriptions for other developing countries to follow. Some countries are deeply interested in learning from China's success.[39] Some are led by authoritarian leaders intent on following China's lead in achieving both growth and continued one-party rule;[40] yet as has been demonstrated elsewhere, there is no one formula of economic success, and what 'works' in China likely will not directly transfer to other circumstances. Those who blindly adopt elements of Chinese policy may very well find themselves in the same place as those who adopted the WC without question, frustrated by economic and political crises.

Finally, there are some who are concerned that the BC may provide a foundation for a new North–South conflict,[41] but a close examination of the substance of the BC and China Model and China's own behavior indicates this is not likely. Although the world's governing institutions are adapting somewhat to China's growing role and may have to make greater allowances for state intervention under certain circumstances, in the grand scheme of things these challenges do not match the ideological conflicts of the Cold War between communism or capitalism or even those pitting the global wealthy North against the poor South. On most fronts, China is far more open and market oriented than when reforms began. At the same time, the Chinese government and industry have striven to learn and play by the rules of the international economic system. Even where the Chinese have interpreted these rules to serve protectionist purposes, they have typically followed the practices of developed capitalist countries. China's self-serving application of the rules has become much more relevant than outright non-compliance with its commitments. As a result of the benefits it has obtained through both liberalization and targeted protection, the international economic system has served China well; and hence, the People s Republic is far more likely to be a tinkerer advocating limited reforms than an outright opponent. Global governance institutions need to be reformed substantially, but the challenge is far less likely to come from a China who has deftly adapted to the capitalist world than from the least developed countries who are still trapped in a vicious cycle of poverty from which no consensus, Washington or otherwise, provides easy escape.

Scott Kennedy is Associate Professor in the Departments of Political Science and East Asian Languages & Cultures and Director of the Research Center for Chinese Politics & Business (RCCPB) at Indiana University. He is the author of The Business of Lobbying in China *(Harvard University Press, 2005). His current research projects focus on the growing role of the Chinese government and industry in global economic governance and the evolution of corporate political activity in China. An earlier version of this paper was presented at the conference, 'Washington Consensus' versus 'Beijing Consensus': Sustainability of China's Development Model, National Taiwan University Center for China Studies and University of Denver Center for China–U.S. Cooperation, Denver. CO, 30–31 May 2008. The author thanks participants from this conference, the National Defense University Institute for International Strategic Studies' China Security Perspective Series, and Indiana University's China Studies Group for their feedback. Special appreciation goes to Wang Qua for his valuable research assistance.*

ENDNOTES

1. Joshua Cooper Ramo, *The Beijing Consensus: Notes on the New Physics of Chinese Power* (London: Foreign Policy Centre, 2004), available at: http://www.fpc .org.uk.

2. Huang Ping and Cui Zhiyuan, eds, *Zhongguo yu quanqiu hua: huashengdun gongshi haishi beijing gongshi [China and Globalization: Washington Consensus or Beijing Consensus?]*(Beijing: Social Science Academic Press, August 2005).

3. As of 2009, Ramo was managing director at Kissinger Associates, an international consulting firm located in New York City. Ramo has published two other monographs: Joshua Cooper Ramo, *Brand China* (London: Foreign Policy Centre, 2007); and Joshua Cooper Ramo, *The Age of the Unthinkable: Why the New World Disorder Constantly Surprises Us and What We Can Do About It* (New York: Little, Brown and Company, 2009).

4. The term BRICs stands for Brazil, Russia, India and China, the world's largest emerging economics. Observers believe Goldman Sachs put forward the BRIC idea as a marketing device in order to generate investment opportunities for itself, but it has become part of the standard lexicon of scholars and policymakers, including in China. See Michael A. Glosny, 'China and the BRICs: a real (but limited) partnership in a unipolar world', *Polity* 42(1), (January 2010).

5. Joshua Kurlantzick, *Charm Offensive: How China's Soft Power Is Transforming the World* (New Haven, CT: Yale University Press, 2007).

6. Dirlik mistakenly dates the term's initial usage to the Fourth World Conference on Women held in Beijing in 1995. At a 1996 meeting in Turkey, Nafis Sadik, Executive Director of the UN Population Fund, commented that the 1994 International Conference on Population and Development (ICPD) had reached a consensus on the importance of achieving sustainable development, which was reconfirmed in Beijing the following year. It is clear that Sadik does not believe he had invented a term because he mentions a 'Beijing consensus' without capitalizing the second word, does not place the two words in quotation marks, and does not elaborate at all on anything distinctive about views reached in Beijing. See Arif Dirlik, 'Beijing Consensus: Beijing "Gongshi". Who recognizes whom and to what end?', Position Paper, *Globalization and Autonomy Online Compendium*, (17 January 2006), p. 9, available at: http://www.globalautonomy. ca; and Nafis Sadik, 'Population and sustainable human settlements', Statement made at the *United Nations Conference on Human Settlements (Habitat II)*, Istanbul, Turkey, 4 June 1996.

7. Ramo, *The Beijing Consensus*, p. 17.

8. *Ibid.*, pp. 22–23.

9. *Ibid.*, p. 33.

10. *Ibid.*, p. 3.

11. Alvin Toffler, *The Third Wave* (New York: Bantam Books, 1980).

12. Dieter Ernst and Barry Naughton, 'China's emerging industrial economy— insights from the IT industry', in Christopher A. McNally, ed., *China's Emerging Political Economy: Capitalism in the Dragon's Lair* (New York: Routledge, 2007). pp. 39–59.

13. Arthur Kroeber, 'China's push to innovate in information technology', in Linda Jakobson, ed., *Innovation with Chinese Characteristics: High-Tech Research in China* (Hampshire: Palgrave Macmillan, 2007), pp. 37–70.

14. Scott Kennedy, Richard P. Suttmeier and Jun Su. 'Standards, stakeholders, and innovation: China's evolving role in the global knowledge economy', *NBR Special Report* no. 15 (Seattle, WA: National Bureau of Asian Research, September 2008).

15. Elizabeth C. Economy, *The River Runs Black: The Environmental Challenge to China's Future* (Ithaca, NY: Cornell University Press, 2004).

16. Chinese Academy for Environmental Planning, *Green GDP Accounting Study Report 2004, Issued,* (11 September 2006), available at: http://english.gov. en/2006-09/11 contet_384596.htm; and Joseph Kahn and Jim Yardley, 'Choking on growth: as China roars, pollution reaches deadly extremes', *New York Times,* (26 August 2007).

17. Ramo, *The Beijing Consensus*, p. 24.

18. The author thanks Arthur Kroeber for providing this scorecard. Personal correspondence, June 2008.

19. On efforts early in the Reform era to Study the experiences of the United Stales, Eastern Europe, Southeast Asia, Ireland, and elsewhere, see Carol Lee Hamrin, *China and the Challenge of the Future: Changing Political Patterns* (Boulder, CO: Westview Press, 1990), pp. 30–63.

20. Randall Peerenboom, *China Modernizes: Threat to the West or Model for the Rest?* (Oxford: Oxford University Press, 2007), pp. 26–81.

21. Unless noted, the views in this paragraph are taken from several of the chapters in Scott Kennedy, ed., *Beyond the Middle Kingdom: Comparative Perspectives on China's Capitalist Transition* (manuscript currently under review).

22. James Fallows, who is also a specialist on Japan, writes, 'China's behavior, and that of its companies, is easier to match with standard economic theories than Japan's'. Fallows' position is rare among specialists of Japan who have turned their attention to China. Chalmers Johnson. Clyde Prestowitz, and Eamonn Fingleton all believe China is following Japan's economic model. See James Fallows, 'China makes, the world takes', *The Atlantic Monthly* 300(1), (July/August 2007), pp. 48–72, and Eamonn Fingleton, *In the Jaws of the Dragon: America's Fate in the Coming Era of Chinese Hegemony* (New York: Thomas Dunne Books, 2008).

23. Joseph Fewsmith, *Dilemmas of Reform in China; Political Conflict and Economic Debate* (Armonk, NY: M. E. Sharpe, 1994).

24. Scott Kennedy, *The Business of Lobbying in China* (Cambridge, MA: Harvard University Press, 2005); Andrew C. Mertha, *China's Water Warriors: Citizen Action and Policy Change* (Ithaca, NY: Cornell University Press, 2008).

25. Kellee S. Tsai, *Capitalism without Democracy: The Private Sector in Contemporary China* (Ithaca, NY: Cornell University Press, 2007).

26. Wang Zhuo, 'Zhongguo gaige shijian dui xifang jingjixue zhuliu liludc juda tiaozhan—Zhongguo moshi shi cujin gongtong fanrong, shixian gongtong fuyuzhi lu' ['The immense challenge China's reform experience presents to Western mainstream economic theory—the China model the road to promote common prosperity and to realize common wealth'], *Zhongguo caizheng [China Finance]* no. 11, (1993), pp. 35–42; Zheng Xia, 'Fazhanzhong guojia jingji fazhan moshi zai tan—"zhongguo moshi" dc lilun sikao' ['Further exploration of developing country economic development model—theoretical thoughts on the "China model"']. *Guangzhou shi caimao guanli ganbu xueyuan xuebao [Guangzhou Municipal Finance and Trade Cadre College Journal]* no. 2, (1999), pp. 39–41; Zhang Jianzhong, '"Zhongguo moshi" zai quanqiuhua zhong jueqi' ['The rise of the "China model" in the midst of globalization'], *Zhongguo guomen shibao [China National Door Times]*, (31 July 2004): and Zhou Jian, 'Zhongguo moshide fazhan daolu: zhongguo tese shehui zhuyj' ['Development road of the China model: socialism with Chinese characteristics'], *Guangdong sheng shehui zhuyixue xuebao [Journal of Guangdong Institute of Socialism]* no. 4, (October 2007), pp. 24–27.

27. Shaun Breslin, 'Capitalism with Chinese characteristics: the public, the private and the international', Murdoch University Asia Research Center, working paper no. 4 (May 2004); and Yasheng Huang, *Capitalism with Chinese Characteristics: Entrepreneurship and the State* (Cambridge: Cambridge University Press, 2008).

28. For one of the more detailed descriptions of the China Model, see Cai Tuo, *Quanqiuhua yu zhengzhide zhuanxing [Globalization and Political Transformation]* (Beijing: Peking University Press, June 2007), pp. 353–355.

29. Qin Fengming, '"Hou huashengdun gongshi" yu zhongguo moshi' ['"Post-Washington Consensus" and the China model'], *Taipingyang xuebao [Pacific Journal]* no. 6, (2005). pp. 40–45.

30. Yao Yang, '"Zhongxing zhengfu": Zhongguo 30 nian fazhan qijide yizhong quanshi' ['"Neutral government": an explanatory note of China's 30 year development miracle'], *Diyi caijing ribao [China Business News]*, (17 November 2008).

31. Wu Zengji, 'Lun "zhongguo moshi" ke chixude tiaojian' ['On the conditions to sustain the "China model"'], *Lilun tantao [Theoretical Investigation]* no. 1, (2005). pp. 5–9.

32. Gideon Rachman, 'Illiberal capitalism: Russia and China chart their own course', *Financial Times*, (8 January 2008); Ian Buruma, 'The year of the "China model"', *The Nation* (Bangkok), (9 January 2008); and Arthur Kroeber, 'Rising China and the liberal West', *China Economic Quarterly* 12(1), (March 2008), pp. 29–44.

33. Wang Yong, 'Domestic demand and continued reform: China's search for a new model', *Global Asia* 3(4), (December 2008), pp. 24–28.

34. Nevertheless, a useful discussion of experimentation is Sebastian Heilmann, 'From local experiments to national policy: the origins of China's distinctive policy process', *China Journal* no. 59, (January 2008), pp. 1–30.

35. Dani Rodrik, 'Goodbye Washington Consensus, hello Washington confusion? A review of the World Bank's *Economic Growth in the 1990s: Learning from a Decade of Reform*', *Journal of Economic Literature* 45, (December 2006), p. 977. Also see Dani Rodrik, *One Economics, Many Recipes: Globalization, Institutions, and Economic Growth* (Princeton, NJ: Princeton University Press, 2007).

36. World Bank, *Economic Growth in the 1990s: Learning from a Decade of Reform* (Washington, DC: World Bank, 2005).

37. There is no indication, however, that such intervention drew any inspiration from China's experience, and the post-crisis policies have been defended as temporary measures in which a return to market principles will follow once the crisis passes.

38. Yao Yang, 'Huashengdun gongshi meiyou guoshi' ['The Washington Consensus is not passé']. *21 shiji jingji baodao [21st Century Business Herald]*, (27 December 2008).

39. Selim Raihan, 'Beyond the Washington Consensus: lessons from China's development experience', Bangladesh Centre for Policy Dialogue, Report No. 12 (May 2000); Garth Le Pere, 'Ties create options for Africa', *China Daily*, (27 February 2008); Barry V. Sautman, 'Friends and interests: China's distinctive links with Africa', Hong Kong University of Science and Technology Center on China's Transnational Relations, working paper no. 12, (1 February 2006); and Drew Thompson, 'China's soft power in Africa: from the "Beijing Consensus" to health diplomacy', *China Brief*, (13 October 2005).

40. Joshua Landis, a Syria expert, reported that in his travels around the Middle East he regularly hears officials express strong interest in the 'China Model' in their quest to maintain authoritarian rule and achieve sustained economic growth. Discussion with the author, May 2008.

41. Dirlik, 'Beijing Consensus'.

CHAPTER 16 THE CONSEQUENCE OF CRISIS: FUNDAMENTAL CHANGE OR ESSENTIAL CONTINUITY?

The Crisis Will Spark Fundamental Change in the Global Political Economy

Advocate: Roger C. Altman

Source: "Globalization in Retreat: Further Geopolitical Consequences of the Financial Crisis," *Foreign Affairs* 88:4 (2009): 2–6

The Future Will Look Much Like the Recent Past

Advocate: Niall Ferguson

Source: "What 'Chimerica' Hath Wrought," The American Interest Online (January/February 2009), http://www.the-american-interest.com/article.cfm?piece=533

Will the global financial crisis produce a fundamental realignment in the global political economy? The last quarter of the twentieth century saw a broad consensus form around market-based liberalism or the so-called Washington Consensus. Across the global South, governments shifted away from state-led development strategies. They liberalized trade, and they opened their economies to multinational corporations. They opened their financial systems to international capital flows. The collapse of the Berlin Wall in 1989 precipitated fundamental economic and political reforms in the former Soviet Bloc. By 1990, market-based liberalism reigned supreme.

The diffusion of this "Anglo-Saxon model" rested upon a clarified global power structure. The collapse of the Soviet Union in the early 1990s eliminated the sole challenger to American military power. The reluctance of European governments to surrender the sovereignty necessary to create a coherent political actor constrained the European Union's ability to transform its economic power into political influence. Emerging market countries—China and India, in particular—remained preoccupied with domestic economic reform. Within this context, the United States emerged as the clear hegemonic power—full of confidence about its model of democratic capitalism and determined to take advantage of the moment in history to extend this model abroad.

THE CRISIS WILL SPARK FUNDAMENTAL CHANGE IN THE GLOBAL POLITICAL ECONOMY

Some analysts argue that the global financial crisis has shattered this system. On the one hand, that the crisis originated and hit hardest in economies that adhered most closely to the Anglo-Saxon model (the United States and Great Britain) has raised questions about this particular model. On the other hand, the fact that the crisis hit the American economy very hard but largely spared China has altered the global power distribution. Government debt in the United States has increased sharply, thereby constraining American policy. In contrast, China has emerged from the crisis with little lasting damage and has thus gained in relative terms.

Roger Altman, a former Deputy Treasury Secretary in the Clinton administration and current CEO of Evercore Partners, argues the crisis is a "seismic global event." He suggests that the ability of the United States to exercise leadership is substantially reduced. Global faith in the U.S. model of capitalism has weakened, while fiscal constraints limit the ability of the United States to conduct a global foreign policy. China, in contrast, has strengthened in relative terms. Although Altman is uncertain about the ability of China to exercise a leadership role, he does believe that the future cannot be like the past.

THE FUTURE WILL LOOK MUCH LIKE THE RECENT PAST

Other analysts argue that the crisis will have mostly a short-run impact. They believe the financial crisis doesn't implicate markets writ large but only raises questions about the merits of liberalized financial markets. One shouldn't forget, these analysts argue, that market-based economic reforms in China have led to a massive reduction of poverty. Nor will the crisis fundamentally alter the global distribution of power. Although China has emerged as an important creditor, it remains a relatively poor society whose continued development requires continued participation in global markets. Consequently, China cannot easily exploit its creditor status to exert power. Moreover, although the United States is more constrained today than in the past, it has always been able to resolve the economic challenges to its political power. There is no reason to believe that this won't occur in this instance.

Niall Ferguson, an economic and financial historian at Harvard University, argues that the future global political economy will not look all that much different than the recent past. He argues that the ten years prior to the crisis had already brought substantial change as "Chimerica"—the China–U.S. economic relationship—came to dominate the global economy. He asserts that although the crisis poses a challenge to this condominium power, he believes that the most likely outcome is the reemergence of this bilateral interdependence rather than the emergence of China or the European Union to supplant American power.

POINTS **TO PONDER**

1. To what extent does the financial crisis pose a challenge to unfettered markets writ large as opposed to financial markets more narrowly?

2. In what specific ways might the financial crisis and governments' responses to the crisis shape the ability of the United States to exercise power? What do these features have for China's power?

3. What do you think the global political economy will look like in ten years?

Roger C. Altman

Globalization in Retreat: Further Geopolitical Consequences of the Financial Crisis

It is now clear that the global economic crisis will be deep and prolonged and that it will have far-reaching geopolitical consequences. The long movement toward market liberalization has stopped, and a new period of state intervention, reregulation, and creeping protectionism has begun.

Indeed, globalization itself is reversing. The long-standing wisdom that everyone wins in a single world market has been undermined. Global trade, capital flows, and immigration are declining. It also has not gone unnoticed that nations with insulated financial systems, such as China and India, have suffered the least economic damage.

Furthermore, there will be less global leadership and less coordination between nations. The G-7 (the group of highly industrialized states) and the G-20 (the group of finance ministers and central-bank governors from the world's largest economies) have been unable to respond effectively to this crisis, other than by expanding the International Monetary Fund (IMF). The United States is also less capable of making these institutions work and, over the medium term, will be less dominant.

This coincides with the movement away from a unipolar world, which the downturn has accelerated. The United States will now be focused inward and constrained by unemployment and fiscal pressures. Much of the world also blames U.S. financial excesses for the global recession. This has put the U.S. model of free-market capitalism out of favor. The deserved global goodwill toward President Barack Obama mitigates some of this, but not all of it.

In addition, the crisis has exposed weaknesses within the European Union [EU]. Economic divergence is rising, as the three strongest EU nations—France, Germany, and the United Kingdom—have disagreed on a response to the crisis and refused pleas for emergency assistance from eastern Europe. The absence of a true single currency has proved inhibiting. And the European Central Bank has emerged as more cautious and less powerful than many expected.

Such lack of strength and unity in the West is untimely, because the crash will increase geopolitical instability. Certain flashpoint countries that rose with the oil and commodity boom, such as Iran and Russia, will now come under great economic pressure. Other, already unstable nations, such as Pakistan, could disintegrate. And poverty will rise sharply in a number of African countries. All this implies a less-coherent world.

The one clear winner is China, whose unique political-economic model has come through unscathed. This will automatically enhance its global position. Yes, its growth has slowed, but to still enviable rates. And measured by financial reserves, it is the world's wealthiest country. China's astute leadership is already making strategic investments that others cannot make.

The expected prolonged severity of the global recession is central to understanding these likely geopolitical impacts. The world's three largest economies, the United States, the EU, and Japan, will not be able to generate a normal cyclical recovery. The pervasive financial damage will prevent it. As a result, nations dependent on those markets for growth, such as those in eastern Europe, will also face a long recovery. And many of the developing economies, which depend on foreign capital, have been hardest hit.

Anatomy of a Crisis

Start with the United States, whose GDP [gross domestic product] is still nearly double that of any other country. Whereas most recessions follow a sequence of rising inflationary pressures, monetary tightening to counter them, and a slowdown in response to higher interest rates, this one is a balance-sheet-driven recession. It is rooted in the financial damage to households and banks from the housing-and-credit-market collapse.

U.S. households lost 20 percent of their net worth in just 18 months, dropping from a peak of $64.4 trillion in mid-2007 to $51.5 trillion at the end of 2008. Approximately two-thirds of this reduction involved lower financial asset values, and one-third was tied to home values. This is a big drop when juxtaposed against a median family income of $50,000 (which has been shrinking in real terms since 2000) and unprecedented household debt (which reached 130 percent of income in 2008).

That debt surged because Americans spent beyond their means. This reflected the wealth effect—households feeling wealthier on account of rising asset values and thus spending more. But consumers are now shell-shocked, and so that effect has been reversed. Household outflows are down, producing the unusual surge in personal savings rates that is now evident. This is why personal consumption expenditures fell by record rates in the last quarter of 2008. But consumer spending dominates the U.S. economy (at 70 percent of GDP). The core question is, When can spending resume growing at cyclically normal levels? With home values still falling and equity prices still 45 percent below their 2007 peak, the answer is not soon.

The other key constraint is the financial sector. Since the crisis broke, global financial institutions (mostly Western ones) have reported $1 trillion of losses on U.S.-originated assets. And the IMF recently estimated that ultimate losses will reach a staggering $2.7 trillion. These losses directly reduce banks' underlying capital and thus their capacity to lend. This explains why U.S. lending volumes have continued to decline and why the lending levels needed to support a normal cyclical recovery are not possible.

A Painful Recovery

The recovery in Europe will be even weaker. Although the United States is expected to register marginal growth in 2010—Goldman Sachs is forecasting 1.2 percent—the eurozone may contract again, by an estimated 0.3 percent. This reflects Europe's more exposed banking systems, historical factors, and the region's weaker policies.

Europe entered the recession later than the United States did and, logically, will emerge later. The housing and credit markets imploded in the United States, and then this implosion moved east. For example. Europe was still growing in early 2008, whereas the United States was not. Europe's banking system is proportionately larger than that of the United States', and its banks were more exposed to weakening emerging markets in eastern Europe and Latin America. And to date, European banks have recognized a smaller share of total likely write-downs than U.S. banks have.

Furthermore, the European policy response has been much weaker. Washington adopted a $787 billion fiscal stimulus program (involving tax cuts and spending increases), representing five percent of GDP. This is expected to raise 2009 GDP (over four quarters) by two percent above the level that would otherwise have prevailed. By contrast, the European Economic Recovery Plan is targeted to provide a stimulus equal to only about 1.5 percent of the EU'S GDP. The resulting boost will be smaller.

When it comes to monetary policy, there has been a similar disparity. The U.S. Federal Reserve lowered the federal funds target interest rate—the rate at which banks lend to one another overnight—to zero percent six months ago. Together with the U.S. Treasury and the FDIC [Federal Deposit Insurance Corporation], the Federal Reserve has provided an astonishing $13 trillion of support to the financial system. This includes guarantees of commercial paper, money-market-fund investments, specific groups of bank assets, and the like. In contrast, however, the European Central Bank has lowered its rates more slowly, only reaching 1.25 percent in April 2009. The comparable figure for overall credit support is 115 billion euros of capital injection for banks and 217 billion euros of funding guarantees—a fraction of what Washington has spent.

There are numerous reasons for this weaker European response. Some have to do with the stronger social security nets across much of Europe and the lesser need for special protection now. Others involve a historical aversion to steps with potentially inflationary consequences. And there is also the inherent difficulty of reaching agreement among multiple nations. The overall implication is that Europe's recovery may be even slower than that of the United States'.

Japan's will be even weaker. Japan remains the world's third-largest economy, but its GDP is expected to fall 6.6 percent this year and to decline again in 2010. This ties directly into Japan's decreasing, but disproportionately important, export sector. Japan also has a limited capacity for fiscal or monetary stimulus, as its national debt is extremely high and its monetary policy has been accommodative—allowing easy access to credit—for years.

The developing world has been hit hardest. Inflows of investment and financing have plunged, exports are very weak, and commodity prices are way down. The countries of central and eastern Europe are particular victims, as they ran large balance-of-payments deficits and depended on external borrowing to finance them. Several of them, including Hungary and Poland, have resorted to emergency loans from the IMF. Meanwhile, Africa has seen capital inflows nearly come to a halt.

The overall picture is a grim one: a deep, truly global, and destabilizing downturn, with world GDP falling for the first time in the postwar period. Given rising populations, such an outright contraction is stunning. As of this writing, it may have bottomed out, but the next three years will be painfully slow. The geopolitical consequences are now coming into view, and they will be profound.

After Globalization

First, the era of laissez-faire economics has ended. For 30 years, the Anglo-Saxon model of free-market capitalism spread across the globe. The role of the state was diminishing, and deregulation, privatization, and the openness of borders to capital and trade were rising. Much of central and eastern Europe adopted this model, as did swaths of East Asia and diverse nations from Ireland to Mexico.

This movement reflected the economic primacy of the United States. Its growth, soaring standards of living, and conservative economic policies were widely admired. Countless societies preferred this model and supported governments that espoused it. The state-centered models, such as the French and German ones, were in retreat.

Now, a page has been turned. The Anglo-Saxon financial system is seen as having failed. The global downturn, and all its human devastation, is being attributed to that failure. Throughout the world, including in the United States, this has turned the political tide in a new direction. The role of the state is expanding again, together with a reregulation of markets. This is evident in the United States, where President Obama has moved toward more activist and bigger government. The quasi nationalization of the banking and automotive industries, as well as the pending reform of the financial system, makes this clear. It is also clear in Ireland, the United Kingdom, and elsewhere, where nationalizations have gone even further. And it is clear in statements made by such leaders as French President Nicolas Sarkozy, who recently celebrated "the return of the state" and "the end of the ideology of public powerlessness."

Second, globalization is in retreat, both in concept and in practice. Much of the world now sees it as harmful. Those nations, especially developing ones, that embraced increased capital flows and open trade have been particularly injured. Those that insulated themselves, such as India, have been less scarred. The global spread of goods, capital, and jobs is reversing. Global exports are falling sharply. The World Bank reports that exports from China, Japan, Mexico, Russia, and the United States fell by 25 percent or more in the year leading up to February 2009. Capital flows are plunging too. Emerging markets are projected to receive only $165 billion in net positive capital inflows this year, down from $461 billion in 2008. Furthermore, financial and trade protectionism are spreading. Both the World Bank and the World Trade Organization recently reported a movement toward higher tariffs, higher nontariff barriers, and an increase in antidumping actions, designed to protect domestic jobs. Brazil, India, Russia, and numerous other states were cited. Moreover, various states' fiscal stimulus plans include subsidies for exporters and "buy domestic" provisions. And discriminatory actions against foreign workers are spreading. Immigrant workers, who are particular victims of this crisis, are returning home in waves. Japan and Spain are offering them cash to leave, and Malaysia is forcing them out.

Third, the world may be entering a new global phase marked by less leadership, less coordination, and less coherence. The world was already moving away from its post–Berlin Wall, unipolar condition, but this crisis has accelerated that process. The United States has turned inward, preoccupied with severe unemployment and fiscal pressures. Its economic model also is now out of favor. President Obama has made a triumphant overseas tour and is hugely popular everywhere. But his attention and political capital must be reserved for domestic issues, such as stabilizing the banking industry, handling the budget, and reforming health care.

Other nations have been rising, especially China. Although the United States' capacity to lead is now diminished and will continue to be so over the medium term, none of these rising powers is capable of full leadership. The outlook for effective multilateral approaches is also cloudy. The G-7 and the G-20 are relatively ineffective, as evidenced by the recent London summit. Yes, the IMF was expanded there, and that is important, but on the more challenging issues—a coordinated global stimulus, global financial oversight, and Afghanistan—the summit failed. Fundamentally, the G-7 is an anachronism—China is not a member—and the G-20 is too large.

On urgent political matters, such as Iran and the Arab-Israeli conflict, multilateralism is in retreat. The economic crisis is requiring most nations, including the United States, to focus inward. Also, other nations' responsiveness to U.S. initiatives has been muted. The case of Pakistan makes that clear: a foiled state with nuclear weapons would threaten many nations, and yet only U.S. diplomacy is fully active there.

Fourth, this crisis will likely increase geopolitical instability. Dennis Blair, the U.S. director of national intelligence, has asserted that the downturn already has produced low-level instability in a quarter of the world. The IMF has warned that millions will be pushed into unemployment, poverty, rising social unrest, or even war.

Key commodity-centered nations, such as Iran and Russia, rose with the oil and resource boom and flexed their geopolitical muscles accordingly. But now, they are coming under severe economic pressure. This year, unemployment in Russia is projected to reach 12 percent, and five million of its people will likely fall into poverty. Nearly half of its monetary reserves, although they are still ample, have been spent to stabilize the ruble and prop up state enterprises. Iran's oil and gas revenues will fall to $33 billion this year, from a 2007 level of $82 billion. At current world oil prices, Iran is actually running a current account deficit. Inflation is at 20 percent in the country, and Iran is unlikely to grow in 2009 or 2010. How these economic pressures will affect its upcoming election and the nuclear issue is unclear.

Countries in Africa have been hardest hit of all, and instability will likely rise there. Fragile states, such as the Democratic Republic of the Congo and the Central African Republic, have seen their social problems exacerbated by the crisis. Foreign reserves in the region have dwindled. The Congolese government will soon be unable to import essentials such as food and fuel. The Central African Republic is already unable to pay the salaries of its civil servants. In 2007, African countries raised $6.5 billion selling bonds on the international markets. This year, the figure will be zero. Private capital inflows could fall by nearly 90 percent, and the Overseas Development Institute, a British think tank, has projected that official aid will decline by $20 billion, as donors retrench. The commodity price crash, combined with the related slowdown in growth, the cutoff of private capital inflows, and diminished official assistance, has pushed the continent's collective current account surplus of four percent to a deficit of six percent in just two years. A World Bank study estimated that 53 million people living in emerging markets will fall back into absolute poverty this year. More frightening, according to the same study, up to 400,000 more children will die each year through 2010 on account of this economic crisis.

The Chinese Model

Only China has prevailed. China's growth did diminish but now may be picking up again. Recently, electricity consumption, freight shipments, and car sales in China have all increased. Its financial system is insulated and relatively unleveraged—and has thus been largely unharmed. This has allowed China to direct a recent surge in lending for stimulus purposes. Beijing's unique capitalist-communist model appears to be helping China through this crisis effectively. And measured by its estimated $2.3 trillion in foreign exchange reserves, no nation is wealthier.

All of this is enhancing China's geopolitical standing. The West is experiencing a severe economic crisis, seen as its own making, whereas China is not. The Chinese leadership is well aware of this relative advantage, even though la priorities are always domestic. Apart from its coal supplies, China is resource poor. But it has recently been making offshore investments in natural resources of a kind that others no longer can make—such as securing future oil supplies from Russia and Venezuela.

It is increasingly clear that the U.S.-Chinese relationship will emerge as the most important bilateral one in the world. The two nations have similar geopolitical interests. Neither wants Iran to acquire nuclear weapons. North Korea to be destabilized, or Pakistan to become a failed state. There is no reason, therefore, why their relationship cannot be a cooperative and globally stabilizing one.

This economic crisis is a seismic global event. Free-market capitalism, globalization, and deregulation have been rising across the globe for 30 years; that era has now ended, and a new one is at hand. Global economic and financial integration are reversing. The role of the state, together with financial and trade protectionism, is ascending.

Pro-growth leaders who seek to limit this phase must lead by example. One key is to promote aggressive stimulus measures to shorten their own countries' recessions and restart world growth. Beijing, London, and Washington are all moving impressively in this direction. Second, financial deregulation went too far, and so moderate reform is now needed to prevent a recurrence of the abuses and regulatory failures that resulted. Washington will shortly launch such a legislative effort, and Europe is moving even faster. A third key is President Obama and the enormous global goodwill he enjoys. He has a uniquely influential podium, which he could use to espouse the benefits of globalization and market liberalization. It is too soon to know whether he will use it that way. Let us hope that he does.

ROGER C. ALTMAN is Chair and CEO of Evercore Partners. He was U.S. Deputy Treasury Secretary in 1993–94.

Niall Ferguson

What "Chimerica" Hath Wrought

The U.S. financial system has been as much a part of American power over the past thirty years as the Sixth Fleet. Yet Wall Street's illustrious investment banks have been either bankrupted, swallowed up or transformed into regular banks in the space of less than a year. So close did the U.S. financial system come to complete meltdown in September that Treasury Secretary Henry Paulson was driven to request emergency powers worthy of wartime: *carte blanche* to spend around $700 billion on the mother of all bailouts. This is in fact less than half the sum the Federal Reserve has already spent through its various "facilities" to banks.

"Why should the rest of the world ever again take seriously the American free market model after this debacle?" a leading British journalist recently asked me. This crisis, he argued, is to economics what the Iraq war has been to foreign policy: a fatal blow to the credibility of U.S. claims to global primacy. "One thing seems probable to me", declared Peer Steinbrück, German Finance Minister. "The United States will lose its status as the superpower of the global financial system." The news magazine *Der Spiegel* called it "The End of Hubris." To the London *Guardian* it was "A Shattering Moment in America's Fall From Power."

Certainly, if the unipolar moment that followed the collapse of the Soviet empire was a very American form of hubris, then the credit crunch has been a very American nemesis. Ten years ago, a strange competition formed in the United States to see who could be more arrogant. Neoconservatives argued that the rest of the world should hurry up and embrace the American political way, or prepare to be bombed into the democratic age. But equally smug were the neo-liberal economists—liberal in the sense of Adam Smith, that is—who argued that the rest of the world should hurry up and embrace the "Washington Consensus", or prepare to be sold short. One lot derided the political failure of the Muslim world; the other lot heaped scorn on Asian "crony capitalism", supposedly the root cause of the 1997–98 Asian financial crisis.

The neocons got their comeuppance in Iraq, where American forces were not, after all, greeted as liberators with sweets and flowers. The neolibs got theirs in September, as a Republican Treasury, headed by the former CEO of Goldman Sachs, nationalized first the country's biggest mortgage lenders and then its biggest insurance company, only to let the investment bank Lehman Brothers fail. One of the few things Barack Obama and John McCain could agree on in the final phase of the presidential campaign was that something was rotten on Wall Street. The stage seemed set for the demise of what has been called "market fundamentalism" by George Soros (paradoxically one of its biggest beneficiaries), meaning the belief in the self-regulating nature of what has turned out not to be self-regulating at all.

That economic policy paradigms are shifting is clear. But is the same really true of the global balance of power as well? To answer that question we need to reflect more deeply on the true nature of this crisis.

We are living through a challenge to a phenomenon Moritz Schularick and I have christened "Chimerica."[1] In this view, the most important thing to understand about the world economy over the past decade has been the relationship between China and America. If you think of it as one economy called Chimerica, that relationship accounts for around 13 percent of the world's land surface, a quarter of its population, about a third of its gross domestic product, and somewhere over half of the global economic growth of the past six years.

For a time, it was a symbiotic relationship that seemed like a marriage made in heaven. Put simply, one half did the saving, the other half the spending. Comparing net national savings as a proportion of Gross National Income, American savings declined from above 5 percent in the mid-1990s to virtually zero by 2005, while Chinese savings surged from below 30 percent to nearly 45 percent. This divergence in saving patterns allowed a tremendous explosion of debt in the United States, for one effect of the Asian "savings glut" was to make it much cheaper for households to borrow money than would otherwise have been the case. Meanwhile, low-cost Chinese labor helped hold down inflation.

The crucial mechanism that bound the two halves of Chimerica together was currency intervention. To keep the renminbi (and hence Chinese exports) competitive, authorities in Beijing consistently intervened to halt the appreciation of their own currency against the dollar. The result was a vast accumulation of dollar-denominated securities in the reserves of the People's Bank of China, which became one of the world's biggest holders of U.S. Treasuries as well as bonds issued by the government-sponsored (now government-owned) agencies Fannie Mae and Freddie Mac. Had it not been for the Chinese willingness to fund America's borrowing habit this way, interest rates in the United States would have been substantially higher. It was Chimerica that kept the Age of Leverage going in its final phase, as total public and private debt as a percentage of GDP [gross domestic product] surged from 250 to 350 percent.

It was not, of course, just the United States that was borrowing, and not just China that was lending. All over the English-speaking world, as well as in countries like Spain, household indebtedness increased and conventional forms of saving gave way to leveraged plays on real estate markets.

Meanwhile, other Asian economies joined China in adopting currency pegs and accumulating international reserves, thereby financing Western current account deficits. Middle Eastern and other energy exporters also found themselves running surpluses and recycling petrodollars to the Anglosphere and its satellites. But Chimerica, above all others, was the real engine of the world economy.

As this tremendous expansion in borrowing proceeded, some economists tried to rationalize what was going on. One school argued that this was "Bretton Woods II", a system of international exchange rate management akin to the one that linked Western Europe to the United States after World War II. Others called it a "stable disequilibrium", something that could be counted on to continue for some considerable time. But then a wave of defaults in the U.S. sub-prime mortgage market revealed just how unstable Chimerica was.

In essence, the rest of the world's savings had helped inflate a real estate bubble in the United States. As is nearly always the case in asset bubbles, easy money was accompanied by lax lending standards and outright fraud. Euphoria eventually gave way to distress and then, in a familiar sequence, to panic. It began in the sub-prime market because it was there that defaults were most likely to happen, but it soon became clear that the entire U.S. property market would be affected. Not since the Great Depression have we seen average house prices declining at annual rates above 10 percent.

What made the property collapse so lethal was that an entire inverted pyramid of novel financial assets had been erected upon the flimsy base of American mortgages. Banks had bundled together the original loans, sliced and diced them and resold them to investors all around the world as "Collateralized Debt obligation" and the like. In a quintessential act of financial alchemy, the rating agencies had pronounced the top tier of these instruments to be AAA-rated. When the supposed gold turned back into lead and then into toxic waste, the consequences were devastating. According to the Bank of England, total losses on the various kinds of securities affected could amount to as much as $2.8 trillion.

So far only around $550 billion of write-downs have been acknowledged by banks around the world. Substantial amounts of new capital have been raised from private investors and governments, but there is still a hole—and it is a hole that threatens to get bigger. Dwindling capital at a time when formerly off-balance-sheet liabilities are coming home to roost means exploding leverage: For Bank of America total leverage (on- and off-book assets divided by tangible equity) is now as high as 134:1; for Citigroup the ratio is 88:1.

This failure among financial firms has had three distinct consequences. First, it has exposed the weaker banks—particularly the investment banks, which could not fall back on the cushion of savers' federally insured deposits—to savage and self-perpetuating share price declines (as the underlying equity declines in value, the degree of leverage rises and illiquidity soon morphs into insolvency, killing bondholders as well as shareholders). Second, it has triggered a further crisis in the market for derivatives. Credit default swaps (CDS) were supposed to be a wonderfully clever form of insurance for bondholders. But it is unclear how the far from transparent derivatives market can cope with defaults on this scale when the notional amount of CDS is $58 trillion.

But third and most importantly, the efforts of banks to stabilize their balance sheets by reducing credit has driven the U.S. economy into a recession—possibly the most severe economic downturn since the early 1980s, if not the early 1930s. Consumers cut spending by an annualized rate of 3.1 percent in the third quarter of 2008, the biggest drop since 1980. Regional surveys are pointing to an annual contraction in production of about 5 percent. What's more, as unemployment rises, consumption is bound to fall further. So will house prices.

The Fed has cut its effective federal-funds rate to very close to zero. The Federal deficit has already exploded, with the increase in public debt in the past year around $1.5 trillion. But neither monetarist nor Keynesian measures seem able to avert a Big Recession, though they may have staved off a second Great Depression.

What are the geopolitical implications of all this? One possibility is that it will speed up the "great reconvergence" between the East and West. If you go back to the very first "BRICs" report that Jim O'Neill and his colleagues at Goldman Sachs produced about the prospects for Brazil, Russia, India and China, China was projected to overtake the United States in terms of gross domestic product in to 2040. But in more recent reports, that has been brought forward to 2027. Maybe it will be even sooner than that, for one inevitable consequence of the credit crunch is that the United States will not only suffer negative growth for at least two quarters (and perhaps a whole year), but will also grow quite slowly for the foreseeable future. By contrast, China's semi-planned economy can probably maintain growth of above 6 percent a year, propelled forward by half a trillion dollars of new state spending on infrastructure and social services. Because, according to the "decoupling" thesis, net exports are no longer the key driver of China's growth, an American sneeze need not necessarily cause an Asian cold.

A second possible implication of the current crisis is that the days when the dollar was the sole international reserve currency may be coming to an end. Reserve currencies do not last forever, as the case of the British pound makes clear. Once upon a time, sterling was the world's number one currency, the unit of account in which most financial transactions were done. It died a slow, lingering death, sliding from $4.86 in 1930 to very near parity with the dollar at the nadir in the early 1980s. The principal reason for that was debt: the huge debts that Britain had run up to fight the world wars. The second reason was lower growth: Britain's economy was the underperformer of the developed world in the postwar decades, right down to the early 1980s.

If, as seems inevitable, the main fiscal consequence of the credit crunch is a huge increase in the liabilities of the Federal government—already substantially increased by the nationalization of Fannie Mae, Freddie Mac, and AIG even before the $700 billion Troubled Asset Relief Program—the United States could find itself in a similar situation. With debt spiraling upwards, the dollar could follow the pound into the category of former reserve currencies. If so, the United States would lose that convenient facility, which it has exploited since the 1960s, of being able to borrow from foreigners at low interest rates in its own currency.

With China decoupled from America—relying less on exports to the U.S. market, caring less about its currency's peg to the dollar—the end of Chimerica would have arrived, and with it the balance of global power would be bound to shift. No longer so committed to the Sino-American friendship established back in 1972, China would be free to explore other spheres of global influence, from the Shanghai Cooperation Organization, of which Russia is also a member, to its own informal nascent empire in commodity-rich Africa.

Yet commentators should hesitate before prophesying the decline and fall of the United States. It has come through disastrous financial crises before—not just the Great Depression, but also the Great Stagflation of the 1970s—and emerged with its geopolitical position enhanced. That happened in the 1940s and again in the 1980s.

Part of the reason it happened is that the United States has long offered the world's most benign environment for technological innovation and entrepreneurship. The Depression saw a 30 percent contraction in economic output and 25 percent unemployment. But throughout the 1930s American companies continued to pioneer new ways of making and doing things: think of DuPont (nylon), Proctor & Gamble (soap powder), Revlon (cosmetics), RCA (radio) and IBM (accounting machines). In the same way, the double-digit inflation of the 1970s didn't deter Bill Gates from founding Microsoft in 1975, or Steve Jobs from founding Apple a year later.

Moreover, the American political system has repeatedly proved itself capable of producing leadership in a crisis—leadership not just for itself but for the world. Both Franklin Roosevelt and Ronald Reagan came to power focused on solving America's economic problems. But by the end of their presidencies they dominated the world stage, FDR as the architect of victory in World War II and Reagan performing a similar role in the Cold War. It remains to be seen whether Barack Obama will be a game-changing president in the same mold. But Americans voted for him in the hope that he is. Would Obama have won without the credit crunch, which destroyed what little remained of the Republican reputation for economic competence?

But the most important reason why the United States bounces back from even the worst financial crises is that these crises, bad as they seem at home, always have worse effects on America's rivals. Think of the Great Depression. Though its macroeconomic effects were roughly equal in the United States and Germany, the political consequence in the United States was the New Deal; in Germany it was the Third Reich. Germany ended up starting the world's worst war; the United States ended up winning it. The American credit crunch is already having much worse economic effects abroad than at home. It will be no surprise if it is also more politically disruptive to America's rivals.

Among the other developed economies, both the Eurozone and Japan are already officially in recession, ahead of the United States. The European situation is especially precarious because, contrary to popular belief, European banks are in worse shape than their American counterparts. Average bank leverage in the United States is around 12:1. In Germany the figure is 52:1. Short-term bank liabilities are equivalent to 15 percent of U.S. GDP; the British figure is 156 percent. Indeed, the United Kingdom runs a real risk of being Greater Iceland—an economy crushed by a super-sized financial sector.

Moreover, unlike the United States, there is no single European Treasury that can implement multibillion-dollar fiscal stimulus. Monetary policy may be uniform throughout the Eurozone, but fiscal policy is still a case of every man for himself.

Emerging markets, too, have been hammered harder by the crisis than the "decoupling" thesis promised. In the year to the end of October 2008, the U.S. stock market declined by 34 percent. But Brazil's was down 54 percent, China's 58 percent, India's 64 percent and Russia's 66 percent. When Goldman Sachs christened these four countries the BRICs, they little realized that their equity markets would one day be dropping like bricks. These figures are scarcely good advertisements for the more regulated, state-led economic models favored in Beijing and Moscow.

The financial crisis is especially bad news for energy exporters: not only belligerent Russia, whose leaders yearns for a reconstituted Soviet empire, but also those other thorns in the side of the United States, Iran and Venezuela. Any oil price below $94 a barrel is bad news for Venezuela's fragile finances; any price below $55 spells trouble for Iran.

In any case, is even the fastest growing of America's rivals really a credible alternative to the United States? Rapidly though it is growing, China is bedeviled by three serious ailments: demographic imbalance, environmental degradation and political corruption. China's military is not remotely ready to mount a serious challenge to American dominance in the Pacific. And, crucially, it is far from clear that China is ready to wean its manufacturing sector completely off the U.S. export market. After three years of very mild renminbi appreciation, the People's Bank of China seems to be contemplating renewed intervention to keep the currency weak relative to the dollar. That means China will continue to sell renminbi for dollars, further enlarging its already large portfolio of U.S. bonds.

There is a paradox at the heart of this crisis. In many ways it is a crisis that has "Made in America" stamped all over it. Yet in the very worst moments of panic this fall, investors made it clear that they continue to regard U.S. government debt as a "safe haven" in uncertain times; hence the recent dollar rally. Huge though the costs of the current crisis may prove to be, there is a way of presenting them that may yet suffice to reassure the rest of the world that America can afford it. After all, the Federal debt in public hands remains equivalent to below 40 percent of U.S. GDP, a significantly lower figure than in many European economies or Japan. (The vastly larger unfunded liabilities of the Medicare and Social Security systems remain, fortunately, off balance sheet.)

Of course, this crisis could yet prove to be the safe haven's last gasp, especially if Congress runs amok with supplementary bailouts and stimulus packages, and the international bond market finally writes the United States off as just another Latin American economy. There seemed very little awareness at the mid-November G-20 summit in Washington that uncoordinated interest rate cuts and stimulus packages could unleash a fresh bout of volatility in international currency and bond markets. The possibility remains, too, that the coming explosion of U.S. Federal debt could finally trigger the dreaded dollar rout, especially if the Chinese decide that the export game is up and their only hope is a policy of "market socialism in one country." Yet this still seems a less likely scenario than a continuation of Chimerica.

True, the financial hubris of recent years has been followed by a terrible nemesis. The age of leverage has ended not with a whimper but with a deafening bang. Nonetheless, it is much too early to conclude that in geopolitical terms the American century is over, or that China solo is about to take over from Chimerica. Power is always relative, and a crisis that hits the periphery of the global economy harder than the core must logically increase the power of the core. Nemesis, too, can be exported.

ENDNOTE

1. "'Chimerica' and the Global Asset Market Boom", *International Finance* (December 2007).

CREDITS

Irwin, Douglas A. "The Employment Rationale for Trade Protection," from *Free Trade under Fire.* Copyright © 2002 Princeton University Press, 2003 paperback edition. Reprinted by permission of Princeton University Press.

Kennedy, Scott. From "The Myth of the Beijing Consensus," in *Journal of Contemporary China,* Vol. 19, Issue 65: 461–477 (June 2010). Copyright © Routledge, reprinted by permission of Taylor and Francis Ltd., http://www.informaworld.com.

Krugman, Paul. "In Praise of Cheap Labor: Bad Jobs at Bad Wages Are Better than No Jobs at All," from Slate, March 21, 1997. Reprinted by permission of the author.

LeGrain, Philippe., and Li Brodsgaard. "The Case for Immigration," from *The International Economy,* Summer 2007. Used by permission.

Miller, John. "Why Economists Are Wrong about Sweatshops and the Antisweatshop Movement." From *Challenge,* Vol. 46, No. 1 (January–February 2003): 93–122. Copyright © 2003 by M.E. Sharpe, Inc. Reprinted with permission.

Rodrik, Dani. "Trading in Illusions," from *Foreign Policy,* March/April 2001. Copyright © 2001 by *Foreign Policy.* Reproduced with permission of *Foreign Policy* in the format Textbook via Copyright Clearance Center.

Rosen, Howard F. "Strengthening Trade Adjustment Assistance," in Policy Brief PBO8-2, January 2008. Used by permission.

Scheve, Kenneth F., and Matthew J. Slaughter. "A New Deal for Globalization," from *Foreign Affairs,* Vol. 86, No. 4, July/August 2007. Reprinted by permission of Foreign Affairs. Copyright © 2007 by the Council on Foreign Relations, Inc., www.ForeignAffairs.com.

Scott, Robert E. "The China Trade Toll," EPI Briefing Paper #219, July 30, 2008. Used by permission of the Economic Policy Institute.

Spar, Debora, and David Yoffie. "Multinational Enterprises and the Prospects for Justice," from *Journal of International Affairs,* 52 (Spring 1999): 557–581. Used by permission.

Stiglitz, Joseph E. "The Anatomy of a Murder: Who Killed America's Economy?" from *Critical Review,* Vol. 21, February–March 2009, pp. 329–339. Used by permission of Copyright Clearance Center.

White, Lawrence H. *How Did We Get into This Financial Mess,* Cato Institute Briefing Papers. Copyright © 2008 by Cato Institute. Reproduced with permission of Cato Institute in the format Textbook via Copyright Clearance Center.

Yunus, Mohammad. "Poverty Is a Threat to Peace," from http://www.nobelprize.org/nobel_prizes/peace/laureates/2006/yunus-lecture-en.html. Copyright © 2006 The Nobel Foundation. Used by permission.